# MY COUNTRY, MY LIFE

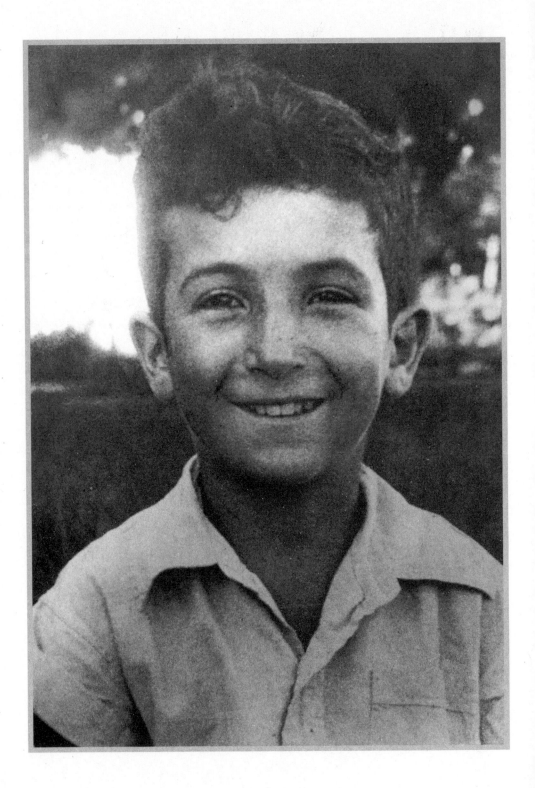

# My Country,

**FIGHTING FOR ISRAEL, SEARCHING FOR PEACE**

# My Life

# Ehud Barak

ST. MARTIN'S PRESS NEW YORK

MY COUNTRY, MY LIFE. Copyright © 2018 by Ehud Barak. All rights reserved.
Printed in the United States of America. For information, address St. Martin's Press,
175 Fifth Avenue, New York, NY 10010.

www.stmartins.com

Maps by Gene Thorp/Cartographic Concepts

Design by Meryl Sussman Levavi

Library of Congress Cataloging-in-Publication Data

Names: Barak, Ehud, 1942– author.
Title: My country, my life : fighting for Israel, searching for peace / Ehud Barak.
Description: First edition. | New York : St. Martin's Press, May 2018.
Identifiers: LCCN 2017060164 | ISBN 9781250079367 (hardback) |
ISBN 9781466892088 (ebook)
Subjects: LCSH: Barak, Ehud, 1942– | Prime ministers—Israel—Biography. |
Generals—Israel—Biography. | Politicians. | Israel—Politics and government—1993– |
BISAC: BIOGRAPHY & AUTOBIOGRAPHY / Presidents & Heads of State. |
BIOGRAPHY & AUTOBIOGRAPHY / Political. | BIOGRAPHY &
AUTOBIOGRAPHY / Cultural Heritage. | BIOGRAPHY &
AUTOBIOGRAPHY / Historical.
Classification: LCC DS126.6.B25 B37 2018 | DDC 956.9405/4092 [B]—dc23
LC record available at https://lccn.loc.gov/2017060164

Our books may be purchased in bulk for promotional, educational, or
business use. Please contact your local bookseller or the Macmillan Corporate and
Premium Sales Department at 1-800-221-7945, extension 5442, or by email at
MacmillanSpecialMarkets@macmillan.com.

First Edition: May 2018

1   3   5   7   9   10   8   6   4   2

To the bereaved families of my young fallen comrades

They say, Whether our lives and our deaths were for peace and a new hope or for nothing we cannot say: it is you who must say this.

They say, We leave you our deaths: give them their meaning . . .

—ARCHIBALD MACLEISH,
"The Young Dead Soldiers Do Not Speak"

# Contents

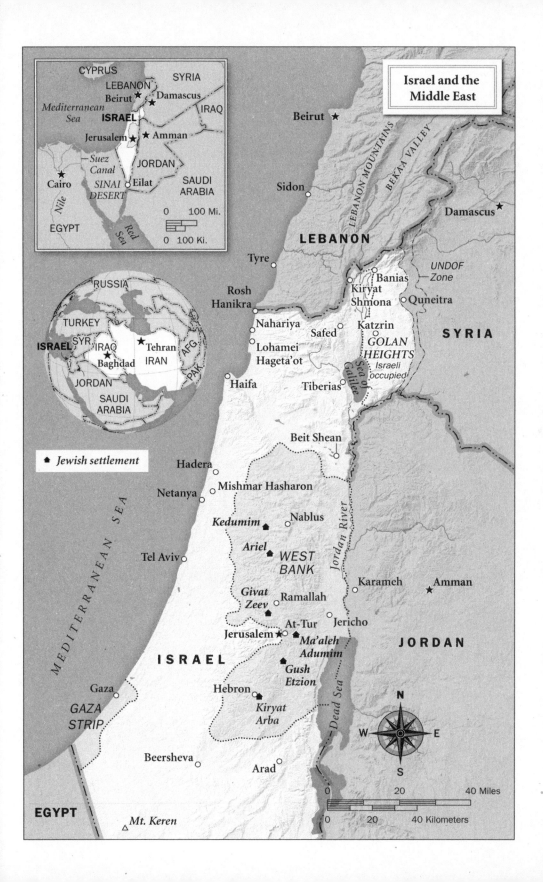

**Israel and the Middle East**

CYPRUS
SYRIA
LEBANON
Beirut ★ Damascus
*Mediterranean Sea*
IRAQ
**ISRAEL**
Jerusalem ★ Amman
*Suez Canal*
JORDAN
*Nile*
*SINAI DESERT*
Eilat
SAUDI ARABIA
Cairo
EGYPT
Red Sea

0    100 Mi.
0    100 Ki.

RUSSIA
TURKEY
ISRAEL
SYR.
IRAQ
Tehran
AFG.
Baghdad
IRAN
PAK.
JORDAN
SAUDI ARABIA

◆ *Jewish settlement*

Beirut ★

Sidon

LEBANON MOUNTAINS

BEKAA VALLEY

Damascus ★

Tyre

Rosh Hanikra

Banias
Kiryat Shmona
Quneitra

*UNDOF Zone*

SYRIA

Nahariya

Safed
Katzrin

Lohamei Hageta'ot

*GOLAN HEIGHTS*
*Israeli occupied*

Haifa

Tiberias

Sea of Galilee

Beit Shean

Hadera

Netanya

Mishmar Hasharon

*MEDITERRANEAN SEA*

*Kedumim* ◆
Nablus

Jordan River

*Ariel* ◆
*WEST BANK*

Tel Aviv

*Givat Zeev* ◆
Ramallah
Karameh
Amman ★

At-Tur
Jericho

Jerusalem ★
*Ma'aleh Adumim* ◆

**ISRAEL**

*Gush Etzion* ◆

JORDAN

Gaza

Hebron
*Kiryat Arba* ◆

*Dead Sea*

*GAZA STRIP*

Beersheva

Arad

N
W    E
S

0    20    40 Miles
0    20    40 Kilometers

EGYPT

△ *Mt. Keren*

# Preface

## Night Flight

THEY SAY YOU CAN READ A PERSON'S FEELINGS ON HIS FACE. IF SO, I must be a very good actor—the opposite of what anyone who has worked closely with me would tell you. Maybe it was just the exception that proved the rule. But I was described as looking defeated. Distressed. Depressed.

As I delivered my brief final statement outside the presidential retreat at Camp David, in the forested Catoctin Hills north of Washington, DC, I felt none of those things. Yes, I was disappointed. I realized that what had happened over the last fourteen days, or, more crucially, what had *not* happened, was bound to have serious consequences, both for me personally as prime minister of Israel, and for my country.

At the time of the Camp David summit in July 2000, however, I'd been a politician for all of five years. Most of my life by far had been spent in uniform. As a teenager, small and slight and not even shaving yet, I was part of the founding core of a unit called Sayeret Matkal, Israel's equivalent of America's Delta Force or Britain's Special Air Service (SAS). Though as a young kid I was quiet, serious, and contemplative, my years in Israel's elite special forces unit, especially when I became its commander, etched those qualities in me more deeply. They also added new ones: a sense that you could never plan a mission too carefully or prepare too assiduously; an understanding that what you thought, and certainly what you said, mattered a lot less than what you *did*; and above all, that when one of our commando operations was over, you had to take a step back and evaluate things honestly, without illusions.

That intense focus and detachment—sometimes to the frustration of politicians and diplomats working alongside me—guided me from the day I became prime minister. In my first discussions with US president Bill Clinton a year earlier, during a long weekend beginning at the White House and moving on to Camp David, I had mapped out in detail the steps I believed we would have to take in order to address the central issue facing Israel: the search for peace.

In choosing to return to Camp David for the summit talks with Palestinian leader Yasir Arafat, I was aware of both the stakes and the risks. Success would mean not just one more stutter step away from our century-long conflict: it would be a critical move forward toward a real, final resolution—in treaty-speak, *end of conflict*. Whatever the complexities of putting an agreement into practice, and no matter how long it might take, we would have crossed a point of no return. After all the suffering and bloodshed on both sides, we would be on the path to two states, for two peoples.

And if we failed? I knew from months of increasingly stark intelligence reports that an explosion of Palestinian violence would be only a matter of time. Indeed, there was every indication the explosion was coming anyway.

I knew something else as well. This was a moment of truth not just for me or for Bill Clinton, who understood our conflict more deeply, and was more determined to help end it, than any other US president. It was a moment of truth for Arafat. The Oslo Accords of 1993 and 1995, groundbreaking though they were, had created a peace *process*, not peace. Over the past few years, that process had been lurching from crisis to crisis. Political support for negotiations was fraying. Yet the core issues had not been resolved. In fact, they'd barely been touched on. The reason for this was no secret. For both sides, these questions lay at the heart of everything we'd been saying for years, to the world and to ourselves, about the roots of the conflict and the minimum terms we could accept. At issue were rival claims on security, borders, settlements, Palestinian refugees, and the future of the ancient city of Jerusalem; none could be resolved without painful and politically difficult decisions.

Entering the summit, I was confident that, along with my team of aides and negotiators, we would do our part to make an agreement possible. I had no doubt that President Clinton, whom I had come to view not just as a diplomatic partner but a friend, would rise to the occasion. But Arafat? There was no way to know. That was why I'd pressed Clinton so hard to convene the summit. That was why, despite the misgivings of some of his closest advisers, he had agreed. We both knew that the so-called final-status issues couldn't be put off forever. Untangling them was getting harder, not easier. We also realized that only in an environment like Camp David—a "pressure cooker" was how I'd described it to Clinton and Secretary of State Madeleine Albright—would we ever discover whether a peace deal could in fact be done.

Now, at least, we knew.

+ + +

Our equivalent of Air Force One, perhaps in a nod to our country's austere early years, was an almost prehistoric Boeing 707. It was waiting on the runway at Andrews Air Force Base outside Washington to ferry me and the rest of our team back to Israel.

As we took off, the mood on board was sober. Huddling with the core of my negotiating team—policy coordinator Gilead Sher, security aide Danny Yatom, and acting foreign minister Shlomo Ben-Ami—I could see that the way the summit ended had hit them hard. It was true, as they often reminded me, that I was the one who ultimately had to decide what we could offer in search for a true peace with the Palestinians. I was the one who would be blamed by the inevitable critics, whether for going too far or not far enough, or simply because the deal had eluded us. Yet these three dedicated men—Gili, by training a lawyer; Shlomo, an academic; and Danny, a former Mossad chief as well as my deputy when I was commander of Sayeret Matkal—had been through dozens of hours of talks with Arafat's top negotiators, not to mention their countless other meetings before we got to the summit. Now they had to come to terms with the reality that, even with the lid of the pressure cooker bolted down tight, we'd been unable to secure the agreement that each of us knew had been within reach.

We'd been ready to contemplate major compromises on every one of the key issues as long as we safeguarded Israel's vital national and security interests. We had been open to an Israeli pullout from nearly all of the West Bank and Gaza, with a support mechanism to help compensate tens of thousands of Palestinian refugees from the serial Arab-Israeli conflicts of the past half century. Most painfully, and controversially, we had agreed to let President Clinton present an American proposal offering the Palestinians sovereignty over all the Arab neighborhoods of Jerusalem as well as "custodial sovereignty" over the Haram al-Sharif, the mosque complex perched above the Western Wall, the holiest site in Judaism. Yet precisely because we had been ready to offer so much—only for Arafat to reject it all even as a *basis* for further talks on a final deal—I knew how gutted my key negotiators felt.

Still, I'm sure none of them was surprised when my old operational instincts kicked in. In my statement to journalists, I had been careful to say that Arafat was not ready *at this time* to make the historic compromises required for peace. In leaving the door open, I wanted to drive home the point that any prolonged deadlock would *not* be because we in Israel had abandoned our commitment to the serious work of peacemaking. But in truth, I thought there was almost no chance Arafat would suddenly prove ready to engage on the major issues in a way he'd failed to do at the summit. Speaking to President Clinton and Secretary Albright before leaving Camp David, I was open about my concerns. It was pretty clear the chances of our getting even a framework agreement on Clinton's watch were vanishingly small. He now had barely five months left in office. Yet my deeper fear was that with Arafat having brushed aside an offer that went much further than any other Israeli had been willing to consider— much further than the Americans had expected—the prospects for peace would be set back not just for a few years, but a decade or two.

As our 707 droned over the Atlantic, I knew that our challenge now was to make sure we were prepared for what came next. Gilead, Danny, and Shlomo left to get some sleep on the long flight ahead. Before long, the plane was full of irregularly slumped bodies, the silence broken only by the drone of the engines and the occasional sound of snoring. I sat, wide awake, in one of the seats at the front. My sleeping habits were another inheritance from Sayeret Matkal. During those years, nearly everything of significance I did had come after sundown. The element of surprise could mean the difference between success and failure in our missions, even between life and death. But all of my planning, all my *thinking*, tended to happen at night as well. The quiet, and the lack of distractions, helped concentrate the mind.

Part of the spadework for our response to Camp David was already in place. Much as I'd hoped that Arafat and I could turn a new page in Middle East history, eight months before the summit I'd directed our military and security chiefs to draw up contingency plans for the likelihood of an unprecedentedly deadly eruption of Palestinian violence. Still, I felt we also had to have a *political* response. Though this would not become our formal, public position for several months, I believed that unless Arafat demonstrated an unlikely change of heart, Israel needed to consider a unilateral change in policy. Though obviously needing to retain the option for our security forces to respond, or preempt, Palestinian attacks, I favored withdrawing from most of the West Bank and Gaza. The territorial terms would be less far-reaching than the proposal Arafat had just rejected. Yet it would still give the Palestinians control of about 80 percent of the area, and all its major towns and cities—sufficient to establish a viable state if they chose to do so. It would also finally give Israel a clearly delineated border with the territory that we had captured in the Six-Day War in 1967—and allow for possible further withdrawals in the future, if the Palestinian leadership ever proved ready for peace.

As I jotted down the outline of the disengagement argument in a pocket notebook, my mind went back to the first time my path had crossed with Arafat's, more than three decades earlier in the spring of 1968. It was nearly a year after the Six-Day War, in which Israel had comprehensively defeated the armies of our three main Arab enemies: Egypt, Syria, and Jordan. Now, our forces were advancing on a Jordanian town called Karameh, across the Jordan River from the West Bank. It was the operational base of a fledgling Palestinian group called Fatah, under Arafat's command. They'd begun staging armed raids into Israel and, in one of their most recent attacks, had planted land mines not far from the Dead Sea. One of the mines destroyed an Israeli school bus, killing a teacher and a school physician and injuring nearly a dozen children.

I had just turned twenty-six and, as a reserve officer, was finishing my studies in physics and mathematics at the Hebrew University in Jerusalem.

I had joined my Sayeret Matkal comrades the night before the assault. Though it was a huge operation, our role was relatively minor. We were to seal the southern entrance to the town. But it proved a tough slog just to get there. Our vehicles got bogged down in mud. By the time we arrived, the Fatah fighters, many in civilian clothes, were racing past us in the other direction. One of them, we later discovered, was Arafat. He escaped on a motorcycle.

It would be nearly three decades later when the two of us first met, shortly after the assassination of my longtime commander and mentor Yitzhak Rabin, when I was foreign minister under Shimon Peres. But in those intervening years, Arafat was rarely off my radar. By the early 1970s, he and his fighters had been expelled from Jordan and were based in Lebanon. Arafat was becoming a significant figure on the Arab and world political stages, and an increasingly uncomfortable thorn in Israel's side. I was head of the sayeret by then. We developed a plan—a raid by helicopter into a Fatah-dominated area in southeastern Lebanon during one of Arafat's morale-boosting visits from Beirut—to assassinate him. But when I took the idea to my main contact in military headquarters, he said no. He insisted that Arafat was no longer the fighter we had encountered in Karameh. "He's fat. He's a politician. He is not a target."

In the early 1980s, the idea would suddenly resurface. In my first meeting, as a newly promoted major general, with then–defense minister Ariel Sharon, Sharon turned to me and the army's chief of staff, Rafael "Raful" Eitan, and said, "Tell me. Why the hell is Arafat still alive?" He looked first at Raful, then at me, and said, "When I was twenty years younger than you are, I *never* waited for someone like Ben-Gurion or Dayan to ask me to plan an operation. I would plan it! Then I'd take it to them and say, you're the politicians, you decide, but if you say yes, we'll do it." I smiled, telling him I'd done exactly that a decade earlier, only to have one of his mates in the top brass say no. Sharon now said yes. But the plan was overtaken: by Sharon's ill-fated determination to launch a full-scale invasion of Lebanon, targeting not just Arafat, but with the aim of crushing the Palestine Liberation Organization militarily once and for all.

I finally met Arafat face-to-face at the end of 1995. Although the Oslo peace process had dramatically changed things, the true prize—real peace—was still far away. We were in Barcelona for a Euro-Mediterranean diplomatic conference aimed at reinvigorating the peace negotiations. The ceremonial centerpiece was a dinner at one of the royal palaces. I arrived early and found myself in a breathtakingly opulent, but otherwise empty, reception room. Empty, that is, except for a dark-brown Steinway piano. From childhood, I have loved music. And while I am never likely to threaten the career of anyone in Carnegie Hall, I have, over the years, drawn enormous satisfaction from playing classical pieces. I pulled back the velvet piano bench and sat down at the keyboard. With my back to the doorway, I was unaware Arafat had arrived, and that he was soon standing only a few feet behind me, watching as I played one of my favorite pieces, a Chopin waltz. My old commando antennae must have been blunted. When I finally realized Arafat was there, I turned, embarrassed, stood up, and grasped his hand. "It's a real pleasure to meet you," I said. "I must say I have spent many years watching you—by other means." We stood talking for about ten minutes. Though time had been set aside for us to meet at greater length after dinner, I hoped to establish a human bond with a leader who held the key to tackling the central issues and negotiating a breakthrough. "We carry a great responsibility," I said. "Both of our peoples have paid a heavy price, and the time has come to find a way to solve this."

At the time, and in our other meetings in the years ahead, he did show a kind of surface reciprocity. He would say the right things: about how he, too, wanted peace, or that he saw me as a "partner." But he never really got beyond viewing me as a career military man more suited to, and interested in, war than in peace. He could never comprehend that for me, as for Rabin, the central imperative was to ensure Israel's *security*. Nor that both of us, over time, came to recognize that military action was just one tool—and not always the best one—to achieve that goal.

+ + +

This book is only partly the story of my life. It's also about Israel, the country whose birth I had the privilege of witnessing, and with which I've shared childhood and adolescence and, now, its increasingly troubled middle age. I want not just to chronicle my country's, or my own, achievements along the way. I am also determined to document the setbacks. The mistakes. Misjudgments. Missed opportunities. And the lessons that we can, and must, learn from them. Though no first-person account can claim to be objective, I hope I've succeeded in resisting the temptation to engage in twenty-twenty hindsight. I wanted to describe the formative challenges in my life and in Israel's *as they appeared at the time*: the 1948 War of Independence, when I was a small child; the Sinai War of 1956, through the eyes of a kibbutz teenager; the wars of 1967, 1973, and the Lebanon War of 1982, which I experienced as an increasingly senior officer in the army. The explosion of violence that became known as the first intifada—when I was deputy chief of staff and Yitzhak Rabin was defense minister—and how it contributed to a change in how both Rabin and I viewed our conflict with the Palestinians. Camp David, too, as well as my equally frustrating effort a few months earlier to negotiate a final peace with Syria's president Hafez al-Assad. Our destruction of a remote reactor facility where Assad's son and heir, Bashar al-Assad, sought to develop a nuclear weapon a few years later, as well as our plan to launch an attack on Iran's program to develop a nuclear weapon, and how and why we ultimately ended up not doing so.

As one of the few surviving public figures to have lived through, and participated in, all of my country's history, I don't want to just describe these and other major events. I've sought to draw the arc of our history—from the early years, all but forgotten even for many Israelis, through all the achievements and errors, challenges and setbacks, to where we now find ourselves. Entering its eighth decade, Israel is incomparably stronger, not just militarily but economically. Yet we are deeply divided and—in recent years, under the most right-wing government in our history, led by my old Sayeret Matkal charge Binyamin "Bibi" Netanyahu—have become unmoored from the principles on which we established our state, fought for it, and built it up against enormous odds and challenges. We are becoming unmoored, above all, from the founding purpose of Zionism: a state where Jews would finally, through self-reliance and self-confidence and self-sacrifice and creativity, take hold of their own destiny.

The dangers Israel faces are real. The "Arab Spring" of less than a decade ago has morphed into an Islamic winter. National frontiers put in place by British and French diplomats after the fall of the Ottoman Empire have been vanishing. Centuries-old conflicts between tribes and rival religious communities have reignited, whether in Iraq or, at a truly terrible human cost, in Syria. Iran's nuclear program is on hold for now, due to a US-led agreement that, however flawed, turned out to be far less flawed than I had feared. But Iran does still pose a danger, not least with its potential ability to move fairly quickly toward resuming its nuclear program once the international agreement expires. The Iranians also remain determined to exert growing power in the region at the expense of major Sunni Muslim states like Saudi Arabia, its Gulf neighbors, and Egypt. Iran is sponsoring terror groups and, through its increasingly well-armed and battle-tested Lebanese proxy Hizbollah, helping to prop up Bashar al-Assad in Syria and threatening Israel's borders. As for our conflict with the Palestinians, the prediction I made to Bill Clinton and Madeleine Albright after Camp David turned out, if anything, to be understated. We are now approaching the end of the "decade or two" of diplomatic deadlock I feared would follow. And the deadlock shows no sign of ending.

That these challenges exist is not where I disagree with Bibi Netanyahu. My concern is the vision he is peddling, at home and abroad, about Israel: the notion that we are too weak to confront whatever dangers might threaten us, that we are, to use his phrase of choice, under "existential" threat. Having spent half my life in the military and nearly a decade as prime minister and defense minister, I'm in a better position than most to know this is nonsense. In regional terms, Israel is a superpower, stronger not just than any one of our potential enemies, but any combination of them we might have to face. Even Iran's nuclear program does not, at least as things now stand, pose an existential threat. The agreement reached with Tehran in 2015, assuming it is complied with, has put key components of the Iranian nuclear program on hold for a decade or so. And here is the critical fact: not only does Israel retain the ability to mount an attack if that were to prove necessary, but the Americans have an even more powerful array of tools at their disposal—no less so now than when I was trying to persuade President Barack Obama and senior administration officials that they should have been prepared to seriously contemplate using them.

Bibi knows all this. Yet in deliberately choosing to ignore Israel's strength in favor of a refrain of weakness and vulnerability, he has opted for a political comfort zone. Rather than take the diplomatic initiative—especially at a time when much of the Sunni Middle East has common interests with Israel because of our shared concerns about Iran—he has retreated into a combination of rhetorical bombast and inaction. Worse, in part perhaps because he or his associates have been facing a series of corruption investigations, he has delegated any serious policy work to the far-right members of his coalition. Nowhere is that more striking than with the Palestinians. With no evident interest in a two-state resolution of our conflict—whether by negotiation or a unilateral Israeli withdrawal from at least most of the territories—senior right-wing cabinet members like Defense Minister Avigdor Lieberman and Education Minister Naftali Bennett are committed to establishing a "Greater Israel" with permanent Israeli control over all the West Bank territory we've held since the Six-Day War a half century ago. That's bad for the Palestinians, of course. But, just as when I went to Camp David, my overriding concern is what it would mean for *Israel*. This Greater Israel will unquestionably be larger in terms of territory. Yet it shows every sign of being smaller in other ways—less cohesive, less Jewish, less open and democratic, and more isolated—both internationally and from diaspora Jewish communities—than the state whose embattled beginnings I witnessed as a child seventy years ago.

# MY COUNTRY, MY LIFE

# Kibbutz Roots

I AM AN ISRAELI. BUT I WAS BORN IN BRITISH-RULED PALESTINE, ON A fledgling kibbutz: a cluster of wood-and-tar-paper huts amid a few orange groves and vegetable fields and chicken coops. It was just across the road from an Arab village named Wadi Khawaret, whose residents fled in the weeks before the establishment of the State of Israel, when I was six years old.

As prime minister half a century later, during my stubborn yet ultimately fruitless drive to secure a final peace treaty with Yasir Arafat, there were media suggestions that my childhood years gave me a personal understanding of the pasts of *both* our peoples, Jews and Arabs, in the land that each saw as its own. But that is in some ways misleading. Yes, I did know firsthand that we were not alone in our ancestral homeland. At no point in my childhood was I ever taught to hate the Arabs. I never did hate them, even when, in my years defending the security of Israel, I had to fight, and defeat, them. But my conviction that they, too, needed the opportunity to establish a state came only later, after my many years in uniform—especially when, as deputy chief of staff under Yitzhak Rabin, Israel faced a violent uprising in the West Bank and Gaza that became the first intifada. And while my determination as prime minister to find a negotiated resolution to our conflict was in part based on a recognition of the Palestinian Arabs' national aspirations, the main impulse was my belief that such a compromise was profoundly in the interest of Israel, whose existence I had spent decades defending on the battlefield and which I was ultimately elected to lead.

Zionism, the political platform for the establishment of a Jewish state, emerged in the late 1800s in response to a brutal reality. That, too, was a part of my own family's story. Most of the world's Jews, who lived in the Russian empire and Poland, were trapped in a vise of poverty, powerlessness, and anti-Semitic violence. Even in the democracies of Western Europe, Jews were not necessarily secure. Theodor Herzl, a largely assimilated Jew in Vienna, published the foundational text of Zionism in 1896. It was called *Der Judenstaat.* "Jews have sincerely tried everywhere to merge with the national communities in which we live, seeking only to preserve the faith of our fathers," he wrote. "In vain are we loyal patriots, sometimes super-loyal. In vain do we make the same sacrifices of life and property as our fellow citizens ... In our native lands where we have lived for centuries, we are still decried as aliens." Zionism's answer was the establishment of a state of our own, in which we could achieve the self-determination and security denied to us elsewhere.

During the 1890s and the early years of the new century, more than a million Jews fled Eastern Europe, but mostly for America. It was only in the 1920s and 1930s that significant numbers arrived in Palestine. Then, within a few years, Hitler rose to power in Germany. The Jews of Europe faced not just discrimination and pogroms. They were systematically, industrially murdered. From 1939 until early 1942, when I was born, nearly 2 million Jews were killed. Six million would die by the end of the war. Almost the whole world, including the United States, rejected pleas to provide a haven for those who might have been saved. Even after Hitler was defeated, the British shut the doors of Palestine to those who had somehow survived.

+ + +

I was three when the Holocaust ended. Three years later Israel was established, in May 1948, and neighboring Arab states sent in their armies to try to snuff the state out in its infancy. It would be some years before I fully realized that this first Arab-Israeli war was the start of an essential tension in my country's life, and my own: between the Jewish ethical ideals at the core of Zionism and the reality of our having to fight, and sometimes even kill, in order to secure, establish, and safeguard our state. Yet even as a small child, I was keenly aware of the historic events swirling around me.

Mishmar Hasharon, the hamlet north of Tel Aviv where I spent the first seventeen years of my life, was one of the early kibbutzim. These collective farming settlements had their roots in Herzl's view that an avant-garde of "pioneers" would need to settle a homeland that was still economically undeveloped, and where even farming was difficult. Members of Jewish youth groups from Eastern Europe, among them my mother, provided most of the pioneers, drawing inspiration not just from Zionism but from the still untainted collectivist ideals represented by the triumph of Communism over the czars in Russia.

It is hard for people who didn't live through that time to understand the mind-set of the kibbutzniks. They had higher aspirations than simply planting the seeds of a future state. They wanted to be part of transforming what it meant to be a Jew. The act of first taming, and then farming, the soil of Palestine was not just an economic imperative. It was seen as deeply symbolic of Jews finally taking control of their own destiny. It was a message that took on an even greater power and poignancy after the mass murder of the Jews of Europe during the Holocaust.

Even for many Israelis nowadays, the physical challenges and the all-consuming collectivism of life on an early kibbutz are hard to imagine. Among the few dozen families in Mishmar Hasharon when I was born, there was no private property. Everything was communally owned and allocated. Every penny—or Israeli pound—earned from what we produced went into a communal kitty, from which each one of the seventy-or-so families got a small weekly allowance. By "small," I mean tiny. For my parents and others, even the idea of an ice cream cone for their children was a matter of keen financial planning. More often, they would save each weekly pittance with the aim of pooling them at birthday time, when they might stretch to the price of a picture book, or a small toy.

Decisions on any issue of importance were taken at the *aseifa*, the weekly meeting of kibbutz members held on Saturday nights in our dining hall. The agenda would be tacked up on the wall the day before, and the session usually focused on one issue, ranging from major items like the kibbutz's finances to whether, for instance, our small platoon of delivery drivers should be given pocket money to buy a sandwich or a coffee on their days outside the kibbutz or be limited to wrapping up bits of the modest fare on offer at breakfast time. That debate ended in a classic compromise: a little money, very little, so as to avoid violating the egalitarian ethos of the kibbutz.

But perhaps the aspect of life on the kibbutz most difficult for outsiders to understand, especially nowadays, is that we children were *raised* collectively. We lived in dormitories, organized by age group and overseen by a caregiver: in Hebrew, a *metapelet*, usually a woman in her twenties or thirties. For a few hours each afternoon and on the Jewish Sabbath, we were with our parents. Otherwise, we lived and learned in a world consisting almost entirely of other children.

Everything around us was geared toward making us feel like a band of brothers and sisters, as part of the wider collective. Until our teenage years, we weren't even graded in school. And though we didn't actually study how to till the land, some of my fondest early memories are of our "children's farm"—the vegetables we grew, the goats we milked, the hens and chickens that gave us our first experience of how life was created. And the aroma always wafting from the stone ovens in the bakery at the heart of the kibbutz, where we could see the bare-chested young men producing loaf after loaf of bread, not just for Mishmar Hasharon but small towns and villages for miles around.

Until our teenage years, we lived in narrow, oblong homes, four of us to a room, unfurnished except for our beds, under which we placed our pair of shoes or sandals. At one end of the corridor was a set of shelves where we collected a clean set of underwear, pants, and socks each week. At the other end were the toilets—at that point, the only indoor toilets on the kibbutz, with real toilet seats rather than just holes in the ground. All of us showered together until the age of twelve. I can't think of a single one of us who went on to marry someone from our own age group in the kibbutz—it would have seemed almost incestuous.

Mishmar Hasharon and other kibbutzim have long since abandoned the practice of collective child rearing. Some in my generation look back on the way we were raised not only with regret, but pain: a sense of parental absence, abandonment, or neglect. My own memories are more positive. The irony is that we probably spent more waking time with our parents than town or city children whose mothers and fathers worked nine-to-five jobs. The difference came at bedtime, or during the night. If you woke up unsettled, or ill, the only immediate prospect of comfort was from the metapelet or another of the kibbutz grown-ups who might be on overnight duty. Still, my childhood memories are overwhelmingly of feeling happy, safe, protected. I do remember waking up once, late on a stormy winter night when I was nine, in the grips of a terrible fever. I'd begun to hallucinate. I got to my feet and, without the thought of looking anywhere else for help, made my wobbly way through the rain to my parents' room and fell into their bed. They hugged me. They dabbed my forehead with water. The next morning, my father wrapped me in a blanket and took me back to the children's home.

To the extent that I was aware my childhood was different, I was given to understand it was special, that we were the beating heart of a Jewish state about to be born. I once asked my mother why other children got to live in their own apartments in places like Tel Aviv. "They are *ironim*," she said. City-dwellers. Her tone made it clear they were to be viewed as a slightly lesser species.

+ + +

Though both my parents were part of the pioneer generation, my mother, unlike my father, actually arrived as a pioneer, part of a Jewish youth group from Poland that came directly to the kibbutz. In addition to being more naturally outgoing than my father, she came to see Mishmar Hasharon as her extended family.

Esther Godin grew up in Warsaw. Born in 1913, she was the oldest of the six children of Samuel and Rachel Godin. Poland at the time was home to the largest Jewish community in the world, more than 3 million by the time of the Holocaust. While the Jews of Poland had a long history, the Godins did not. Before the First World War, my mother's parents made their way from Smolensk in Russia to Warsaw, which was also under czarist rule. When the war was over, the Bolshevik Revolution had toppled the czars. Poland became independent under the nationalist general Józef Piłsudski. The Godins had a decision to make: either return to now-Communist Russia or stay in the new Polish state, though without citizenship because they had not been born there. No doubt finding comfort, community, and a sense of safety amid the hundreds of thousands of Jews in the Polish capital, they chose Piłsudski over Lenin. They lived in what would become the Warsaw Ghetto, on Nalewski Street, where Samuel Godin eked out a living as a bookbinder.

My mother came to Zionism as a teenager, and it was easy to understand why she, like so many of the other young Jews around her, was drawn to it. She saw how hard her parents struggled economically, on the refugee fringes of a Jewish community itself precariously placed in a newly assertive Poland. She saw no future there. Though she attended a normal state-run high school, she and her closest friends joined a Zionist youth group called Gordonia, which had been founded in Poland barely a decade earlier. She started studying Hebrew. Each summer, from the age of fourteen, she and her Gordonia friends would retreat deep into the Carpathian Mountains, where they worked for local Polish landowners and learned the rudiments of farming and the rigors of physical labor. Late into the evening, they would learn not just about agriculture but Jewish history, the land of Palestine, and how they hoped to put both their newfound skills and Zionist ideals into practice.

She had just turned twenty-two when she set off for Mishmar Hasharon with sixty other Gordonia pioneers in the summer of 1935. It took them nearly a week to get there. They traveled by train south through Poland, passing not far from the little town of Oświęcim, which would later become infamous as the site of the Auschwitz concentration camp. Then, on through Hungary and across Romania to the grand old Black Sea port of Constanța; by ship through the Bosphorus, past Istanbul; and on to Haifa on the Palestinian coast, from where they were taken by truck to their bunk-bed rooms in one of a dozen prefab structures on the recently established kibbutz. Though the water came from a well and the kibbutz lacked even the basic creature comforts of the cramped Godin apartment in Warsaw, to my mother, it was just part of the challenge and the dream she'd embraced, which had come to define her. It was, she confided to me many years later, as if only then was her life truly beginning.

That feeling never left her. Yet it was always clouded by the memory of the family she left behind. When the Second World War began in September 1939, the Germans, and then the Soviets, invaded, overran, and divided Poland. Two of my mother's three sisters fled to Moscow. Her teenage brother Avraham went underground, joining the anti-Nazi partisans. All three survived the war. But in the autumn of 1940, the rest of her family found themselves inside the Warsaw Ghetto with the city's other 400,000 Jews. My mother's parents died there, along with her thirteen-year-old brother Itzik and her little sister Henya, who was only eleven.

When my mother arrived at the kibbutz, her Gordonia friends assumed she would marry a young man named Ya'akov Margalit, the leader of their group back in Warsaw. But the budding romance fell victim to the Zionist cause. As she embarked on her new life, Margalit was frequently back in Poland training and arranging papers for further groups of pioneers. He continued to write her long, heartfelt letters. But the letters had to be brought from the central post office in Tel Aviv, and the kibbutznik who fetched the mail was a quiet, diminutive twenty-five-year-old named Yisrael Mendel Brog—my father. Known as Srulik, his Yiddish nickname, he had come to Palestine five years earlier. He was an ordinary kibbutz worker. He drove a tractor.

My father's initial impulse in coming to Palestine was more personal than political. He was born in 1910 in the Jewish shtetl of Pushelat in Lithuania, near the mostly Jewish town of Ponovezh, a major seat of rabbinic learning and teaching. His own father, the only member of the Pushelat community with rabbinical training, made his living as the village pharmacist. Many of the Jews who lived there had left for America in the great exodus from Russian and Polish lands in the early 1900s. By the time my father was born, the community had shrunk to only about 1,000.

When he was two years old, a fire destroyed dozens of homes, as well as the shtetl's only synagogue. Donations soon arrived from the United States, and my paternal grandfather was put in charge of holding the money until rebuilding plans were worked out. The problem was that word spread quickly about the rebuilding fund. On the night of September 16, 1912, two burglars burst into my grandfather's home and stole the money. They beat him and my grandmother to death with an axle wrenched loose from a nearby carriage. Their four-year-old son Meir—my father's older brother—suffered a deep wound where the attackers drove the metal shaft into his head. He carried a golf-ball-sized indentation in his forehead for the rest of his life. My father had burrowed into a corner, and the attackers didn't see him.

The two orphaned boys were raised by their paternal grandmother, Itzila. Any return to normalcy they may have experienced was cut short by the outbreak of the First World War, forcing her to flee with them by train ahead of the advancing German army. They ended up some 1,500 miles south, in the Crimean city of Simferopol. Initially under czarist rule, then the Bolsheviks, and from late 1917 until the end of the war under the Germans, they had to deal with cold, damp, and a chronic shortage of food. Uncle Meir quickly learned how to survive. He later told me that he would run after German supply carriages and collect the odd potato that fell off the back. Realizing that the German soldiers had been wrenched from their own families by the war, he began taking my father with him on weekends to the neighborhood near their barracks, where the soldiers would sometimes give them cookies, or even a loaf of bread. But they were deprived of the basic ingredients of a healthy childhood: nutritious food and a warm, dry room in which to sleep. By the time Itzila brought them back to settle in Ponovezh at the end of the war, my father was diagnosed with rickets, a bone-development disease caused by the lack of vitamin D in their diet.

In another way, however, my father was the more fortunate of the boys. The lost schooling of those wartime years came at a less formative time for him than for his brother. Meir never fully made up the lost ground in school. My father simply began his Jewish primary education, *cheder*, a couple of years later than usual. He thrived there. Still, when it was time for him to enter secondary education, he decided against going on with his religious education. Meir was preparing to leave for Palestine, so my father enrolled in the Hebrew-language Zionist high school. When he graduated, one of the many Brog relatives who were by now living in the United States, his uncle Jacob, tried to persuade him to come to Pittsburgh for university studies. But with Meir signing on as his sponsor with the British Mandate authorities, he left for Palestine shortly before his twentieth birthday. Jacob did still insist on helping financially, which allowed my father to enroll at the Hebrew University in Jerusalem.

He did well in his studies—literature, history, and philosophy—but abandoned them after two years. His explanation for not staying on, when

I asked him years later, was that with the accelerating activity of the Zionist pioneers, it felt wrong to him to spend his days going to lectures, reading books, and writing essays. I am sure he also felt isolated and alone, with Meir, the only link to his life before Palestine, working in Haifa on the coast, four hours by bus from Jerusalem. When he began looking for a way to become part of the changes going on around him, Mishmar Hasharon didn't yet exist. Its founding core—a dozen Russian Jewish pioneers—was still working on agricultural settlements near Herzliya, north of Tel Aviv, until they found a place to start their kibbutz. But they had been joined by several young men and women who, though a year or two older than my father, had been with him at the Hebrew High School in Ponovezh. He decided to join them.

Late in 1932, the Jewish National Fund, supported financially by leading Jewish figures in Western Europe and the United States, bought 2,000 acres from an Arab landowner near Wadi Khawaret. The area was set aside for three Jewish settlements: a moshav called Kfar Haim, where the land was divided into family plots, and two kibbutzim. One was called Ma'abarot. Next to it was Mishmar Hasharon. My father was among the seventy youngsters who set off in three trucks with everything they figured they would need to turn the hard, scrubby hill into a kibbutz. They built the core from prefab kits: wooden huts to sleep in and a slightly larger one for the dining hall. They dug a well and ordered a pump from Tel Aviv, at first for drinking and washing, but soon to allow them to begin a vegetable garden, a dairy with a dozen cows, and a chicken coop with a few hundred hens, and to plant a first orange grove and a small vineyard.

Still, by the time my mother arrived three years later, there were not enough citrus trees, vines, cattle, and chickens to supply a membership that now numbered more than 200. Along with some of the others, my father worked outside the kibbutz, earning a regular paycheck to help support the collective. On his way back, he would stop at the post office in Tel Aviv to pick up letters and packages for the rest of the kibbutz— including Ya'akov Margalit's love letters to my mother. That was how my parents' friendship began, how a friendly hello led to shared conversation at the end of my father's workday, and how, a few years later, my mother decided to spurn her Gordonia suitor in favor of Srulik Brog, the postman. It was not until 1939 that they moved in together. They didn't bother getting married until the summer of 1941. Perhaps because this was less than nine months before I was born, my mother always remained vague when asked their exact wedding date.

My parents were an unlikely pair. My mother—bright, lively, and energetic—was a *doer*, who believed passionately in the grand social experiment of kibbutz life. Having helped her mother raise her siblings in Warsaw, and with a natural affinity for children, she became the main authority on issues related to childbirth and early childcare. She actively partook in the kibbutz's planning and politics, and reveled in its social life. My father was more detached both politically and socially. He was more contemplative, less assertive, less self-confident. Though he agreed broadly with the founding principles of the kibbutz and wanted to play his role in making it a success, I could see, as I grew older, that he was often impatient at what he saw as its intellectual insularity and its ideological rigidity.

As a result of his childhood illness, my father never grew to more than five foot four. Still, he was a powerful presence, stocky and strong from his work on the kibbutz, with a deep, resonant voice and wise-looking, blue-gray eyes. It was only through Uncle Meir that by the time I was born, he had moved on from driving a tractor to a more influential role on the kibbutz. Meir worked for the Palestine Electric Company, and when Mishmar Hasharon installed its own electricity system, the PEC was in charge of the work. Meir trained my father and put him forward as the kibbutz contact for maintaining and repairing the equipment. He was well suited for the work: a natural tinkerer, a problem-solver. He was good with his hands, and his natural caution was an additional asset as the kibbutz came to grips with the potential, and the potential dangers, of electric power. Once the system was installed, he became responsible for managing any aspect of the settlement that involved electricity: water pumps, the irrigation system, the communal laundry, and our bakery.

My parents were courteous and polite with each other, but they never showed any physical affection in our presence. None of the adults did. This was part of an unspoken kibbutz code. Not only for kibbutzniks but for all the early Zionists, outward displays of emotion were seen as a kind of self-indulgence that risked undermining communal cohesion, tenacity, and strength. Because I'd known no other way, this did not strike me as odd. Only in later years did I come to see the lasting effect on me. It would be a long time before I became comfortable showing my feelings beyond my immediate family and a few close friends. When I was in the army, this wasn't an issue. Self-control, especially in high-pressure situations, was a highly valued asset. But in politics, I think that it did for a considerable time inhibit my ability to connect with the public, or at least with the news media that played such a critical intermediary role. And it caused me to be seen not just as reserved or aloof, but sometimes as cold, or arrogant.

I got much that I value from my parents. From my mother, her boundless energy, activism, her attention to detail, and her focus on causes larger than herself—her belief that politics *mattered*. Also her love for art and literature. When I would come home from the children's dormitory to my parents' room—just nine feet by ten, with a wooden trundle bed to save space during the day—there was always a novel or a book of verse sharing the small table with my parents' most prized possession: their kibbutz-issue radio.

As a child, however, I spent much more time with my father. He was my guide, my protector and role model. Like my mother, he never mentioned the trials they and their families endured before arriving in Palestine. Nor did they ever speak to me in any detail about the Holocaust. No one on the kibbutz did, as if the memories were scabs they dared not pick at. Also, it seemed, because they were determined to avoid somehow passing on these remembered sadnesses to their sons and daughters. Still, when I was ten or eleven, my father—once, inadvertently—opened a window on his childhood. Every Saturday morning, we would listen to a classical music concert on my parents' radio. One day, as the beautiful melodies of Tchaikovsky's Violin Concerto in D major came through the radio, I was struck by the almost trancelike look that came over my father's face. He seemed to be in another, faraway, place. When the music ended, he turned and told me about the first time he'd heard it. It was on the train ride into Crimean exile with Itzila and Meir in the early days of the First World War. The train took five days to reach Crimea and sometimes halted for hours at a time. Every evening, a man at the far end of their carriage would take out his violin and play the second movement of the Tchaikovsky concerto.

I have heard the piece in concert halls many times since. When the orchestra begins the second movement—with the violin notes climbing higher, trembling ever so subtly—it brings tears to my eyes. I can't help thinking of the railway car in which my then-four-year-old father and other Jews from Ponovezh escaped the Great War of 1914. And of other trains, in another war twenty-five years later, carrying Jews not to safety but to death camps.

My father encouraged me, when I was eight, to learn the piano. I took lessons once a week throughout my childhood along with several other kibbutz children. When we got old enough, we took turns playing a short piece—the secular, kibbutz equivalent of an opening prayer—at the Friday night meal in the dining hall. I have always cherished being able to play. Sitting down at the piano and immersing myself in Bach, Beethoven, Schubert, or Chopin never ceases to bring me a sense of calm, of freedom, and—especially nowadays, when I have finally worked to master a particularly intricate piece—a feeling of pure joy.

+ + +

As a young child, I spent most of my waking hours in the company of my several dozen kibbutz "siblings" in the children's home, in the dining hall, or running through the open spaces in the center of the kibbutz with our metapelet, Bina, who would often take us through the orange groves in the afternoon, and sometimes across the main road to the Arab village.

Wadi Khawaret consisted of a few dozen concrete homes built back from a main street bordered by shops and storehouses. Bina would buy us sweets in the little grocery store. The man behind the counter had a kindly, weathered face and a dark mustache. Dressed in a gray *galabiya* and a keffiyeh, he smiled when we came in. There was always a group of Palestinian women, in full-length robes, seated on stoops outside breastfeeding their babies. We saw cattle, bulls, even the odd buffalo being led to or from the fields. I sensed no hostility, and certainly no hatred, toward us in the village. The people seemed warm and benignly indifferent to the dozen Jewish toddlers and their metapelet. My own attitude to Wadi Khawaret was of benign curiosity. I did not imagine that within a couple of years we would be on opposite sides of a war.

I enjoyed these visits, as I enjoyed every part of my early childhood.

Each age group on the kibbutz was given a name. Ours was called *dror*. It was the Hebrew word for "freedom." But *dror* was also the name of one of the Jewish youth movements in the Warsaw Ghetto, heroes in their doomed uprising against the Nazis. Little by little, from about the age of five, I became more aware of the suffering the Jews had so recently endured in the lands my parents had left behind, the growing tension around us, and the sense that something momentous was about to happen as the prospect of a state got closer.

The memories remain with me to this day, like a series of snapshots. On a spring morning in 1947, I got my first real sense that the Jewish state was something we would have to fight for, and that youngsters not that much older than me would play a critical role. I got a close-up look at the elite of the Zionist militias, the Palmach. It numbered something like 6,000, from a pre-state force totaling around 40,000. The Palmachniks were highly motivated activists, almost all of them in their late teens. They had no fixed base. Each platoon spent five or six months at a time on various kibbutzim. For the first two weeks of each month, they would earn their keep by working in the fields. They spent the other weeks training. I had just turned five when I watched three dozen Palmach boys and girls, in their T-shirts and short khaki pants, rappel confidently down the side of one of our few concrete buildings. The building was only twenty-five or thirty feet high, but it looked like a skyscraper from my perch on the grass in front, and the feat of the young Palmachniks seemed nothing short of heroic.

A few months later, on a Saturday afternoon in November 1947, I crowded into my parents' room as the Haganah radio station crackled out its account of a United Nations debate on the future of Palestine. The session was the outcome of a long train of events starting with Britain's acknowledgment that its mandate to rule over Palestine was unsustainable. The British had proposed a series of arrangements to accommodate both Arab and Jewish aspirations. Now, the UN was meeting to consider the idea of splitting Palestine into two new states, one Arab and the other Jewish.

Since the partition was based on existing areas of Arab and Jewish settlement, the proposed Jewish state looked like a boomerang, with a long, very narrow center strip along the Mediterranean, broadening slightly into the Galilee in the north and the arid coastline in the south. Jerusalem, the site of the ancient Jewish temple, was not part of it. It was to be placed under international rule. By no means were all Zionist leaders happy with partition. Many, on both the political right and the left, wanted a Jewish state in all of Palestine, with Jerusalem as its centerpiece. But David Ben-Gurion and the pragmatic mainstream argued that UN endorsement of a Jewish state—no matter what its borders, even with a new Palestinian Arab state alongside it—would represent a historic achievement. The proceedings went on for hours. At sundown, we had to return to the children's home. But we were woken before dawn. The vote for partition—for the Jewish state Herzl first dreamed of fifty years before— had been won. A huge bonfire blazed in front of the bakery. All around us the grown-ups were singing and dancing in celebration.

On the Arab side, there was no rejoicing. Every one of the Arab delegations at the UN voted against partition, rejecting a Jewish state even if it was created along with a Palestinian Arab one. Violence erupted the next day. An attack on a bus near Lydda, on the road up to Jerusalem, left six Jews dead. Similar attacks occurred around the country. Shooting broke out in mixed Arab-and-Jewish towns and cities: Jaffa on the southern edge of Tel Aviv; Safed, Tiberias, and Haifa in the north; and in Jerusalem.

I followed all this with curiosity and trepidation through my halting attempts to read *Davar le Yeladim*, the weekly children's edition of the Labor Zionist newspaper *Davar*. We children felt an additional connection to what was going on. One of our former housemates, a boy named Giora Ros, had left the year before when his father took a job in Jerusalem. As the battle for the city raged through the end of 1947 and into 1948, its besieged Jewish residents fought for their lives. Throughout the *yishuv*, the Jewish community in Palestine, food was being collected to relieve the city. We sent our friend packages of clothing and food, which we saved up by eating only half an egg at breakfast and smaller portions at dinner.

The mood darkened further at the end of January 1948, four months before the British departed. A cluster of settlements known as Gush Etzion, south of Jerusalem near the hills of Bethlehem, also came under siege. Around midnight on January 15, a unit of Haganah youngsters— they would become known as "The 35"—set off on foot to try to break through. Marching through the night, they made it only within a couple of miles of Gush Etzion before they were surrounded and attacked by local Arabs. By late afternoon, all of them were dead. When the British authorities recovered their bodies, they found that the enemy had not simply killed them. All of the bodies had been battered and broken. Rumors spread that in some cases, the dead men's genitals had been cut off and shoved into their mouths. Since I was still a few weeks short of my sixth birthday, I was spared that particular detail. But not the sense of horror over what had happened, nor the central message: the lengths and depths to which the Arabs of Palestine seemed ready to go in their fight against us. *"Hit'alelu bagufot!"* was the only slightly sanitized account we children were given. "They mutilated the corpses!"

Even after the partition vote, statehood was not a given. In the weeks before the British left, two senior Americans—the ambassador to the UN and Secretary of State George C. Marshall—recommended abandoning or at least delaying the declaration of an Israeli state. Ben-Gurion, however, feared that any delay risked the end of any early hope of statehood. After he managed to secure a one-vote majority in his de facto cabinet, the state was declared on May 14, 1948.

And hours later, the armies of five Arab states crossed into Palestine.

# 2

# Picking Locks, Stealing Guns, Growing Up

WHEN THE WAR BROKE OUT IN EARNEST IN THE SPRING OF 1948, MY focus, like that of all Israelis, was on the fighting, which even the youngest of us knew would determine whether the state would survive. Day after day, my father helped me to chart each major advance and setback on a little map. Dozens of kibbutzim around the country were in the line of fire. Some had soon fallen, while others barely managed to hang on. Just five miles inland from us, an Israeli settlement came under attack by an Iraqi force in the nearby Arab village of Qaqun.

But inside Mishmar Hasharon, I had the almost surreal feeling that this great historical drama was something happening everywhere else. If it hadn't been for the radio, or the newsreels we saw in the dining hall, and the little map on which I traced its course with my father, I would barely have known a war was going on. The only Arab army that got near us was the Iraqis, in Qaqun. If they had advanced a few miles farther, they could have overrun Mishmar Hasharon, reached the coast, and cut the new Jewish state in half. I can still remember the rumble of what sounded like thunder one morning in June 1948 as the Alexandronis, one of the twelve brigades in the new Israeli army, launched their decisive attack on the Iraqis. "No reason to be afraid," our metapelet kept telling us. That only made me more scared. Yet within a few hours, everything was quiet again, and never again did the shell fire get near to us.

It wasn't until well into 1949 that formal agreements were signed and "armistice line" borders drawn with the Arab states. By the measure that mattered most—survival—Israel had won and the Arab attackers had lost. Still, Jordan ended up in control of the West Bank, as well as the eastern half of a divided city of Jerusalem, including the walled Old City and the site of the ancient Jewish temple. The new Israel remained, at least geographically, vulnerable. It was just eleven miles wide around Tel Aviv and even narrower near Mishmar Hasharon. Egypt-held Gaza was seven miles from the southern Israeli city of Ashkelon and just forty from the outskirts of Tel Aviv.

Israel secured control of the entire Galilee, up to the prewar borders with Lebanon and Syria, and of the Negev Desert in the south. The territory of our new state was about a third larger than the area proposed under the UN partition plan rejected by the Arabs. Yet the victory came at a heavy price: more than 6,000 dead, 1 percent of the Jewish population of Palestine at the time. One-third of the Israeli dead were Holocaust survivors.

The Arabs paid a heavy price too, and not just the roughly 7,000 people who lost their lives. Nearly 700,000 Palestinian Arabs had fled—or, in some cases, been forced to flee—towns and villages in what was now Israel. The full extent and circumstances of the Arabs' flight became known to us kids at Mishmar Hasharon only later. But it did not take long to notice the change around us. Wadi Khawaret was physically still there, but all of the villagers were gone. As far as I could discover, none had been killed. They left with a first wave of refugees in March or April 1948, and eventually ended up near Tulkarem on the West Bank. After the war, the Israeli government divided up their farmland among nearby kibbutzim, including Mishmar Hasharon.

The absence of our former neighbors in Wadi Khawaret seemed to me at the time simply a part of the war. From the moment the violence started, I understood there would be suffering on both sides. When we sent our care packages to Giora Ros in Jerusalem, I remember trying to imagine what "living under siege" would feel like, and what would happen to Giora if it succeeded. Especially after the murder and the mutilation of The 35, I assumed the war would come down to a simple calculus. If there was going to be an Israel—if there was going to be a Mishmar Hasharon—we had to win and the Arabs had to lose. At first, even the fact that our kibbutz had been given a share of the land of Wadi Kha-waret seemed just another product of the war. After all, Ben-Gurion had accepted the plan for two states. The Arabs had said no and attacked us instead. *Someone* had to farm the land. Why not us?

+ + +

Yet events after the war led me to ask myself questions of basic fairness, and whether we were being faithful to some of the high-sounding ideals I heard spoken about with such pride on the kibbutz. The Palestinians were not the only refugees. More than 600,000 Jews fled *into* Israel from Arab countries where they had lived for generations. More than 100,000 arrived from Iraq, and several hundred thousand from Morocco, Tunisia, and Algeria in North Africa. Immediately after the war, about 50,000 were airlifted out of Yemen, where they had endured violent attacks after the UN partition vote.

The reality that greeted the newly arrived Yemenis in Israel was more complex. Most were initially settled in tented transit camps. I'm not sure how several dozen Yemeni families made their way to Wadi Khawaret, but it made sense for them to move into the village's vacant homes. But a few nights after the Yemenis moved in, a posse of young men, including some from Mishmar Hasharon, descended on them and, armed with clubs and wooden staves, drove them away.

I was shocked. I'd seen the photos in *Davar le Yeladim* celebrating the airlift, with the Yemenis kissing the airport tarmac in relief, gratitude, and joy at finding refuge in the new Israeli state. Now, for the "crime" of moving into a row of empty buildings in search of a decent place to live, they'd been beaten up and chased away. By *us*. I realized Wadi Khawaret no longer belonged to the Arabs, but surely our kibbutz had no more right to the buildings than Jews who had fled from Yemen and needed them a lot more than we did. For days, I tried to discover who had joined the vigilante attack. Though everyone seemed to know what had happened, no one talked about it. In the dining hall, I ran my eyes over all the boys in their late teens and early twenties. They all looked the same as before, eating and talking as if nothing had happened.

The Yemenis also needed jobs. This led to a challenge for Mishmar Hasharon. The core of the kibbutz ethos was that we lived from our own labor. Yet Ben-Gurion insisted we and other kibbutzim provide work for the Yemenis and other new arrivals from the Arab states. We began hiring Yemeni workers when I was about ten, when we kids started working for an hour or so each day in the fields. We worked alongside several dozen Yemeni women who lived a few miles north in a *maabarah*, a transit settlement that later evolved into a village called Elyakhin.

I don't know whether I expected to feel a Gordonian sense of joy at the redemptive value of physical labor when I began working in the fields. Our first assignment was to plant long rows of flower bulbs—gladioli—spaced at intervals of four inches or so. But as I joined the other children and the Yemeni women, what I felt was more mundane. Heat. Fatigue. Boredom. To make the time pass, I thought of it as a competition. Each of us began together, planting the bulbs in furrows stretching to the end of the field. The point was obviously to do it right. But I found it interesting to see who finished first, and how much longer it took the rest of us.

The same worker always led the way. She was a Yemeni in her early thirties named Baddura. Short and stocky, with dark curly hair, she was nearly always smiling, whether we were planting bulbs, sowing seeds, or picking oranges and grapefruit and lemons, potatoes, or peppers and tomatoes. When I remarked to her how much better and faster she was than the rest of us, she laughed. Still years away from growing into my adult body, I looked more like an eight- or a nine-year-old. She took me under her wing. The next day, we were picking tomatoes. "Do the row next to mine," she said. Watching the almost balletic grace with which she moved made it easier. I decided it was like mastering a new piece on the piano. The secret was to achieve a kind of unthinking fluidity, to think a few notes ahead of the ones you were playing. Before long, I was finishing my sowing or reaping a good ten yards ahead of the other kids, and not too far behind her.

Though the Yemenis worked in our fields, they were not members of the kibbutz. They were paid a day rate. Though they were by far the most productive workers, they got no share of what we produced or possessed. A few years later, I raised this at one of the separate aseifa meetings held by young people on the kibbutz, only to be told we'd never wanted to employ outsiders in the first place. It was only because of Ben-Gurion that we felt unable to refuse. I'm sure that was true, but it struck me as an exercise in finding a verbal rationale for a situation that was obviously unjust.

It was an accidental glance up from picking carrots that focused the sense of unfairness. We were working on a tract of about seven acres where we also grew tomatoes and potatoes and eggplants. I think I was eleven or twelve. We had piled onto a flatbed trailer, a dozen kids and a dozen Yemeni women, and were towed by a tractor driven by a man named Yankele. Like my father, he was one of the original group at Mishmar Hasharon. Before the Yemenis came, he had worked planting and harvesting. Now, he was responsible for "managing" the Yemenis, and us kids as well, during our fieldwork. It was a hot, dusty summer's day, and he paced among us every half hour or so to make sure the work was going smoothly. I'd been working for an hour or so, crouching alongside Baddura, when I looked up. On the edge of the field, under the shade of a clump of banana trees, stood Yankele. He was twirling a big set of keys around his finger, first one way, then the other, as his eyes tracked us. Like a kibbutznik-turned-plantation-owner.

✦ ✦ ✦

In the tiny world of the kibbutz, there were not enough children to organize separate school classes for each year. When I started school, I was five and a half. Most of the others were six. A few had already turned seven. Maybe it was this age pressure, or maybe something inside me, but from the outset, I had a thirst for knowledge. I was aware early on that some of the schoolwork came easily, almost automatically, to me: numbers and math and reasoning most of all. I also began reading books, even if I could not fully understand them. By the time I was eight or nine, I was burying myself in volumes of the children's encyclopedia at the kibbutz library, trying to untangle the mysteries of airplanes and automobiles or the creation of worldly wonders, from the Hanging Gardens of Babylon to the Empire State Building and the Golden Gate Bridge.

At first, I got many of the answers from my father. On Saturdays, we would walk around the kibbutz as I plied him with questions. In many ways, he lacked self-confidence. I remember decades later, after he had passed away, asking my mother how come they had spent their entire lives on the kibbutz and never moved away. She replied: "What would your father have done outside?" But he had a quick mind and, despite having left Hebrew University early, had secured enough credits to get his degree—one of a handful of men on the kibbutz to have done so. He delighted in acquiring, and sharing, knowledge.

How come the moon wasn't always round, I remember asking him in one of our first educational strolls. How did anyone *know* that the saber-toothed tigers I'd seen in the encyclopedia actually existed? And where were they now? There was not a single question he did not try to help me answer. When I was nine or ten, he took me to see the first water pump on the kibbutz. I watched as he disassembled the casing, then the power unit, which had a big screwlike element in the middle. I wanted to know how it worked, how it was designed. How it was made. A few months later, he took me to the factory near Tel Aviv where the pumps were manufactured.

I was an introverted child, not so much shy as self-contained, contemplative, at times dreamy. Though I became aware of how quickly my mind seemed to grasp numbers and geometric shapes and music notes, I was small for my age and awkward at the sports we'd play on the dusty field at the far edge of the kibbutz. I did over time become a remarkably effective left defensive back on our kids' soccer team. But that wasn't because I miraculously discovered a buried talent for the game. Physically, I was like my father—with a natural hand coordination that made delicate tasks come easily, but otherwise, often haplessly, hopelessly, uncoordinated. My soccer prowess was down to the fact that no opposing player in his right mind, once I'd inadvertently cut his knees out from under him, felt it was worth coming anywhere close to me.

Bina, our metapelet from when I was three until age eight, was the mother of twins a year younger than me. She was more handsome than beautiful, with wavy dark hair. But she was full of warmth. She was especially kind to me, which was no doubt one reason I felt the effects of my collective upbringing less dramatically than some other kibbutz children. When we were both much older, she used to tell a story about my slightly ethereal approach to life when I was in her charge. One winter afternoon when I was four, she took our group onto the gentle rise on the northern edge of the kibbutz, which at that time of year was full of wildflowers. When she got there, she realized I had gone missing. Retracing her steps, she found me standing in front of a rock in the middle of the dirt path. "Ehud," she said, "why didn't you come with us?" I apparently replied: "I'm thinking: which *side* of the rock should I go around?"

Still, important though Bina was as a presence in my life, it was the influence of another figure—another youngster—who mattered more and for longer. His name was Yigal Garber. In first grade, every child got a mentor. Yigal was mine. Solidly built and self-confident, with a knowing smile, he would go on to become one of the most respected members of the kibbutz. Though I was the only child he mentored, he was also in charge of our class's extracurricular educational program. It began when I was ten, and Yigal was sixteen. It was a mix of ideological training—the kibbutz equivalent of what my mother had done with her Gordonia friends in Poland—and a scouting course.

One evening a week, he would spend several hours with us. He began by reading us a story or a poem. One that I remember with particular clarity involved a slave who had a nail driven into his ear in hopes of remaining in his master's service forever. He had become enslaved not only in body, but in mind. Another night, Yigal read us an account of a Palmach unit stranded on a hill they had taken, with anti-personnel mines all around them. The readings were gripping and were always an entry point for a discussion: How did we understand the story? What would *we* do if faced with a similar choice?

When that part was over, he walked us into the fields outside the kibbutz. The only sound we heard was the occasional screech of a jackal. Sometimes, he would split us into twos and have each pair set off from a far edge of the field and find our way back. Yigal stationed himself at the center. We would have to sneak up and see which of us could get closest without his seeing or hearing us approach. In his last year with us before leaving for his army service, he gave each of us a narrow wooden stick and began drilling us in the teenage introduction to martial arts.

+ + +

Shortly after I turned thirteen, I overheard a conversation between a couple of older kids in the dining hall. They said there was this guy in Gan Shmuel, a kibbutz to the north of us, who had an "amazing" ability. Using a strip of steel shaped to work like a key, he could open locks—even chunky Yale padlocks, the gold standard in those days—in less than a minute.

I was intrigued by the mechanical puzzle and managed to locate two slightly rusted locks. One was a Yale, the other an Israeli-made lookalike called a Nabob. One evening after dinner, I searched the ground around the kibbutz garage for shards of metal that looked like they might fit into the key slot, and spent the next half hour or so propped against a tree, trying and failing to coax either lock to open. I realized I would need to discover how the locks worked. But how to get inside to see?

Saturday afternoons in Mishmar Hasharon were a quiet time, like the old Jewish neighborhoods and shtetls back in Europe but minus the religious trappings. I waited until midafternoon and walked past the bakery toward the garage. Its roll-down, corrugated door was locked. So was the structure next to it, where the blacksmith and metalwork shop were. But attached to the blacksmith's was a hut where our scrap metal was dumped. I doubted it would be locked, and it wasn't. Pausing to let my eyes get used to the dark, I made my way into the metalwork area. I crossed to the cabinet where the tools were kept. I took out a steel jigsaw used for cutting through metal and, hiding it under my shirt, made my way out.

Fortunately, the saw was up to the task of cutting into the softer alloy that made up the body of the locks. Once I'd cut inside them, I saw they shared the same basic construction. There was a series of springs and shafts that, in response to the indentations of a key, aligned in such a way to allow the lock to open. I sneaked back into the metalwork shop five or six times. By trial and error, I managed to shape one of the jigsaw blades into a pick tool that seemed like it should do the job. For days, I manipulated it into each of the padlocks. I knew I had the principle right, but I still couldn't get it to work. Blisters formed on my thumb and fingers. Then, finally, the Yale sprung open! With each successive try I got better at knowing how to put the blade in, when and where to rotate it, and how much pressure to apply. After fashioning a half dozen other tools, each slightly different in width and shape, I could get the mechanism to work on my first try. Other locks—doors, trunks, closets—were even easier after I made picks for them as well.

I couldn't resist sharing my newly acquired skill with a couple of the boys in my class, and word gradually spread. There was a handful of slightly older boys whom we referred to as the "rogues." They weren't delinquents. They were free spirits, bridling at the uniform expectations and rules of kibbutz life. Over the next few years, as coconspirators more than close friends, I found myself drawn to two of them. Ido and Moshe were eighteen months older than me. Though Ido was just a few inches over five feet, he was strong and athletic, a star even on the basketball court. Moshe was taller, if a bit overweight. He was nowhere near as strong as Ido but still stronger than me, and had a streetwise intelligence and a sardonic sense of humor. Both had tested the patience of our teachers to the breaking point. Ido had been sent off to a vocational school in Netanya. Moshe was moved to Mikveh Israel, a school that focused mostly on agriculture. On Friday evenings and Saturdays in the kibbutz, however, they filled their time with a variety of minor misdeeds. My role—the cement in our budding partnership—was as designated lock-picker.

Our first caper targeted the concrete security building near the dining hall. It contained the kibbutz's store of weapons, protected by a metal door secured by a padlock. Late one Friday night, with Ido and Moshe as lookouts, I crouched in front of the lock and took out my tools. In less than a minute, I had it open. We darted into the storeroom. There were about eighty rifles, along with a few machine guns, on racks along the walls. Ido took a rifle from the farthest end of the rack and wrapped it in a blanket. Moshe pocketed a box of ammunition. As the others hurried back to our dormitory, I closed the lock, making sure it was in the same position I'd found it, and joined them. The next afternoon, we stole away through the moshav of Kfar Hayim into a field on the far side. We test-fired the rifle until sunset, when we returned to the kibbutz and replaced it in the armory. It felt like the perfect crime: foolproof, since no one was likely to notice anything. Essentially harmless. And repeatable, as we confirmed by returning on Friday nights every month or two.

This modest preadolescent rebellion never extended to doubting the national mission of Israel. Growing up on a kibbutz in a country younger even than we were, we all felt a part of its brief history, and its future. That was especially true after my kibbutz mentor, Yigal, left for his military service and joined one of the Israeli army's elite units.

The 1948 war had been won, but it had not brought peace. Palestinian irregulars, fedayeen operating from Jordan and the Gaza Strip, mounted hit-and-run raids. In armed ambushes or by planting mines, they killed dozens of Israeli civilians and injured hundreds more. The country was in no mood for another war. The newly created Israeli armed forces— known as Tzahal, a Hebrew acronym for the Israeli Defense Force—also seemed to have lost the cutting edge, or perhaps the desperate motivation, of the pre-state militias. At first, Ben-Gurion relied on young recruits in the infantry brigades to counter the fedayeen attacks. Nearly ninety reprisal operations were launched in 1952 and early 1953. Nearly all ended with the soldiers failing to reach their target or taking casualties. Sometimes both.

By mid-1953, the army decided to set up Israel's first dedicated commando force. It was called Unit 101. It was led by a twenty-five-year-old named Ariel Sharon, who had been a platoon commander in 1948. With Ben-Gurion and especially the then army chief of staff, Mordechai Maklef, determined to hit back hard at the fedayeen attacks, Sharon took a few dozen handpicked soldiers and began mounting a different kind of retaliatory attack. The largest, in October 1953, was in the West Bank village of Qibya in response to the murder of a woman and her two children in their home in central Israel. Sharon and his commandos surrounded and attacked the village, destroying homes and other buildings—and killing at least forty villagers sheltering inside them. Israel came under strong international condemnation and was accused of allowing its troops to unleash a massacre. Unit 101 was soon disbanded. It had lasted only half a year. But that was not because of Qibya. While realizing the importance of avoiding civilian casualties, Maklef's successor as armed forces chief, Moshe Dayan, was convinced that only units like 101 offered any realistic hope of taking the fight to the fedayeen. He made Unit 101 the core of a larger commando force that was merged into Battalion 890 of the paratroopers' brigade, and he put Sharon in overall command.

This was the force that Yigal Garber joined. He became part of its elite commando team, Company A, and took part in a series of attacks in the West Bank and Gaza. While avoiding a repeat of Qibya, they inflicted heavy casualties on Jordanian and Egyptian army and police units, and also suffered casualties of their own. Battalion 890 was based just a couple of miles from Mishmar Hasharon, and Yigal returned to the kibbutz every few weeks. He never talked about the commando operations. But with every report of Israelis killed in a fedayeen attack, I knew there would be a retaliation raid, with Yigal almost certainly involved—and, I hoped, returning unscathed.

He did. And in 1956, two years into his military service, he was part of Israel's second full-scale war. For a while, our reprisal attacks seemed to be working. The fedayeen attacks decreased. But that didn't last, especially in the south along the border with Gaza. Egypt's pro-Western monarchy had been toppled in a coup organized by a group of army officers led by a stridently pan-Arabist—and anti-Israeli—lieutenant colonel named Gamal Abdel Nasser. Egypt began to provide support for the fedayeen in Gaza, arming and training them and helping organize cross-border attacks. Then, in the summer of 1956, Nasser nationalized the Suez Canal, which had been owned by the British and French.

Ben-Gurion was convinced to go to war when both Britain and France decided to retake the canal. Under an agreement reached beforehand, Israel would begin the hostilities, after which the British and French would enter under the guise of separating Israeli and Egyptian forces. Ben-Gurion's hope was to end the threat of fedayeen strikes, at least in the south, by taking control both of Gaza and the enormous natural buffer afforded by the Sinai Desert. Militarily, it went as planned. On October 29, 1956, Yigal and other paratroopers from Battalion 890 dropped deep into the Sinai. They landed near the entrance to the Mitla Pass, a sinuous route between two lines of craggy hills twenty-five miles from the canal. British and French air strikes began three days later. Nasser pulled most of his forces back across the canal. By early November, Israel was in control of Gaza and the whole of the Sinai.

Politically, however, Ben-Gurion and his European partners had catastrophically miscalculated. Britain and France were fading imperial powers. The balance of power after the Second World War rested with the United States and the Soviet Union. Both were furious over the obviously prearranged seizure of Sinai, Gaza, and the canal. It took a while for the message to sink in. In a speech to the Knesset soon after the conquest was complete, Ben-Gurion declared the post-1948 armistice null and void, and said Israel would never return the territory it had captured to the Egyptians' control.

A few days later, however, he had no choice but to deliver a different message in a radio address to the country. In making his forced retreat, he did at least secure a concession with the help of the Americans. The Sinai and Gaza border area would be placed under the supervision of a UN force, and he got a US assurance of Israel's right of passage through the Straits of Tiran to the Red Sea as well as an agreement that if the Egyptians blocked Israeli shipping we would have the right to respond. But he also announced we would leave every inch of territory taken in the war. By early 1957, we did so. The one lasting gain came in Gaza. On their way out, Israeli troops destroyed the fedayeen's military installations, and cross-border attacks from the south ceased.

Unlike in 1948, the Sinai War touched me directly. I never felt Israel's existence was in danger. The fighting was brief and far away. But Mishmar Hasharon had a small role in the war plan. Ben-Gurion and Dayan were concerned that the coordinated attack might lead to a wider war, with the possibility that Egyptian warplanes might attack as they had in 1948, or that the Jordanians might be drawn into the fighting. As one precaution, they based several hundred reservists from the Alexandroni Brigade in a defensive position near the Mediterranean: the eucalyptus grove at the top end of our kibbutz, where the cover was so dense they were all but invisible from the air.

We kids seized on the chance to see Israeli soldiers at close hand. I can't remember whether it was Ido or Moshe who noticed an area at the back of their encampment, on the other side of the kibbutz cemetery, where neatly stacked boxes of munitions were kept. We spent the next several afternoons on reconnaissance. A soldier was always on guard, but there were times the area was unwatched, either when one guard handed over to the next, or on their cigarette breaks.

We struck the following Friday. Nowadays, the cemetery consists of a half dozen rows of headstones. Walking through it, as I still do at least once each year, is like revisiting my past. Almost all the grown-ups I remember from my childhood now rest there, including my parents. My father died in 2002, at the age of ninety-two. My mother passed away only a few years ago, a few weeks after her one-hundredth birthday. But in 1956, the cemetery was tiny. The chances of anyone being there at midnight on a Friday were close to zero. Crouching in the shadow of the headstones, we could see the guard. We waited until he left for his break.

Each of us took a wooden box and one of the slightly larger metal boxes. Inside, we found a treasure trove: thousands of bullets for all kinds of weapons. The metal cases held heavier firepower: grenades and mortars. We returned those. We were mischievous, but not crazy. Yet each of us now had a crate full of ammunition, even including belts for machine guns.

+ + +

My experience at school began to change in my early teenage years. Shortly before my fourteenth birthday, our age group was sent to a school outside Mishmar Hasharon. The kibbutz had decided that since there were only a dozen or so children in each class, it wasn't economically viable to provide a quality education. They sent us to the regional high school.

It was several hundred yards down the road in the direction of Tel Aviv, and far more rigorous. I was no longer the only kid in my class who liked to read or could do math problems in his head. It was there I first got truly interested in science. When I came across concepts I couldn't understand, our teachers always seemed able to answer my questions or help me find the answers myself. I liked the school enormously. I might well have gone on to finish my secondary education there. I probably should have. But the next year, the kibbutz brought us back.

One of the reasons for the U-turn was financial. Like many kibbutzim, Mishmar Hasharon embarked on a scheme to make its school more economically sustainable—by taking in a number of "outside children," or *yeldei chutz*, from towns and settlements around Israel. Yet this latest policy change also triggered a debate over what *kind* of education kibbutzim should be providing. Should a kibbutz school offer a curriculum tailored to passing the *bagrut*, the matriculation exam, and going on to university? Or should it limit itself to a fairly basic education geared to developing the talents needed for a productive life on the kibbutz? In a series of heated debates in the dining hall, almost all of Mishmar Hasharon supported the model of a basic, kibbutz-oriented education.

My father was the leading voice among the dissenters, and though it seemed obvious he was fighting an uphill battle, I remember feeling a sense of pride at watching him. Not only was he opposed to the new policy, he was aghast. In the only time I can recall him speaking out at one of the weekly kibbutz meetings, he asked how Mishmar Hasharon could take upon itself the right to constrain an individual child's life potential. "We are Jews!" he said. "We are people who have left our impact on history through our scholars, not our peasants. I can't understand how we, who came here to open a new chapter in the history of our people, can choose to keep our sons and daughters from studying. We should *encourage* them to study!" He accepted that the interests of the kibbutz mattered. But what kind of "model society" would we be creating if we chose to "doom our own children to ignorance, and cut them off from the great forward momentum of history in Israel and the whole world?"

In a kibbutz, however, the majority ruled. In this case, it was nearly unanimous, my mother included. I could see she felt torn, whether because she agreed with my father or because she realized how deeply he felt. But she accepted the decision. For her, this was what it meant to be part of the larger kibbutz family. Still, my father didn't give up. He couldn't change the kibbutz's ruling. But he tried to get me to stay at the regional high school. A couple of years earlier, examiners had fanned out across Israel to administer its first aptitude tests. I finished among the top two-dozen results in the country. "How can you throw your gifts away? For *what*?" he asked me. "If you leave that school, and give up on going to university, it will be like betraying yourself." At one point, he walked me out to the patch of hard-packed soil where we parked the tractors and farm machinery. "What do you want to do with your life?" he asked. "Do you want to be a *farmer*?"

I thought about it before answering. "I don't know what will happen in the future," I said. "But if you ask me now, I would say I want to drive one of the kibbutz trucks."

I could see the shock and disappointment in his eyes. But it was the truth. I did imagine that at some point I might want to make a life outside the kibbutz. But I'd never lived anywhere else. If I was going to remain a part of it, I could think of no better way than to join our little corps of drivers. Though they lived on the kibbutz, they spent most of their time delivering or picking up goods in places like Tel Aviv, Holon, or Ashkelon. As the US Marines might have put it, I guess I figured I'd join the truck drivers and see the world.

The deeper reason I said no to my father, as I am sure he suspected, was that I felt a need to take control of my own life. That was simply a part of growing up, a process that probably happened more quickly for 1950s kibbutz children than for town or city kids. We loved and respected our parents, but we were living with other teenagers. We weren't just residents of the kibbutz. We were part of the economic collective, working in the fields or orchards, the garage and the metal shop. This bred a sense of independence. I listened to my father's arguments, but this was a decision about *my* future.

So I returned to the kibbutz school. The level of teaching was nowhere near that of the regional school. But we did begin to study new subjects like economics and politics. There were two other welcome surprises as well. The first was the arrival of a new history teacher. Knowledgeable, enthusiastic, and eloquent, he had a rare gift for igniting excitement in his students. We studied the French Revolution. He brought it to life with insights into Montesquieu, Rousseau, and John Locke; Louis XVI and Marie Antoinette; Robespierre, Danton, and Napoleon. He traced the dynamics that led to the revolution, and the way its ideals descended into the bloodshed and terror that followed. He presented history as a human process that raised as many questions as it answered, as something we could learn from.

The second high point was a couple named David and Leah Zimmerman. Though Mishmar Hasharon, like other kibbutzim, was secular, they introduced us to the Talmud, the ancient compendium of rabbinic discussion and debate on the meaning of passages from the Bible. We focused on two tractates, Baba Kama and Baba Metziah, in which the rabbis drew on verses from Exodus to devise a system of rules for resolving civil disputes. It was the Talmud of torts. The intricacy and the depth of the rabbinical debate fascinated me.

+ + +

Yigal returned from the army a few months after the 1956 war, when, like other teenagers, I was about to enter a pre-military program known as Gadna, a Hebrew acronym for "youth battalions." There were several options kids could choose. One was linked to the air force, another to the navy. But most of us joined the reconnaissance and scouting group, Gadna Sayarim. It involved studying topography and navigation, as well as field exercises that were a lot like the ones Yigal had put us through a few years earlier. At year's end, we took part in a national exercise. It was called, a bit grandiosely, Miyam el Yam: from sea to sea. We had to find our way from the Mediterranean, near Haifa, across northern Israel to a lake that was a sea only in name, the Sea of Galilee. It lasted three days. All of us from around the country were divided into groups of four. Each was given a topographical map and a compass, with landmarks marked along the way, which we had to find and draw in a notebook to prove we'd been there.

A couple of hours in, my three new fellow scouts and I faced our first challenge. We were making our way along a shepherds' trail, with brush and bramble on either side, when the path split in two. We had to decide which fork to take. The map didn't help: each inch covered the equivalent of a mile and a half. The key was to match the map with what we were seeing around us, to use points we *could* identify from the map—Haifa and the sea in the receding distance, and a taller hill to our northeast— and figure out which path was more likely to take us in the right direction. I enjoyed this mix of calculation and imagination. As my trek-mates turned to me for this first decision, and then on each successive stage as we crossed the Galilee, I realized it was also something I was naturally good at.

Still, the closest thing to real military activity remained my excursions with Ido and Moshe. We stowed our ammunition trunks under our beds. The final piece of our arsenal fell into place in May 1958. For the tenth anniversary of Israel, there was a national exhibition celebrating the achievements of the state. It was held in Beit Dagan, on the other side of Tel Aviv, and I paid a first visit on my own, curious to see what was on display. But as I walked through, I couldn't help noticing the lack of security. Two days later, I returned with Ido and Moshe. There was a stand devoted to the Israeli military industry. We already had a supply of ammunition for an Uzi submachine gun, courtesy of our raid on the Alexandroni Brigade. Now, when the guy in charge of the stand was busy chatting with other visitors, we came away with an Uzi.

Then the trouble began. Along with Ido, Moshe, and the other older boys, I now lived in a larger dormitory under the cursory gaze of an older metapelet. She was doing routine cleaning when she decided to dust around the boxes under our beds. When she tried to move one of them, she was amazed by its weight. She got one of her sons-in-law to help. I think the box he pried open first was Moshe's. But within a few minutes he'd opened Ido's and mine as well. Inside each were hundreds of bullets and the machine-gun belts. Inside mine was our prized Uzi. It would not exactly have taken the KGB to work out the rest. The kibbutz leaders ordered an inquiry. Ido was summoned first and attempted a brief show of defiance. "What's the big deal?" he asked. "It's just stuff we collected. Why should you care?" But separately questioning Moshe, then Ido again, the inquisitors worked out every detail. That the ammunition had come from the Alexandroni Brigade, the reservists sent to *defend* us, was bad enough. But the Uzi was stolen from the National Exhibition. That was even worse. It was left to the core of young men in their late twenties and thirties to figure out how to punish us. Everyone agreed we could not be reported to the police. That would risk a scandal for the kibbutz. They decided to beat some sense into the offenders, in front of all the rest of the teenagers in the dormitory.

Fortunately, I wasn't there. One afternoon each week, I boarded a bus into Tel Aviv for my piano lesson. But when I returned after sundown, I sensed immediately something was wrong. Yigal was waiting at the bus stop outside the kibbutz. He told me what I had done was terrible. Not just because it involved weapons, but because it was a *breach of trust*. Did you really *steal ammunition from the army*? he asked, his voice rising. And from the *National Exhibition*? I didn't bother denying it. I suppose I felt lucky they hadn't found out about our raids on the kibbutz armory. He did not administer my beating. That came a few weeks later from one of the kibbutz elders. He simply took me by the shoulders and shouted, "You must *never* do this again."

It was worse for my parents. At first, they were convinced I couldn't have got involved in something like this without being dragged in by the others. My father even asked me whether the reason I'd been "drafted" by Ido and Moshe was because I was small and able to squeeze through tight spaces in windows and doors. As it happened, that did sometimes come in handy. But I told them no, I was not an unlucky bystander. I was as much a part of it as the others. My father was angrier than I had ever seen him. My mother, faced with what must have seemed like a betrayal of every one of her Zionist principles, told me that if the kibbutz had decided to report us to the police, she would not have objected.

Their mood had lifted slightly by the time I began my final year of high school in September 1958. After two years back in the kibbutz school, our age group was sent out again in another shift in policy, this time in response to signs of growing support in Mishmar Hasharon and other kibbutzim for the argument my father had made against the quality of education we were offering. In order to go at least some way toward meeting that objection, Mishmar Hasharon would band together with two-dozen other kibbutzim and send all twelfth-graders to one of two outside high schools. The first, Beit Berl, was a Labor Zionist institution focusing on the humanities. In addition to a few of the less academic boys, most of the girls were sent there. The rest of us went to a place called Rupin. It was a few hundred yards past the regional high school. It specialized in agricultural scientific research.

A few of the teachers were enormously gifted, and they worked in the areas that most interested me: math, physics, and biology. Yet the rest of the curriculum was almost numbingly *un*inspiring. I did not miss a single math or science class. Otherwise, I began setting my own schedule. Some days, I would sleep late, or not go at all. When I did go, I'd often show up without having done the homework. Neither Ido nor Moshe was with me at Rupin. They were starting their military service. But I assembled a new band of mischief-makers, and it was not hard to entice them to go AWOL.

I was warned several times by the school administrator. He said he could not accommodate a student who seemed oblivious to, or dismissive of, the rules. He was especially upset because my attitude seemed to be infecting others. A few months into the school year, he told the leaders of Mishmar Hasharon, and then my parents, that I would have to leave. My father was especially upset. A couple of years earlier, he'd had visions of my staying on in the regional high school and going to university. Now, I'd been unable to hold my own in Rupin. Still, both he and my mother were relieved when Mishmar Hasharon and the school worked out a compromise that did not end my studies altogether. The expulsion stood, but I was allowed to continue attending math and science classes.

For my mother, the blow was softened when I began to work almost full time on the kibbutz, alongside Yigal, driving a tractor. I woke up early and accompanied him to the fields of wheat, barley, or rye. We also made a series of trips 130 miles south into the Negev to a moshav called Patish. It had been set up by newly arrived Moroccan Jews. Since they didn't have the equipment or know-how to cultivate all their fields, they rented out some of the land. Mishmar Hasharon had contracted to farm a parcel of 450 acres.

For ten days at a time, Yigal and I would place a tractor on the back of a pickup and head to Patish. We worked from four in the morning until sundown. After work, we ate at a tiny family-run restaurant a few miles away in Ofakim, a so-called development town populated by Moroccan Jews who were sent there as soon as they arrived in Israel. Far from regretting not being in school, I drew satisfaction, and pride, from knowing that I was functioning as an independent adult. It also gave me time to think. My whole life had been circumscribed by the struggle to create and secure the state. But I again found myself pondering issues of basic fairness in our young country, and the challenge of reconciling our words and principles with our deeds amid the difficult *realities* of building the state.

Back on the kibbutz, the kindly and hardworking Baddura had caused me to question how we were treating the Jews who had arrived from Yemen. In the Negev, I met members of the even larger postwar influx from Morocco. One image struck me above all. It was from the place Yigal and I ate dinner. Ofakim was a development town that had yet to develop. It had no visible means of support, and there was no sign the government was doing much to remedy that or integrate the new immigrants economically and socially. The "restaurant" was a side business a family had set up in the dining room of their tiny home. The sixth or seventh time we went there, I was startled by sudden movement a couple of feet away from where we were sitting. Looking more closely, I saw a wooden box, the kind we used in Mishmar Hasharon to crate oranges, filled with hay. At first, I thought the stirring inside was a family pet. Then I saw it was a baby. I said nothing until we had left. "Was that really a child?" I asked Yigal. "A *baby*?" He replied, with a tinge of sadness but also a look that seemed to convey surprise at my naïveté: "Yes. They don't have room for him."

+ + +

My evolving feelings about the Arabs, the other people with dreams of what they still saw as Palestine, became more complex as my childhood drew to an end. It is true that, amid Israel's struggle to be born and survive, the fate of absent Arabs from villages like Wadi Khawaret barely registered with me. Yet as I got older—in my teens—I came to understand *why* the Palestinians were fighting us. Before the 1956 war, Dayan gave a brief speech that had a powerful impact on many of us. It was a eulogy, but it was for someone Dayan didn't know personally. His intended audience was the rest of the country. He spoke in Nahal Oz, a kibbutz on the border with Gaza often targeted by fedayeen. In April 1956, a group of Arabs crossed from Gaza and began cutting down the wheat in Nahal Oz's fields. The kibbutz security officer, a twenty-one-year-old named Roi Rotberg, rode out on horseback to chase them away. The intruders opened fire as soon as he got close. They beat him, shot him dead, and took the body back over the armistice line. The corpse was returned, mutilated, after an Israeli protest through the UN.

With Israeli newspapers full of agonized accounts of what had happened, Dayan's message was that we should not blame the *Arabs* for Roi Rotberg's death. We should look at ourselves, and the neighborhood in which we lived. "Why should we talk about their burning hatred for us?" he asked. "For eight years, they have been sitting in the refugee camps of Gaza, while before their eyes we have been transforming the lands and the villages where they and their fathers dwelt." Of course they hated us and the state we were building. Rotberg had allowed his "yearning for peace to deafen his ears, and he did not hear the voice of murder waiting in ambush." Dayan said the danger was that other Israelis had become similarly naïve. "How did we shut our eyes, and refuse to see, in all its brutality, the destiny of our generation?" A generation that was settling the land but that "without the steel helmet and the barrel of the gun, will not succeed in planting a tree or building a home."

Still, if I was part of a generation that understood the need for military preparedness, strength, and a readiness to fight, the 1956 war also brought home to me the need to consider *how* we fought. This meant grappling with a contradiction wired into Zionism from the start: the need to take up arms to defend our state, while recognizing the Jewish moral code that was its foundation. When the Israeli armed forces were established in 1948, Tzahal's doctrine included the principle of *tohar haneshek*—"purity of arms"—and an explicit requirement for our soldiers to use the minimum necessary force and do all they could to avoid civilian casualties. Putting "purity of arms" into practice was always going to be hard. All arms kill. In all wars, civilians die. But that did not make the principle, or the need to be aware of it in combat, any less important.

Even if the soldier called on to make that judgment was someone who had mentored me from the time I was six, and whose military prowess I had come to respect. Yigal Garber's parachute jump on the first day of the 1956 war went smoothly, but the battle for control of the Mitla Pass became the most deadly of the war, costing the lives of nearly forty Israeli soldiers and leaving around 120 wounded. It was also unnecessary. Under Israel's prewar choreography with the British and French, our landing near the Mitla Pass was to be the trigger for an Anglo-French attack. In fact, Ariel Sharon, better known as Arik, the commander of Battalion 890, received orders from Tel Aviv *not* to take the pass. Only grudgingly did they let him send in a reconnaissance force to establish whether it was safe to cross.

The reconnaissance team walked into a trap. Machine-gun and mortar fire rained down from Egyptian troops dug into the caves and other natural defensive positions above the pass. It took hours to extricate the stranded men. Yigal's unit fought its way in from the eastern side of the pass. A small group from the reconnaissance force managed to get a foothold on the western side. Almost 250 Egyptians were killed, but thirty-eight Israeli paratroopers also died, the largest single toll in any battle since 1948. Battered and bitter, the surviving men from the reconnaissance force parachuted into the southwesternmost part of the Sinai, near Et-Tur on the Red Sea.

Yigal and the others headed overground to join up with them. By the time they got there, Egyptian resistance had all but ended. They had a brief exchange of fire with several dozen holdouts in the Egyptian force. The Egyptians surrendered. But rumors began to circulate after the war that at least some of them were then shot dead.

I never discovered whether that was true. I asked my friends what they'd heard. I asked some of the older men on the kibbutz, my father included. All of them responded with a slightly different, and unfailingly vague, version of events. When I asked Yigal, he abruptly changed the subject, leaving me with a sense of uneasiness.

When Yigal and I made our final trip to Patish in 1959, I knew it would be pointless to ask him about it again. Whatever he said wouldn't change anything. I still respected his courage and his fighting spirit, and the part he'd played in defending Israel. I appreciated what he'd done for me as I grew up. But what mattered now wasn't what Yigal had done. It was what I would do, and how I would live my life.

Especially since I, too, was about to begin my army service.

# 3

# Accidental Commando

I REPORTED FOR INDUCTION ON THE SECOND SUNDAY OF NOVEMBER 1959, three months short of my eighteenth birthday. Military service was a near-universal rite of passage for Israeli teenagers. For children of the kibbutz, it held even greater significance. Now that we had a country, the kibbutzniks' role as the avant-garde in taming and farming the land was less important. But the sense of mission we'd been raised with drove us to aspire, maybe even assume, we would still leave an imprint in other spheres of the new state's life. I doubt it's an accident that nearly every one of the boys with whom I grew up in Mishmar Hasharon went on to become an officer during his time in the military.

At first, I had hoped to join the air force. But a question on the application form asked whether I ever suffered from breathing discomfort. Like almost everyone on the kibbutz, I did get a bit clogged up when the weather turned cold and damp. So I naïvely answered yes, not realizing that this ended any chance of training as a pilot. My fallback choice was a tank unit, but when I joined the hundreds of other draftees at the processing center near Tel Aviv, about a hundred of us were shunted, by alphabetical lottery, into training for armored personnel carriers (APCs). Known as battle taxis, the APCs Israel had at the time were lumbering, World War II–vintage half-tracks.

Our training battalion was based in a large hillside army camp outside Beersheva in the Negev. I had expected our *tironut*—basic training—

to be demanding. That was the whole point. But I was less prepared for the seemingly endless array of inspections, under the watchful eye of a corporal who meted out punishments for the tiniest scuff on a boot, a belt, or a rifle. The rest of the time was spent in physical training. I found that hard, too, at least at the beginning. I still weighed barely 130 pounds, and by no means was it all, or even most of it, muscle. My military career, such as it was, looked very likely to involve spending my required couple of years baking inside an APC in the Negev before moving on to something more useful, and certainly more fulfilling, with the rest of my life.

But a series of accidents, in Israel's life and in mine, would soon point me in a different direction. The first became known as the Rotem Crisis, from the Hebrew name for the Israeli military response, and it delivered a jolting reminder of our vulnerability to a surprise attack from neighboring Arab states. Militarily, Israel was much stronger than in 1948. But we were still a young country, at an early stage in our economic development. Our defense strategy rested on a recognition that we could not afford to sustain a large standing army, relying instead on a pool of trained reservists. The problem was that a full call-up of the reserves would require something like forty-eight hours. That meant some form of early warning was critical.

Rotem erupted in February 1960, about halfway through my tironut, and began almost farcically. The chief of military intelligence, Chaim Herzog, was at a diplomatic reception in Tel Aviv when he began chatting with a guest he knew well: the head of the local CIA station. What, the American asked, did he make of the fact that Egypt had moved its two main army divisions into the Sinai, toward the border with Israel? Herzog came up with a suitably woolly reply, about how it was obviously a situation that bore watching. But the truth was that neither he nor anyone else in Israel had any idea about the Egyptian redeployment. He left the party as soon as he could to tell Ben-Gurion and Chaim Laskov, who had succeeded Dayan as chief of staff. When a reconnaissance flight the next day confirmed that Egyptian infantry units had indeed moved deep into the Sinai, Ben-Gurion and the generals scrambled for a response.

They did not want a war. Ben-Gurion was particularly worried that in responding to Nasser's buildup, he might inadvertently escalate things. He vetoed the idea of a full mobilization, but he did order a more limited call-up of about 7,000 reservists. He placed the air force on alert. He directed the four brigades responsible for the defense of southern Israel, including our armored brigade near Beersheva, to deploy along the border. That meant that munitions convoys had to be sent out to equip the hastily assembled border force.

The first sign I saw that anything extraordinary was going on was the sudden movement of tanks and APCs inside our camp. At first, no one told us raw recruits anything. We looked on and stayed out of the way. But with our operational units preparing to move forward, there seemed no one else with the expertise, experience, and local knowledge to lead the supply columns. So our training unit was summoned before the platoon commander. "Any volunteers?" he asked. When none of us raised a hand, he said, "Come on. One of you must have grown up around here." That meant the first part would be familiar territory. He left unspoken the obvious postscript: the need to negotiate the final ten miles or so, through open desert, and to find the right area, on our side of a border that wasn't even marked. "Can't *any* of you," he barked, "lead a convoy of a few trucks?"

I'm not sure what possessed me. But I thought to myself: yes, I probably can. I'd trained with Gadna Sayarim, the high school scouting and reconnaissance program. And while I'd never lived in the south, the cooperative farm where I'd worked along with Yigal Garber after getting kicked out of high school was not far from the route the conveys would have to take.

So I raised my hand.

"Can you lead a convoy?" he asked.

"Yes, sir, I can," I said. "But I'll need a map. And a compass."

"Why do you think you're qualified?" he prodded. I'd been in Gadna Sayarim, I said. I had some experience navigating and reading maps. "OK," he replied, and he sent me, along with two of the company's junior officers, to the battalion commander.

Someone phoned ahead, because he was clearly expecting us. Still, I could see the surprise in his eyes when he looked at me: only just eighteen, but looking closer to fifteen, my uniform sagging on my slender frame. He gazed at the officers, then back at me, then at the officers again, as if trying to figure out whether he was about to approve something utterly crazy. But he had little choice. Three convoys had to be dispatched within the next couple of hours. So far, with me, he had a sum total of one guy to lead them. "Fine," he said, and waved us out.

The column consisted of eight American-made six-wheelers, each packed with ten tons of munitions and other supplies. I was in the lead truck. The driver was a reservist in his midthirties. So were most of the men in the rest of the transport trucks, one driver and one soldier in each. A staff sergeant, in the second vehicle, was in command, at least in theory. Surreal though it felt, I was actually in charge, since I was the only person who might, conceivably, get us to the right place.

The first part, on paved roads, was fairly easy. But shortly after night-fall, we reached open desert, the beginning of more than three hours of picking and weaving, calibrating and recalibrating our way across a wide expanse of sand and occasional scrub bushes that, every mile or so, would suddenly give way to a windswept series of dunes and wadis. The map and compass helped, but I soon realized it was almost impossible to get an accurate reading from inside the truck. Every few minutes, I waved the convoy to stop, got out, and walked fifty or sixty yards into the sand and calibrated our progress from there. My fallback was the stars. From them, I could at least make sure we were headed in generally the right direction. But the need to navigate around the dunes meant we were never moving in a perfectly straight line. The miles ticking by on the truck's odometer couldn't tell me exactly how far we'd traveled. A couple of times, I was concerned we might be wandering off course—not by much, but enough to risk leaving us either a mile or two south of where we were supposed to go or, worse, on the Egyptian side of an unmarked desert frontier that, especially at night, would look pretty much the same on either side.

Finally, a few hours before dawn, I brought the convoy to a halt. I climbed out, walked back to the staff sergeant, and told him, with more confidence than I felt, "We're here." I had no way of knowing for sure, but I felt we were more or less in the right place. Before we'd set off, I was briefed by the officer in charge of one of the operational APC battalions. He told me that once we got there, we should stop and wait. He would follow our tracks the next morning and link up with us. An hour after sunrise, we saw his jeep bobbing over the sand toward us. He pulled to a stop, shook hands with the staff sergeant, and then turned to me. "Unbelievable," he said. "We're exactly where we need to be."

Our role in the grand scheme of things was hardly decisive, but the rest of the border mobilization also went as planned. That, along with some frantic diplomatic activity and a healthy dose of common sense on both sides, ensured that a new war with Egypt was averted, at least for now. By the time war did come, in 1967, the lesson of Rotem had been learned: our need to find a reliable way to tap into the battle plans of the hostile Arab states around us. And through another wholly unexpected turn of events starting just a few weeks after the Rotem Crisis, I would play a personal role in making that happen.

+ + +

Under army regulations, training recruits got a five-day leave every few months during basic training. My first one came a bit later than usual, due to Rotem. But in April 1960, shortly before the Passover holiday, I headed back to Mishmar Hasharon. I still had every reason to believe I'd be spending the next couple of years in an APC unit in the Negev; I couldn't pretend I was looking forward to it. Still, the idea of returning home in my army uniform, at least a bit stronger and bulkier than before, gave me a sense of pride.

On my third day back, I was in the dining hall with a half dozen schoolmates-turned-soldiers when Avraham Amon sat down and joined us. He was one of the *yeldei chutz*, the "boys from outside" who had joined our class when we were taken out of the regional high school. He, too, was now in the army. As we were finishing lunch, he asked me, "How's tironut?"

"Tough," I said. "Boring."

Smiling, he said, "How would you feel about joining a sayeret?"

In Hebrew, a sayeret is a special unit that carries out missions behind enemy lines or under particularly exacting conditions. In the early 1960s, there were only two of note. One was Sayeret Golani, attached to the Golani Brigade near the northern border. The truly elite one was Sayeret Tzanhanim, the paratroopers' sayeret. It had been developed from Company A of Battalion 890, the successor to Arik Sharon's Unit 101, where Yigal had served in the 1950s.

"Which sayeret?" I asked.

"It's called Sayeret Matkal," he replied.

I'd never heard of it. When I asked what it did, he said, "I'm not allowed to say. But are you interested?" The air of mystery made it seem only more enticing. And no matter what it did, it had to be a step up from what lay ahead of me in the Negev. "Yeah. Sure," I replied.

I heard nothing further for several weeks. Then, at the end of the month, I was ordered to report to a small hut in an army base near Tel Aviv. It belonged to Maka 10, the personnel department of military intelligence. Two men in their late twenties greeted me. One, shorter even than me, introduced himself as Sami Nachmias. The other was tall and slim and said in a surprisingly quiet voice, "I'm Shmil Ben-Zvi." They were two names that I, like most kibbutz teenagers at the time, knew well. They were among the earliest recruits to Company A. They shook my hand and motioned me into a jeep. As we drove out of the base, they peppered me with questions about almost anything except the army: the kibbutz, school, sports. Then, Ben-Zvi pulled the jeep to the side of the road, turned around to face me, and asked, "Is it true you can pick locks?"

Yes, I said. "Do you want me to show you?" He said that wouldn't be necessary.

"Is it true you can navigate? Read maps?" Nachmias asked. I nodded.

The interview thus concluded, they drove me back to the base in silence. Nachmias supplied the parting words: "OK. You'll probably hear from us."

I didn't. But as basic training was winding down, I got a further order: to report to an address in Tzahala, a neighborhood in north Tel Aviv where a lot of military officers lived. It was a small house with a metal gate outside. I was met at the door by a man about thirty in shorts and a T-shirt, who introduced himself as Avraham Arnan. He led me inside. He unfurled a map of Jerusalem and the surrounding hills and pointed to a spot on the southwest of the city. He drew a wide, curving line through the hills to a second point. "You know how to read a map?" he asked. When I nodded, he said, "I want you to describe to me—just as if you were walking on this line—exactly what you see, as you make your way to the place I marked." I used the elevation lines on the map as a guide, and the positioning of the hills and woodland and villages on the map, and began describing how each stage would look. When I was finished, his only response was the hint of a smile. When he spoke, it wasn't about the map. It was, again, about picking locks. "How did you learn?" he asked. I explained how I'd cut into the locks, figured out how they worked, and made a set of tools to open them. "Thank you," he said. "You can return to your unit."

Though he hadn't said so, I got a feeling this was the Sayeret Matkal equivalent of a final interview. When I got back to Beersheva, I dug around as discreetly as possible for details about Avraham Arnan. I learned he had served in 1948 in the hills around Jerusalem, so he would have known firsthand the terrain he asked me to describe. That, I guessed, explained the half smile. But I was entering my last week of tironut. I still had no idea whether I'd be spending the next couple of years inside an APC or in a sayeret whose function was a mystery, beyond the fact it seemed less interested in whether my boots were shined than whether I could pick a lock.

The day before the end of basic training, I was told to return to Maka 10. A jeep was waiting. The soldier at the wheel mumbled hello and drove me to a sprawling military base about a half hour away. It was built by the British in the Second World War. At the far end was a pair of domed concrete shelters used by the British for munitions storage. Five tents. Two field toilets. And a single-story brick structure with a tin roof. It contained offices for Avraham Arnan, a couple of other officers and a secretary, a kitchenette, and a room for storing weapons. This was the home of Sayeret Matkal, although the first thing I was told was that no one, outside a handful of senior officers in military headquarters, knew we existed.

+ + +

Avraham Arnan was the heart and soul of Sayeret Matkal. Even from my brief first encounter with him in his living room in Tzahala, I was struck by his physical presence, his almost movie-star looks, and a face made even more intriguing by different-colored eyes, one brown and one a piercing green. But what really set him apart, as I got to know him and came under his spell in the sayeret, was his playful, almost bohemian disregard for the normal strictures and structures, rules and regulations, of the armed forces. What mattered to him was what actually needed to get done and how best to accomplish it despite all the bureaucratic obstacles, and he made me and his other teenage recruits feel we were equal partners with him in getting there.

Years later, he confided that if his life had not led him into the military, he would have probably chosen something in the arts or culture, either architecture or maybe directing films. But he had volunteered for the Haganah at age seventeen, a year before the 1948 war. As the losses mounted in Jerusalem, he found himself in the Palmach's crack Harel Brigade, under the command of a future Israeli chief of staff, David "Dado" Elazar.

His vision for Sayeret Matkal became Israel's answer to the dangers identified by Rotem. It had its origins, though, in his experiences in the years after 1948, when he joined a military intelligence unit running a loose network of Arab agents across Israel's northern border. They provided occasional bits of information, but in talking with his wartime friends, he realized this kind of low-level intelligence could never address the *real* need for Israel: to ensure we had early warning if Syria, Jordan, or Egypt were preparing to go to war against us.

He began to toy with the idea of training a small force of Israeli soldiers to go on cross-border intelligence missions. The initial response from the *kirya*—military headquarters in Tel Aviv—was so frustrating that anyone else would have given up. None of the generals saw any reason to believe his scheme would work. The real obstacle, however, was their continuing trauma over what had happened the last time Israeli soldiers crossed the border on an intelligence mission. It happened in 1954, and it ended in a failure even more serious than Rotem. The target was the Golan Heights, inside Syria. The special technology unit attached to military intelligence had developed a bugging device designed to be placed on a telephone pole on the Golan. The task of installing it was given to the most respected commando unit in the army: Company A in Sharon's paratroop battalion, led by its commander, Meir Har-Zion.

On a spring night in 1954, Meir led his team onto the Golan. They rigged the bugging unit to the telephone pole, buried the bulky transmitter, and made their way back. And it worked. Israeli intelligence could listen in on military communications on the Heights. The hitch was that the batteries had to be replaced every few weeks. Several more times, Meir and his men sneaked back into Syria to keep the bug working. But as commander of Company A, Meir was a key part of Israel's anti-fedayeen operations. So Moshe Dayan decided to transfer the task of replacing the batteries to a regular unit from the Golani Brigade.

In December 1954, a handover mission was organized. Three men from Company A, including one of Meir's sergeants, joined three from the Golani Brigade. But the preparation was perfunctory. They didn't even hold a joint live-fire exercise before setting off. There was also a lack of clarity about who was in charge. Though the Golani commander was nominally the senior officer, only the Company A men had any firsthand experience of this kind of mission. A half mile onto the Heights, they were intercepted by Syrian soldiers. If this had been a Company A operation, the response would have been automatic. They would have wheeled, opened fire, and attacked. But when the Syrians ordered the team to drop their weapons, one of the Golanis did so, and the Company A men followed suit. They were all taken to Damascus and held in solitary confinement.

One of the captured Golani soldiers was a nineteen-year-old named Uri Ilan. His mother, Fayge Ilanit, was a member of the Israeli Knesset whom Ben-Gurion and the whole of the government knew well. The soldiers' captivity dragged on until they were finally returned to Israel in March 1956. By then, however, Uri Ilan had hanged himself. He managed to hide a number of notes in his uniform, and they were found when the body was being prepared for burial. *"Lo bagadeti,"* was his message. *"Nekamah."* "I did not betray anything . . . Revenge."

Ever since the Uri Ilan mission, there had been a de facto ban on cross-border intelligence operations by Israeli soldiers. Ben-Gurion and his military commanders knew, of course, the importance of getting early warning of an enemy attack. But Ben-Gurion decided the price of possible failure was simply too high.

Sayeret Matkal was born three years later. Avraham was still part of the unit running low-level agents in Syria and Lebanon, but his commander reluctantly agreed to allow him to set up his new intelligence group. His initial "headquarters" was a sparsely furnished Tel Aviv apartment. The first two people he brought in were veterans of the Palmach's Arab Platoon, pre-state fighters who trained themselves to pass as Arabs and gather intelligence. Next, he invited friends who had served in Unit

101 and Company A. Finally, he enlisted a core of them to help train recruits to his new sayeret. He hoped the involvement of these commando veterans would also give the unit credibility inside the kirya. One of them, Micha Kapusta, had been part of 101, as had Yitzhak Gibli, who had been a teenage Palmachnik in 1948. A third was another Company A officer named Aharon Eshel, known as Errol, in part for his Errol Flynn–like swagger, but also because it was an acronym of his Hebrew name. Also drafted was a young, physically imposing Company A officer named Moshe Levin, known by his childhood nickname, Kokla. But the crowning addition to the group had the distinction of having led the last *successful* Israeli bugging mission on the Golan, in addition to being the most respected commando in Israel, a man whom Dayan would later call the country's greatest soldier. It was Meir Har-Zion himself.

+ + +

I was part of the second group of recruits to Sayeret Matkal, in the early summer of 1960. The unit had been given its own base barely a year earlier. It had yet to carry out a single mission, and there was no sign of when, or if, the generals in the kirya might give Avraham the go-ahead. Still, he was convinced that if we could demonstrate a toughness, commitment, and competence that offered an obvious addition to Israel's intelligence capability, even they would recognize the folly of not using it.

He made every one of us feel a part of making this possible. I was one of ten new recruits, bringing the size of the sayeret to twenty. We were almost all teenagers; the oldest of our officers was twenty-one. A number of the men were Sephardi Jews, acquainted with Arabic language and culture. I was the sayeret's only lock-picker. All of us had been recruited in much the same way. It was how the top Palmach units had been formed, and the way Sharon assembled Unit 101: friends recommending friends.

We trained in the whole range of commando skills. We used not only Uzis, but Soviet-made Kalashnikovs and machine guns. We worked with detonators and explosives. We staged raids on Israeli airfields. We conducted exercises using rubber dinghies to practice attacking from the sea. But mostly we *walked*. For hundreds of miles, almost always at night, the length and breadth of the country, with only a compass as a guide. Before setting off, we would study a map of a given area, committing every trail, hilltop, or dry creek bed to memory. I can still remember what Meir Har-Zion told us: to be truly prepared, you needed to spend "an hour for an hour"—an equal time mastering and memorizing the lay of the land to the amount you'd need to navigate your way, in darkness, to your destination. It was a grueling regimen designed to push us to the limits of endurance. On one series of exercises, we were limited to a single canteen of water a day as we trekked deep into the Negev Desert. The first time Errol set eyes on me after I joined the unit, he had turned to Avraham, laughed, and said, "Are we taking high school kids now?" But before long, I was a "high school kid" no longer.

Meir Har-Zion rarely took a direct part in our exercises. On his final Company A mission, a month before the 1956 war, he had been shot in his throat and arm. A military doctor saved his life by performing a tracheotomy, but his speech was affected and he still had almost no use of his right arm. Errol, Micha Kapusta, Yitzhak Gibli, and Kokla were more actively involved with us. They were there not only to help train us, but to instill a commando attitude, a spirit of confidence bordering on bravado.

Kapusta was our guide on our punishing five-day treks through the Negev. Though Avraham would see us off at the start, he stayed back at the base. In a couple of the exercises, we relied on carrier pigeons to keep in touch with the base, until we began killing them for dinner. Once, on a searingly hot desert afternoon, hours from the nearest hospital, Kapusta spotted a poisonous snake. He used pieces of wood to pry its head up from the sand, grabbed its neck, and strangled it.

We also studied Arabic, though most of the sayeret recruits already spoke the language. My tutor was a Cairo-born Jew named Amin. In part because he enjoyed mathematics and played the violin, we hit it off immediately. He was also nearly deaf in one ear. Languages have never been my forte. Even in Hebrew, I have a slight lisp. That made speaking Arabic even harder. Still, Amin frequently complimented me on my accent, at which point the others in the class would point out that I was lucky he was hard of hearing.

A year in, we were given a classroom briefing on what to do if we fell into enemy hands. The gist was to tell them only our name, rank, and serial number. But we had a special session with Gibli, who told us about what captivity was really like. He had been shot and wounded during a retaliation operation in 1954 and was captured by the Jordanians. Until his release, he was kept in solitary confinement and tortured. The details of his imprisonment, the beatings and the cigarette burns, were lurid. Partly because we were developing a bit of commando self-confidence— but mostly to hide the discomfort of wondering how each of us would react to being in enemy hands—we heckled him over an account that seemed to get more heroic with each retelling. He wisely ignored us. He emphasized that survival would be down to not just physical strength: it required strength of mind.

A few weeks later, the whole sayeret held a four-day exercise in the Galilee, the mountainous region in the north of Israel on the border with Lebanon. On the second night, at about four in the morning, we shook off our backpacks and settled in for a few hours' sleep. The first thing I heard was shouting in Arabic. I saw a guy hovering over me, his face covered. He handcuffed me, pulled a burlap sack over my head, yanked me to me feet, and led me off. We were piled into the back of a truck. From the whispered comments around me, I assumed all twenty of us had been taken. We drove for nearly four hours. Twice, I got a slap across the face, more painful because of the burlap. I kept telling myself this *had* to be part of our training. If it was for real, we'd have been more badly beaten, or killed. Still, how could we know for sure?

The truck lurched to a stop. We were led into a building, down a hallway, and into a large room. The walls were bare except for a series of iron rings. Our captors tore the sacks from our heads for a few moments and tied our wrists to the manacles. For the first six or seven hours we were kept together, arms shackled and raised. Then they took us away one by one. I was the last to be led out. I was taken to a room so small there was not even space for a cot. After the last shaft of light disappeared from the slit-like window near the top of wall, the first interrogator showed up. He unlocked the door, entered, and unfolded a metal chair. He wanted answers: what unit was I from, what did our unit do, who were our commanders, what were our orders, and what was our designated role in the event of war.

I told him my name, rank, and serial number. After each question, I repeated them, or shook my head in silence. "You *will* answer, sooner or later," he shouted in heavily Arabic-accented Hebrew, hitting me across the face. "All of you will." Over successive days and nights, other inter-rogators shouted out the same questions. I was slapped dozens of times. Punched in the stomach. One of the captors uncuffed me and bent my arm behind my back, wrenching it upward. Though I was determined not to cry out, I grunted in pain. Over and over, I told myself: "This is *not* for real. They can hurt me. But they have limits. They can twist my arm. They can hurt me. But there's no way they can *break* my arm."

I was not allowed to sleep. I was never left alone for more than a half hour. If I crouched on the stone floor, I would be yanked to my feet and punched or slapped. Twice a day, I was taken from my cell to a primitive toilet and given a minute to relieve myself. There were only two changes to the routine. On a few occasions, five or six of us were brought back into the large room. Every few moments, we could hear moans or shouts of pain from down the hallway. We were told we wouldn't be let go until we had given them *more* of what they wanted—the implication being that some of us had already talked.

Once or twice, the interrogators sent in a good cop. "I can *help* you," he told me. "But you have to give me *something*."

But when it was over, none of us had talked. We didn't fool ourselves into thinking that meant we could hold up in genuine captivity. There, they *could* break your arm. They could burn your chest with cigarettes, rip out a fingernail or a tooth. They could kill you. The main value had been to give us some sense of what we might face. We might still be afraid, but at least it would no longer be fear of the totally unknown.

Challenging though our training was, I found every bit of it enthrall-ing and, with each new test passed, somehow empowering and exhilarat-ing. This was all the more remarkable because we had yet to carry out a single operation. If anyone other than Avraham had been in charge, I think the unit might have unraveled. He imbued us with an ethos, a feel-ing that we were a special breed with a critically important purpose, and that sooner or later we would be called on to do special things. When we were in uniform, it was camouflage dress. When we were on the base, we mostly wore sandals and shorts. We called each other by our first names, even the officers.

In fact, in its first few years the sayeret sometimes felt less like an army unit than a college fraternity. Every spring, we organized a feast in a cavernous hangar on the edge of our compound. It was called Chag ha Pri, the Feast of the Fruit. For days ahead of the event, we would mount night raids on kibbutzim, "liberating" crates of every kind of fruit imaginable, and chicken and lamb if we got lucky. The only rule was that none of us would steal from our own kibbutzim. Among the guests at the Feast of the Fruit was an unsuspecting selection of senior officers whom Avraham knew. A few of them got into the spirit, like Dado Elazar, his Palmach commander from 1948, who was by this time commander of Israel's armored corps. Since our sayeret was always short of gasoline for our exercises, he would divert surplus supplies to us. But other guests were less impressed with the pyramids of oranges and avocados and mangoes and watermelons. I could almost hear a voice screaming inside them: these are *Israeli soldiers*. They're *stealing* this stuff.

+ + +

In the autumn of 1961, nearly eighteen months after I arrived, it seemed we might actually be given a real mission. This was largely due to a change at the top of the military. For much of the 1950s, when Moshe Dayan was chief of staff, his right-hand man was a Haganah veteran named Meir Amit. In 1961, the term of Dayan's successor as chief of staff, Haim Laskov, was coming to an end and Amit was in the mix to get the top job. He was already head of operations. In practical terms, that made him the number two man in the armed forces. But when the job went to Tzvi Tzur, Laskov's deputy, Amit decided to accept the post of head of military intelligence. He had been part of the top military leadership during Rotem, so he knew the importance of intelligence, and the potential cost of Israel being taken by surprise in a future war. He was energetic, bright, and exuded an infectious sense of self-confidence and authority. He also had clout at headquarters. If *he* decided the time had come to revive cross-border intelligence operations, there was every chance it would happen.

By the time my period of military service was drawing to an end, it still hadn't happened. And yet I did not seriously think of leaving. Though my two years in Sayeret Matkal had been the most physically demanding of my life, they were also the most fulfilling. I did not want to forfeit the chance of being part of it when it finally became an operational unit. So I committed to at least two more years in the military. I joined my closest friend among the recruits, Uri Zakay, for six months in officers' school as we waited.

In the summer of 1962, shortly after I returned to the unit from officers' school as a second lieutenant, the green light finally came.

# 4

# Turn Off the Radio

At first, it was only "approval in principle." It's impossible to overstate the trepidation with which Israel's military brass, and Ben-Gurion himself, approached the decision finally to send Sayeret Matkal into action. It was not just that we were a unit utterly untested in the field. The stakes were enormous. For the first time since Uri Ilan's desperate act of suicide in a Damascus jail cell, Israeli soldiers would be crossing into Arab territory on an intelligence mission. Amid continuing tensions with the increasingly militant rulers of Egypt and Syria, there seemed little doubt that at some stage we would again have to fight to defend our security, perhaps even our existence as a state. The Rotem debacle had highlighted the danger of a surprise attack. But the memory of Uri Ilan remained a haunting reminder of the risks of failure.

My role, again, came down partly to accident. The man initially chosen to lead the operation was someone I'd liked from my first days in the sayeret. Ya'akov Tal, known as Tubul, was a year older than me. He came from Tiberias in the north of Israel. As a teenager, he'd worked for extra pocket money alongside shepherds in the hills above the Sea of Galilee, picking up a near-fluent command of Arabic. He was self-confident without a trace of arrogance, with a natural talent for connecting with his soldiers.

But Tubul had applied to the leading technology institute in Israel, the Technion near Haifa. As he began training his four-man team to cross onto Syria's Golan Heights, he received word that he'd been accepted. The academic year wouldn't begin until September, and it had been assumed at first that the operation would happen before then. But even though Meir Amit was pressing the rest of the military brass for a final go-ahead, it hadn't arrived by early August, and Avraham decided he needed a fallback plan. He ordered me to join the team's training as Tubul's deputy, and to be ready to step in as commander if that proved necessary. When we next heard from Amit, a week later, it became clear the mission would not happen in time for Tubul to lead it.

We would set out from the northeast corner of Israel, a patch of parkland near a kibbutz called Dan, only a mile or so from where Uri Ilan's group had begun its mission. This time, however, we intended to gather information deeper in the Golan. That meant taking a longer route, beginning with a climb onto a plateau about 200 feet high and crossing the Banias River toward a Syrian army base in the northern part of the Heights.

We had nearly three weeks for our final preparations. After two years of sayeret training, I was confident that, physically, we would be up to the task. But even without the obvious jitters emanating from headquarters, I could not help but be aware of the possibility, and the cost, of failure. Every evening, I would stake out time to go through everything that might conceivably go wrong. Years later, when I did my graduate studies at Stanford, I was exposed to words of wisdom from a non-kibbutznik— Benjamin Franklin—that probably best summed up what drove my planning for the sayeret's first operation, and the others that would follow. "By failing to prepare," he wrote, "you are preparing to fail."

Running into Syrian soldiers was top of my list of concerns. Land mines were a close second. I got a map of the area from military intelligence, which, in theory at least, showed the location of troop positions and mines all along the edge of the Golan. But it had been compiled over a period of nearly two decades on the basis of information from shepherds, smugglers, and the occasional Arab agent. Whenever they reported seeing a military outpost, or the telltale combination of fencing and yellow danger triangles denoting mines, the place was marked. Once it was marked, no one in intelligence headquarters dared erase it. The result was that the map now showed an almost unbroken stretch of potential dangers. Within the amount of time that we had to get ready, there was no way of knowing which of them were still actually there.

The operation was set for the final days of September. Unlike Tubul, who had been commanding the team from the moment they had joined the sayeret, I'd been working with them for only a few weeks. My deputy for the operation, Avi Telem, was also a newcomer. But he was smart and steady, and he had served in the Golani Brigade, so he knew the terrain along the border.

Avraham could not hide his own nervousness as the operation drew nearer. A week before we were due to set off, he asked whether we were planning a further, full-scale exercise. When I said the final run-through was set for the following night, in the Negev, he told me he wanted Meir Har-Zion to attend. During the exercise, Meir said nothing at all. I couldn't help wondering whether, despite our nearly daily exercises and my nightly stock-taking, I'd somehow missed an obvious detail in our planning. When we got back to the sayeret base, Avraham was waiting for us. "Well?" he asked Meir. "They don't need me," he said. "They know what they're doing." It was not just a source of reassurance for me, but a huge relief for Avraham.

The team I'd inherited from Tubul included three gifted soldiers with different backgrounds and different skills. Avi Muchtar was born in Iraq. He was powerfully built, quick-thinking, and almost always smiling. Kuti Sharabi grew up in a Yemeni family in an impoverished neighborhood in Tel Aviv. He had a self-deprecating sense of humor, a quick mind and sometimes an even quicker tongue, but an extraordinary ability to focus on the task at hand. The third member was a kibbutznik. His name was Moshe Elimelech. We called him Moshiko. Utterly self-contained, a man who spoke only when absolutely necessary, he brought two different qualities to the mission. One would be indispensable: a combination of raw physical strength and almost elastic flexibility. The other, of which I was a bit more leery, was a total, deeply irrational absence of fear.

Though none of us needed a further reminder of the weight being attached to our mission, the night before we headed north, Avraham got a call from the chief of staff's office. Tzvi Tzur wanted to see me the next morning for a personal briefing. I tried to get Avraham to say no. I pointed out that if we didn't get going by ten o'clock at the latest, we'd risk throwing everything off schedule. But "no" was not an option. After some further back-and-forth, it was agreed that I would meet the commander of Israel's armed forces at nine the next morning at a gas station north of Tel Aviv and join him for the thirty-minute drive along the coastal road to a speaking engagement he had in Netanya.

I saw Avraham again before I set off. "We are beginning an extremely critical twenty-four hours for our unit, the intelligence corps, in fact for the armed forces as a whole," he told me. "I don't know what might happen. No one does. Just remember two things. First, out there, in the field, *you* are the *ramatkal*"—the chief of staff. Only I and my team could judge and respond to what we encountered once the operation started. "And second, this mission *has to be accomplished.*"

I left to see the real ramatkal. Before we began the drive to Netanya, he asked me to unfold the map I'd brought with me and talk him through, step by step, how we planned to get onto the Golan, complete our mission, and get back again. The more I talked, however, the more I sensed that, more than the details, General Tzur wanted to gauge whether *I* felt confident. He wanted to reassure himself he wasn't taking any more than the obvious risks in sending us, in Uri Ilan's footsteps, back into Syria. Fortunately, he didn't ask whether I was sure we'd succeed. If he had, I would have said yes, we were prepared. But there was no way we could be certain. Still, he must have got what he wanted. When we reached the edge of Netanya, he shook my hand, wished me luck, and went on his way.

The rest of the team was waiting at the crossroads. Two teams, in fact: mine, with whom I'd be crossing into Syria in less than ten hours' time, and our *hillutz*, or backup. A hillutz was always a part of any operation across the border. The backup group would stay on the Israeli side. If we got into trouble, they'd come in after us.

Even after my briefing for the chief of staff, we had one last stop to make on the way north. It was at the headquarters of the army's northern command. It was in a Tegart fortress overlooking Nazareth, one of dozens of such encampments built by the British around the country, with watchtowers on each corner of the outer walls. The northern commander was an equally forbidding figure. Avraham Yoffe had served in the British artillery in the Second World War and the Golani Brigade in 1948.

He used to joke with other officers that while they looked like a bunch of kids, he was the only one with the true bearing of a general.

He must have been busy when we arrived, because we ended up hanging around in the courtyard for nearly twenty minutes. Just as I was beginning to worry that the timetable for what really mattered—our climb up onto the Golan—was being put at risk, I noticed a beautifully polished jeep off to the side. I assumed it belonged to General Yoffe, who was known to be an avid hunter and would later become the head of Israel's National Parks Authority. It had a padlocked metal grille on the back, which held two jerricans of gasoline. Yori Cohen, the commander of the backup team, and I spotted the fuel containers at the same time. We couldn't help smiling. Yes, we were about to embark on an operation that, assuming we didn't fail, would finally give Israel relevant intelligence from across our border for the first time since the 1950s. But we were still Sayeret Matkal, still chronically short of gasoline for our field exercises. And I still knew how to pick a lock. As Yori stood guard, I broke into the grille and removed the jerricans, one for each of us, and closed it again. Then, after briefing the general, we headed to our setting-off point. Yoffe left to join Avraham Arnan and Meir Amit's intelligence deputy, Ahraleh Yariv, in the command post for our mission, near a hilltop kibbutz overlooking the whole of Israel's northern border.

The sun set at around seven, but we waited for darkness. It was nearly eight when we set out. Fifteen minutes later, we crossed the border. I led the way, with Avi Muchtar, Moshiko, Kuti Sharabi, and, finally, Avi Telem behind. We carried our operational equipment and tools in our backpacks. Avi and I had a pair of binoculars. Mine were bulkier but offered a slightly better view in the darkness. Each of us had an Uzi and a pair of grenades. All our planning had been aimed at getting onto the Golan, deploying the equipment, and getting out again. If all went well, no one would even know we'd been there. But we had practiced what to do if things went wrong. If challenged or ambushed by a Syrian patrol, we would operate by old Company A rules. We would open fire and charge.

The climb onto the plateau wasn't too tough, not nearly as hard as our sayeret training treks. When we reached the top, there was no obvious sign of any Syrians. Still, we had to move slowly. Even with my binoculars,

I could see barely thirty yards into the darkness, and I had to scan the route ahead, back and forth, to make sure there were none of the troop outposts or minefields that had been marked on the map. Soon, however, we found an obviously well-used footpath, which I figured was likely to be safe.

When we had walked a few minutes, we found ourselves going through a tangle of bushes and reeds, some of them up to two feet high, still dry and crackly from the summer. Aside from the risk of tripping, I knew the noise we were making might attract attention. I told the rest of the team to hang back twenty yards behind me. I moved forward to make sure the route was clear before signaling them to follow. I had been slightly nervous on the climb up, not so much because I expected trouble but because there was no way of knowing *what* to expect. I tried to put the concerns of the generals from my mind. Almost immediately, the nerves were gone, and I was focused only on getting us through the next minute, the next twenty or thirty yards of the Golan.

As soon as we'd made it across the plateau, we ran into trouble. We needed to cross the Banias River. On our map, I'd picked out what looked to be a shallow ford, but the water was much higher than we expected. After spending thirty minutes scouting the bank for 150 yards in either direction, we settled on what seemed to be the shallowest part. Yet we hadn't anticipated the need to cross a river in full flow; worse, we'd never trained to do it. Nor had we brought any special equipment. Unless we could figure out a way to cross—and quickly—the timetable for the whole operation would be at risk.

The only remotely useful tools I could find were two twenty-five-foot lengths of parachute wire. We spliced them together. I took the lead end and waded in. I sunk up to around my chest but managed to get across. With Avi Telem on the other bank holding his end of the wire, the others used it to help them cross, so they at least managed to keep the sensitive equipment dry. Finally, Avi followed. All of us were soaking wet. We were also behind schedule. We had covered less than half of the three-mile route to the destination. Even if we did manage to complete our mission, the delay meant we might be spotted on our way back to Israel. We had strict orders to turn back by 1:15 a.m., even if that meant we had to abort. And it was already past midnight.

We began the climb into the heart of the Heights, planning to go around the southern edge of the Syrian base at Banias. The vegetation was sparser, but we still ran the risk of making noise from the stones and larger shards of rock as we weaved our way up. Within ten minutes, I could see the vague outline of the army camp: several large buildings for several hundred Syrian troops, ringed by trenches with security outposts and a barbed-wire fence on the perimeter.

For a half hour or so, we moved forward in a kind of rubber-band formation. I would advance as quietly as I could, listen for signs of Syrian troops, scan the area ahead with my binoculars, and wave the others to follow. But as I prepared to move forward again, I suddenly felt a tug on my shoulder. It was Moshiko, and the very fact of his speaking was proof of his alarm. "Ehud, we've got to go faster," he said. "We won't get there in time." I said I understood. But I told him to wait for the others to catch up and stay behind with them as I scouted the way ahead. Still, by the time the outer fence of the base came into view, the others had picked up their pace. They were only fifteen feet behind me.

Suddenly I heard the sound of movement. I motioned the others down. At first, I thought it was a wild boar. But then I noticed, twenty feet in front of us and a bit off to our right on a slight rise, three Syrian soldiers. They were lying on rocky scrubland fifty yards outside the fence. One was tossing and turning. Another was snoring. I maneuvered my Uzi into firing position just in case. We waited for a minute. Then two. But it seemed clear they really were sleeping.

Then, from directly behind me, came another sound: the hiss of Avi's bulky two-way radio. I was worried we'd wake the Syrians. But just as I was figuring out how to make sure we got past them before that happened, Avi drew up beside me.

"Ehud," he whispered. "It's one fifteen. The command post ordered us to turn back."

"Turn off the radio," I said, my hand on his elbow, reassuringly I hoped, as I led him and the others back a full one hundred feet from the Syrians. We took a wider route around the camp. We moved much more quickly on the final mile to our target. We were now well clear of the camp, and I felt it was unlikely we'd run into a patrol. I was also confident we'd have an easier return trip. I knew what had held us up on the way in:

finding a path on the plateau clear of mines, figuring out how to cross the river, and the general unfamiliarity of the terrain. None of those applied now. I felt we could get the job done and still be back before dawn. As we got nearer the road, Avi asked me a few more times whether he should turn the radio back on. "No," I kept telling him. "It's OK. I'll tell you when."

It was about two thirty when we reached the target, on the edge of a field, and Moshiko, Kuti, and Avi Muchtar managed to complete the work within fifteen minutes. We moved more quickly on the way back. It was nearly 4:00 a.m. when we crossed the river. "You can turn on the radio now," I told Avi, who was obviously relieved. He handed it to me. Using our agreed code words, I reported our location, and added the phrase for "mission accomplished."

When we began our final descent, it was starting to get light. I assumed we were near enough to the border to make it unlikely we'd be shot at. Still, there was a danger we'd be spotted by a patrol, so I was relieved when we reached the mound of boulders, more than ten feet high, that served as a tank barrier outside Kibbutz Dan. When we stepped behind it, I saw Avraham and Meir Amit waiting. The head of military intelligence said nothing. He didn't have to. He just shook my hand, beaming. Avraham grabbed each of us, one by one, in a bear hug.

Then, drawing me aside, Avraham said I had only narrowly missed landing in deep trouble. I assumed my transgression was shutting off the radio and disobeying the order to return. That was just part of the problem, however. Despite General Yoffe's protests in the command post, Avraham and Ahraleh Yariv had managed to convince him to rein in his frustration until they knew what was actually happening on the ground. But Yoffe had also discovered that his jerricans of gasoline were missing. He insisted that if and when I returned safely from the Golan, I be handed over to the military police.

In the mix of celebration and relief that the Syrian operation had succeeded, I got off with what amounted to a plea bargain. I promised both Meir Amit and Avraham—at least one of whom believed me—that it would not happen again.

# 5

# Out of the Fog

ALMOST NO ONE IN ISRAEL KNEW WHAT WE HAD DONE. BUT THE NEXT morning, a package arrived at the Sayeret Matkal base from one of the few people who did. We opened it in Avraham's office. It was a nearly full carton of real French champagne. Inside was a handwritten note from the chief of staff. "For the success of the operation," General Tzur had written. "Minus two bottles . . . to teach Ehud Brog not to shut off his field radio."

I assumed that his reprimand was tongue-in-cheek, for the same reason I'd escaped being locked up on General Yoffe's orders as a gasoline thief. Had we been captured on the Golan, the very future of the sayeret as an operational intelligence unit would have been put at risk. Tzur, and Ben-Gurion as well, would have faced a reopening of all the old wounds from the Uri Ilan mission. Instead, not only had we managed to get in and out of Syria in one piece, but we had taken a first step toward erasing the blind spot in our intelligence capabilities shown so dramatically by Rotem. A few days later, I received a letter from the chief of staff informing me that I was to receive my first *tzalash*, or operational decoration, in recognition of "a mission which contributed to the security of the state of Israel."

I was proud of what we had accomplished. But while Avraham, General Tzur, and our other military and intelligence chiefs celebrated our mission, I felt not so much triumph as relief. I didn't kid myself: I knew the operation could just as easily have gone wrong. In fact, it very nearly did, through errors or omissions I had made. I made that point, in general terms, when we joined Avraham and the rest of the sayeret in a formal debriefing. That very night, just as I had in the days before we set off, I wrote down a series of crucial points in my notebook, detailing oversights that I knew I'd have to correct if we were to succeed in further missions.

Why hadn't I chosen a route that took us further away from the Syrian base? How had I let us arrive so unprepared, untrained, and unequipped for crossing the swollen river? Why hadn't I checked the current several miles downriver inside Israel? And couldn't we have moved more quickly on the way in, even with the delay in crossing the river?

I was aware of, and grateful for, the confidence Avraham had shown in choosing me to lead the sayeret's first, critical operation. Years later, I asked him why he'd picked me. He told me he'd been relying on intuition. He realized that, like all the other young officers in the unit, I'd had no experience of a real cross-border mission. But he said he'd seen in me the tools needed for success: self-confidence, attention to detail, and an ability to think and act swiftly in response to what actually happened on the ground.

With the sayeret's initial success, there was a demand for us to mount further operations elsewhere on the Golan. Though Sayeret Matkal's existence has long ceased to be a secret, some key details of its intelligence missions remain known, to this day, only to those who have served in it. That understanding was central to the way we worked from the start, and it has not only protected sensitive missions over the years. It has protected lives. I was involved in nearly all the missions we were asked to undertake in the months that followed, either as commander of the main force or the hillutz. I was also soon training a new team of recruits for future operations. But perhaps the most important sign of Avraham's confidence was to involve me in early efforts to broaden Sayeret Matkal's experience and reach beyond pure intelligence missions, to create a true special forces unit.

Back in 1961, the unit had hosted a visit by Colonel Albert Merglen, a veteran of France's colonial wars in Indochina and Algeria and leader of the airborne commando force known as the 11th Demi-brigade Parachutistes de Choc. As the colonel looked on, I was part of a sayeret team that mounted a live-fire raid in a training area not far from Lod Airport. We attacked a position protected by trenches and concrete barriers and stormed a two-story building. Eager to impress Merglen, Avraham even insisted on our wearing French-style red berets in place of helmets. I assume it was the attack more than the berets that did the trick. Now, two years later, Merglen proposed a series of exchanges with Sayeret Matkal. The first would involve a sayeret officer spending eight weeks on a counter-guerrilla commanders' course with the *parachutistes*, and Avraham selected me to go.

I had just turned twenty-one. I'd never been outside Israel, at least legally. I had no passport. I didn't own a suit or a tie. But within days, I was kitted and fitted. I boarded an El Al flight to Paris and, on a storm-tossed Caravelle, flew to Perpignan in southeastern France. The base was in a seventeenth-century fortress near Mont Louis, in the Pyrenees along the Spanish border. There were eighteen "shock parachutists" on the course. Most of them were about a decade older than me, and they were the epitome of toughness. The guy who taught us how to set booby traps had parachuted behind German lines in the Second World War. All of the men had fought in Indochina and Algeria. One had operated a thousand miles behind Vietminh lines, surviving for a year and a half on nuts, berries, tree bark, and snakes. With the benefit of my sayeret training, I was at least their equal in fitness. I had also not spent years consuming prodigious amounts of alcohol and smoking Gitanes. But I'd never experienced anything nearly as demanding or risky as some of the training we were put through.

With backpacks crammed with Alpine military gear, we hiked to the peaks overlooking the fortress, covered with snow and ice from about 6,500 feet upward. We trudged for hours, shifting to snowshoes with cleats for the ice. We learned how to dig caves in the snow and to use ice axes to keep from tumbling down the steeper inclines. We scaled cliff faces, without safety cables or nets. Our training inside the fortress always included a break for lunch. Since the *parachutistes de choc* were, after all, French, it was a Paris-restaurant-standard meal, often lasting more than two hours and including copious quantities of alcohol. I didn't drink at the time, but could hardly abstain altogether. The first exercise after lunch was usually pistol marksmanship. The instructors kept well clear when it was my turn.

However impressed, even at times awestruck, I was by the toughness of the French commandos and the obvious closeness they had built during combat, I began to sense a darker side in them as well. They didn't talk much. Even if they had, my few words of French would not have been much help in deciphering what made them tick. But every few nights, I would accompany them when they walked into the small village down the road for a movie or a few drinks, and the locals would literally cross the street to avoid us. Later, I discovered that every one of my French comrades had been involved in the Organisation Armée Secrète, or OAS, the far-right anti–de Gaulle opposition in the French army in the late 1950s. In Algeria, they had mounted freelance attacks on the insurgents, and on civilians as well. Though Algeria had been granted independence the year before, these men were unreconciled to it. In fact, a few months after my time in Mont Louis, the Demi-brigade was dismantled when several of its top officers were found to be involved in an assassination plot against President Charles de Gaulle.

After my return in late June 1963, Avraham asked me to share my experiences with the other sayeret officers. I began with the positives. I singled out the sense of self-confidence, allied with individual strength and teamwork, that the French commandos had developed from exposure to almost incredible extremes of danger. I believed their success depended not on eliminating risk. We all knew that was impossible. It was about professionalism developed over a period of years by men who had served together in the toughest of circumstances. But I also mentioned their darker side, which seemed to me a reminder of the danger of the misapplication of the very qualities that made them a formidable military force. "The ethos of a unit like theirs, and like ours, is essential to making us strong," I said. "But what I saw in France was an entire ecosystem that these guys had created, extremely patriotic in their own minds, reinforced by one another. But dangerous for society as a whole."

+ + +

It would be nearly a decade before Sayeret Matkal became not just a military intelligence unit but a fighting force, and I would have a central role in making that happen. But there was an almost equally daunting challenge we were called on to tackle first—a critical one, if Israel was going to be truly prepared for another war. Our bugging missions on the Golan had reduced our vulnerability to a surprise attack in the north, but the real challenge of Rotem had yet to be addressed. Egypt—with its hundreds of battle tanks, and hundreds of thousands of men under arms—was by far our most powerful Arab enemy. President Nasser wasted no opportunity to flaunt his determination to fight, defeat, and ultimately erase the state of Israel. Yet we still had no reliable, real-time intelligence on his forces.

Fixing that, if such an operation was even possible, would make our bugging operations on the Golan look like mere Boy Scout missions. We couldn't simply walk into Egypt with our backpacks, find a telephone pole on one of the few roads crossing the vast expanse of the Sinai Desert, and attach a bugging device. The idea was to tap into the communications networks in the Sinai. That meant using a more powerful, and far bulkier, intercept apparatus. It weighed many hundreds of pounds. Just getting it into Egypt would be a problem. Even if we could get it there, we'd have to deploy it, make sure it was working, and then get back into Israel again undetected. Otherwise, there was the risk the Egyptians would discover what we'd done, which would very likely tip off Syria to our operations on the Golan as well.

Two years before leading the first mission on the Golan, I'd been involved in preliminary planning, and fairly detailed training, for such a mission in the Sinai. We abandoned the idea at the time as obviously unworkable. But now Meir Amit, our unit's overall commander in the kirya and chief of operations at the time of the Rotem crisis, recognized that getting intelligence access to Egypt was central to Israeli security. He was intent on reviving a plan to improve Israel's early-warning capabilities in the Sinai. So was Avraham Arnan, who enlisted the backing of an old friend, Uri Yarom, who was now commander of Israel's sole helicopter squadron and was eager to put our fleet of recently acquired Sikorsky S-58s to operational use. When Avraham called me in to tell me what he had in mind, he began by saying it would be "by far the greatest challenge we've contemplated"—typically disarming candor, but also a challenge I'm pretty sure he knew would only increase my determination to at least try. The flight in would be difficult enough. Israel had never before tried such a heliborne mission, but he told me that wasn't my problem. "That will be Uri's job." The real test would be to carry out a mission at night, deep inside Egypt, and get out again in one piece without being discovered. "Still, I know we have to succeed," he said. "And I want you and your team to do it."

Even now, more than half a century later, most of the details remain classified. But once I'd chosen my team of sayeret soldiers for the mission, we trained for nearly nine months. We drafted in geologists to identify areas of the Negev similar to the terrain we'd find in the Sinai. We developed a series of methods to prevent Egyptian soldiers or scouts from discovering that we'd been there—assuming, of course, we managed to get in, carry out our mission, and return safely. It was a relentless process of trial . . . and error.

One of the many reasons we'd abandoned the plan a couple of years earlier was that, in a nighttime exercise to see whether we could avoid detection by Israel's own crack desert scouts, we'd failed. Now, after many weeks of training in the Negev, we finally succeeded—in a test that ran four straight nights and replicated, as nearly as we could, what we intended to do across the border in the Sinai. It was as if we'd never been there at all.

Yet there were setbacks and frustrations too. Many months into our training, we conducted a series of exercises in which we simulated the mission in the sandscape of the Negev, not too far from the camp where I'd done my basic training. Though most of them went as planned, one of our last run-throughs highlighted two problems we realized we would still have to crack if we were going to have any realistic chance of success. The first problem was worryingly fundamental. When we deployed the equipment in a trial run-through in the Negev, it began to malfunction only hours later. The reason: rain. We'd failed to fully waterproof it. We did make sure we fixed that.

The main problem, however, was the sheer weight of the equipment. The helicopter could get us, and it, into Egypt. But we couldn't fly directly to the place where we planned to install it. We might as well just tell the Egyptians we were on our way. It was much too heavy for us to carry, even for a few miles. And if we were going to go ahead with the mission, time was running short. A tentative date for the mission had already been set: February 1964. I was not alone in believing that, unless we cracked the challenge of getting the equipment to the site, the operation was impossible.

The solution came from a staff officer in military intelligence. Meir Amit visited our base once a month to hear how the preparations were going. With the date getting closer, he brought along his entire staff. When I raised my concern about the weight problem, a colonel from his personnel section said, "Why not build a lightweight rickshaw, small enough to get in the door of the helicopter, but which can carry all or most of the equipment once you're on the ground?" Within days, they had a prototype made of airline-standard tubing and designed to be pulled by two men. We held another exercise in the Negev, but it proved almost impossible for two men to pull the contraption through the sand. It also left deep zigzag imprints that would surely raise the suspicions of the Egyptians.

But prototype number two was a four-wheel, chrome-alloy cart. The technology experts had made the axles telescopic, so the vehicle would get through the door of the chopper. They had also borrowed nosewheels from a training jet and figured out a way to make sure it wouldn't leave telltale tracks in the Sinai sand.

We were as ready as we were ever going to be. We got the final go-ahead. Our backpacks were crammed with the whole array of equipment we'd designed, commandeered, or purchased for the mission—some of it from a hobby shop in Pennsylvania. All the cargo, except our personal gear, our weapons, and our communications equipment, was loaded onto the cart. A command post was set up in a few wooden huts on Mount Keren in the Negev, complete with equipment to receive new intelligence from the Sinai. Not since the first Golan operation had the attention of the military headquarters been so keen, or the stakes so high. In addition to Meir Amit, and of course Avraham, also flying down to Mount Keren would be General Tzur's successor as armed forces chief of staff. He was a gruff Palmach veteran whom I'd met very briefly at the end of my officers' course but whom I would come to know well, and work closely with, in the years ahead: Yitzhak Rabin.

✦ ✦ ✦

The helicopter lifted off immediately after dark. Compared to today's special forces operations, the mission had a somewhat improvised feel about it. Certainly, that was true of the equipment we were ferrying in, and the array of tools we'd devised. But I'd trained the men in my team from the day they arrived in the sayeret. Achihud Madar was unfailingly sure-footed, whether finding his way alone at night on unfamiliar ground or in a firefight inside a building. He also had a natural dexterity. He and another of the soldiers who was also gifted with his hands, Nissim Jou'ari, would perform the most technically delicate part of the operation. The third member was Oded Rabinovitch. Tall, thin, and quiet, he was absolutely reliable in whatever part of an operation he was given to execute. I chose a sayeret officer named Kobi Meron, who'd been with me on a number of Golan missions, as my deputy commander. Over six feet tall, he was probably the strongest man in the unit, quick-thinking and utterly unflappable.

When we landed, we telescoped out the axles on the cart. The roar of the departing chopper was replaced by silence. Under the soft light of the stars, I led the way deeper into the desert. It took nearly an hour to reach the road near the site that we'd chosen. Though traffic was light, I posted Oded and Nissim as lookouts. Kobi, Achihud, and I got down to work on the first stage of the operation, which, under our tight timetable to get the equipment deployed and running, we'd assumed would be straightforward and fairly easy. It wasn't. The details still haven't been declassified. But they boiled down to geography. Conditions in the Sinai were different from the Negev, and even our team of scientists couldn't predict precisely how that might affect the mission.

What mattered now, however, was that we were falling behind schedule, putting the whole operation at risk. I called back Oded and Nissim from lookout duty. All five of us now pitched in with every tool in our backpacks that could conceivably help. It took nearly three hours in all. But we finally managed to get to the stage where our two close-in experts, Achihud and Nissim, could complete the work. They managed to get the main part done fairly quickly, meaning we almost certainly had accomplished enough to get some useful intelligence. But the full complement of the equipment was not yet deployed, and we were fast approaching a point where we'd risk missing our rendezvous time with the helicopter to take us back into Israel. I was briefly tempted to stop while we were ahead. But I told them to keep going, make sure we got the job fully done.

We had to be out of Egypt by first light, and we were now more than an hour behind. There was another problem, too, which I at first sensed more than saw. A bank of fog was closing in. It had come in patches at first but was getting denser. We had the same radio we had taken onto the Golan. We'd worked out code words for each part of the operation but agreed to break silence only if absolutely necessary. Now, I had no choice. If the fog continued to thicken, it would block any chance of the helicopter getting in. I radioed the command post and said as calmly as I could, "Milk is coming." It wasn't elegant. But "milk" was our code word for fog. The chopper would now try to bring us out within thirty minutes.

Moving more quickly now that the cart was nearly empty, we made our way eastward. As conditions worsened, I radioed again with a short series of numbers: directions for a new pickup point. Even that seemed like it might not work. The fog now enveloped us completely. I brought the team to a stop. I stayed with the cart while the other four outlined a landing area with kerosene flares. It was another five minutes when we heard the thump of chopper blades. Though we couldn't see more than a few feet, I suddenly saw the outline of the landing gear and then the underbelly. But the helicopter did not seem in control. It was drifting toward where I was standing with the cart. It was just seconds away when its nose wrenched upward and its landing lights suddenly blazed on. It landed with a judder only a half dozen yards away from me. Later, I learned that the navigator had realized the craft was drifting and, just before impact, had violated operational rules by turning on its lights, and shouted a warning to the pilot.

We piled in, secured the cart, and took off. Within a minute, the murky blanket of fog was below us. As we swooped back into Israel, I could see the first pink of daylight.

A few days later, one of the sayeret soldiers gave me a firsthand insight into the mood in the command post during the final stages of the operation. Avsha Horan's role had been to act as security guard for the top brass in Mount Keren. He occasionally took a peek inside. He described the atmosphere when I radioed my "milk is coming" message: solemn faces, hushed conversations between Avraham and Meir Amit. And off to the side, the recently elevated chief of staff, Yitzhak Rabin, chain-smoking and biting his nails. Finally, the audible sighs of relief when the pilot radioed in with a final, coded message from the chopper: "Out of the fog. Heading home."

+ + +

With the rest of the team, I was invited to see Rabin ten days later. We were being given a further tzalash. This was the first time I'd met him since leaving officers' school two years earlier, when, with a few terse words, the then deputy chief of staff congratulated me and several other cadets who graduated with top honors. I had felt a bit overwhelmed in his presence. Now, I was struck by his shyness. He greeted each of us with a tentative handshake and seemed uncomfortable making eye contact. Yet once he began asking me about the Sinai operation itself, it was as if he was transformed. He was hungry for every detail, anxious to know the way we'd had to adapt on the ground. And obviously pleased, and proud, that we'd found a way to make the operation work.

The Sinai mission marked a transition for me and others in Sayeret Matkal. Avraham Arnan finally left the unit he'd imagined, created, and built. He became the head of the technology unit in military intelligence. His deputy, Dovik Tamari, succeeded him, serving the first in what would become two-year stints for each of his successors as the sayeret's commander. I, too, got a wider role. Though I was still just a young lieutenant and too junior for the job, Dovik made me his de facto deputy, with responsibility for operational oversight of our missions.

Though the tzalash was gratifying, what gave me more satisfaction was the importance of the Sinai operations themselves. They had significantly improved Israel's intelligence capabilities. But in truth, I didn't actually believe there would be another war. Sure, the threat remained. Egypt, in particular, still seemed determined to find a way to hobble, and if possible eliminate, Israel. But especially since the 1956 war, the military balance seemed to be tilting in our favor, and fedayeen attacks and cross-border skirmishes had subsided. Not long after the Sinai mission, I was chatting with other officers on the sayeret base and remember turning to one of them and saying I was sure that by the time I was married and had a teenage child, we'd be able to take a skiing holiday in Lebanon.

I began to think about what peace would mean not just for Sayeret Matkal or Israel, but for my future. By the autumn of 1964, I'd decided to end my active service in the unit that had been central to my life since joining the military. Dovik persuaded me to delay, for nearly a year, but at the end of the summer of 1965, I left Sayeret Matkal, and the army altogether. I studied physics and mathematics at Hebrew University in Jerusalem. I remained involved in the sayeret as a reservist, but I couldn't see devoting my adult life to military service in a country that, fortunately, seemed on a trajectory toward peace.

Something else also colored my thinking about my future. For the first time in my life, I had fallen in love.

# Six Days in June

THE FRENCH HAVE AN EXPRESSION FOR LOVE AT FIRST SIGHT: *COUP DE foudre*. A thunderbolt. That was how it felt when I set eyes on nineteen-year-old Nili Sonkin in mid-February 1963.

It was my first visit to the kirya, central military headquarters, in Tel Aviv. I'd been told to report to the administrative section to register my formal change of status from a mere draftee to a staff officer, something I'd managed to overlook amid the demands of our first sayeret operations on the Golan. Since I didn't know which office to go to, I approached a girl sitting at a desk near the entrance. She looked up with a wide smile. When she directed me to the second floor, it wasn't just her voice that struck me: alluringly multi-timbred, almost like a musical composition. It was her eyes. Bright, radiant, green. Full of playful, unapologetic self-confidence.

In the weeks that followed, I invented a series of excuses to return. I introduced myself to her, with as much composure as I could muster, and on each visit stayed a bit longer. I told her about growing up in Mishmar Hasharon, about math and music, and how, as a soldier, I'd walked almost every inch of the land of Israel—in short, about everything except our still-secret sayeret and our nighttime forays across the border. She, too, opened up about her home and her family and her friends. Though there was another girl I'd been going out with—the younger sister of my old kibbutz coconspirator, Moshe—I'd never before felt anything like the connection I sensed with Nili.

I also found myself gripped by an unexpected, and unfamiliar, lack of self-assurance. I was twenty-two. I had the inbred confidence of a kibbutznik who'd had some success in the military. Yet with Nili, I felt unmoored, totally out of my depth. She was part of a different Israel. She was a *Tel Avivit*, born and raised in the largest and brashest city in our young state, a place that was everything the kibbutz was not. She had graduated from Alliance, a high school in north Tel Aviv set up with French backing and an accent on French language and culture. Unlike the girls on the kibbutz—proud of their plain, utilitarian clothes and sensible shoes—she wore makeup and perfume and, when she was out of uniform, bright print dresses. She never tried to make me feel out of place. Still, it was sometimes hard not to wonder whether she saw me as a country bumpkin— a nice, interesting, bright county bumpkin, perhaps, but still an interloper or a curiosity in her world.

In April, the day before I was due to leave for the French commando fortress in Mont Louis, I plucked up the courage to ask her out. I needn't have worried. She smiled. In fact, she proposed that since I was about to leave the country, she should be the one doing the asking. She invited me to dinner that evening at the apartment she shared with her parents and younger sister, about a half mile from the kirya and a few blocks from the Mediterranean. Dinner was less awkward than I feared, but I still felt nervous, until the dishes were cleared and Nili and I went out to chat on the apartment balcony and, just before I left, to share a first kiss.

We wrote each other almost every day while I was away in France. Once I got back, we met whenever I wasn't preparing for a sayeret operation. This was the first girl I'd known whom I could talk to, and listen to, on almost any subject with a feeling that it was natural and somehow meant to be. But in the second half of 1963, I was working almost nonstop on preparing for a sayeret operation. I still saw Nili when I could: sometimes at her apartment, or occasionally going out to a movie, a meal, or a concert in Tel Aviv. Yet what I most wanted was an acknowledgment that we were not just dating, a commitment that we intended the relationship to last. I didn't say this to Nili. Years later, she would say this was down to my pride. In fact, I was afraid she would say no. And in the periods when we were apart, I couldn't help asking myself why *she* hadn't raised the question of a deeper commitment.

Even more frustrating, by the time I entered Hebrew University in September 1965, our relationship was again conducted by mail. After her military service, she took a three-year posting in Paris. I could understand the attraction, not just because of her taste for all things French. She was working with the Mossad to help Moroccan Jews skirt an official emigration ban and get to Israel. Still, it meant that charting our future together, if we had one, would have to wait.

+ + +

The intellectual experience at university was everything I hoped. The challenge was finding a way to juggle my studies with my military reserve duty. In other units, most reservists could schedule their one-month annual stint for when classes weren't in session. Yet to be of use to Sayeret Matkal, I'd have to report whenever I was most needed, and four weeks were unlikely to be enough. Near the end of my first term, I was away for nearly six weeks. The next winter, and into the early part of 1967, I was called up for nearly two months on another operation. It was deemed especially urgent, because it was prompted by a concern that the Egyptians might be close to discovering a large, booby-trapped device we'd installed in one of our later operations in the Sinai. Our job now was to defuse it and bring it back to Israel.

The officer in overall command of the mission was Nechemia Cohen, a good friend and one of the finest officers in the unit. Before I left for university, I'd mentored him so he could take over my role under Dovik Tamari as the officer in charge of our core operational activities. Nechemia, too, was now about to leave the sayeret, though not for university. He was about to become deputy commander of a paratroop company.

Since I was the one who had installed the device, I was given the role of making it safe and bringing it back. With the help of a twelve-foot-long metal tool designed by the technology unit, I was fairly confident I'd manage. But when Chief of Staff Rabin heard about the mission, he summoned me and Eliezer Gonn, the scientist from the technology team who was working with us. Rabin was with a half dozen other officers when we arrived. Gonn had brought along a model of the device, which he proceeded to place on Rabin's office table. But as I was explaining how I was going to defuse it, Rabin turned to Gonn and asked, "Could it blow up spontaneously?"

"Yes, of course," he said.

"What?" Rabin barked.

Gonn replied matter-of-factly, "It is a physical device. It obeys the laws of physics. When, for instance, there's a thunderstorm in Turkey, a flash of lightning could discharge at precisely the frequency needed, or one of its higher harmonics, with enough energy to activate the fuse."

I was far junior to everyone else in the room. But as a physics student, I was probably the only one who could fully follow the argument he was making. Looking at Rabin's expression, it was clear he was about to cancel the operation on the spot. "Excuse me, sir," I said. "Could I ask Dr. Gonn another question?"

I pointed at an unopened bottle of orange soda on Rabin's desk. "Tell me," I asked the physicist, "is it possible that the fluid in that bottle is spontaneously leaking through the glass even as I'm speaking?"

"Sure," Gonn said. "It might take years before even a fraction of a centimeter of the soda goes missing. But glass is like a 'frozen' liquid, and liquid water, or the molecules, are seeping into, and through, the more viscous 'liquid' of the glass. It's just physics."

Rabin looked at me, then at Gonn. He'd got the message. "The operation is confirmed," he said in the deep, gravelly voice that would become more familiar to me in the years ahead. "Good luck."

The device didn't explode, but I couldn't defuse it either. I did manage to get the remote metal tool locked onto the bolt of the booby trap. But it had apparently rusted solid. It wouldn't budge, even when I waved Nechemia and the others back—in case it *did* explode—and tried with an ordinary wrench. Though this was the first sayeret mission in which I'd been involved that ended in failure, that wasn't what worried me. It was the possibility the Egyptians might discover why we'd put it there in the first place. I also felt as if we'd let down Dovik, since this was one of the last operations during his period as head of the unit. He was about to hand over command to a veteran paratroop officer, Uzi Yairi.

Yet the Egyptians never found the device. What saved it was the very thing I was so confident would *not* happen when I left for university: another Arab-Israeli war.

+ + +

Tension began building in the north in the spring of 1967, initially set off by Syrian efforts to divert water from the upper reaches of the Jordan River, an important water source for Israel. In a series of exchanges, Syrian troops on the Golan fired on Israeli tractors in the demilitarized zone below and shelled our agricultural settlements in the Galilee. We responded with tank fire and then airpower, scrambling our jets and shooting down six Syrian MiG-21s.

The first indication we might be headed toward war came as I returned to university for the spring term. Ben-Gurion's successor as prime minister was the undeniably capable, if far less charismatic, Levi Eshkol. During Israel's Independence Day parade on May 15, Eshkol received word that Egypt had moved many thousands of troops into the Sinai, nearer to the border with Israel. When the Soviets warned Nasser of what they said were Israeli plans for a preemptive strike against Syria, Nasser went further and expelled the United Nations force put in place after the 1956 war. On May 23, he closed the Straits of Tiran, Israel's trading gateway to the Red Sea and the source of virtually all our oil imports.

I was told to report to Sayeret Matkal the following day, as part of the first group of reservists called up. When I reached the base, Uzi Yairi, who was now in charge of the unit, organized us into four teams and placed me in command of one of them. We were ordered to prepare ourselves to helicopter into the Sinai, attack a series of Egyptian air bases, and put the runways out of commission. My team's target was not far from where I'd led one of our earlier Sinai missions.

With each passing day, war looked more likely, and there was no confidence we would win without a costly struggle. In 1948, Arab attacks had killed about 170 people in Tel Aviv. Now, word got out that a park in the center of the city had been set aside to allow for the burial of as many as 5,000. With Israel's military commanders pressing Eshkol to take the initiative and launch a preemptive strike, he delivered a radio address at the end of May, intended to reassure the country the situation was under control. But due to last-minute, handwritten changes to his typescript, he

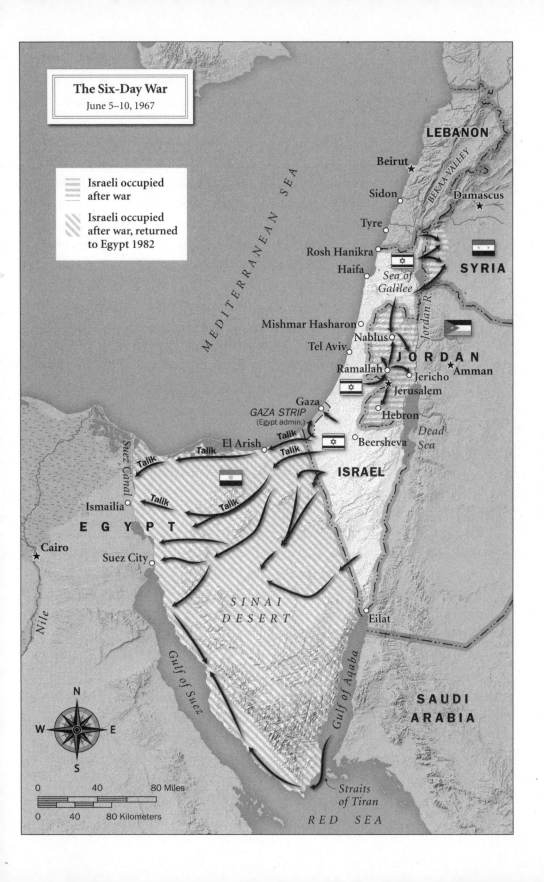

The Six-Day War
June 5–10, 1967

Israeli occupied
after war

Israeli occupied
after war, returned
to Egypt 1982

LEBANON

Beirut

Sidon

Damascus

Tyre

BEKAA VALLEY

SYRIA

Rosh Hanikra

MEDITERRANEAN SEA

Haifa

Sea of
Galilee

Mishmar Hasharon

Jordan R.

Nablus

Tel Aviv

JORDAN

Ramallah

Jericho

Amman

Jerusalem

Gaza

Hebron

GAZA STRIP
(Egypt admin.)

Dead
Sea

Talik

El Arish

Talik

Beersheva

Talik

Talik

ISRAEL

Suez Canal

Talik

Ismailia

Talik

Talik

EGYPT

Cairo

Suez City

SINAI
DESERT

Eilat

Gulf of Aqaba

SAUDI

Gulf of Suez

ARABIA

Nile

N

W        E

S

Straits
of Tiran

0        40        80 Miles

RED  SEA

0        40        80 Kilometers

faltered while reading it. He sounded anything but under control. Within days, he bowed to political pressure and brought back Moshe Dayan, now a member of the Knesset, as defense minister.

I still vividly remember a visitor to the sayeret a week before Eshkol's radio address. Colonel Eli Zeira was head of the "collection department" of the intelligence corps, the rough equivalent of America's National Security Agency and the headquarters unit responsible for Sayeret Matkal. He summoned all the officers. There had so far been three periods in the Zionist project, he began. The first stretched from the early settlements in Palestine at the end of the nineteenth century until the establishment of Israel in 1948. The second stage was from 1948 until the 1956 war, and the third from 1956 until now. "There will soon be a war," he said confidently. "Three Arab countries will take part. Within a week, we will defeat all of them. And a new chapter in the history of Zionism will begin."

The Six-Day War began on June 5, 1967. As Zeira predicted, Egypt, Syria, and Jordan all joined forces against us. The final outcome—Israel's victory—was sealed by noon on the first day, with wave after wave of preemptive bombing sorties destroying the air forces of all three Arab countries. But the fighting that followed was brutal in places: especially around Jerusalem, but also in the south at the outset of the war, and later on the Golan Heights.

The first effect back in Israel of our air force attacks was to make our sayeret helicopter missions into the Sinai superfluous. In fact, it left the entire unit at loose ends—especially hard for veterans or reservists like me who had been part of our nearly decade-long development into Israel's sole, dedicated cross-border infiltration force. At this point, we were still just an intelligence unit, not an elite commando force like Britain's SAS. The aim of our missions into Syria and Egypt was to *not* fight. It was to get in and get out, unseen and undetected. But we were equipped to fight if necessary. From the unit's earliest days under the sway of Meir Har-Zion, Kapusta, Kokla, Gibli, Errol, and the other grizzled vets from Unit 101 and Company A, we had been steeped in the spirit of commandos. Our training involved not just a punishing endurance regimen but learning to fight: staging raids under a variety of conditions, firing a range of weapons, and deploying makeshift explosives or land mines.

The frustration we felt on the first morning of the war was not because we were itching to fight, for the hell of it. But even on the first day of the war, it was clear this would be by far the most consequential conflict in our country's history. There was no mission for Sayeret Matkal, nor, it seemed, any prospect of our playing any significant part.

My own role was slightly less peripheral due to Avraham Arnan. He phoned me almost as soon as we'd got news of the Israeli air victory and said he had been told to take a few men from the sayeret to complete our failed attempt to defuse the booby-trapped device in the Sinai. I drafted in two others from the unit: Danny Michaelson, a soldier in Nechemia Cohen's team and a friend from Hebrew University, where we had been lab partners; and Rafi Friedman, our paramedic, who had been with me on several of our missions on the Golan.

Avraham arrived at the base around noon. I got a jeep and we set off. We crossed into Egypt around four o'clock in the afternoon and headed for the field headquarters of Israel Tal. Known as Talik, he was the commander of Israel's armored corps, and Avraham knew him well. His wartime division consisted of the country's premier tank unit, the Seventh Armored Brigade, and a reserve brigade, as well as the 35th Paratroop Brigade under the command of Rafael "Raful" Eitan. We accompanied them the next day to an abandoned Egyptian camp not far from El Arish, in the northern Sinai. At least, we'd assumed it was abandoned. As Talik and Avraham were talking in his command post, we heard a burst of gunfire, which seemed to come from just a few dozen yards outside. As everyone inside the command post looked around, Avraham turned to me and said, "Ehud, don't you think we ought to deal with it?" Then, to Talik: "Make sure none of your guys shoots him."

I got Danny and Rafi. We made our way toward an underground bunker, which seemed the most likely source of the gunfire. Hugging the wall as I led the way down a series of concrete steps, I clicked off the safety on my Uzi. But with the main Egyptian forces in obvious retreat, I figured that whoever was doing the shooting would have to be shell-shocked, or insanely brave, to put up a fight. We found eight men crouched inside: soldiers and several staff officers cradling Kalashnikovs, and an Egyptian army general. In what was obviously at least serviceable Arabic, I told them all to raise their hands, which they did. I made a brief attempt to interrogate the general, but quickly reached the limits of my linguistic proficiency. So we marched them away and handed them over to Talik's intelligence officers.

This interlude instantly conferred on us the desert equivalent of street cred. The next morning, Talik agreed we could accompany the Seventh Brigade as it moved deeper into the Sinai, and peel off when we got closer to the area where we had to complete our sayeret mission. Given the early course of the fighting, and our forces' rapid advances in the Sinai, I couldn't help wondering whether there was any real need to deal with the booby trap. But the fact that the kirya, in the early hours of the war, still wanted us to try was a reflection of the deep apprehension in Israel before the war. Even now, it seemed, there was a concern that the Egyptians might reclaim the parts of the Sinai we had now captured.

When the armored column got near to the area where the sayeret device had been installed, I pulled our jeep aside and we headed off to try to complete the mission. Yet I was no more successful in broad daylight than in the desert darkness a few months earlier. Finally, I told Avraham we'd be better off just blowing it up. I attached an explosive charge, set a two-minute delay, and we watched from a couple of hundred yards away as the whole thing disintegrated.

Before sunset on the third day of the war, we reached the vicinity of the Egyptian air base at Bir Gafgafa in the heart of the Sinai. Even had the war ended then, we would have been in control of a large chunk of the desert buffer zone that Ben-Gurion had hoped to retain after the 1956 war. But now we heard on the radio that Israeli troops had also broken through in fierce fighting with the Jordanians and taken the whole of east Jerusalem, including the Old City and the site of the remains of the ancient temple. I was only twenty-five, a kibbutznik raised on the assertively secular creed of Gordonian Zionism. But I was old enough to remember the war of 1948, the bitter struggle for the ancient city in which Judaism had been born, the packages of food we sent to try to help break the siege, and the division of Jerusalem at the end of the war, leaving us with only its newer, western half. And while I may not have read the Torah in the same way as a religiously observant Jew, the meaning of Jerusalem was no less powerful for me. On hearing the news that the city was in our hands, I shivered with emotion. I felt goose bumps all up my arms. Jerusalem was part of our people's history, of who we were, where we'd come from. It was an inseparable part of the story of Israel. This was no less true of the biblical sites of Judaea and Samaria—the West Bank of the Jordan River. Places like Bet El, Shiloh, or Hebron. They represented the historic wellspring not just of the state we'd created, but of Jewish civilization, our heritage.

In the Sinai, our early advances prompted Talik to move further as well—toward the Suez Canal and the main towns and cities of Egypt. As the Seventh Brigade billeted down in Bir Gafgafa, he sent his reserve brigade westward, in the direction of the canal, and we joined them.

The battalion was more mobile than a pure tank force, but also more vulnerable: lightly armored French AMX-13s and a collection of the half-tracks that I dimly remembered from my basic training. A few of the AMXs led the way, then a line of half-tracks, and more tanks at the rear. I nosed our jeep into the middle, behind the battalion commander, a lieutenant colonel named Ze'ev Eitan. Groups of Egyptian soldiers were scattered on either side of us, and they aimed an occasional burst of fire in our direction. But there seemed little point in shooting back. We didn't need to fight, and it was clear that the Egyptians didn't really want to.

Shortly before dark, Lieutenant Colonel Eitan halted our column. The road we were on cut through sand dunes on either side. We knew there were still Egyptian soldiers around us, though I doubt any of us expected trouble. Still, there were well-established rules for setting up a defensible position when an armored force halts for the night. As Eitan briefed his officers, I stood a few feet off to the side and listened. Suddenly, the commander of his AMX company interrupted. "Sir," he said, "why are we staying here—right on the main road? There are Egyptians still out there. Behind us, for sure. And any force ahead of us will run straight into us. Why not a few hundred yards off to the side, in a place that gives us a view of any enemy movement, or allows us to ambush an approaching force?" He was obviously right, and I expected Eitan to agree and alter the arrangements. But he didn't. Having ordered his men to encamp on the road twenty minutes earlier, he was reluctant to get his tanks and half-tracks moving again. No doubt, some of the exhausted crews were already asleep.

I parked our jeep a few yards off the road. We organized a series of watches: Avraham, then Rafi and Danny, with me taking the predawn stretch. A few hours later, Rafi nudged me awake. "I heard something," he said, pointing west toward the Suez Canal. "It was faint. But I think so." I told him to keep listening. For a while, everything seemed fine. Then, Danny woke me up. He said he was sure he heard a faint tremor, as if from tanks or APCs. I put my ear to the ground. I heard it too. I told him to go to Eitan's command half-track, insist he be woken up, and tell him. When he got back, Danny said, "I told him."

"And?"

"Don't know," he replied. "He said I could go." I tried to grab a bit more sleep before my watch. But barely fifteen minutes later, Danny jostled me awake again. "I'm *sure* now," he said. "Whatever it is, it's closer." I went off to find Eitan. But before I got there, a column of Egyptian T-55 tanks suddenly appeared on the road, fifty yards from the front of our column. I'm sure they were as surprised as we were to be face-to-face with enemy armor. But they knew what to do. They opened fire.

Had we been deployed a few hundred yards off the road, we'd have seen them coming. If the battalion commander had acted on Danny's warning, we'd have had an extra twenty minutes to prepare. The shells jolted our crews awake. Within thirty seconds, they were returning fire. But our tanks barely dented the heavily armored T-55s. Nearly every one of theirs seemed to score a direct hit. Within minutes, a number of our half-tracks, and one of our tanks, were in flames.

Now that we were in a fight—the single fiercest battle in Israel's advance across the Sinai—Lieutenant Colonel Eitan reacted swiftly. Coolheaded and courageous amid the shell fire, he radioed for supporting fire, only to be told that none of our artillery batteries was within range. Realizing we couldn't penetrate the front armor of the Egyptian tanks, he ordered a platoon from the rear to leave the road and fire on the Egyptians from their flank. When one T-55 was hit and started to burn, the Egyptians' fire finally began to slacken, and Eitan ordered the rest of us to collect the dead and wounded and retreat.

As we pulled back, we encountered a company of Centurion tanks from the Seventh Brigade, sent in to relieve us. The battle would rage for another hour, and by the time it was over, the Egyptian tank unit was nearly destroyed. But almost two dozen of Eitan's reservists had been killed. Later that morning, I learned that Shamai Kaplan, the commander of the Centurions, had also been killed. Though I didn't know him personally, he was married to one of my kibbutz "sisters" from Mishmar Hasharon.

+ + +

A few hours later, I drove back to Tel Aviv with Avraham and the others. After dropping Avraham at headquarters, we returned to the sayeret base, but it was nearly empty. The main fighting was now with Syrian armored units on the Golan Heights, and most of the men in the unit had gone north in the hope of joining what seemed likely to be the final stage of the war. Although the precise outcome was not yet clear, there was a dawning certainty, almost surreal, that Israel was gaining control of all the areas across our 1948 borders from which the Arab states around us had shelled Israeli farming settlements, or facilitated fedayeen attacks and ambushes against our citizens—the very border areas where I'd led intelligence operations in Sayeret Matkal.

I, too, now drove north. Not far from Kibbutz Dan, the staging point for our first Golan operation, I linked up with a group of other sayeret reservists. Israeli tanks and the Golani Brigade had already broken the main resistance of the Syrians, but fighting was continuing in a few parts of the Golan. In the western corner of the Heights, which bordered Lebanon, several villages still lay beyond the Israeli advance. We got an order to see if we could take them. It took barely two hours, against barely more resistance than I'd met in capturing the Egyptians in the Sinai bunker. By the time we made our way back across the Golan to the now-abandoned Syrian headquarters on the Heights, it was sunset, and the war was drawing to a close.

I gave my jeep to a couple of paratroopers and hot-wired a more comfortable mode of transport back home: a sleek, black Mercedes that had obviously belonged to a senior officer. If only because of the Syrian license plates, I avoided the main road back into Israel. I found a dirt track running along the southern edge of the Golan and descended toward the fruit groves of Kibbutz Ha'on, near the Sea of Galilee. I then headed for Givatayim in east Tel Aviv, to a place I knew well: the home of Menachem Digli, who had been Avraham Arnan's deputy in the sayeret when I left for my stint in officers' school. Before I returned to the unit, he had a motorcycle accident and badly damaged his leg. He'd been temporarily reassigned to a post in intelligence. I figured a Syrian Mercedes would make a nice gift. Not wanting to wake him, I left it in front of his house. Sadly, he never got to use it. The next day a couple of military policemen knocked on his door and asked what he knew about the car outside. "Nothing," he said. "It's not mine." They took it away.

As much as Sayeret Matkal had wanted to play its part on the battlefields of the Six-Day War, we had to accept that, at best, we'd been freelance support troops. In some cases, mere spectators. Yet while it would be years before this was openly acknowledged, we did make an important contribution to the outcome. Because Dayan had been called back as defense minister only days before the war, he had no reason to alter the plan for the preemptive air strikes. But he made major adjustments to our ground advance. Just as with Eshkol's knowledge of the initial Egyptian advance in the Sinai before the war, his judgments were informed by detailed intelligence on where enemy tanks and troops were located, what they were doing, and how and when they might be planning to advance.

Speculation mounted after the war about how Israel seemed to know so much about the Arab forces. Meir Amit's successor as head of military intelligence, Ahraleh Yariv, was anxious to avoid jeopardizing future sayeret missions, so he engaged in some misdirection. In a speech on how the war had been won, he included a reference to a "high-ranking spy" in the Egyptian army who, he implied, had leaked critical information. The "spy" was the intelligence-gathering equipment we'd installed in Egypt and on the Golan Heights.

On a deeply personal level, too, the war left its mark on Sayeret Matkal. Though the fighting had been brief, people died. Thousands of Egyptians, Syrians, and Jordanians, but also about 650 Israelis, including people we knew well. Nechemia Cohen, the officer I'd joined in our failed attempt to defuse the booby trap in the Sinai, entered Gaza on the first day of the war. He was in his new role as deputy commander of a paratroop company, under another veteran sayeret officer whom I knew well, Yehiel Amsalem. Amsalem was killed very early on, and Nechemia took command. He, too, was shot and killed fifteen minutes later. To this day, he and I share the distinction of being the most decorated soldiers in Israel's history. I have no doubt that, had he lived, he would have held that honor himself.

These were the first close friends from the unit we'd lost. We did not mourn them openly. For young soldiers of my generation, there was an embedded sense that such individual displays of emotion were an indulgence, a luxury even. In the early years of the state, the model Israeli mother or father stood silent and strong as their son's coffin was lowered into the ground.

Nechemia's death hurt, of course. I was friends not just with him, but his older brother, Eliezer. Known by his army nickname, Cheetah, he was for some time in charge of the air force's main helicopter squadron and had flown me on sayeret missions into the Sinai. Several days after the war was over, before returning to university, I drove up to Jerusalem to see his family. Cheetah was at the door when I arrived. Neither of us spoke. But as we embraced, I could feel my eyes dampen, and as I pulled back I saw tears in his eyes as well.

"Our squadron was the one that got the call to bring out the casualties," he said. "They ordered the pilot who brought out Nechemia not to tell me he was dead . . . until the war was over."

"He was a wonderful man," I told Cheetah. "There was no one better."

+ + +

When I returned to Hebrew University, the country felt completely different. It was not just the sudden realization that, in military terms, Israel had eliminated any realistic threat to its existence, important though that was. The more profound change was physical. The country in which I'd grown up felt not just small, but pinched, especially in its "narrow waist" near Mishmar Hasharon. Pre-1967 Israel was about three-quarters the size of the state of New Hampshire. Now, within the space of less than a week, the territory Israel controlled had more than tripled. It included the whole Sinai, up to the edge of the Suez Canal. The entire Golan. The ancient lands of Judaea and Samaria: the West Bank. And the reunited capital city of Jerusalem.

Suddenly, we had a sense that we could *breathe*. Wander, explore. Few of my classmates were religiously observant. But none of us could help feeling the sense of connection as we walked through the Old City of Jerusalem, or parts of Judaea and Samaria, whose place-names resonated from the Bible. I felt especially moved when I first visited the Old City with my friends, stopping and chatting and buying things at the colorful market stalls—and when I stood in front of the surviving Western Wall of the ancient Jewish temple. No Israeli had been able to visit the wall after the 1948 war. From nowhere in the western, Israeli-controlled half of the city had it even been visible.

In my personal interactions with Palestinians in the weeks after the war, I sensed no obvious tension, much less hostility. They were often friendly. Looking back, I'm sure that was one reason—along with simple human nature, a desire to enjoy Israel's new sense of both security and size—that none of us was inclined to look too deeply, or too far ahead, and contemplate the implications of the new borders for our country's future.

I was aware, of course, that the pleasantries we exchanged with the Palestinians of Jerusalem or the West Bank were superficial: a few words across a market stall or a restaurant counter. I didn't pretend that our Arab neighbors were now suddenly inclined to be our friends. But I did believe that, having come face-to-face with our overwhelming military supremacy, the Arab states would, over time, grant Israel simple acceptance. From there, we could begin the process of building genuine, lasting human relationships and, eventually, peace.

There was a brief period after the war when Prime Minister Eshkol cautioned his ministers about the implications of holding on to the vast new area. The government formally agreed to treat most of it, with the exception of Jerusalem, as a "deposit" to be traded for the opening of peace talks. Yet within weeks, the emphasis in the Israeli political debate shifted to which parts we would keep: the Sinai and the Golan almost certainly, as well as the Jordan Valley and a number of areas of past Jewish settlement on the West Bank. The drift away from any serious talk of trading land for peace was accelerated by the Arab states' response to the war. Perhaps that, too, was simply a matter of human nature, a reluctance on their part to accept defeat. But they appeared no more ready than before to contemplate peace. Throughout the summer, there were clashes along the Suez Canal, our new "border" with Egypt. In a summit in Khartoum in September, the Arab states adopted a platform that became known as the "three no's": they rejected not just the idea of peace, but peace talks, or recognition of the State of Israel. And in October, Egyptian missile boats attacked and sunk the Israeli navy's flagship, the destroyer *Eilat*, killing nearly fifty people on board.

Without this renewed violence, and the hard line adopted by the Arab states, we in Israel might have been able to consider more deeply the future implications of our victory in the Six-Day War. The gains on the battlefield were clear to everyone. We were no longer a small, constricted country beset by a sense of vulnerability. We were not only much bigger. We were stronger militarily than the combined armies of the Arab states. Still, very few people asked themselves at the time what *kind* of Israel would result from our holding on to land on which many hundreds of thousands of Arabs lived. Nor did we ponder the limitations of military strength, alone, in addressing these questions. We—and I must include myself—were too caught up in a sense of postwar relief, celebration, and, as the months passed, a certain complacency.

But within only a few years, we would face a dramatically different series of challenges. First, a campaign of Palestinian terror. Then another full-scale war, beginning with a surprise attack by Arab armies that we had assumed would not dare to fight us again.

# 7

# Back in Uniform

IF YOU'D VISITED TEL AVIV IN JULY 1967, YOU WOULD HAVE SENSED A new spirit of confidence: not cockiness exactly, but a sort of spring in the collective step. This was not just due to the Six-Day War. It was because the city, if not yet the rest of the country, had shed the economic austerity of Israel's first two decades and was beginning to experience at least some of the consumer comforts that Western Europe, or America, took for granted. But we were still a decade away from the first shopping malls, or the upscale cafés and restaurants that today give places like Dizengoff Street, a few blocks back from the seafront, the feel of London or Paris on a summer's day. Television had been introduced only a year after the war. *Color* TV was still nearly a decade away. I can't say I was surprised to learn, when the archives were opened a few years ago, that a committee of moral arbiters in our Ministry of Education vetoed plans for the Beatles to perform in the city. "No intrinsic artistic value," they pronounced. "And their concerts provoke mass hysteria."

Even in Tel Aviv, and certainly the rest of Israel, a kind of cultural austerity still prevailed. A legacy of 1948, it reflected the years of shared sacrifice, physical labor, and the life-and-death struggles that I, like most Israelis at the time, had experienced within our own lifetimes. That may help explain why elements of my character that would later attract frequent comment, and sometimes criticism, never came up: the fact that I seemed so *self-contained*, reluctant to engage emotionally with people beyond a circle of close friends or confidants. To the extent those around me would have taken note—family, university classmates, sayeret comrades, or officers in the kirya—my slight emotional aloofness, and the way I internalized even tragedies like the death of Nechemia Cohen, were not exceptional. They were, in many ways, simply Israeli.

Yet as Israel, Israeli society, and my place in them changed, it would be suggested to me more than once—and not always kindly, when it was from critics or rivals—that I had a "touch of Asperger's," a reference to those on the more benign reaches of the autism spectrum, marked by both this aloofness and a special facility for math, music, and abstract ideas. I would always smile in response, suggesting that such diagnoses were probably best left to the professionals. I couldn't pretend, however, that emotional engagement with new acquaintances, even with people I knew and liked but were not close friends, came easily. And it's true that from my first experience of the world of numbers as a child on the kibbutz, and as I tackled ever more elaborate pieces on the piano, I did become conscious of the ease with which my brain translated the complexities into pictures in my mind. And the joy, at times, with which it allowed me to play around with, and develop, what I saw.

By the summer of 1967, I had experienced that feeling again, in my first real encounter with theoretical physics at Hebrew University. After the Six-Day War, I seriously contemplated a future as a research scientist, or perhaps eventually a professor of physics. Two months after the war, I enrolled in a summer program at the Weizmann Institute, Israel's preeminent postgraduate research facility. Being surrounded by some of the country's, even the world's, leading scientists, and by postdoctoral students determined to follow in their footsteps, was intellectually enthralling. But it also exposed me to the way in which pure science sometimes got submerged in simple routine or, more discouragingly, in the politics and positioning and backbiting of the academic world.

I think what finally deterred me from taking a path into academia or research was a feeling, nurtured on the kibbutz and solidified by those many nights leading sayeret operations across our borders, that I would find my true purpose in life trying to make some special contribution to the future course of Israel. I didn't remotely consider politics at that point. Instead, I thought of going back into the military. I realized that in order to make a significant mark, if indeed I could, I would need to serve in the regular army, not just an extraordinary unit like Sayeret Matkal. But I did hope that at some stage I'd have the opportunity to finish my time in the sayeret as its commander, carrying on Avraham's vision and, ideally, building and expanding on it as well. If that part proved possible, I felt that, by comparison, a career in academia would be somehow blinkered, and surely less fulfilling personally. My sayeret experience had also taught me something else: that protecting Israel's security was not just a matter of muscle, or firepower, indispensable though they sometimes were. It also called for mental application, an ability to assess risks, to find answers, sometimes within the space of seconds when, inevitably, things went wrong. It required not just brawn, but brains.

A week before I began my final year at Hebrew University, I went to see Eli Zeira, the senior intelligence officer who'd so brashly predicted the course of the Six-Day War, in hopes of sounding out my prospects. Despite a yawning gap in rank and age—Eli was nearly fifteen years older—I felt I could be open with him. I knew him from Sayeret Matkal, which came under his purview in the kirya. He was also a scientist manqué and was eager, as soon as I arrived in his office, to hear about my physics studies. When I did manage to turn the conversation to the army, I told him I was thinking of returning, but that I wanted his honest opinion about my chances of eventually being given command of the sayeret. He began with a series of caveats. The choice of future leaders of the sayeret was not his to make. When the current commander, Uzi Yairi, ended his term in roughly eighteen months' time, I'd still be too young to have a realistic chance. "Maybe even next time around," he said. And in any case, I would first need to get some experience in the regular army. "But then," he concluded, "my opinion is that you have a very good chance of becoming commander of the unit." That was more than enough. Whether it actually happened would now ultimately be down to me.

My last year at university was the closest thing I would have to a normal student existence. I was called away only once, for a battle that ultimately had a lasting impact on the course of our conflict with the Arabs, and on the prospects of eventually finding a way to make peace. It was Israel's largest military action since the war, across our new de facto border with Jordan. It was directed at a new enemy: a fledgling army of

Palestinian guerrillas called Fatah. It was led by a man few Israelis had heard of at the time: Yasir Arafat. Although Fatah had nominally existed for nearly a decade, it was only now emerging as a political force, in large part because of the Arab armies' humiliating defeat in the Six-Day War. A Palestinian political leadership already existed, in the shape of the Palestine Liberation Organization (PLO). But it was based in Cairo. Its chairman was, for all practical purposes, an adjunct of Egyptian president Gamal Abdel Nasser's leadership role in the Arab world. Though Arafat had not yet explicitly challenged this state of affairs, his, and Fatah's, rise after the war carried a powerful message for the existing Arab presidents and prime ministers: after their hollow promises of victory before the 1967 war, it was time for a new generation, and a new, more direct form of confrontation with the "Zionist enemy."

Arafat had set up camp with nearly a thousand men just across the Jordan River, in a town called Karameh. From early 1968, they had been launching hit-and-run raids, not just on the West Bank but into the Negev in southern Israel. Eshkol's cabinet was initially divided on whether to attack his base in Jordan, both as an act of retaliation and a signal to King Hussein that if his army didn't rein in Arafat's men, Israel would take whatever action necessary. But the decisive moment came on the eighteenth of March. A school bus not far from Eilat, in the far south, hit a Fatah land mine, killing a teacher and a school doctor and injuring ten children.

I was called up the night before Israel's retaliation strike, as part of a small Sayeret Matkal contingent that was supposed to play a support role. The main Israeli forces—including a full paratroop brigade, the Seventh Armored Brigade, and the paratroopers' sayeret—mounted a pincer operation around the Fatah camp and Karameh itself. But the resistance they met, both from Fatah and Jordanian troops, was much fiercer than expected. One of the paratrooper commandos, Mookie Betzer, who later joined Sayeret Matkal, told me how they landed by helicopter and immediately came under a hail of AK-47 fire. Within minutes, several of his men had been killed. Mookie was wounded. The tanks of the Seventh Brigade advanced from the south. Battling the Jordanian army, they took losses as well. Amnon Lipkin, who would also later become a friend and colleague in both the army and Israeli politics, was in command of a unit of lightly armored French tanks called AMLs. They, too, were hopelessly outgunned.

Our sayeret assignment was to block the southern entrance to Karameh as the Israeli armored force advanced. But we got bogged down in mud as we made our way from the Jordan River. By the time we arrived, hundreds of Arafat's men had already fled the area. Arafat, too, had escaped, on the back of a motorcycle.

By the time the fighting was over, some 200 Fatah fighters had been killed. But nearly thirty Israeli soldiers lost their lives as well, and more than twice that number were wounded. Politically, the outcome was even murkier. Most of Israel was still basking in our victory in the Six-Day War. Now, we had deployed many of the same units, only to fight to what looked like a costly draw. Arafat and Fatah could claim—and soon did— that they had stood and fought, and inflicted losses on the victors of 1967.

+ + +

In retrospect, given all the interruptions, I'm a little surprised I managed to finish my university studies. My classmates helped me, going over what I'd missed and sharing their notes, whenever I returned from an extended stint of reserve duty. Working hard in the final year, I even managed to finish in the upper 15 percent of the class, and several of my math and science professors strongly urged me to go to graduate school.

But my mind was made up to return to the army. And as I balanced my studies with plans for the future during my final months, I still hadn't given up hope that Nili would be there with me. When she returned from Paris, we started seeing each other again. Whenever I could, I would take the bus down to Tel Aviv and spend the weekend with her. Everything I'd loved about her since that first meeting in the kirya, everything I valued in our relationship, was still there. Yet so, too, were the doubts: whether she was ready to commit herself to sharing our lives together; whether a kibbutznik like me could ever truly fit into her *Tel Avivi* world. Shortly before the 1967 war, she'd invited me to a Friday-night party with a group of her friends. It was the first time she was including me as part of a couple in her social circle, and I couldn't help feeling it was a kind of test. Unfortunately, from the moment we got there, I felt out of place. For her, it was just another party. For me, it was another universe. I didn't drink at the time. I couldn't dance. Her smartly dressed friends carried themselves with the blasé indifference of young urbanites, talking about things that, to me, seemed unimportant. And so I dismissed them as self-indulgent and superficial. The unfortunate thing is that I would turn out to be wrong about that: most would go on to play important roles in their chosen fields, in Israel and beyond. But at the time, I couldn't see past the jarring differences between us.

None of that, however, had changed my feelings for Nili, and I now decided there was no point in just waiting and wondering whether we could make a life together. I figured I would borrow a car from an army friend, with the idea that Nili and I could spend three or four days together in the Galilee: to be alone, to walk, to talk, to see whether we actually had a future. I wrote her a note, took the bus to Tel Aviv while she was at work, and dropped it through the letterbox. "I am going on this trip," it said. "I'd love it if you could come with me. I think it's important for us."

As the days passed, I heard nothing back. I felt crushed. But at least it was better to know where we stood, or so I told myself. Later, she told me the envelope had ended up under a pile of mail. She hadn't seen it until a week afterward. She said that of course she would have come with me. She felt angry with herself, and with me too, for not simply having phoned. But since I didn't contact her in the weeks that followed, she figured this was just another one of our times apart. Or another example of my "stupid pride." A few months later, I heard she was engaged to be married, to a young man she'd known since their high school days at the Alliance.

I had first met Nava Cohen, the woman I would go on to marry, the previous year. It was through another Cohen, though they were not related: Nechemia, my sayeret friend who was killed in the 1967 war. He invited me to Tel Aviv for a party in the spring, on the Jewish holiday of Purim, and introduced us. Nava was just nineteen, five years younger than me. She was attractive, but I was struck also by her poise, warmheartedness, and obvious intelligence. Yet she had her boyfriend with her, and I still hoped that Nili and I would be partners for life. Now, Nava was beginning her studies at Hebrew University as well, and, in a way, it was again Nechemia Cohen who brought us together. Since his death, those of us who knew him from the sayeret had been looking for a fitting way to honor him. We finally decided to set up a living memorial in his name: a Moadon Sayarim, a center to train young people from all over Jerusalem in scouting and navigation. We spent six months getting it up and running, and Nava pitched in.

Several months after I heard of Nili's engagement, I finally asked Nava on a date. We were in the university library, which had a space where you could listen to tapes through headphones. I would go to hear classical music. Nava was studying English literature, and I'd sometimes see her there engrossed in recordings of Shakespeare with the text of *Hamlet* or *Macbeth* in front of her. Since I wasn't shackled by the need to follow the alacks and alasses, I read the newspaper as the music washed over me. I turned to the movie section. I circled three films, drew a question mark in the margin, and passed it to her. She looked puzzled for a second. Then she smiled and put a checkmark next to one of them.

While we came from different backgrounds, the gap was narrower than it had been with Nili. Her parental home was in Tiberias. Her parents were from old Sephardi families, with a centuries-long history in Palestine, and were also solid Ben-Gurion Labor supporters. Her father fought in the British army in the Second World War. He now ran the branch of Bank Leumi in Tiberias. Her mother ran a shop in what was then the city's best hotel, the Ginton.

We were married there, in the spring of 1969. My parents and brothers came with two busloads of friends from the kibbutz. Avraham Arnan was there, of course. Ahraleh Yariv and Eli Zeira, two of the military intelligence heroes of the Six-Day War, also drove up for the wedding, which touched both Nava and me, not to mention her family and our guests. Years later, as I rose higher in the ranks of the military, I would sometimes be invited to weddings by officers under my command. Remembering how much we appreciated Ahraleh's and Eli Zeira's gesture, I always said yes.

+ + +

I'd returned to Sayeret Matkal a few months before our wedding. Both Nava and I were aware of the pressures my military commitments might place on our family life. But she understood why I'd chosen to go back and was supportive. I was, if anything, more certain that I'd made the right decision. Israel faced a whole new set of challenges to its security. Given the decisiveness, and speed, of our victory in 1967, there seemed no immediate danger of Egypt's risking another full-scale war. In Israel, where Golda Meir had become prime minister after Eshkol's death from a heart attack, there was also little appetite for returning to the battlefield. Yet the postwar skirmishes with the Egyptians along the Suez Canal had escalated into far more than that: what would become known as the War of Attrition. Nor could there be any doubt, after Karameh, that Fatah's influence, militancy, and determination would only grow, not least because more-radical factions within the PLO were ready to step into the breach if Arafat faltered. Israel needed an answer for all these threats.

Uzi Yairi's term as Sayeret Matkal commander had by now ended, but his successor was someone I knew well. Menachem Digli was the officer on whom I'd bestowed my stolen Syrian Mercedes at the end of the war. His leg had recovered from the motorcycle accident, and I returned to the sayeret as his deputy. He delegated full responsibility to me for operational issues. I believed that the new kind of challenges we were confronting, particularly the prospect of intensified attacks from the new generation of Palestinian fedayeen, meant that the sayeret would sooner or later have to broaden its reach and move beyond the kind of intelligence operations we'd done before the 1967 war to become the SAS-like special forces unit Avraham ultimately envisaged. But that was not going to happen soon, if only because the intelligence missions now required were going to be a lot tougher. Israel had control of the entire Sinai and the Golan, meaning that we would have to push deeper inside Egypt and Syria.

Soon after my return, we began to plan the sayeret's most ambitious mission so far. The aim was familiar: to ensure effective intelligence from inside Egypt. But that would mean crossing the Suez Canal and operating deeper inside Egypt. We'd have to go in by helicopter, and the steady buildup of Egyptian forces along the Suez Canal now included Soviet-made antiaircraft missile batteries.

The mission struck the generals in the kirya as so risky as to border on the insane. But my experience of earlier airborne missions, and my knowledge of physics, made me confident we could find a way to make it work. I talked to the few senior air force officers who seemed more receptive, as well as to officers in the helicopter units. We also called on the help of several soldiers from our units with a background in math, and a gifted engineer from the air force. Together, we developed a plan, using the contours in the desert terrain, to calculate a flight route that would avoid our helicopters being detected by Egyptian radar. Or shot down by Egyptian missiles. As an extra fail-safe, we added a layer of deception: the sayeret team, under my command, would stage a pair of diversionary attacks. We would plant explosive charges on a high-voltage electricity cable, and on the main oil pipeline from Suez City to Cairo.

Still, for weeks, the answer from the kirya was no. The man who had succeeded Rabin as chief of staff after the war, Chaim Bar-Lev, dismissed it as "a plan built on chicken legs." In the end, what got us the green light was a further escalation, on both sides, in the War of Attrition. In January 1970, Israeli warplanes began a series of deep-penetration bombing raids, for the first time striking targets dozens of miles, in some case hundreds of miles, beyond the canal. The Israeli bombing campaign reduced the chance we'd get shot down and provided cover for our operation. Since we'd been operating on the assumption, or at least the hope, that the generals would eventually approve the mission, when the word did come from the kirya, we were ready to go.

Our helicopters took off after sunset, nearly skimming the water and weaving their way among the dunes and wadis on the far side of the canal. We weren't spotted, or at least we weren't shot down. We landed with my team of ten men, unloaded a pair of jeeps, and headed off to plant our diversionary charges. Within an hour, we had placed time-delay explosives on the electricity tower and the oil pipeline. But then came the core intelligence part of the operation, and from the start we ran into difficulty. As with our first operation in the Sinai, before the 1967 war, we found that while we could plan for almost every other eventuality, there was no reliable way of knowing the exact terrain and physical environment in which we'd have to operate. Nor did it help when one of the array of tools we'd brought with us—from the mail-order shop in Pennsylvania—gave up the ghost. We did manage to make headway, but it was painfully slow. We were running nearly three hours behind schedule, and the deadline we were working against—daybeak—was immovable. My instinct was to abort. We'd placed the explosives on the electricity tower and the pipeline. That would at least divert attention from our main mission. Having demonstrated our ability to elude Egyptian detection in crossing the canal, I figured we could always return in a few months and have another attempt.

Digli and several other sayeret officers were following the mission from their command post in the Sinai, part of the intelligence base our military engineers had built after the 1967 war into a 2,400-foot-high mountain called Gebel Um-Hashiba, twenty miles back from the Suez Canal. When I radioed in to tell him that I recommended abandoning the operation, I could hear the surprise in his voice, and what seemed reluctance as well. "If that's your judgment . . ." he said. But before I could reply that, yes, I felt withdrawal was the wisest course, I heard him speaking to someone whose voice I recognized: Avsha Horan. He had been the soldier on guard duty in the command post for our first operation in the Sinai, the one who later told me how Rabin was chain-smoking and biting his nails when it appeared we might be in trouble. Now, he was a sayeret officer. Digli came back on the radio. "We can see more from here," he said. Then, pausing, he added, "Avsha says he thinks you can still do it."

I had grown to respect Avsha's judgment. And while Digli hadn't explained what "more" they saw from the command post, I didn't have the time to probe if we were going to have any chance of completing the operation. Both he and I knew it ultimately had to be my call. Whatever happened, I'd be the one responsible. "We'll do it," I said, and signed off.

We'd planned for the work to take several hours, time that we now couldn't afford. With all of us pitching in, sweat drenching our uniforms, we managed to finish it more quickly, but we we were still behind schedule. Dawn was now twenty-five minutes away. I radioed the helicopter pilot with a new pickup point, closer to where we'd installed the equipment though still far enough, I hoped, to avoid giving away what we'd done. It was just after daybreak when our chopper began its sinuous desert flight back into Israel. We could see flames leaping up from the oil pipeline, and then a thick, dark cloud of smoke.

There could be no doubt the prize had been worth it. By the time we returned, for the first time since we'd captured the Sinai, Israel was again receiving relevant information from inside Egypt. With the War of Attrition showing every sign of getting even fiercer, it was an important intelligence achievement. When we landed, Digli and Ahraleh Yariv were there to meet us. Digli, smiling broadly, handed me a small cloth insignia. "You've earned it," he said, adding that Bar-Lev himself had endorsed my promotion from captain to major.

+ + +

With the Egypt mission, and a series of other operations I helped run nearer to the canal, there now seemed every possibility I would be chosen to succeed Digli as commander when his term expired. But that was still more than a year away, in the spring of 1971. With his agreement, I decided to use the time to do what Eli Zeira had advised before I made my decision to return: to get experience in the regular army. The War of Attrition created a demand for qualified officers who could command tank units, since they were playing a key role against the Egyptians along the canal. Along with about a dozen other middle-ranking officers who had volunteered to move into the armored corps, most of them friends of mine, I embarked on a course covering every facet of tank warfare: how each system on an individual tank worked, how to pilot one, load in the shells, and then calibrate its main gun, aim, and fire. We studied communications protocols, even tank maintenance. We learned how to command an armored platoon—a group of three tanks—and then an armored company of eleven tanks and APCs. Finally, in July 1970, we were given command of actual companies, with the aim of deploying us against the Egyptians.

My company was part of Brigade 401, in the Sinai. It was one of two armored forces that were rotated every three months into action on the front line. In a stroke of good fortune, the brigade commander was Dovik Tamari, Avraham Arnan's first successor as commander of the sayeret. While we awaited our forward deployment, due in September, he included me in his discussions with his senior officers on tactics and planning. This inevitably included the core of our existing strategy: a line of fixed fortifications we had built on our side of the canal after the war. They were known as the Bar-Lev Line, because the chief of staff ultimately had to sign off on them. But the main impetus had come from Avraham Adan. A former Palmachnik, known as Bren, he had commanded forces in the Sinai at the start of the War of Attrition and was now the overall head of the armored corps.

There were strong critics of the Bar-Lev Line, but few more vocal than Arik Sharon. The very qualities that had made him the perfect choice to lead Unit 101 and its successor commando units—a natural instinct to favor bold, preemptive attacks, allied with an absolute confidence in his own judgment and little patience for those who challenged it—had stalled his rise up the military ladder for a few years. But now he was head of Israel's southern command. He was convinced that in the event of another full-scale war with Egypt, the Bar-Lev Line would be worse than useless. We'd find ourselves forced to defend a string of fortifications that could serve no real purpose in repelling a concerted Egyptian attempt to retake the Sinai. Arik's preferred strategy was to let the Egyptian armored divisions cross the canal and then confront them on terms where Israeli forces had a proven advantage: a mobile battle in the open desert.

When the debate came up in our brigade strategy discussions, I said I believed Arik was right. I said there was no way the Bar-Lev fortifications could block a major Egyptian advance. I knew from my sayeret experience that we'd been able to operate unseen between Egyptian positions on the other side of the canal, and they were only a few hundred yards apart. On some parts of the Bar-Lev Line, there were seven or eight *miles* between outposts, plenty of room for a whole Egyptian brigade to pass through.

Very few in the kirya, however, seemed ready to recalibrate our strategy against the Egyptians. Only later, when the damage had already been done, would it become clear that the navy was alone in acting on lessons learned from the fighting since the 1967 war. Having lost its flagship to a smaller, more agile Egyptian missile boat at the outset of the War of Attrition, it refocused on deploying mobile missile boats of its own. But the air force was showing no sign of dealing with the implications of the Egyptians' increased antiaircraft capability—even though we'd begun to lose planes and pilots to the new surface-to-air missile batteries Nasser had received from the Soviets. I could see that a similar myopia, or denial, was affecting the armored corps. On patrol along the canal, I would sometimes see the hulk of an Israeli tank destroyed by Soviet-made AT-3s. Known as Saggers, they were portable and allowed a single soldier to fire wire-guided missiles. Their range was nearly a mile and a half, which was farther than the main guns on our tanks could operate with any reliability against such a small target. Yet no one appeared to have addressed the question of what would happen if the Egyptians used Saggers on a much greater scale in a future war.

I remained in the Sinai through early 1971, but by the time my tank company was due for our forward deployment, the War of Attrition was suddenly over. Neither we nor the Egyptians wanted a return to full-scale war, and with Washington taking the lead and pressing the Israeli government to agree, a cease-fire was signed. Both sides claimed victory. But both were exhausted. Certainly, many Israelis had ceased to see a compelling reason for the 1,000 days of fighting. We had lost about 900 dead: more than in the Six-Day War.

In one respect, the Egyptians won. Under the terms of the truce, their antiaircraft missiles were barred from a roughly thirty-mile strip along the canal. Within days of the truce, however, Nasser began moving his SAM batteries forward. Before long, there were nearly one hundred missile sites in the "prohibited" zone, giving the Egyptians control of twenty miles or more of the airspace on our side of the canal. Golda was incensed. So was Bar-Lev. But there was no way, and no will, to reopen the fighting and force Nasser to move the missiles back.

The cease-fire took effect at midnight on August 7, 1970. I've never had trouble recalling the date because of a phone call almost exactly twenty-four hours later. It was from my mother-in-law, to tell me Nava had gone into labor with our first child. Since I was due for deployment on the front line, we had agreed weeks earlier that the best thing would be for her to have the baby in Tiberias so her parents could be with her. Now, I got a jeep and raced north. I reached Tiberias the next morning. I opened the door to the hospital room and saw Nava, obviously tired but beaming, cradling our daughter Michal in her arms.

I managed to stay with them for several days before returning to the Sinai. With Nava and Michal soon settled back into our apartment in the north Tel Aviv neighborhood of Ramat Aviv, I made weekend visits home whenever I could. Still, I saw nowhere near as much of our daughter's first few months as most fathers. As Nava and I would discover even more jarringly over the next few years, that was an inescapable part of being an army officer.

But at least my next posting was closer to home. It was only twenty minutes from our apartment, on a former British base from World War II. On April 1, 1971, I was promoted from major to lieutenant colonel and received the assignment I'd hoped for when I returned to the army.

I became the commander of Sayeret Matkal.

# 8

# Uzis and Eye Shadow

I REPORTED TO THE SAME JUMBLE OF BUILDINGS ON THE SAME BASE where I'd arrived a decade earlier as an eighteen-year-old fresh from basic training, when Sayeret Matkal was still a gleam in Avraham Arnan's eye. Now, I would be the first sayeret commander to have served in the unit as a soldier and young officer. Avraham's initial ambitions had been more than met. We had helped erase the traumas of Uri Ilan and Rotem, and restore the morale and effectiveness of Israeli military intelligence. Time and again, we had successfully mounted operations that had been dismissed as too dangerous, or impossible. Yet as I told the team leaders and our other officers on my first day in command, this was no longer enough.

Our intelligence missions gave Israel an important edge in the Six-Day War. I assumed—naïvely, it would turn out—that they would be put to use in any future war. But if we were to retain our unique role, we had to become an elite *fighting* force as well. One reason—beyond the fact that even our intelligence missions always carried the risk of discovery, interception, ambush, and combat—I didn't even have to mention. It was the legacy of the 1967 war, when we had found ourselves as little more than bit players in the most important conflict since the establishment of the state. But the main argument for change was what had happened *since* the 1967 war: Israel now faced a new range of security challenges that other army units, trained to engage and defeat enemy troops on the battlefield, were not equipped to meet.

In the War of Attrition, we might not have lost a single inch of territory. But we *had* lost tanks and planes, and Israeli soldiers and pilots were being held prisoner in Egypt and Syria. While Arafat's Fatah and the other armed Palestinian groups might not present a *conventional* threat, they posed an insurgent challenge to Arab states on our borders and, increasingly, were turning to *nonconventional*, asymmetrical warfare, and acts of terror. While I'd been with my tank company in the Sinai, full-scale civil war had erupted in Jordan as King Hussein confronted Palestinian fighters who directly threatened his rule but also left the country open to retaliatory attack from Israel.

In forging a sayeret that could confront this new challenge, I assured our officers, we would not be starting from scratch, and I could see some of them nodding in agreement. We would rely on the qualities that had proved our doubters wrong in our first intelligence missions. "We have to stay true to the *spirit* of Sayeret Matkal," I said. Every one of the officers knew what I meant: our inbuilt sense of teamwork, of family almost, and the way we valued brains, creativity, and focus more than formal lines of authority; the rigor we applied to training for, preparing for, and executing each mission; and no less important, to criticizing, and trying to fix, everything that had gone wrong on an operation or that we'd failed to anticipate.

Though I expected to lead many of the operations myself, I knew that we'd succeed or fail on the strengths of the officers around me. I was incredibly fortunate on that score. Some I already knew well from my time as Digli's deputy. Smart, self-confident, *self-starting* officers like Amiram Levin, the stocky kibbutznik from the north with whom I'd worked most closely and most often as deputy; Avshalom Horan—Avsha—who'd convinced me to risk completing the mission inside Egypt; Giora Zorea, who, like me, had come up through the unit and was one of our most experienced team leaders; and Danny Yatom. Born not far from Mishmar Hasharon but a city boy from Netanya, Danny was smart, levelheaded, and a sure-handed organizer, and we'd somehow clicked from the time he arrived in the sayeret. I made him my deputy for my first year in command.

There were two others as well, both related to Moshe Dayan but with a self-assurance all their own: Uzi Dayan, the son of Moshe's brother who had been killed in the 1948 war when Uzi was only months old; and Mookie Betzer, who was married to Uzi's cousin. Family ties had been a part of Sayeret Matkal's development from the start. It had been friends bringing friends. But also, not infrequently, a cousin bringing a cousin, or a brother bringing a brother.

This would also prove to be the case later during my period of command with two other officers who would become important members of my team. In their case, it was the younger one who joined first. Binyamin Netanyahu—Bibi, as everyone called him—had been a member of Amiram Levin's team when I was Digli's deputy. He'd also been a part of one of our several operational failures along the canal at the beginning of the War of Attrition. Our men were spotted by an Egyptian patrol as they were crossing the canal in rubber boats held together by nylon cord, with the assistance of Shayetet 13, Israel's equivalent of the US Navy SEALs. The Egyptians opened fire, and we responded from our side of the waterway as the unit moved to extricate itself and pull back. But one of the dinghies got tangled up in the nylon cord and Bibi found himself in the water being tugged down by the current and the weight of his equipment. Only the SEALs, and Bibi's mix of strength, endurance, and luck, averted disaster.

By the time I returned as commander, Bibi had been given a team of his own, making him one of a half dozen core operational officers with whom I worked from the planning stages of each mission, through the training and the operation itself. Bibi was smart, tough, and self-confident. He also understood my determination to build the unit into a military strike force—which was one reason why he urged me to bring in his older brother. Bibi was twenty-two at the time. His brother—Yonatan, or Yoni— was twenty-five. He had led a company of paratroopers in the 1967 war before going off to university. He'd taken a bullet in the elbow while helping to rescue one of his soldiers facing the Syrians on the Golan. "He wants to return to the army, and he's exactly the kind of officer you want," Bibi said.

I brought Yoni in for a chat. Over the next several years, I would get to know him much better, becoming not just friends but neighbors, too, when he bought a flat one floor below ours. But even in this first meeting, I found him a contrast to his younger brother. Bibi was practical, detail-oriented. Yoni was a more complex character. He was interested in history and philosophy. He read poetry. He would sometimes feel the need to go off by himself and just think. He was a man of action, too. Shorter and trimmer than Bibi, with a thick thatch of dark hair swept back from a craggy face, he was the central casting image of a soldier. He also had real battlefield experience. I invited him to join Sayeret Matkal and put him in charge of our training teams. When Danny Yatom left the following year to train as an armored officer, I made Yoni my deputy.

However different they were, the Netanyahu brothers were close. They shared a drive to excel and to succeed. As I got to know them, I learned that this did not come merely from within, but also from their upbringing, their family background, and in particular their father. Ben-Zion Miliekowsky, as he was then known, studied at Hebrew University at the same time as my father, in the early 1930s, and was an impassioned supporter of Ben-Gurion's main right-wing Zionist rival, Ze'ev Jabotinsky. My father remembered him gathering bemused groups of students during breaks from classes, standing on an upturned wooden box, and proclaiming that the Arabs would *never* willingly accept a Jewish state. Long before the 1948 war, and nearly four decades before our capture of the West Bank in 1967, he insisted that we needed to create a Jewish state in all of biblical Israel: from the Mediterranean to the Jordan River and beyond.

Following Yoni's death—in the Entebbe rescue operation a few years later—I got to know their father. After 1948, he had led a frustrating existence. A specialist in medieval Jewish history, he could not find a place on the faculty at Hebrew University. He was convinced that his outspoken advocacy for Jabotinsky's Zionism in a country defined by Ben-Gurion's had frozen him out. He left Israel to pursue his academic career in America, where both Yoni and Bibi spent much of their youth. He always remained bitter about what he felt were unfair, politically inspired roadblocks to his academic advancement in Jerusalem.

He was teaching at Cornell when his sons were officers under my command in Sayeret Matkal. But while there was a physical distance between father and sons, he loomed large in both of their lives. They bore an almost adolescent admiration for him, bordering on worship. I remember once remarking to Nava that it was as if Bibi and Yoni were tethered to their father by some mental umbilical cord. They were capable and ambitious, but seemed weighted down by a struggle to live up to his lofty expectations, and perhaps to right the wrongs he felt had been done to him in Israel's early years. In a poignant postscript, decades later when Bibi first was elected prime minister, Ben-Zion was asked by a journalist for his reaction. "He would make an excellent minister of *Hasbarah*," he replied, a Hebrew word that translates as something between public relations and propaganda. "Or a very good foreign minister." But how about *prime minister*, the reporter pressed. Ben-Zion replied, "Time will tell."

+ + +

As we mounted a series of intelligence operations deeper into Egypt and Syria, I made sure that we trained as if we were already the broader strike force I hoped we would become. We mapped out detailed plans for commando operations against the new kind of security challenges the country faced, and prepared rigorously to make sure we'd be ready to act if called upon. Yet there was no guarantee that would actually happen. A bit like Avraham in the unit's infancy, I had to deal with the frustration of trying to convince the generals in the kirya to give us the go-ahead. Some agreed that Israel needed a specially trained commando force. But not everyone felt Sayeret Matkal could, or should, take on that role. Rafael "Raful" Eitan was perhaps the most strident opponent. He had fought with the Palmach in 1948, and was a veteran of both Arik's Unit 101 and the parachutists' Battalion 890. He was now *katzhar*, the head of all infantry and paratroop forces. He insisted that such work required a *real* sayeret, by which he meant the paratroopers.

Yet the need for a special forces unit was becoming increasingly hard to ignore. By the summer of 1971, a couple of months after I became sayeret commander, King Hussein's army had defeated the insurgency of Fatah and a pair of even more militant partners, the Democratic Front and the Popular Front for the Liberation of Palestine, and forced them out of Jordan. That meant a quieter eastern frontier. But the Palestinian groups had rebased across our northern border in Lebanon. When Jordanian prime minister Wasfi al-Tal was assassinated in November, it

**Nurtured on the kibbutz** (from top): As a four-year-old, engrossed in an early engineering puzzle with one of our few toys on the floor of my parents' one-room apartment. With my mother, from whom I got not only unwavering love but my emotional connection with the early, pioneering ideals of Zionism. With Bina, our *metapelet,* or kibbutz carer, on our first day of school.

**In uniform**: BACK HOME, as a twenty-year-old officers' school cadet, with my parents and my brothers (l-to-r) Shmuel, then thirteen; eight-year-old Reuven; and Avinoam, nearly three years younger than me but looking three years taller. TRAINING BREAK, with a makeshift garrotte that, thankfully, I never found occasion to use. MY FIRST LOVE, Nili Sonkin, as I encountered her on duty at the *kirya*, military headquarters, in Tel Aviv.

**Preparing for combat:** Meeting General Yitzhak Rabin, with whom I'd become ever more closely involved in the decades that followed, as one of six top graduates in my officers' training class shortly after my twentieth birthday.

**The Six-Day War:** Briefing my sayeret team on the eve of the June 1967 war on a mission—made unnecessary within hours by Israel's early air attacks—to disable an Egyptian air base in the Sinai. With (l-to-r) Danny Michaelson, Sayeret Matkal founder Avraham Arnan, and Rafi Friedman as we followed Israeli armored units into the Sinai, then peeled off to disable a booby-trapped device that we'd deployed two years earlier.

**Rough cut:** SEVERING AN
EGYPTIAN TELEPHONE LINE
on our way into the Sinai at
the start of the 1967 war.

**Cutting edge**: MEETING, AS A LIEUTENANT IN THE SAYERET, with members of the military intelligence's technology unit a few months before our first operation into the Sinai in February 1964. Seated to my left are Sayeret Matkal commander Avraham Arnan and Uri Goren, then head of the technology unit. The tech unit's work was also indispensable, when I became commander of the sayeret in 1970, to our first operation beyond the Suez Canal (below). WITH ME, ALONG WITH OUR HELICOPTER CREW BEFORE TAKEOFF, are: at far left, Uzi Dayan; to my right, Amit Ben-Horin, the sayeret officer posted inside Israel during our operation to abduct Syrian officers in 1972 and who was later killed in the Yom Kippur War; and, crouching in front, Yoni Netanyahu (second from right), Bibi Netanyahu's older brother, who would lose his life during the commando operation to free a hijacked Air France jet in Entebbe, Uganda.

**Commando force:** LEADING MY DEPUTY SAYERET COMMANDER Danny Yatom and our fellow "Angels in White," as the Israeli newspapers called our then top-secret unit, and some of the hostages we freed from a hijacked Sabena airliner at Tel Aviv's international airport in 1972. A YEAR LATER, a final training session aboard an Israeli missile boat for our operation against Black September terror leaders in the heart of Beirut.

**New battlefields:** As SAYERET COMMANDER, during an exercise in the Negev in 1972. IN SUEZ CITY, at the southern end of the canal, on the final day of the Yom Kippur War in 1973. THE "UGANDAN ARMY" MERCEDES being loaded onto one of our military transport planes for the raid to free hijacked hostages being held in Entebbe in 1976.

**Mark of the sword**: WITH AVRAHAM ARNAN, formally inducting a new member of the Order of Sayeret Veterans in a ceremony deliberately, if ironically, patterned on the British army. COMMANDER'S FAREWELL, on my final day in charge of the unit, with (l-to-r) chief of staff David "Dado" Elazar and Israel Tal, his number-two, smiling on. I was presented with the traditional leaving gift—a photo of sayeret men marching into the night, as well as my fifth *tzalash*, or military commendation.

proved to be the start of a series of killings and terror attacks by a new group within Fatah called Black September. There was at least some potentially encouraging news from Egypt. Nasser had died in September 1970, and his successor was his less flamboyantly militant vice president, Anwar Sadat. Yet in both Egypt and Syria, a number of our air force pilots were still being held prisoner.

I felt an especially strong motivation to help bring the pilots home. They had risked their lives for us. It seemed to me we owed them the same. One of the men being held in Syria, Pini Nachmani, had a personal connection to many of us in the unit: he had flown us on sayeret missions. I came up with a plan that, while undeniably risky, seemed to me to have every chance of success. We would land transport helicopters a few miles from Damascus and unload a pair of armored cars. Then, we'd abduct a number of Syrians from an officers' club on the western edge of the city with the aim of exchanging them for the captive pilots. But Raful's view prevailed: I could not get the approval of the kirya. I did take heart from Avraham Arnan's support. He was now Golda Meir's counterterrorism adviser. Also from the fact that Chaim Bar-Lev's successor as chief of staff was an old friend of the sayeret: Dado Elazar, Avraham's Palmach comrade from 1948. Yet winning over the remaining doubters in the kirya was obviously going to take time.

As so often during my years in uniform, however, Sayeret Matkal's birth as a special forces unit came by force of circumstance: not in an officers' club near Damascus, but on a runway at Lod Airport.

+ + +

I was sitting down to dinner with Nava a little before seven on May 8, 1972, when the phone rang. We'd just fed Michal, who was almost two, full of energy, and showed no sign of wanting to go to bed. "It's Manno," said the voice on the line. Brigadier General Emanuel "Manno" Shaked was Dado's chief of operations. "A plane has been hijacked," he said. "It's heading for Lod. It will land in about thirty minutes. They've got hostages. Get to the airport." He said Dado and the defense minister, Moshe Dayan, were on their way there.

I called Danny Yatom and told him to get whoever was at the sayeret base to Lod as soon as possible. But most of the men were on training exercises, including one team with Yoni deep in the Negev Desert. Danny immediately began recalling them. When I got to the airport, I found Dayan and Dado huddling in a room below the control tower, unfurnished except for a small table in the corner. Talik, the armored commander in the 1967 war, was with them: he was now head of all military operations in the kirya. Rechavam Ze'evi, the head of the central command area, which included Tel Aviv, was there, as was Ahraleh Yariv, who had succeeded Meir Amit as head of military intelligence. He nodded glumly as I joined them.

The plane had landed. A Sabena Boeing 707 bound from Brussels to Tel Aviv, it had been hijacked after a stopover in Vienna. All we knew at this point was that the hijackers were Palestinians and that there were about a hundred passengers on board. Dado said that while we figured out how to respond, we had to make sure, at all costs, the plane didn't take off again. It would presumably go to an Arab country, where we'd be powerless to act. Though only a handful of my men had arrived, I took the only officer who had, Shai Agmon, and an El Al engineer to see whether we could disable the hijacked jet. It was parked about a mile from the main terminal area. With the El Al man just behind us, we approached from the rear, crouching low. The engines were still running, but at least the deafening noise kept anyone from hearing us as we ducked under the fuselage and the engineer removed a stabilizing pin from the front wheel. It was an eerie feeling, envisaging the captive crew and passengers, and the terrorists, a few feet above our heads but knowing that, at least for now, we were powerless to do anything more to help.

Manno hadn't called me because I'd won my argument to expand the role of the sayeret. It was the luck of the draw. With the growing threat of terrorism, the kirya had drawn up a list of installations that might be targeted. Next to each, they'd put the name of the military unit to be called up in an emergency. We'd been allocated Lod Airport because our base was closer than other units. As I accompanied the engineer back to the control tower, I tried to work out in my mind whether we could plan, prepare, and train quickly enough to mount an operation to free the plane later that night.

About a dozen members of the unit had now arrived, and more were joining us every half hour or so. I arranged for El Al to give us a hangar and a 707 identical to the Sabena plane. Shai, Danny Yatom, and I took two airline technicians with us for a closer look at the Boeing. We studied up on it as quickly as we could, beginning with the cockpit and the front door, which we saw was too high to reach without a large ladder. But making our way back, we realized the wings were low enough to climb onto. When, with the help of Danny, I clambered onto one of them, I managed to get one of the emergency doors to open by banging hard on the top end with my open fist. I asked the technicians whether we could expect the Sabena doors to give way as well. Yes, he said, but cautioned me that on some airlines, there were passenger seats next to the two doors above each wing.

Walking up into the cabin, I tried to work out how we might attack the hijackers before they were able to harm the passengers, or us. With the rest of the sayeret still making its way to Lod, I put Danny in charge of briefing the new arrivals, familiarizing them with the 707, and preparing for the possibility of an assault operation. I also told him to get hold of a couple of dozen small, .22-caliber Beretta pistols, of far more use in a close-quarters battle with the hijackers than our usual Uzis. I knew we'd have to get up to speed quickly on using the Berettas. None of us had trained on them. But many of the air marshals on board all El Al flights were Sayeret Matkal reservists, and they did use Berettas. I told Danny to check for any sayeret marshals arriving on El Al flights and get them to join us.

As I headed back to see Dado, we were nowhere close to a detailed plan on how to confront the hijackers. Nor did we have any orders. The people who would give them—Dado, Dayan, and ultimately Prime Minister Meir—were still deciding how to respond. But when I reached the control tower, at about 9:30 p.m., we got the go-ahead to at least prepare for a possible assault. "Talk to Talik," Dado told me. "See what the options are to take over the plane if that's the decision." I sat down with Talik and ran through what I'd learned from my brief look at the hijacked plane and the work we'd been doing on the Israeli 707. I told him I'd need another two hours to make sure my men had practiced climbing up on the wings and forcing open the doors, and another hour for preparations and briefings for the teams who would be participating in the operation. "By about half an hour after midnight, we'll be ready to deploy," I said, though from his stoic, nearly silent response I couldn't be sure whether he was in favor of an assault. "By 0100, we'll be ready to act."

Both of us went back to see Dado. He seemed encouraged, especially when I said we'd be ready to move by one in the morning. He told me the pilot of the plane had been in contact with the control tower. He was an RAF veteran and, though the terrorists seemed unaware of this, he was also Jewish. The hijackers were demanding more than 300 Arab prisoners be released and flown to Cairo. "And they seem quite nervous."

Returning to the hangar, I sent Shai Agmon with four soldiers to set up a lookout and sniper post about seventy yards to the side of the Sabena jet. I ordered him not to open fire unless they were sure there had been shooting inside the plane and could positively identify an armed hijacker. By now, we had three-dozen soldiers and officers, including Uzi Dayan and his full team. I took all those who were already briefed and divided them into four groups, each with an officer and five soldiers and assigned to deal with one of the two doors above each of the wings. I left the others to continue training.

When midnight came, I was far from certain we could meet the twelve-thirty deployment target I'd given Talik. I was also disappointed that we hadn't managed to bring in any air marshals, with the experience both of the Berettas and the inside of a 707. But all incoming flights had now stopped for the night, and the next chance we'd get to bring them in would be the next morning. Yet I didn't want to risk Dado's trust in a sayeret operation by failing to meet our agreed deadline.

From Shai's lookout post to the side of the plane, I learned that the front cabin door of the plane was open. He said he'd seen a couple of hijackers walking by it, silhouetted by the dim cabin light. But otherwise, there was no sign of activity inside. I called Talik and told him I was taking my assault teams to the area behind the plane. About a half hour later, I confirmed we were ready to begin the operation. Although the plane's engines were off now, our approach had been masked by the drone of the generator brought in to supply power to the cabin. We were lying face-down on the tarmac, directly behind the tail of the plane but well back. Two rows of twelve men, plus me and a soldier in charge of the communications. We'd brought along four small ladders to help us onto the wings.

"We want to exploit the darkness, and the sound of the generator, to cover us," I said in my final briefing before we'd left the hangar. "If they realize we're there, we get into the cabin as quickly as possible, any way we can. The first five seconds will be critical. Act decisively."

But more than an hour passed as we waited for the green light to storm the plane. My main concern wasn't that the hijackers would see us. It was dark, and there seemed little reason to believe one of them would suddenly decide to take a walk around the plane. But sunrise was around five in the morning, and there was no way I could see mounting our assault in broad daylight. If we didn't get the go-ahead soon, the chance would be lost. I called Talik several times, making the point that if we *were* going to do it, we needed darkness. The sayeret was a breed of night animals. Other people, even terrorists, would be less alert and effective at night.

Finally, an hour before sunrise, he called back. "The big boss is on his way," he said. I left the others and crept back to meet the defense minister, a good forty yards away. Moshe Dayan greeted me with a whispered hello. In a way, his arrival reminded me of my first operation in the sayeret when, before heading north to the Golan, I'd been summoned to brief the chief of staff. Back then, he'd appeared less interested in the details than in confirming that *I* was confident the mission would work. Dayan, of course, had as much operational knowledge and experience as anyone in Israel. Yet it seemed that he, too, wanted to satisfy himself that I honestly felt we could succeed. Though he never so much as hinted at this, he also knew that one of the officers I would be taking in with me, Uzi, was his own nephew.

"How do you plan to do it?" he asked. I explained how we would get into the plane simultaneously, in four teams, and confront the hijackers. "We can do it," I said. "Better now than in daytime." Dayan merely nodded. He stood there, silent, for another few moments. "I'll let you know," he said, then shook my hand and returned to the control tower. But fifteen minutes later he sent his reply, via Talik. It was brief and explicit: "Not tonight."

For the first but not the last time in uniform, I felt the frustration of finding my preparation and judgment trumped, without explanation, from above. When I got back to the control tower, I made no attempt to hide my view that we should have moved against the hijackers while we had the chance. But Dado sat me down and filled me in on what was obviously a changing situation. He said the terrorists had allowed the pilot, Reginald Levy, to come see Dayan and press their demands. He had brought with him a slab of light-yellow material to demonstrate the seriousness of the risk of saying no. When tested, it turned out to be exactly what the hijackers said it was: plastic explosive.

The pilot said there were four terrorists—two men with pistols and two women with explosives and grenades—and that they appeared increasingly nervous. There were ninety-five passengers and seven crew. He'd confirmed that none of the exits above the wings was blocked by a passenger seat. He'd returned to the plane without any clear answer from Dayan on the prisoner release. But before leaving, he revealed that his own wife was among the passengers. He asked Dayan to promise that Israel would help care for their daughter if the hijack ended tragically.

By the next morning, that was looking more and more likely. Though the hijackers were still in contact with the tower, the only visible movement was the arrival of a representative of the Red Cross. The lead hijacker, who called himself Captain Rifa'at, was making increasingly forceful demands for the prisoner release. Our negotiating team did its best to buy time by giving the appearance we were considering the demand. It was Dayan who proposed going a step further. He told Rechavam Ze'evi, as the head of the central command area, to begin rounding up hundreds of young Israeli soldiers. He wanted them dressed in prison uniforms and then bused to the airport, within sight of the hijacked jet. Dayan also arranged for another Boeing 707, ostensibly to take the "freed prisoners" on to Cairo.

"What then?" Ze'evi asked Dayan. "We're not really going to put them on a plane and take off!"

It was after he'd had no real reply that he in effect answered his own question, inadvertently leading us to the idea of attempting a daytime attack after all. Talking to Dado and me, he said, "Since we're going to such lengths to deceive them, why not just add another layer? Why can't Ehud's people take the role of the airport mechanics?" Looking at each other, Dado and I realized it was a stroke of brilliance. Dado went to brief Dayan, confident that he would share our enthusiasm for the idea, which he did. I remained with Ze'evi and his deputy to work out the details. We agreed they would take care of the pantomime with the prisoners, as well as arranging for El Al to get us the ladder trucks that airline maintenance crews used, which would allow us access not just to the jet's wing doors, but the front and rear doors as well. That left me free to concentrate on preparation and training.

We had just a few hours to adapt our plan. We'd trained in close-quarters fighting before, when working on the plan to attack the officers' club near Damascus in an effort to free our captured pilots. But that idea had been vetoed, and we'd never had to use those skills in a live mission. Nor had we ever used the Berettas. And this would be the first time we would be taking on the personae of civilian engineers, with the need to fool armed terrorists on the lookout for any sign of danger. And for the first time in *any* of our major operations, we would be operating in daylight.

Now that nearly all our soldiers and officers had arrived, I began arranging the final line-up of attack teams. We would need six rather than four, since the new plan would give us access to the front and rear doors. Danny now also told me that a couple of the El Al technicians had shown him a way of climbing up from inside the nosewheel into the cockpit. One of the toughest and strongest of our soldiers, Uri Koren, had tried it successfully on the El Al 707. I assigned Danny, Uri, and another officer to attack through the front door and the nosewheel. I put Uzi Dayan in charge of the tail door. The emergency doors above the wings, however, still gave us the quickest way in. I planned to take overall command of the operation from the left of the aircraft, because both the front and tail doors also faced that way. I entrusted Bibi Netanyahu and his team with the wing doors on the far side of the plane.

By noon, we got a further boost. With the resumption of incoming flights, we began collecting air marshals. One in particular raised my confidence. I knew Mordechai Rachamim well from the sayeret. He was a Yemeni from Elyakhin, the moshav near Mishmar Hasharon where Baddura and the other Yemeni workers lived. He was tall, strong, and athletic, naturally agile and quick to respond in situations of danger. He was also no ordinary air marshal. In 1969, he'd been posted on an El Al flight from Amsterdam to Tel Aviv. On a stopover in Zurich, four gunmen from Fatah's main radical rival in the PLO, the Popular Front for the Liberation of Palestine, leapt out of a car, opened fire with AK-47s, and began throwing grenades. The PFLP assault injured four of the crew and killed the copilot. Armed with his Beretta, Mordechai rushed to the cockpit window and returned fire. Seeing the attackers were too far away, he slid down the emergency chute. Once on the tarmac, he shot one of the terrorists in the head and kept the rest of them at bay.

As additional air marshals arrived, I slotted each of them into an assault team in place of one of our sayeret soldiers. The next to arrive was Marco Ashkenazi, a Cairo-born veteran with whom I'd worked on a mission inside Egypt. With Mordechai slated to spearhead our attack on the front left-side wing door, critical for the opening moments of the operation, I added Marco to Bibi's team on the other side of the aircraft.

It was then that Yoni arrived back from the Negev. He insisted on being added to one of the assault teams. In one respect, that made sense. He had more combat experience than almost everyone in the unit. But there was an unwritten sayeret rule never to place two brothers together in the line of fire. "It's too late," I told him, with an arm on his shoulder. "Bibi has already been training his team." He went off to find Bibi. I thought there was little chance of Bibi standing down, but didn't feel I could stop Yoni from trying. Five minutes later, they came to talk to me. Bibi said, "Yoni wants to replace me. We want you to decide." I assumed both of them knew what I'd say. "Today, it's Bibi," I replied. "But Yoni, this is not our last operation. I will make sure you are there the next time."

The last marshal to join us was a tall, thin redhead named Zur. He'd had only fifteen minutes to begin training when I got word that Dado— along with Ze'evi and Ahraleh Yariv—were on their way to see a runthrough. As they filed into the hangar, I quickly explained the operational plan. I showed them how we would push in the wing doors, and then ushered them inside the 707. Two minutes later, the emergency-door teams climbed onto the wings. When I gave the agreed two-finger whistle, they stormed the plane. "OK, gentlemen," Dado told the team leaders when it was over. "We've seen what we needed." Before returning to the control tower, however, he took me aside. "You know they have explosives, right?" he said solemnly. When I replied that yes, I knew that, his tone softened. "You don't have much time, Ehud," he said. "Don't waste it. *BeHatzlakha*." Good luck.

We still had to outfit ourselves in mechanics' white overalls and swap the sayeret's paratroop-style red boots for black ones. I directed all the men to conceal their Berettas on a waist-belt inside their overalls. We got acquainted with our mechanics' toolboxes. Finally we organized our maintenance motorcade: four electric buggies in front, towing four ladders, two short ones for the wings and taller ones for the front and rear doors. Waiting for the order to move, I said a final few words. Seeing the determination and nervous anticipation on the faces of the men around me, I began by reiterating that the first five seconds would be critical. "We all know that nothing ever happens exactly according to plan. Each and every one of us has to focus on speed, momentum, and precision. No one can wait for anyone else to act. From the moment I give the signal, or if we come under fire, each team has to act as if they have to accomplish this all on their own. *All* of us must assume that. Keep cool. Stay focused. Rely on your instincts. We're ready for this mission. And we are going to accomplish this."

One minute after four in the afternoon, we got the word to go. I was in the lead buggy, consciously trying to look like a civilian, not a soldier. It was about a mile and a half to the aircraft. I glanced back at the others. Like me, many of them had been awake for thirty hours or more, in some cases nearly forty-eight hours. The air marshals had been plucked off long-haul flights on which relaxation, much less sleep, was not an option. As before any mission, I knew some of the men would be thinking about what was about to happen. They also realized that if we failed, the passengers trapped inside the plane would be at the mercy of terrorists armed with AK-47s and explosives. But I was confident that any apprehension would be overtaken by adrenaline when the assault began and the first shots were fired.

As we got closer, Shai Agmon radioed me. He said two or three people, not the terrorists, had come out of the plane. One seemed to be the Red Cross man. They were about 120 yards away from the aircraft. As soon as he'd signed off, I got word from the command post in the control tower that it was indeed the Red Cross representative, along with two of the flight crew. They'd been chosen by the terrorists to do security checks on the "maintenance" men.

I brought the convoy to a halt. The Red Cross man gave each of us a fairly cursory body search before waving us on. When he got to Bibi, it turned out that for some reason he had left on his red sayeret boots. In Israel, that was the equivalent of a neon sign saying: "I am a paratrooper." Although the Red Cross man noticed the boots, he at first made no comment. Then, rolling up the pants leg of Bibi's overalls, he saw his Beretta—not inside his waist-belt, but inside the boot. The next thing I heard was an angry spurt of French as the man called the control tower. For a moment, I feared the mission was over, with potentially fatal repercussions for the hostages. But whatever explanation the Red Cross man was given—presumably by Dayan himself, who would not have held back in conveying what was at stake—it dissuaded him from taking further action.

As we were returning to the buggies, the Red Cross man told me that Captain Rifa'at had ordered us to pull up to the generator on the side of the plane. Each of us would then have to walk forward and open the front of our overalls so he could make sure we weren't armed. I passed back four orders to the rest of the men. First, with no exceptions, move your pistol to the *back* of your belt. Second: I'll be the first to go through the inspection. Third: watch what I do and do the same. Finally, if our cover is broken, or if you hear gunfire, we all storm the plane.

I felt as I always did as an operation was about to begin. Amid the undeniable tension, there was a sense of what I can best describe as focused calm. I had a keen awareness of everything happening around me, almost as if I was watching things from above the fray, in slow motion, high resolution. When our motorcade approached the generator, Rifa'at leaned out from the copilot's window. He was pointing a pistol at us. He seemed to be in his late twenties or early thirties. He had dark hair and a mustache and the hint of a stubbly beard. We stopped beside the generator. I got out and walked toward the cockpit, halting about ten feet away. Looking up at the hijacker, I made a conscious effort to appear curious rather than worried. His eyes seemed a mix of intense focus and tension. I opened the front of my overalls. Because of the heat, I was wearing nothing else on top. He nodded to signal he was satisfied. I refastened the overalls and moved off. One by one, the other men passed inspection. Then we went back and brought the two smaller ladders to the side of each wing, and the "mechanics" set down to work. I delayed bringing in the large ladders so as to minimize any risk of arousing the terrorists' suspicions.

The fact that at least so far they seemed to suspect nothing was in large part down to Dayan's misdirection plan. As we began working on the plane, the "Palestinian" prisoners were disembarking from buses about 300 yards away. As Rifa'at watched, several hundred men formed long rows. A few of them waved in his direction. The Boeing that was ostensibly going to take them on to Cairo, to be followed by the Sabena jet minus the hostages, was being towed into position.

One by one, our assault teams were moving into place. All that remained was for me to give a short, sharp whistle and the attack would begin. Yet just as I was raising my fingers to my mouth, I saw Bibi coming toward me from under the fuselage. He motioned to me to wait. Zur, the last of our air marshals, had a problem. Having spent ten hours in the air on the way back to Israel before being immediately plugged into an assault team, he had something to attend to. "He has to take a shit," Bibi said. Can't it *wait*? I asked. No, was the answer. So I said OK, leading to the most surreal "operational" moment I would witness during all my years in the military.

The "prisoner release" was now in full flow. Dozens of military vehicles, and a small army of fire engines and ambulances, had also pulled to the far end of the runway, out of sight of the hijackers, in case our attack on the Sabena jet went wrong. Tel Aviv hospitals were on alert. And Zur was crouching and relieving himself. He nodded in gratitude when he'd finished and returned to Bibi's team on the far wing. I gave him a full minute to be certain he was in place.

Then I whistled. From my initial position beside the plane, I saw Danny Yatom and his team begin to move one of the tall ladders toward the front door. Shifting my eyes toward the wing doors as the crucial first five seconds ticked by, I saw both the ones on my side of the plane were still shut. I climbed up on the wing. When I got to the smaller, rear door I saw the main one cave inward and Mordechai Rachamim rush in. But the soldier on the other door was trembling and frozen in place. I slapped him, hard, on the back. "Move!" I shouted. Instantly, he pushed and rushed inside. I then noticed Uzi and his team had still not entered from the rear. I jumped from the wing and ran toward the ladder at the back, but by the time I got there, they had made it inside, and I followed them in.

Everything was over within ninety seconds. As I'd expected, the planning and training turned out to matter less than instinct and initiative. Within seconds, Uri Koren managed to get into the nosewheel assembly. Though he couldn't dislodge a metal-mesh panel separating it from the cockpit, he spotted the outline of a man's foot above him, fired, and wounded Captain Rifa'at. The other members of Danny's team in front were less lucky. With the ladder, they had no trouble getting to the passenger door, but they struggled to force it open. When they did nudge it open a crack, one of the hijackers opened fire, slightly wounding one of the men and forcing them to abandon the attempt.

Mordechai went in shooting through the front wing door on my side of the plane, but immediately drew fire and had to retreat. But Omer Wachman, another air marshal I'd posted on the rear wing door, was in just a couple of seconds later. Coming face-to-face with one of the hijackers, he shot him in the head. That allowed Mordechai to get back inside. He quickly exchanged fire with the hobbled Captain Rifa'at, hitting him in the side. As Mordechai ducked down to reload his pistol, Rifa'at managed to lock himself inside one of the toilets near the cockpit. Mordechai ran after him. He fired through the bathroom door, then kicked it open and confirmed that he was dead. Rushing back toward the center of the plane, he spotted the main woman hijacker, wearing a bulky explosive vest. Grabbing her hands, he reached inside the vest and yanked out the battery pack. With two of the hijackers already dead, Mordechai had now subdued the third. But knowing that there was still another woman unaccounted for, he handed her over to Bibi and Marco Ashkenazi. Bibi grabbed her by the back of her hair, but it turned out to be a wig, which came off in his hand. As she began screaming, Marco instinctively struck her across the face, but he used the hand in which he had his Beretta. The gun went off, and the bullet grazed Bibi in his upper arm.

When Uzi Dayan got in through the rear door, he'd run up against a stocky, suntanned man blocking his way, and fired—thankfully, only into his midsection. He turned out to be one of the passengers, a filmmaker from Austria. Still, there was the other woman hijacker to deal with. Several of the passengers pointed to the floor just ahead of Uzi, where she lay curled up, holding a grenade with the pin out. Ordering her loudly, sternly, not to move, Uzi wrapped his hand over hers, extracted the grenade from her grasp finger by finger, replaced the pin, and had one of his men lead her out of the plane and down the stairs.

All the hijackers had been either killed or captured.

Tragically, in the initial cross fire a twenty-two-year-old passenger named Miriam Holtzberg had been hit. Although the man whom Uzi had mistakenly shot recovered, she did not. The remaining passengers and crew were now free and safe, alive and unharmed.

The day after the rescue, Israeli newspapers devoted acres of newsprint to how the operation had succeeded. Since Sayeret Matkal's existence was still an official secret, the headline writers called us, variously, a "special" unit, a "select" unit, and even in one case, because of our El Al coveralls, "angels in white." I felt a mix of emotions: pride, a sense of achievement against all the odds, and, above all, relief. Without my saying so, everyone in the unit understood that my inaugural comments, about our need to become a full special forces unit, were no longer a distant wish. We did, briefly, celebrate back at the sayeret base. But as with every other operation, we went through a self-critical assessment of what we could have done better. How could we make sure in future hostage situations that none of the captives was harmed? How could we improve coordination among the assault teams? And minimize the risk of shooting *each other*? Why had I, as commander of the operation, had to wait for someone *else* to suggest the idea of disguising ourselves as aircraft technicians? And why had we failed to train with Berettas as well as Uzis?

They were not just academic issues. Even if we were never again called upon to free a hijacked airplane, we would face other operations with equal urgency, without the weeks or even months of preparation we'd always insisted on in the past.

+ + +

We would meanwhile need to be proactive. It wouldn't be up to us to decide which operations we'd take part in. But it *was* up to us to identify and understand potential threats and frame ways in which we might provide a response, something I'd been doing almost from the day I became sayeret commander. Every few weeks, I would go to Ahraleh Yariv, who was now head of military intelligence, with a mission I felt confident that we were ready to carry out. Several of the most complex centered on the new threat posed by Palestinian groups in Lebanon. Before the civil war in Jordan, King Hussein had accused Fatah, the PFLP, and the Democratic Front for the Liberation of Palestine of trying to create "a state within a state" and deliberately weakening his government. Now, they were doing much the same in Lebanon. Their headquarters buildings in southern Beirut were spawning hijackings or terror attacks. From bases in southern Lebanon, the Palestinians were also firing Soviet-made Katyusha rockets into Israel. But every one of the plans I proposed—even one that targeted Yasir Arafat himself—was dismissed as too risky, especially for a sayeret that, as far as the kirya was concerned, had yet to prove itself as a full special forces unit.

After Sabena, Dado and the other senior officers in the kirya seemed more receptive to our trying to initiate operations, especially the plan to seize Syrian officers and trade them for the Israeli pilots. But such a mission required not just military or intelligence approval. Dayan, and possibly Golda as well, would have to sign off, and there was little immediate sign of that happening. Once again, however, events on the ground forced the issue. Early on the morning of June 9, our intelligence reports gave us notice that the next day, a group of senior Syrian officers would make an inspection visit to the eastern part of the Lebanese border area with Israel. We would have to move quickly. Within the space of twelve hours, we'd need to plan the attack; organize, equip, and brief the assault teams; make the three-and-a-half-hour drive north; and cross into Lebanon.

Still, I was determined to try, which marked the start of two of my most frustrating weeks as Sayeret Matkal commander. The place where we planned to abduct the Syrians was an area I knew personally: the sparsely settled strip of land where Lebanon, Syria, and Israel met, not far from where I'd helped "capture" several Syrian villages on the final day of the 1967 war. With the convoy expected to pass through the next morning, we crossed the border around nine o'clock at night on June 9. Our plan was to lie in ambush in dense vegetation a few yards off a curve in the road, further reducing the time the Syrians would have to react once they saw us, with two other sayeret teams a couple of hundred yards away in either direction, so they could cut off the road once we attacked. But as we made our way through a deep gorge and were about to begin our climb up toward the road, I was contacted by the sayeret officer we'd stationed in the operational command post, on the slopes of Mount Hermon on the Golan Heights. He relayed a message from Motta Gur, the head of the northern command. Its intelligence unit said there was a Lebanese army checkpoint a quarter mile from the planned ambush site. Motta himself was further south—in fact in the same British Mandate fort from where we'd commandeered the jerricans of gasoline before our first sayeret operation on the Golan. So I was not in direct contact with him. I replied through the officer in the command post. "Tell Motta we know about it," I said. "We've planned for it." That wasn't true. But I figured there were at most four or five Lebanese soldiers manning the checkpoint, and that the last thing they'd want to do is get involved in a firefight between us and a convoy of Syrians. But Motta's reply was unequivocal. The mission was off.

When we'd climbed through a bramble-filled ravine back into Israel, it was nearly midnight. I left a message for Motta. I found it hard to disguise my frustration, and anger, at being ordered to abort the attack, especially after my assurances that the Lebanese roadblock was not a problem. It was only when we got back to the sayeret base that I learned there was more to his veto than I'd thought. He and Dado had received intelligence saying the Syrians were likely to make a series of further visits to the border area, so this might not be our last chance. A couple of days later, we received word they'd be making a further inspection tour, on the western part of the border. On the Lebanese side it was known as Ras Naqoura, on ours as Rosh Hanirkra, where the Mediterranean coastline rose dramatically to a ridge and, once into Israel, sloped steeply down again in the direction of Acre and Haifa.

Again, we made our way across the border. I took in two main assault teams, one led by Mookie, the other by Uzi Dayan. We hid in a tangle of bushes about halfway along the road that climbed up toward the border ridge. A third team, to provide support, was under Bibi, who was nearing the end of his military service and—despite my hope that he would stay on—had decided to pursue graduate studies in America, at MIT. I stationed Bibi and his men at the bottom of the road, equipped with rifles and rocket-propelled grenade launchers.

We waited, knowing we'd be able to see the convoy as it made its way up toward us. Again, I had no direct link to Motta. Yet both he and Dado were following the mission from a command post on the far side of the Naqoura ridge in northern Israel. We were in nearly real-time contact through a sayeret officer named Amit Ben-Horin, right across the border. A first vehicle appeared at around ten thirty in the morning. Bibi radioed us. It was a Lebanese army armored car with a single machine gun. It drove past and halted 150 feet on, at the point where the road began to climb. The two guys inside took out a small table and a couple of chairs and began brewing up coffee on the side of the road. "All OK," I said when I radioed Amit to tell him. "Pre-deployment." The convoy arrived two hours later and began to climb. "We're taking it," I radioed Amit.

"Wait," he replied. And as I kept pressing him for the final go-ahead, another thirty seconds passed.

"Not approved," he finally barked back at me, clearly wanting to make sure I got the message.

"What the hell is going on?" I replied in a mix of a shout and a whisper, since I knew the convoy was getting closer. Within a minute, we spotted the lead Land Rover, which was soon past us on the way up to the ridge. It was followed by two large American cars with the Syrian officers, and then a trailing security vehicle. It was too late. I was fuming. The convoy had passed within a couple of yards of us, moving slowly because of the incline. But, regaining my composure, I realized we'd get another opportunity, when the officers returned from their inspection visit. We now knew exactly how the convoy was deployed, and with any luck, the security men would be less alert by the end of the day. Even better, it would be nearer to nightfall, perfect conditions for the ambush.

As we were waiting for the Syrians to return, I considered not even telling Amit a further, unexpected, development: a Lebanese shepherd, with a half dozen sheep, suddenly stumbled on us. One of Uzi's men, fluent in Arabic, quickly tied the startled man's arms behind his back, scattered the sheep, and told him: "It's fine. Another hour or so, we'll be gone, and we'll let you go." It turned out to be less than an hour. Forty-five minutes. During which, not once but twice, Amit told us that Dado and Motta were worried: not just about the armored car, but now about the shepherd. I assured him everything was fine. We'd do the operation. The guys in the armored car would be helpless. Bibi and his team had it in their sights. And the shepherd, like us, was just waiting for it to be over so we could all go home. Minutes later, Amit called again. He told us the convoy was on its way down. But barely sixty seconds later, he said, "It's off. Don't do it. Dado told me to repeat it twice: do *not* execute the operation."

When we got back to the command post, Dado and Motta were not the only ones there. Since Motta was within days of leaving to become Israel's military attaché in Washington, they'd been joined by his successor as head of the northern command, Yitzhak Hofi. Three times I suggested to Dado that we speak without my officers present. I did not feel it was right to have Uzi, Mookie, and Bibi hear me telling the generals how I felt. But Dado insisted there was no reason for them to leave.

"This is a serious issue," I said, trying to keep my emotions in check. "What happened out there is unacceptable. An effective special forces unit cannot operate this way. For the second time in a week, you've made us stop an operation. Both times, it was an operation that we, the ones who have to do it, knew could succeed. An operation on which the fate of three Israeli pilots depends. Now, again, with no real reason, you've stopped us. I see this as a breach of trust." When neither Dado nor Motta replied, I went on: "I have to tell you openly. You can't possibly judge the situation on the ground. Only we can. And you're behaving as if you *know.* You *can't* know from here. There was no reason for us not to grab those officers. I don't want to reach a point when I have to start thinking about what to report back, or not report, just to make sure we're free to complete a mission that you *ordered*, after agreeing it was necessary for Israel."

No one said anything for a few moments. I could see that Uzi, Mookie, and Bibi were shocked at having heard me speak in this way to three of the top commanders of the armed forces. But I meant every word. If Sayeret Matkal was to function as a special forces unit, it needed to have the trust of those who'd authorized an operation in the first place. It was Dado who finally replied. Sort of. Trying to defuse the tension, he told us a joke from his Palmach days. "There are two bulls who come into a field full of cows. A young one and old one. The young one says to the old guy: 'Let's run over there to the far end of the field, where the prettiest cow is, and we can fuck her.' The old bull replies: 'No need to rush. Let's go slowly, and fuck them all.'"

I guess we were meant to be the young bulls.

I doubt Dado knew whether we'd get a third chance at the Syrian officers, though I'm sure he hoped so. A few days later, we got word there would be a final inspection visit, to the central sector of the border area, on June 21. Ordinarily, I would have led that operation as well. Now, I made an exception. To Dado's obvious surprise, I decided to remain behind in the command post. "A commander has to be in the best place to ensure a mission is successfully completed," I told him. "I've come to the conclusion the only way I can do that is to be here with you. Because the real bottleneck isn't out there in the field. It's here."

I placed Yoni, who had just become my deputy, in overall command of the two main teams: Uzi Dayan's and another led by one of our most impressive young officers, a kibbutznik named Danny Brunner. He reminded me a lot of Nechemia Cohen: he spoke little, and softly, but once an operation began he was calm, clear minded, and able to anticipate and avoid trouble before it materialized. Two other teams, one led by Mookie Betzer and the other by Shai Agmon, would be concealed half a mile away on either side of the ambush to act as blocking units once the attack force intercepted the convoy. We chose a spot across from the Israeli moshav of Zar'it. We equipped Yoni's force with a pair of jeeps and had them hide overnight in the moshav's orchards, a hundred yards from the road on the Lebanese side of the frontier. The next morning, when we got confirmation the convoy was on its way, they crossed and stationed themselves on the road, lifted the hood of one of the vehicles, and made as if they were trying to repair engine trouble. Both the blocking forces were in halftracks with heavy machine guns in case the convoy chose to stand and fight. Mookie's even included a Centurion tank.

What we didn't count on was a Lebanese driver, in a VW Beetle as I recall, puttering along the road shortly after Yoni's team crossed. The man waved at them. Quite rightly, Yoni let him drive on. Along with the other obvious reasons not to fire on a civilian VW, he didn't want to alert the Syrians and their hosts there was danger ahead. But the Lebanese motorist, as well as a group of nearby farmers, were suspicious enough to deliver a warning that there were a couple of stalled jeeps on the road. The convoy halted shortly after passing Mookie's force, hidden in an orchard about a quarter of a mile away.

Had I not been in the command post, I suspect the mission would again have been called off. This time, I was the one in direct contact with all three teams. Even before I gave the order, Yoni had anticipated it. He and Uzi turned west to confront the convoy. In a brief initial exchange of gunfire, one of Uzi's men was wounded, not seriously, in the leg. But with Mookie's team closing in from behind and Yoni's and Uzi's men in front, the convoy was trapped. Three Lebanese soldiers were killed in the exchange of fire, and one of the Syrian officers managed to flee on foot, but the rest of the Syrians were captured.

The safest way back into Israel would have been the way the force had entered. But Yoni and Uzi felt the main imperative was to get the Syrians out as quickly as possible. At a not inconsiderable cost to a pair of American limousines, Uzi drove each of them, with a total of five Syrian officers, through a boulder-strewn field across the border.

The Syrians included three senior members of the Operations Department of the General Staff, and two from air force intelligence. Israel made an immediate offer to swap them for our pilots, though how enthusiastically I'm not sure. With this kind of leverage on our side, it seemed unlikely the Syrians would do further harm to our pilots. *Our* intelligence officers were keen to get every bit of information they could before sending the Syrians home. It would be a year later before the exchange was done.

+ + +

Barely two months after the ambush operation in south Lebanon, another event drove home the rising threat of Palestinian terrorism. Black September, the terror organization formed by a small group inside Yasir Arafat's Fatah during the civil war in Jordan, seized and murdered members of the Israeli Olympic team at the 1972 games in Munich.

As soon as the news broke on the morning of September 5, I phoned Ahraleh Yariv, head of military intelligence. "You need to send us," I said.

I tried to persuade him that if it came down to an operation to free our hostages, Sayeret Matkal offered the best hope for avoiding a bloodbath. We had the mind-set, the background, the training, and now the experience. I also knew the *German* military had no special forces unit. Ahraleh told me it was too early to say what involvement, if any, Israel might have. He'd get back in touch with a decision when it came.

I called a few of my officers together for preliminary planning. We collated what little information we could from the stream of media reports about the building the terrorists had attacked. As for the attackers, I said we had to assume there were at least half a dozen, and that they had AK-47s and probably grenades or other explosives. Like the Sabena hijackers, they would probably be prepared to die, but hoping to live. All of that turned out to be true. None of it, however, could alter the reply I got from Ahraleh a couple of hours later. "We decided to send Zvika," he said. Zvika Zamir was the head of Mossad, Israel's national intelligence agency, and he would be going only as an observer. Any operation against the terrorists would still be in the hands of German units. In fact, under the postwar German constitution, which barred the army from operating on domestic soil in peacetime, it would fall to the German police. Later, I learned that German law would also have prevented any foreign military unit, such as ours, from playing a role.

Still, the German police's bungled attempt to end the ordeal was especially painful because it was so predictable. I believe that if we *had* been there, at least some of the eleven Israelis killed might not have lost their lives. The Germans launched an ambush at a NATO airfield outside Munich, when the terrorists and hostages were ostensibly on their way to board a flight for Cairo. We know now that there was no properly coordinated plan. Too few police were deployed for the operation. They were inappropriately armed. They lacked relevant training or experience. The result was a bloodbath. As a final insult to the memory of the murdered Israelis, although the three surviving terrorists were jailed, the German government released them to meet the demands of the hijackers of a Lufthansa airliner the following month.

Added to the Israeli public's shock over the massacre, there was anger at having to watch the murderers go free. In the weeks afterward, I got occasional hints that a sustained Israeli response was under way, though

I didn't know the details. I was not aware that Ahraleh, at the direction of Golda herself, was coordinating it. Nor that a special Mossad team was at the center of the operation. Yet from news reports of a series of attacks on suspected leaders of Black September, I and most Israelis assumed we were determined to convey a message the Germans had not: that terror killings of the sort perpetrated in Munich would not go unanswered.

It was not until late 1972 that I knew the full scale of the operation. We had no formal ties with the Mossad, but our intelligence work occasionally overlapped. In mid-December, the sayeret's intelligence officer was approached with a "theoretical question" by a couple of guys from the Mossad. Did we have the capability to attack three separate flats in a pair of apartment buildings in Beirut? I sent back my preliminary answer a few days later. I said it was possible, but there was no way I could say for sure without more information. Would the people in the apartments be armed? Were there guards outside? Was there a caretaker or concierge? Was there only one way into the buildings, or also rear entrances? Would we be able to get a plan of the interior of the apartments?

In another month, they came up with most of the answers. The buildings were fairly new, with glassed-in lobby areas and concierges. The Mossad men also gave us a fairly detailed layout of two of the three apartments. They did not know whether there were back entrances. They thought it was likely there were bodyguards, or at least some security detail posted outside. As for the people living in the apartments, all of them were likely to have at least small arms.

Over the next week or so, we raised a series of other questions. Mainly, I wanted to know whether they were sure the people we'd be looking for would be at home. The Mossad officers said they were still working on that, but believed they would be able to confirm this before any operation happened. They also told us the identity of the people they were targeting: Palestinian leaders with ties to Black September. "I think it's possible," I finally told them. "We'll start planning. We can finalize the arrangements if you come back with the rest of the information we'll need."

Nothing happened for several months. By the early spring of 1973, with my two-year term as sayeret commander winding down, I assumed the operation had been vetoed. I could understand why. As we worked on our plan, it became clear that getting into the heart of the Lebanese capital, hitting the apartments, and getting out again without finding ourselves in a major firefight would be by far the most difficult mission we had attempted.

I was on a weekend away with Nava and Michal in the Red Sea resort of Eilat when things suddenly began to move. At around noon on Saturday, I got a call from Talik's deputy in the kirya. "Ehud," he said, "we need you back here as soon as possible." Since we were talking on an open phone line, when I asked him why, he replied simply, "You remember how you were approached by someone with some questions from our colleagues?" It seemed the Beirut plan was on again.

I told Nava I'd been summoned to a meeting at the chief of staff's office and grabbed the first commercial flight north. The meeting was already under way when I arrived at the kirya early that evening. Dado was in his usual seat at the table he used for staff discussions, flanked by Talik. Across from them was Manno Shaked, the officer who had phoned me to tell me about the Sabena hijacking and who had now succeeded Raful Eitan as katzhar, overall chief of the infantry and paratroopers. Beside him were the two Mossad officers with whom I'd had most of my dealings about Beirut. They were all staring at an aerial photo of the Lebanese capital, with an area marked in blue pen around a street called Rue Verdun.

I entered and took one of the remaining chairs. Gesturing toward the image of Beirut, Dado turned to me. "Do you know this place?" he asked. Yes, I said. I'd seen the photo. Nodding toward the Mossad men, I said, "These two officers showed it to me a while ago."

"Do you have an idea how to do this operation?" I told him that we didn't have a fully detailed operational plan. But I said we'd looked into the problems we'd face. "We believe we can do it." When he asked how, I outlined the approach we'd settled on: a small force, thirteen men, plus two from Mossad to act as drivers. We would need the Mossad men to go to Beirut ahead of us and rent a pair of nice American cars, the kind typical tourists would use. We'd land on the waterfront, well south of the most built-up parts of the city coastline, and meet up with the rental cars. When we reached the apartment blocks, three squads of three men each would take care of the apartments. Four more would remain outside to deal with security guards or any other interference, and to command and coordinate. We'd leave the same way we came in, by sea.

Dado nodded and smiled. I found out later that he'd asked the same question of Manno, who had proposed a classic regular army raid. They would block the road with ten armed paratroopers on each end with the aim of holding off resistance, while another two dozen went into the apartments and attacked. I could only assume Dado concluded that this almost certainly wouldn't work, at least not without major trouble. It would certainly forfeit any chance of surprise.

"The mission is yours," he said. "Manno will be in overall command, offshore. Because we're also planning to hit several other targets."

The reason for the urgent summons was that the Mossad had concluded that all three of the Palestinians would be in their apartments within the next couple of weeks. Everyone involved realized that—given its complexity, the obvious risks, and the inevitable unknowns—the operation could well go wrong. In fact, one reason for Dado's "other targets" was to ensure that if it did, there would be successes elsewhere to provide a credible justification for having sent Israeli forces into Beirut. We would be operating in a crowded, up-market residential area. We could only hope that at the hour we struck, most people would be in bed. Or out partying. This was, after all, pre–civil war Beirut, the "Paris of the Middle East."

In the years since, an extraordinary array of stories has grown up around the sayeret's final and best-known mission during my term as commander, culminating in the dramatic version in Steven Spielberg's movie *Munich*. I remember reading in one earlier book, otherwise surprisingly accurate, about our *five weeks* of intensive training. Even the full ten days I thought we'd been given would have been a bonus. In fact, we had half that as a full team, since our Mossad drivers had to make their way to Beirut as tourists, rent the cars, and scout out our route from the seashore to Rue Verdun.

There were four other operations planned alongside ours: three by paratroop units and one by the Shayetet 13 SEALs, against a series of Fatah and Democratic Front installations. Though all of them, like ours, would need help from the SEALs in getting ashore, only one required direct coordination with us. This was an attack on a DFLP building a mile or so away in southern Beirut, led by Amnon Lipkin, the friend whose unit had faced one of the toughest battles at Karameh five years earlier. Amnon's paratroop force would land with us and also pile into Mossad rental cars. Our attacks would begin at the same time, with the maximum prospect of retaining the advantage of surprise.

As we began intense preparations for the mission, I did make one change in the plan I'd outlined to Dado. When Yoni pressed to be included, I added him to Mookie Betzer's force. I put the other two attack teams under a pair of young officers named Amitai Nachmani and Zvika Gilad. Both were self-confident, natural leaders, and had other qualities I also knew we'd need: focus and calm. I would take charge on the street outside the targeted apartments, along with Amiram Levin. With us would be Dov Bar, a Shayetet 13 officer, and our medic, Shmuel Katz.

At the sayeret base, we made mock-ups of the layout of the apartments using bedsheets for the walls and adjusting the dimensions as further bits of intelligence came in from Mossad. But the even more critical work involved simulating the whole operation, from the moment of our landing on jet-black rubber dinghies piloted by the SEALs. We found a new building development in north Tel Aviv with a pair of apartment blocks under construction. For two nights, we ran through the whole thing: setting off in the dinghies from a missile boat off the Israeli coast before midnight, meeting up with our Mossad drivers onshore, making our way through the center of Tel Aviv to the apartment complexes, and simulating the attack. I wanted to ensure we could pull off the whole thing without anyone raising an alarm. The one problem came during the second run-through. A policeman drove by as we were making our way toward the Tel Aviv apartments. Manno managed, just barely, to persuade him that reporting us to his superiors would not be an especially good idea.

In our debriefing discussions after that exercise, Dado identified a problem I'd overlooked. We would be entering Beirut dressed as civilians. Once we got to the top end of Rue Verdun, we planned to approach the apartments as if we were partygoers returning from a night on the town. "It doesn't look right," Dado said. "More than a dozen young people walking, all of them *men*?" Mookie came up with the solution, one that would have the unintended effect of elevating our mission further in Israeli lore, and I immediately agreed. The three least burly-looking of us would go in as women: a boyish-looking guy named Lonny Rafael, Amiram Levin, and me.

We had black-and-white photos of the three men we would be targeting: Mohammed Youssef al-Najar, or Abu Youssef, Black September's chief operations officer for the West Bank; Kamal Adwan, one of Arafat's top military planners; and Kamal Nasser, a member of his leadership circle and his spokesman. Black September, and Arafat's Fatah more broadly, were not only at war with the existence of Israel; they were behind an escalating campaign of terror. As I explained to the men I'd be leading on the Beirut operation, the Mossad, Dado, and ultimately Golda had concluded that these three men were appropriate targets in the wake of Munich. I said that what we were being asked to do in Beirut was not an act of revenge but a preemptive attack, and a deterrent. It was a way of preventing the people we were targeting from unleashing further Munichs, and leaving no doubt in the minds of potential future terrorists that their acts would carry a heavy price.

For Amitai Nachmani, who would lead the attack on one of the apartments, my words were not enough. Twice, he came to see me. Before leading his team into Beirut, he said he wanted to satisfy himself that the people we were attacking, and the way we were attacking them, had been properly thought through by the people giving the orders. I told him I understood. I did not tell him that I was proud of him for asking—which, although I'm sure he sensed it, was an omission I regretted when he lost his life in the Sinai Desert a few months later. But the next time I saw Dado, I told him what Amitai had said. He needed no convincing when I urged him to address the entire Beirut team and answer their questions at our final briefing before the mission. He did so, explaining how and why the decision to target these three Palestinians had been reached, to the satisfaction of Amitai and the others.

We set off by missile boat from Haifa on the afternoon of April 9. To my relief, since I suffer from seasickness, the Mediterranean was calm as we headed west toward Cyprus before circling back in the direction of the Lebanese coast after nightfall. I ran through key elements in the plan with several of the officers and then joined Amiram and Lonny in transforming ourselves as best we could into credible dates for the evening. I'd vetoed dresses or high heels in favor of flared slacks and flats. We used standard-issue army socks to pad out our bras. Two of the women soldiers in the sayeret helped us with our lipstick, blue eyeliner, and eye shadow. The final touch was our wigs. Amiram and Lonny were blondes. I went as a stylish brunette.

I'm reluctant to take issue with the Spielberg version of events, if only because he had my part played by someone undeniably better looking than I was, even as a thirty-one-year-old. But in *Munich*, we are shown zooming into a crowded harbor area on a line of motorboats, changing into drag only once we've sprinted ashore, opening fire on a dockside kiosk and shooting our way into town like something out of the Wild West. Had any of that happened, we would have started a small-scale war, not to mention almost certainly losing any chance of finding the terrorists at home when we got to Rue Verdun.

In fact, we left the missile boat, Manno's offshore command post, in motor dinghies out of earshot of Beirut and powered down the engines as we got closer to the shore. All of us, including the "women," were wrapped in ponchos and were carried ashore by the SEALs to make sure we stayed dry. All of us had loose-fitting jackets. The attack teams used them to conceal Uzis, explosive charges to blow the locks on the apartment doors if they couldn't be forced open, a hand grenade or two, and flashlights for the dash up the stairs. One member of each team had a large plastic bag, with orders to take away any easily accessible documents. As the "mother" of the brood, I also had a large purse, in which I carried our radio to communicate with the team leaders and with Manno on the missile boat if necessary.

Our SEAL pilots steered us well away from the more built-up part of the seafront toward the Coral Beach, one of the private clubs on the southern end of the shoreline. Four rented station wagons were waiting, two of them for us and two for Amnon's squad. Amnon set off toward the DFLP target. We headed north toward the center of town. In the Spielberg film, my speaking role consisted of two words, my name, as I introduced myself to my driver. In fact, we had already met: during the run-through exercises in Tel Aviv. After we got into the cars, I asked him how his scouting of the route had gone. He looked worried. He said there was always an armed guard in front of the Iraqi consulate, which was on our way, and that there was a Lebanese police post at one end of Rue Verdun itself. I assured him it would be fine. There would be no reason for the consulate guard, or a policeman, to suspect what we were up to, or who we were. Still, I could tell he was still nervous. "What's wrong?" I asked. He hesitated before replying. "I've never been in a place where you're being shot at," he said. I told him not to worry: he *still* wouldn't be. "You're going to be parked around the corner, until it's over. Then, it's just about getting home."

When we reached the top of Verdun, it was about ten minutes after one in the morning. Our cars pulled over. I took Mookie's arm as we began walking the 200 feet or so to the first of the apartment buildings. The others followed in knots of two or three. Both Mookie and I saw two policemen approaching on the sidewalk. "Ignore them," I whispered. We weaved a few inches to the side to let them pass. The buildings were as we'd expected, with their lobbies set back from a covered terrace in front. As the other teams made their way to the second building, Mookie, with Yoni in his expanded team, went to find Abu Youssef, the Black September operations officer. The concierge must have been in his room, or on a coffee break, because the lobby was empty. The door was unlocked, so they sprinted toward the interior staircase and made their way up to the fifth floor.

Adwan, the Fatah military man, and Kamal Nasser lived next door. Adwan, Amitai's target, was on the second floor. Nasser was on the third. As the teams raced into the other building, Amiram and I posted ourselves near one of the terrace pillars, occasionally exchanging a few words of what we hoped would pass as girl talk. The SEAL officer and Dr. Katz were a dozen yards further up the street, as lookouts. We seemed seconds away from what had all the makings of the operation we'd rehearsed back in Tel Aviv. The main problem I'd expected—security guards posted outside—hadn't materialized. We'd been told by the Mossad to look out for a gray Mercedes, but it wasn't there either.

The next stage was for each squad leader to press the transmit button three times on his radio once he was in place and they'd attached small explosive charges to the apartment doors. When I'd heard from all of them, I would send a signal back. Then, at the count of five, each of them was supposed to detonate their explosive charges, burst into the apartments, and attack. Mookie's signal came first. Yet before either of the other two teams checked in, the trouble began. Suddenly, the door of a red Renault flew open almost directly across the street from where Amiram and I were standing. A tall, sturdy, dark-haired man with a neatly trimmed mustache climbed out. He looked across at us. He opened his leather jacket. He pulled out a pistol and started to approach us. *"Ein breirah,"* I whispered to Amiram. "No choice." To this day, I remember the shock on the man's face as he watched us—a pair of young women—open our jackets and pull out Uzis. Fortunately for him, we'd had to make allowances for concealment, over accuracy, in choosing our weapons. We'd left the Uzis' stabilizing shoulder stocks behind. As our first shots hit, he had half turned to run. Though wounded, he somehow got back in the car. We kept shooting, but he managed to drag himself out of the far door and roll behind a knee-high wall on the other side of the street. One of our shots obviously hit the electrical innards of the Renault, because the car horn began blaring full-blast, as if someone had set off a modern-day car alarm. So much for the element of surprise.

I saw three sets of lights suddenly come on in the otherwise dark apartment buildings. They were in the flats the Mossad had identified. At least that part of the plan was intact. These were the terrorists we were after, and it seemed they were at home. Seconds later, I heard an explosion. It was from Abu Youssef's apartment, the one Mookie had been assigned. Then, bursts of gunfire from the other building.

A Lebanese police Land Rover was now approaching from the bottom of the road. We waited until it was about fifty feet away. Amiram and I opened fire, then Dov and Shmuel Katz as well. The driver lost control and crashed into the side of the Renault. There were at least four policemen inside. They, too, rolled behind the wall on the far side of the street. Using the terrace columns for cover, we kept shooting. Within a minute or so, only a couple of the cops fired back.

Although the three Palestinians could not know the reason for the gunfire and the wailing of the car horn, they were now on their guard. When Mookie had blown open the door to Abu Youssef's flat, he saw the Black September man peering out from the bedroom. Mookie raised his Uzi, but the Palestinian ducked inside and shut the door. Mookie and another in his squad fired through the door. When they went in, they found

Abu Youssef and his wife, both dead. When Zvika's team burst in on Kamal Nasser, he was ready. Crouching under his bed, he aimed his automatic pistol and fired, grazing one of the team on the leg. But in a burst of Uzi bullets he, too, was killed. Sadly, the force of the explosive charge on the door also blew open the door of the next-door flat, killing an elderly Italian woman. When Amitai and his squad broke into Kamal Adwan's apartment, he was standing, in civilian clothes, with an AK-47 raised and ready to fire. Amitai fired first.

Mookie's team came down first. They joined us, crouching behind the columns, as sporadic shots continued from one of the policemen behind the wall across the street. When a second police Land Rover approached and it suddenly accelerated toward us, we opened fire. It swerved, crashing into the rear bumper of the other one.

The other teams were back down now. I shouted for Dov to have the drivers bring the station wagons from around the corner. When we began to pull away, a third police Land Rover appeared. It sped up behind us. We all piled out of the cars and opened fire. Mookie tossed a grenade. We then got back in and sped away, dropping hollow, needle-sharp spikes out the back window of the car as we left; any other pursuing vehicle would be in no shape to follow for very long. Still, we had to avoid trouble on our way back out. We took the shortest route to the sea, straight out to the Corniche, the city's main avenue along the Mediterranean. As we got closer we could hear gunfire. Obviously, the police, and the Palestinian militias, realized *something* was not right. The advantage we had was that they would have no idea what exactly had happened on Rue Verdun, who we were, or where we were going.

No sooner had we joined the Corniche than I saw another police Land Rover about a hundred yards ahead of us. This one had a spotlight on the roof, panning the coastline. I told the driver to slow down. About a hundred yards or so later, reaching the place where we'd arranged for the SEALs to meet us, he and the other station wagon pulled over to the side of the road. The Land Rover kept driving. We slid down a steep embankment nearly thirty feet to the sea. Two of the three assault teams had bags full of documents as well. We swam out to the dinghies. When we had hoisted ourselves in, we headed out to the missile boat. The whole operation had taken about a half hour, less than ten minutes on Rue Verdun.

I radioed Manno on the way to the missile boat a half dozen words, the agreed code phrase for "mission accomplished, targets achieved." I could hear relief in his voice when he replied. At first, I assumed that was because they hadn't heard from us during the operation. Our radio link to the missile boat had gone down when we entered the built-up area around the apartment blocks—genuinely, despite Manno's suspicion that I'd cut the connection. Yet he had other reasons to exhale when he heard we had got out safely. Amnon's team had had a much tougher time, and it could have been even worse were it not for his courage and leadership under fire. They met resistance from the moment they arrived at the DFLP building. Two of his men were killed, another wounded. They had to fight their way in, and out again. They only barely managed to carry out their fallen comrades and link up with another team of SEALs near the Coral Beach.

It was a little before six in the morning when I got home. I was careful not to wake Nava. I'd changed out of my slacks and flats and surrendered my wig on the missile boat. But the small matter of my makeup completely slipped my mind. By the time we got back to Israel, I was exhausted. The next thing I remember was my wife standing by our bed as I stirred awake around noon the next day. She looked at my eye makeup and the remnants of my lipstick, shook her head, and smiled. She didn't need to ask where I'd been. Israel radio had been full of news about a major operation in Beirut.

+ + +

A few weeks later, my term as commander ended. The handover to my successor, Giora Zorea, turned out to be more elaborate than my arrival, though not at my instigation. With both Talik and Avraham in attendance, Dado presented me with my fifth tzalash. It was not for Beirut, nor for the operation against the Syrian officers, nor the intelligence our cross-border operations were providing. Dado said it was for all of the above, and for "operational leadership leading to important achievements for Israel's security." When I replied, I am sure everyone knew I spoke from the heart in saying that my every moment with Sayeret Matkal had been a privilege. And that this latest commendation was an award for the achievements of the whole sayeret.

Dado did me another good turn. As my stint as commander drew to an end, I knew what I hoped to do next in the army: to use my tank training to work my way up the command chain in the armored corps. But like past sayeret commanders, it was assumed I would first spend time at the US Marine Corps staff college in Quantico, Virginia. I had other ideas. I was now thirty-one, and I wanted to exercise other parts of my mind by doing graduate work at a normal American university. Dado agreed.

I still had to get accepted. The first step was to take the postgraduate entry exam, the GRE. There were two parts to it. The first involved mathematics and abstract thinking, the second the English language. If my fate had rested on my English grade, I'd have ended up at Quantico: I finished in the 28th percentile. But in the other part, I was in the 99.7th percentile. That proved enough to get me into the four universities to which I applied: Harvard, Yale, MIT, and Stanford. I chose Stanford, mainly because it allowed a far greater latitude in choosing my program of study. Also, the weather.

In early August 1973, Nava and I joined my parents and hers on a sunny afternoon in Mishmar Hasharon to celebrate Michal's third birthday and say goodbye. We were heading to Palo Alto, California, with every expectation of two years of intellectual stimulation, new friends, new experiences, and something approximating a more normal family life. My "other" family, the Israeli army, also had reason to believe a period of new possibilities lay ahead. The threat of terror remained, of course. There had also been a brief bout of nerves over military maneuvers by Anwar Sadat a few weeks earlier. But that had come to nothing. In no small part due to the success of operations like the raid on Rue Verdun, Israel's leadership believed the balance of strength and security was on our side; at least for a while, the country could breathe a bit more easily.

But we were all about to be proven spectacularly wrong.

# 9

# Wake-Up Call

I ONLY VAGUELY RECOGNIZED THE VOICE ON THE OTHER END OF THE line, but her words instantly jolted me awake: "The boss is busy," she said. "But he wants you to know. A war has started back home."

The call came at four thirty in the morning. It was the sixth of October, 1973: Yom Kippur, the holiest date on the Jewish calendar. I was still a bit groggy from the night before. We had been out at a get-to-know-you event for some of the several dozen Israelis, and several hundred American Jewish students, at Stanford. We had been in the United States for barely six weeks.

The "boss" in question was Motta Gur, who was now Israel's military attaché in Washington and my nominal commander for my period in the United States. "I need to talk to Motta," I said. She passed him the phone. "I want you to know I'm going back," I told him. Motta's reply took my mind back fifteen months, to our on-again-off-again mission to abduct the Syrian officers, with Motta and Dado in the command post, intent on reining in the "young bulls" of the sayeret. "Ehud," he said, "from what I'm hearing, I don't think we are missing a major war."

"What's this *we*?" I said. Motta was a general at the upper reaches of the armed forces, officially posted to Washington. I was a young officer, just starting to work my way up the chain of field command. "I can't afford to miss even a *nonmajor* war," I said. "I'll check in with you when I get to New York."

"Major" would turn out to be, if anything, an understatement. All I knew, as I kissed Nava and Michal goodbye and got a cab to San Francisco Airport, was that Israel was again at war. By the time I joined the swarm of Israelis around the El Al desk at Kennedy Airport eight hours later, the picture was clearer, and more worrying with each new report from back home. Surprise attacks by Syria and Egypt—armies we'd not just defeated, but humiliated, six years earlier—had pinned down and pushed back our forces on the Golan Heights and in the Sinai. Without any advance call-up, many reservists were only now reaching the front lines.

As hundreds of people pressed for seats on the El Al flight, I was fortunate to receive a boost up the pecking order from another man in line. Since the Sabena operation, the existence of Sayeret Matkal had become a bit less secret. Still, the identity of the sayeret commander was known to just a few people outside the unit. So skittish were the army security people that before I'd left for Stanford, they even insisted I change my name. I was no longer Ehud Brog. I'd Hebraicized it to Barak, which seemed near enough to the original. Among the few dozen outside the unit who did know about my role, however, were paratroopers who'd joined us on various missions. One of them now told the El Al people who I was. Not only was I given a seat on the first overnight plane back to Tel Aviv, but I found myself helping the airline establish a priority for assigning seats to others: first, active officers in fighting units—armor, infantry, the air force; then reservists, with the emphasis on those who'd seen active service most recently.

As we were waiting to board, I phoned Uzi Dayan and asked him to meet me at Lod Airport the next morning. Then I called Motta again. "Ehud," he said, with no trace of irony, "it is an *extremely* serious war. Syrian tanks are getting close to the outer fences of Nafakh"—our main command post on the Golan. "Good luck."

Uzi was waiting for me when we landed. Walking to his car, we ran into two reserve armored officers who had also just arrived home. They expected to be sent north to help beat back the Syrian advance. When they asked me where I thought I'd be going, I said, truthfully, I had no idea. "Wherever I can help," I said. Uzi drove us to the *bor*, the underground bunker in the kirya. Usually, it functioned as the day-to-day operations center, but it was also where the commanders operated during times of war.

At officers' school, we learned about the importance of throwing the enemy "off balance." Now, *we* were off balance. The faces I saw around me were gray and drawn. There were dead looks in the eyes of the commanders and their staff. Some thirty hours after the surprise attack, the self-confidence we'd felt since 1967 seemed to have evaporated. I looked into several of the rooms where, months earlier, I'd run through operational plans as sayeret commander. Inside each, a large wall map traced the course of the fighting. Israeli forces were marked in blue, the Syrians and Egyptians in red, with a time stamp for each position report scribbled at the side in black marker. But the latest addition was from *ten to twelve hours* earlier. It was as if we'd lost track of what was happening, or were simply overwhelmed by the pace of events.

I spoke briefly with Talik as he walked along the corridor. He looked ten years older than when I'd last seen him. Then I spotted Ahraleh Yariv, who had been called back into military intelligence at the start of the war. Looking surprised to see me back in Israel, he pulled me close to him. "It's important that you came back," he said. "We'll need each and every one of you to get the job done." Then he hugged me again. It was as if, knowing I would soon be heading for the front line, he wondered whether we'd see each other again.

I made my way to the office that the chief of staff used in the bunker and asked Dado's secretary if I could see him. As she was deciding whether to let me in, he emerged. Though obviously aware of the seriousness of the situation, Dado projected his usual calm and confidence. For the first time, I felt a bit more hopeful. "*Ma nishmah*, Ehud?" he asked, an everyday Israeli greeting. "What's up?" I told him I'd just come from the airport. "I can help in special forces, infantry, armor. Whichever is most needed."

"Leading a tank unit," he said. "They've suffered heavy losses. Go see Tzipori." Motke Tzipori was in charge of organizing the armored units. He sent me to Julis, the training base between Tel Aviv and Beersheva, where tanks from maintenance units around the country were being brought. Once they were reasonably operational, and as more reservists arrived from abroad, I would lead a makeshift unit, dubbed Battalion 100, to help reinforce our badly depleted forces in the Sinai.

+ + +

I was just one of dozens of officers in command of thousands of tireless and courageous troops called on to try to turn the tide. Most were reservists. Many, like me, had rushed home from abroad, feeling for the first time since 1948 that there was a real risk Israel would be defeated. By the time I got my battle orders—October 14, the ninth day of the war—Israeli forces on the Golan, at enormous cost, had managed to turn back the Syrian attack. In this war, the men from Sayeret Matkal were not bystanders. Most of the unit joined the fightback in the north, where, under Yoni Netanyahu's command, they took on and defeated a Syrian commando force in the heart of the Golan. Yoni himself risked his life to rescue a wounded officer from another unit behind enemy lines.

In the Sinai, however, the situation remained dire. An initial counterattack, launched while I was on my way to Julis, ended up in tatters, with whole battalions all but destroyed as our tanks came under fire, mainly from wire-guided Saggers. Israel's main advantage in 1967—our command of the skies—was all but gone. By moving their surface-to-air missiles to the bank of the Suez Canal after the truce in the War of Attrition, the Egyptians had created an effective no-fly zone a dozen miles into the Sinai. A few days after the failed counterattack, with the situation still hanging in the balance and the commander of the air force warning that we were nearing our minimum "red line" number of fighter jets, Golda contacted the Americans to express Israel's readiness to negotiate a cease-fire in the south. But having retaken the Suez Canal and pushed into the Sinai, President Sadat was in no mood to call a halt to the fighting. The only way we were going to end the war was to retake the canal and defeat the even larger Egyptian forces on the other side.

When I rushed back from Stanford, I was still just a thirty-one-year-old lieutenant colonel. But I had spent two years in command of Israel's elite special forces unit. So I knew, and in many cases had worked with, the men at the very top of the armed forces, including Dado, the chief of staff. I also knew, or at least had met, many of the generals who were now

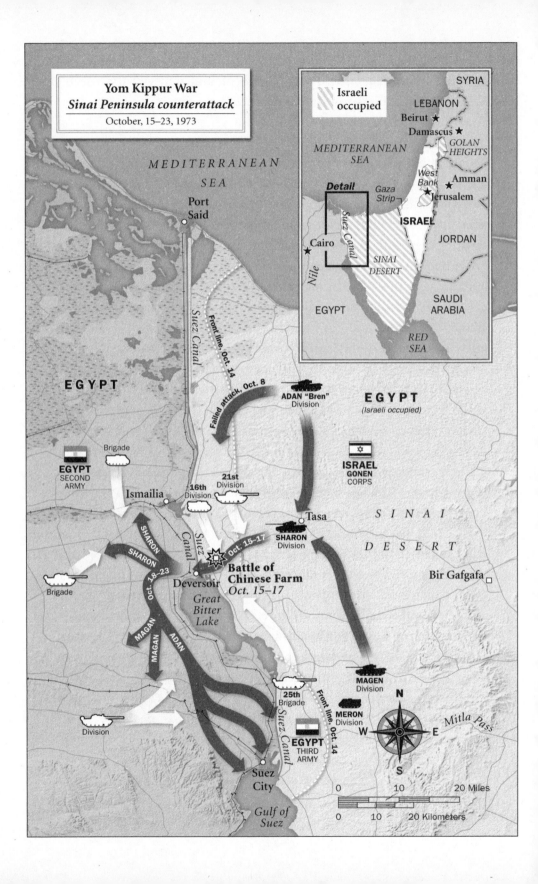

Yom Kippur War
*Sinai Peninsula counterattack*
October, 15–23, 1973

Israeli occupied

SYRIA
LEBANON
Beirut ★
Damascus ★
GOLAN
HEIGHTS
MEDITERRANEAN SEA
Detail
Gaza Strip
West Bank
Amman ★
Jerusalem ★
ISRAEL
Cairo ●
Nile
Suez Canal
SINAI DESERT
JORDAN
EGYPT
SAUDI ARABIA
RED SEA

MEDITERRANEAN SEA
Port Said

EGYPT

Suez Canal

Front line, Oct. 14

Failed attack, Oct. 8

ADAN "Bren" Division

EGYPT
(Israeli occupied)

EGYPT SECOND ARMY
Brigade
Ismailia
16th Division
21st Division

ISRAEL
GONEN CORPS

Tasa
SHARON Division

S I N A I

D E S E R T

Bir Gafgafa

SHARON
SHARON
Oct. 15–17
Oct. 18–23
Brigade
Suez Canal
Deversoir
Battle of Chinese Farm
Oct. 15–17
Great Bitter Lake
MAGAN
MAGAN
ADAN
MAGEN Division
MERON Division
Division
25th Brigade
Suez Canal
Front line, Oct. 14
EGYPT THIRD ARMY

N
W    E
S
Mitla Pass

Suez City
Gulf of Suez

0        10        20 Miles
0    10    20 Kilometers

plotting the counteroffensive in the command bunker in the south: Shmuel Gonen, known as Gorodish, who was head of the southern command; Arik Sharon, who'd left the same job for politics a few months earlier but was now commanding a division near the canal; and Chaim Bar-Lev, the former chief of staff, whom Golda had called back into service at the outbreak of the war. I even knew the bunker: Um-Hashiba, the command and intelligence post from which we ran our sayeret operations into Egypt after 1967. I spent two nights there before receiving battle orders for my battalion, and I found myself in the extraordinary position of witnessing firsthand the top-level debates over how and when to seize back the initiative from the Egyptians and cross the canal.

During the last, decisive two weeks of the war, as part of one of our main armored divisions, my tank battalion took part in the crossing of the canal. We staged a raid beyond enemy lines on the other side to take out Egyptian missile sites, helping restore our jets' command of the skies, and participated in a major battle with Egyptian armor. Late that night, realizing that we'd lost one of our armored personnel carriers, I struck out on foot, through the Egyptian troop positions, to locate our surviving soldiers. As the fighting began to wind down, I was also tasked with guiding the forward units in a large Israeli armored force across the Egyptian desert—terrain I knew well from sayeret missions—to complete the encirclement of Sadat's Third Army. That effectively brought the war to an end.

Still, the memory that has stayed with me longest was the fight for an experimental agricultural facility located just a few miles back from our side of the Suez Canal.

+ + +

In Israel, it was known as the Chinese Farm. In fact, it was Japanese experts who helped set it up in the then–Egyptian Sinai before the Six-Day War. When we captured it in 1967, deciphering the characters on the equipment had evidently proven beyond our linguistic capabilities. Thus, *Chinese* Farm. Now, it was back in Egyptian hands. The sprawling complex, with its web of irrigation ditches, controlled the main transport corridor from the Sinai to the bank of the canal.

Before dawn on October 16, one of the battalions in Arik Sharon's division, under a veteran paratroop commander named Danny Matt, had crossed the canal on rubber rafts with an advance force of some 750 men and a few dozen tanks. But it was a precarious beachhead, vulnerable to Egyptian air strikes, artillery, and Sagger fire. Hopes for any large-scale Israeli counterattack rested on moving forward an enormous roller bridge, and hundreds more tanks, to complete the crossing—impossible without retaking the Chinese Farm.

The first I knew of the scale of Egyptian resistance there was about four in the morning on the seventeenth. I got a radio call ordering me to get my battalion ready to move, ASAP. We'd been attached to the other main armored division, along with Arik's, assigned to lead the canal crossing. It was under the command of Avraham "Bren" Adan, the head of Israel's armored forces. "You're going north of Tirtur 42," Bren's operations officer told me. This was the road running along the upper edge of the Chinese Farm. He told me that parachutists of Battalion 890, under Yitzhik Mordechai, were in trouble. "Go. Find them. Help get them out."

I had known Yitzhik for years, and he was now in command of the paratroopers' elite Battalion 890. I knew the overall commander of the paratroopers' brigade even better: Uzi Yairi, who had been in charge of Sayeret Matkal during my final years of reserve duty at Hebrew University. Helicoptered into the area near the canal just hours earlier, the paratroopers had been sent to the Chinese Farm shortly before midnight. As I soon learned, they had no more idea than I did about what they were about to face. They were told they were going in simply to clear out squads of "tank-hunters." They *weren't* told of repeated attempts by some of Arik's top tank, paratroop, and reconnaissance units to take the farm over the previous thirty-six hours—attacks that not only failed but cost a large number of tanks, armored personnel carriers, and dozens of Israeli lives. Without artillery or armor support, Yitzhik's men immediately faced close-range rifle, machine-gun, and mortar fire from the Egyptians.

Ordering my battalion to get ready for our first combat mission of the war, I immediately found myself face-to-face with a distraught and determined friend from military intelligence. Lieutenant Colonel Yishai Yizhar had arrived at Bren's headquarters the day before. When he saw me, he'd asked to join my unit. He was a brilliant electronics engineer and was about to assume command of the technology unit in military intelligence. I told him we already had our complement of tank crews, and since he'd never had any armored training, I found him a place in one of our armored personnel carriers. But before joining military intelligence, he'd been a company commander in Battalion 890; hearing that we were going to rescue his old unit, he insisted on joining me on the lead tank. I tried several times to refuse, but he argued I had no moral authority to stash him in an APC when we were going in to rescue his comrades. Aware that each wasted minute might cost more of the paratroopers' lives, I relented. I told Yishai he'd be sitting across from me on the turret, right above Yasha Kedmi, another friend who, having served under me in my first tank company in the War of Attrition, had asked to join back at Julis. Yasha was our loader and radio operator. He got Yishai a machine gun, extra magazines for his Uzi, and a box of grenades.

We moved out through wavelike dunes in total darkness. After the first few miles, the terrain leveled out a bit. Still, the sand was deep and the going slow. When we got within a couple of miles of where I assumed Yitzhik and his men would be, I radioed him. His tone of voice alone was enough for me to realize how tough the situation must be, especially coming from an officer I knew to be experienced and unflappable under pressure. "They're very close to us, shooting," he said. "I've got many wounded. Get here as quick as you can."

As we got closer, I could still see no sign of them. As dawn was about to break, I radioed Yitzhik to suggest he fire off a flare, but he thought that would put them at even greater mercy of the Egyptians. Instead, he tossed out a smoke grenade. We spotted it, more than half a mile away, slightly below us and to our right. I ordered us forward, leaving my second tank company behind for covering fire. I led Company A, which included my most experienced tank commander, Moshe Sukenik. Immediately behind us were our APCs, including one carrying our medical team. My aim was to engage the Egyptian fire while starting to evacuate Yitzhik's men to one of the long, dry irrigation ditches 600 yards behind us.

We moved forward in a broad line with my command tank in the center. We held our fire until we got closer. I still couldn't see exactly where the men of Battalion 890 were and didn't want to risk hitting them. Only when we got within about seventy yards did I spot the first of the paratroopers. They were in groups of three or four in a thin line stretching

200 or 300 yards on either side of us. They lay behind whatever cover they could find: a bush, a clump of debris, a small rise in the sand. Some were firing. Others were wounded. From just a few yards away, Egyptian infantrymen raked them with rifle and machine-gun fire. The Egyptians were now shooting at us as well, and we returned fire. But the Egyptians, far outnumbering Yitzhik's men, were spread out in a network of foxholes, in some places connected by trenches. As we halted at the Egyptians' line, I ordered my APC commander to start evacuating the paratroopers back to the irrigation ditch, aided by another group of reservists from a nearby APC unit.

A shell suddenly exploded twenty yards ahead of me. Others rained around our tanks. The source of the fire was straight ahead, about 1,300 yards away: three SU-100s, Soviet-made World War II "tank destroyers." I trained the main gun of my tank on one of the SU-100s and ordered the gunner to fire. I used the battalion-wide radio frequency so the others would hear the order. But when the dust and smoke had cleared, the SU-100s were still there. I ordered a sight correction and ordered, again: "Fire." Still, we missed. It was only then I realized why. Almost none of the tanks brought into Julis from the maintenance units had included their "commander's notebook" with their checklists for calibrating and firing—a major problem, since many of the reservists had last been in a tank years before. I ordered the gunners to use their telescopes, parallel to the main gun, instead and our shells finally began to find their targets.

We were under attack not just from the tank destroyers, but from small-arms and RPG fire. On the turret of our tank, Yishai and I were firing back, our Uzis on automatic, and throwing grenades. Bullets pinged off the turret and the body of the tank. Then, from our right flank, came the shoulder-mounted Saggers, homing in with their eerie blue-red glow, juddering toward us as the Egyptian soldiers corrected their trajectories. One of the missiles barely missed us, and the silky wire from its guidance mechanism was tangled over our turret. I tried using my binoculars to identify where they were coming from, but it was no use. I radioed for artillery support, only to be told there was none available.

To my right, the APCs had completed their first evacuation run and were coming back for more of Yitzhik's men. There was a raggedness about it all: one APC, then a couple of others, then a gap, then another one or two. They were doing whatever they could, whenever they could, as the Egyptian fire continued to intensify. A few of Yitzhik's men, whether desperate or dazed, simply stood up and started walking, defenseless, back toward the irrigation ditch.

I directed Moshe Sukenik to take half the company and head toward the Saggers to try to take them out, even though we both knew that he'd have to risk heavy fire before they got close enough. He had two-inch mortars on his turret, but their range was only 500 yards, far less than the Saggers. Every forty-five seconds or so, a salvo of Saggers zeroed in on our tanks and APCs. Within a few minutes, two of the tanks were hit. One was on fire. Two of the SU-100 tank-destroyers were still there as well. Egyptian infantrymen were spraying us with small-arms fire. The whole area was swathed in grayish smoke. Every minute or two, another tank or APC took a direct hit. There was a smell, too—once experienced, it never leaves your memory: the scent of burnt human flesh.

The fire from the foxholes was getting worse. "Run over them," I ordered my tank driver. "Start with the foxhole in front of us." He jerked us forward and we plowed over the first Egyptian position. "Reverse, get the one to the right," I said. As he backed up, I was shocked to see a surviving Egyptian soldier, shrugging off a thick blanket of sand from his shoulders, raise an RPG launcher at us from just fifteen feet away. We were close enough to look into each other's eyes. I raised my Uzi and shot him before he could fire. Rifle and grenade fire continued from along the line of foxholes. A second length of the Saggers' guidance wire tangled over our main gun. Yishai was firing at the Egyptians from the other side of the tank. We both tossed grenades in the direction of the worst of the gunfire.

It was then that I saw Yishai had taken a bullet in the side of his neck. Blood was gushing from the wound. His face was contorted in pain. He looked at me, raising his hands upward, as if to say: "I did my best. It's over now." I pressed hard on the wound, trying to stem the flow. But he slipped out of my grasp and collapsed into Yasha Kedmi's arms. Yasha propped him up and kept trying to stanch the bleeding. I turned toward the Egyptian soldier who had shot Yishai, less than twenty feet to my left. Keeping myself as low as possible above the turret, I fired into his chest. He tumbled into the foxhole. As I kept shooting, Yasha told me Yishai was dead. "Are you sure?" I asked. When he said yes, I ordered the driver to back up. We drove a few hundred feet, to where the medics were taking cover with a group of wounded paratroopers. With their help, we lowered his body from the tank and then returned to the battle.

Barely ten minutes had passed since it began. Two SU-100s were now spewing smoke and out of action. The third had withdrawn. But the Egyptians were still firing. Five of our tanks had been hit. Two were on fire. One APC was smoldering, its company commander seriously wounded. I knew that if we stayed much longer, we would end up like other armored units during Israel's first, failed counterattack in the early days of the war. We would risk being wiped out. As far as I could tell, all the surviving paratroopers had been brought out or had managed to hobble to the irrigation ditch. I ordered Sukenik to abandon his attempt to take out the Saggers, and we withdrew behind the irrigation ditch.

It was only then that I realized that alongside two of our crippled tanks there was still a group of a dozen men: six crew members from my battalion and six of Yitzhik's men. It took nearly two hours to get them out. We used our tank guns to try to reduce the intensity of the fire from the Egyptians around them. I ordered one of our APCs to go get them. I rounded up all our smoke grenades, and the APC crew used them to create a smokescreen, the only way I could think of to reduce the danger of being targeted by the Saggers. It worked, but it required incredible guts for the men in the APC to pull it off.

The battle had required guts of every man in the battalion. All of them had found a way to conquer the first and most powerful enemy on a battlefield: fear. I felt it too. But even at the height of the fighting—with fire raining down, vehicles on fire—I'd experienced the same, almost slow-motion, sense of detached focus I'd found during the most difficult moments in our sayeret operations. I fired back, tossed grenades, while also issuing orders to my own tank and the rest of the battalion. In some ways, it is easier for a commander. When you lead people into combat, you don't have time to surrender to fear. You have to assess and evaluate, second by second, everything going on around you. You have to make instant decisions, give orders, and ensure they're carried out, and then begin the cycle all over again. Your soldiers are waiting to hear your voice, and they're watching your actions as well. If you lose control at any point, not only is your life at stake—theirs are too.

Early that evening, we were ordered to rejoin Bren's division to be ready for the crossing. When I reported that three of my soldiers were still missing, I was ordered to inform the commander of the battalion replacing us to find the missing men. The fight for the Chinese Farm was still not over. It would be another twelve hours before, in a coordinated push by a strengthened armor and infantry force, Israeli forces finally drove most of the Egyptians out. What tenuous gains we'd made until then had come at an enormous price. Of Yitzhik's 300 men, nearly 40 were killed, and many others wounded. I'd led around 130 people into battle. More than 35 were injured. Eleven were dead, including Yishai Yizhar and Motti Ben-Dror, our medical officer. And though one of our missing soldiers was found alive, the other two could only be brought home for burial.

As I began to hear the details of the previous days' fighting, I became more astonished, and angry. Taking, or at least neutralizing, the Chinese Farm was undoubtedly important. Despite the tragically steep price paid by my battalion and others, the battle we fought there did make it possible to keep moving forces toward the canal and to begin the crossing. But Israel's tactics had involved a series of piecemeal strikes by units that were obviously too small, and inadequately supported or coordinated, to succeed. The problem wasn't the choice of units. No one could doubt the record of Battalion 890, or of the men Arik had sent in the day before Yitzhik arrived. But there was no way they were going to take the area on their own. I couldn't understand why there was no attempt to assemble a force that might actually have been strong enough: parachutists, tanks, artillery. I felt I knew at least part of the answer from the two nights I had spent in the Um-Hashiba command post before joining Bren's division. By dawn on October 16, the first of Arik's men had crossed the canal. By the afternoon, although our big roller bridge was still not ready, a smaller pontoon bridge was available. Everyone knew we needed to get control of the Chinese Farm. But all the field commanders were focused on the *real* task, the real prize: crossing the canal and defeating the Egyptians on the other side.

Now, at least, the main crossing was under way. Bren had chanced the fact that, with Yitzhik pinned down at the Chinese Farm and the Egyptians concentrating their fire on his men and mine, he could get the pontoon bridge through. From late afternoon on October 17, his first units began to cross. On the morning of October 18, my battalion joined them. There was still fighting ahead, and we were part of it: taking out the SAM sites, engaging units of the Third Army, and—with *Sadat* now pressing the Americans for a cease-fire, *his* military commander thrown off balance, and many units clearly losing the will to fight on—racing against the clock to encircle and defeat it five days later.

When the guns finally fell silent, I had time to give full rein to my thoughts. Above all, there was a sense of enormous relief, and pride, in knowing Israel had survived and finally triumphed in its toughest battlefield challenge since 1948. Yet there were also fundamental questions about how the war had happened, starting with why our political and military leaders hadn't known that two neighboring states were about to attack us—despite huge investment in intelligence, including our sayeret intercepts, which should have given us time to call up all our reserves. Disentangling the details would take months. But we already knew the human cost of those failures. Many hundreds of Israeli soldiers had been killed. The final number would be around 2,800, nearly four times our losses in 1967. Thousands were wounded, some crippled for life. Many of the dead were men whom I'd grown up with or served with, including more than twenty in my own battalion. Some of the dead in other units were close friends.

I felt exhausted. I also realized that Nava, thousands of miles away in Palo Alto, and my parents on the kibbutz could still not be sure I had escaped the fate of so many others. I learned later that my parents had been making daily calls to Menachem Digli, the former sayeret commander, who was now working in intelligence in the kirya. Though he had no way of knowing where I was, he kept assuring them that he had checked with my commanders and that I was alive and well. Nava had been relying on American news reports and the relayed assurances from my parents, which she was seasoned enough as an army wife to treat with skepticism.

I missed her badly, and little Michal. I needed to hear their voices. I drove to one of the brigade communications units. There was a long line in front of the radio telephone. But within a half hour, I managed to get a crackly connection to California. Nava burst into tears when she heard my voice. I told her I was fine, and that I couldn't wait to see her and our little girl. Then, my own eyes dampening, I reeled off the names of friends who had been killed. In addition to the brave men I'd lost in my own battalion, there were dozens of others I already knew of. A pair of brothers from Mishmar Hasharon, a couple of years younger than me, in separate units, killed within hours of each other. Yoav Brum, a gifted economist and close friend who'd been with me during my tank training. And Shaul Shalev, a philosophy postgraduate and a brave tank commander whom I'd become friends with at officers' school. He'd rescued three-dozen troops from one of the Bar-Lev fortifications in the first hours of the war, only to be killed trying to get to a tank crew who had taken refuge a few miles back from the canal.

I'd lost two wonderful sayeret comrades, too: Amit Ben-Horin, the officer who'd relayed the order from Motta to abort our attempt to abduct the Syrian officers in Lebanon, and Amitai Nachmani, the team leader who had demanded a meeting with Dado before our attack in Rue Verdun. Ben-Horin was killed in the fighting near Ismailia, at the northern end of the canal, as Sharon's units pushed on after the crossing. The day before the end of the war, both Amitai and Amiram Levin were part of an operation to take over the Fayid Air Base across the canal. When an Egyptian RPG hit their jeep, Amiram was wounded. Amitai was killed.

I thought, too, of Yishai Yizhar: the friend struck down beside me, whom I'd cradled in my arms on the top of my tank, trying to stop the bleeding.

"Oh, Ehud," Nava said. "It's like 1967 all over again."

"No," I said. "Worse. Much worse."

A few weeks later, I was coming out of the kirya when I ran into another friend, whom I'd first met at Hebrew University. Like me, he had been a junior officer in 1967. His name was Ron Ben-Ishai. He was one of the country's leading journalists, covering the armed forces for the bestselling daily newspaper, *Yediot Achronot*. In the early autumn of 1967, we were still transfixed by the idea of being able to visit areas of biblical Israel, which for years had been under Jordanian rule. With a few university friends who were young officers, nine of us in all, Ron and I embarked on a trek from the southern edge of Jerusalem, weaving our way through the Judaean Desert toward Kumeran, on the Dead Sea.

Now a very different war had come and gone. I'd fought in it. Ron, as what is now called an embedded journalist, had been with Danny Matt's paratroopers when they'd crossed the canal. He was alongside another of Arik's units fighting out of the bridgehead on the far bank of the canal. Both of us had seen terrible suffering, and enormous moments of courage as well, over the past few weeks. But Ron said he wanted to show me something. Fishing into his wallet, he took out a carefully folded photograph. He had taken it in 1967, just six years earlier, to mark our Judáean trek. There we were. All nine of us. Young. Full of optimism. And probably a bit full of ourselves as well.

Ron and I were the only two left alive.

+ + +

We had won the war, and not just because our forces were now within sixty miles of Cairo, and only twenty-five miles from Damascus. We had been attacked by two huge armies: one-and-a-half-million soldiers. Thousands of tanks. Hundreds of fighter jets. Other, much larger nations had endured months, even years, of hell before prevailing in such circumstances: the Soviet Union, for instance, with its huge strategic depth, or France, finally rescued by its American-led allies, during World War II.

The pride and the relief in having prevailed—and the reality that, for all Israelis, avoiding defeat, with all it would have meant for Israel's survival, would have been worth even greater pain and more casualties—could not erase the sadness felt over friends lost. Nor over the failure of our generals and political leaders to prepare the country for the surprise attacks or, at least at the beginning, respond to them. Dozens of meetings were held in military units after the war to discuss what had gone wrong. I was not the only young officer to notice that the higher up the command chain they went, the more unedifying they became. After we'd heard one too many senior officer fine-tuning his account with each retelling, minimizing his share of responsibility, a new phrase entered Israeli army slang. *Sipurei kravot*—"battle stories"—were the words usually used to describe a normal debriefing process. That expression was now amended, to *shipurei kravot*. Battle *improvements*.

After the war, I was assigned to convert my makeshift force into a regular training unit for tank commanders: Battalion 532. That slightly delayed my reunion with Nava and Michal. But before we'd left for Stanford, we had bought a larger apartment in the Tel Aviv suburb of Ramat

Hasharon. Nava and I now agreed that at the first opportunity, I'd return to California and we'd fly back together to move in. I went at the end of the year. We bought a refrigerator and a washing machine for the new flat—better models, and cheaper, than those available in Israel—and came home. The two weeks in Palo Alto were a jumble of emotions. Happiness at being back together. But also a sobering sense, now that I was outside Israel for the first time since the war, of the enormity of the threat we'd faced and the frustration and fear Nava must have felt as we'd fought to defeat it. The year-end news retrospectives we watched on American TV were full of film clips from the first days of the war, when it looked very possible we would lose. I remember being struck by the thought that, if we *had* lost, if Israel had ceased to exist, ceremonies of memorial and mourning would have been held across America, probably also in Stanford. But even amid the shock and sadness, Israel's disappearance would not have impinged on a single NFL Sunday, or delayed a single family shopping visit to J. C. Penney.

My command of Battalion 532 lasted only a few more months. On April 1, 1974, an official commission of inquiry published its initial report on the war. It was scathing in its assessment of our intelligence failings, for which it placed the main blame on the officer who had been promoted the year before as head of military intelligence: Eli Zeira, the man who had addressed us on the sayeret base and so confidently predicted the outcome of the 1967 war. It also took aim at two other commanders. Gorodish, as head of the southern command, was one. The other was Dado. As chief of staff, he was held ultimately responsible for the lack of preparation, and for not having ordered at least a partial call-up of our reserves.

In Eli's case, the very fact of our being caught by surprise made his position untenable. In fact, as I learned more details about what had happened, I realized the commission had, if anything, understated the seriousness of his errors. There was some logic in his attempt to minimize the use of "special sources." However, during the run-up to the war, Eli had resisted several requests from more junior intelligence officers to activate what the commission called these "special sources" of intelligence. Not only had he failed to do so, he had indicated to the few generals who were aware of their existence that he had in fact activated them, implying that his lack of concern about the possibility of an attack was based on all our available intelligence.

Because Dado was one of the people misled, his fall struck me as profoundly unfair. He had devoted his whole adult life to the defense of our country. In the toughest, early moments of the war, he had stood firm and strong, and his leadership was critical in turning the tide of the war and ultimately winning it. After the inquiry report, he was never again the same person. He developed a near obsession with fitness and exercise. Psychologists might have called it displacement activity. I wondered whether it was a kind of self-punishment. Either way, it may well have killed him. At age fifty, less than three years after the war, he died of a heart attack following a day of tennis and swimming.

Almost every level of command was thrown into flux after the inquiry report. So was the political landscape. Though Labor did manage to weather an election held shortly after the war, both Golda and Dayan now bowed to growing public pressure and resigned. The premium was on finding replacements who were sufficiently experienced but did not bear responsibility for the errors of the war. For prime minister, the choice fell on Yitzhak Rabin. He had strong military credentials, of course. But he had left the army and entered politics, and had been out of Israel for several years as Israel's ambassador to Washington. He had joined Golda's government only weeks before the war, in the relatively minor role of minister of labor. Much the same thing happened in the army. Only one of the generals who had been in the running to succeed Dado before the war was unscathed: Motta Gur. He, too, had been in Washington. In the wake of the inquiry report, he was called back to replace Dado as chief of staff.

Not everyone emerged from the war with his reputation diminished. The lion's share of the credit for Israel's eventual victory went to the rank and file of our citizen army. But in the officers' corps, there were also examples of coolheadedness in crisis, and leadership. One was Raful Eitan. As a division commander, he had led the counterattack against the Syrians on the Golan and was now made head of the northern command. Another was Moussa Peled, who became head of the armored corps. My overall wartime commander, Bren, replaced Gorodish as head of the southern command. Dan Shomron, whose 401st Armored Brigade played a critical part in defeating the Egyptians, was another. Dan and I had first got to know each other well at Karameh, then during my period as sayeret commander. In the years ahead we would work more closely together than almost any senior officers in the military. He was now promoted as well. He became katzhar, overall head of infantry and paratroop forces, and he recommended me as his successor in Brigade 401.

Still, Motta had the final word on whether I'd get the post, with input from the two senior officers most directly affected: Peled and Bren. I don't think either of them had anything against me personally. But both were tank officers through and through, and there were other candidates to succeed Dan who, unlike me, had spent their whole careers in the armored corps.

I heard formally that I was being considered as I was about to return to my battalion from Ramat Hasharon one Sunday morning. I was ordered to report to Motta's office. When I got there, he gestured toward the small table at the side. He already had two other visitors: Peled and Bren. "You probably know you're a candidate for taking over 401," he said. "These two gentlemen think you're not yet ready. What do you say?"

If I'd had more time to prepare, I might have answered more subtly. But I did believe that I would be a worthy commander of the 401st. "I don't know exactly what the two gentlemen mean by whether I'm ready," I replied. "So I have a proposal. Find a battle-tested officer whom you trust. Have him check who among the three of us, me or the two gentlemen, is more familiar with the tank and its systems. Who of us knows better the terrain, in Syria or Egypt, day or night, where we have to fight? Who knows the operational procedures, and the armored doctrine these gentlemen signed off on? Finally, which one of us has spent more time in a turret of a tank, on the battlefield, shooting at enemy forces and being shot at by the enemy?"

There was silence, a grave look from Peled and Bren, the hint of a smile on Motta's face, and the meeting was over. Several days later, I was notified of his verdict. I was named the commander of the 401st Armored Brigade in the Sinai, and promoted to full colonel.

Our base was fifteen miles from the canal. We spent three months at a time in this forward deployment and three months in our rear base, fifty miles from the canal. During one of our forward deployments, Motta came on an inspection visit. He wanted to discuss how we planned to defend the area near the canal in the event of a repeat of the 1973 war. I told him everything we were doing in the brigade was aimed at ensuring *flexibility*. I had also been thinking about some of the broader issues relating to our defenses in the south. "No matter how good our tactics or plans," I said, "what worries me is that we're still not looking at our overall approach to our defense against Egypt. It's as if we've forgotten that in 1967, when we captured the Sinai, it was in order to have a buffer zone. We had *one hundred fifty miles* of sand between southern Israel and the canal. But when the Egyptians attacked in 1973, we defended the desert front line as if it was the walls of Jerusalem!"

Since the 401st was one of two regular brigades on the Egyptian front, it was not easy to make the four-hour drive home to Ramat Hasharon. When I got word Nava was going into labor with our second child, I was leading a training exercise five or six miles from our base. As she was on her way to the hospital, I grabbed my car and headed north. Unlike Michal's birth, this one was not easy. When the baby emerged, she was struggling to breathe. The immediate danger passed, but she was placed in an incubator. When I got to the hospital, Nava was asleep. I was taken to see our tiny daughter, Yael. When the nurse left, I noticed the baby's pinkie trapped in the plastic cover of the incubator. I started banging on the window of the room. The nurse rushed back. With a look of sympathy mixed with world-weary experience of other fathers in similar panic, she raised the cover, folded Yael's tiny hands onto her stomach, and all was well.

It was another health crisis that hastened the end of my period as brigade commander. But this time, I was the one in the hospital, for ten nightmarish days. I'd nearly collapsed from high fever and exhaustion. The initial suspicion was some kind of contamination linked to the rudimentary sanitation in the Sinai. When the symptoms persisted, several doctors suggested I probably had hepatitis B, and a couple of others even said it might be a form of leukemia. Years later, better diagnostic tools ruled all that out. I've never discovered what the illness was. But for nearly six months, getting through the day, or sometimes a single task, remained a struggle.

I did not want to leave my post. I was still barely eighteen months into the role and anxious to get further command experience. But just as I was feeling at my weakest, another aftershock of the 1973 war, this one involving Uzi Yairi, forced the issue. No one could reasonably have held Uzi responsible for the losses suffered by Battalion 890 at the Chinese Farm. I'm certain that if he had known what happened to the other Israeli forces that had tried to take it over, he would never have allowed Yitzhik Mordechai to go in without adequate armor and artillery support. Still, he blamed himself. In obvious distress after the war, he was reassigned as an operational officer in military intelligence in the kirya.

He was still at his desk when Fatah terrorists landed on Tel Aviv's seafront a little before midnight on March 4, 1975. They were spotted by a police patrol, which opened fire. The Fatah men ran from the beach, firing Kalashnikovs and tossing grenades. A block in from the sea, they burst into a modest, three-story building: the old Savoy Hotel. They shot and killed three people in the lobby and took the rest of the staff and guests hostage.

Sayeret Matkal was called in. As the unit went through final preparations for its assault, Uzi showed up. He had a rifle. He was in his everyday officer's uniform, unlike the sayeret team, which was weighted down by special forces gear. As a former commander of the sayeret, he persuaded them he could help. Shortly before dawn, led by Amiram Levin, they attacked. They killed three of the Fatah men within seconds. But another terrorist set off an explosion that collapsed most of the top floor. Uzi joined a couple of the other sayeret men in search of the hostages. He was shot in the head and neck. Seven of the eight terrorists were killed, the other captured. Though five hostages were freed, five lost their lives. One of the sayeret men was killed in the firefight in the hotel. Shortly after the ordeal was over, Uzi died on the operating table of Ichilov Hospital, a few hundred yards from the kirya.

+ + +

Still shocked and saddened by what had happened, I was hardly enthusiastic when Motta told me that he now wanted me to take Uzi's headquarters job. I accepted that since I'd had similar background and sayeret experience, there was logic to the decision. But I was still gaining brigade command experience and couldn't help feeling that the move was at least partly intended as a kind of rest-and-recovery cure because of my illness, not dissimilar to the circumstances under which Uzi had been given the assignment. Still, I *did* need rest and recovery. Even if fully healthy, I'm not sure I could have convinced Motta to change his mind. In my weakened state, I had no chance.

Skeptical though I was about the job, it opened up a new world to me as I learned how the huge range of intelligence information we gathered was collated, evaluated, assessed, and ultimately applied. My new assignment was to help with this process, in tandem with Shai Tamari, the younger brother of Dovik, Avraham Arnan's first successor as commander of Sayeret Matkal. Though we were both colonels, Shai had the slightly more senior role. I was part of the military intelligence department while he was in the operations department, with a more direct link to the units actually carrying out the missions. Once a week, the two of us met to organize the intelligence and operational coordination for the following week. Then, we'd join Motta's meeting with the general staff, sometimes followed by a further meeting with Shimon Peres, who'd succeeded Dayan as defense minister.

Our intelligence analysis team included separate desks for Egypt and Syria, Jordan and Lebanon, Iraq and other neighboring states, as well as other countries, and superpower relations. We relied on all the raw material we could get, not just from military intelligence and Mossad, but academic and specialist literature as well. I was responsible, along with Shai and a few others, for bringing all of this together. This meant frequent meetings with members of the analysis teams. For the first six months or so, I barely uttered a word in these sessions. I listened, absorbing the information and getting to understand the way the analysts worked and thought.

Our whole intelligence department was responsible for drafting an annual strategic assessment for the army and the government. The final report was written by Shlomo Gazit, who had succeeded Eli Zeira as head of military intelligence. Before we sent it to print, he held a long meeting, inviting the views of all the military intelligence officers. The focus in December 1976, just three years after the war, was on the risks of a new surprise attack. At the end of the discussion, however, he said, "We know we run a real danger for the country if we fail to spot the signs of a war. But have any of you asked yourselves something I find myself wondering from time to time? Is there not a similar risk if we miss the signs of an opportunity for *peace*?"

His words had a powerful impact on me. One of the benefits of my job was that I could read the full inquiry report from the 1973 war, including the portions that had been kept classified. Some dealt with the political situation before the war. Golda had relied heavily on a kitchen cabinet of trusted ministers and close advisers. The inquiry described how Sadat had been extending negotiation feelers before the war. And how Golda, Eli Zeira, Dado, and Dayan had responded. It was like an exercise in collective reinforcement. They agreed the Arab countries would not simply go on living with the humiliation of their defeat in 1967. At some stage, they would move to regain the initiative, on the battlefield. But none appeared to think through the implications of this for our *political* approach. Perhaps, like Eli Zeira in 1967, they assumed a kind of historical inevitability of Israeli triumph. Though we'd ultimately prevailed in 1973, it was impossible not to wonder whether, as Shlomo suggested, we had missed the signs of a possible peace beforehand.

Now, however, we were facing an ever-growing challenge from an enemy with no interest in peace: the armed Palestinian groups. The Democratic Front took over a school in northern Israel a half year after the war, murdering twenty-five hostages, including twenty-two children, during an unsuccessful Sayeret Matkal attempt to free them. In March 1975, Fatah had seized the Savoy. And about a year into my posting in the kirya, the Popular Front for the Liberation of Palestine launched an even more audacious operation.

It became known by the name of the airport where the ordeal ended: Entebbe. And when it began I, like Uzi Yairi, was sitting at my desk in the kirya.

# Entebbe

SUNDAY IS AN ORDINARY WORKING DAY IN ISRAEL. THE FIRST SIGN that June 27, 1976, would be any different came shortly after noon. It was an urgent message from Lod Airport, now renamed in honor of David Ben-Gurion, who passed away after the 1973 war. Radio contact had been lost with Air France Flight 139 from Tel Aviv to Paris, shortly after a stop-over in Athens.

We couldn't know for sure what had gone wrong. But we did know there were roughly 300 passengers and a dozen crew on board. Many of the passengers were Israelis, and others were Jews from abroad. Ever since the Sabena hijacking four years earlier, whenever a civilian airliner was thought to be under attack within three hours of Israel, step one in our response to a suspected hijacking had been automatic. Sayeret Matkal was ordered to the airport.

As the unit assembled at Ben-Gurion, its current commander—Yoni Netanyahu, my former deputy—was hundreds of miles away in the Sinai, preparing for an operation across the canal. So it was Mookie Betzer, now Yoni's deputy, who began briefing the men for a possible hostage rescue. Motta was at a meeting outside the kirya, but his deputy—the head of the operations branch, Kuti Adam—buzzed me on the intercom at two in the afternoon and summoned me to his office.

By now, we knew the plane had been hijacked and it wasn't heading back to Israel. The terrorists had dubbed it "Arafat," and it was on its way to Libya. I took the stairs down to Kuti's office, two floors below mine, and he immediately handed me a large, black-and-white aerial photo. It showed the Libyan air force base in Benina, just outside Benghazi on the eastern edge of the country. "Can we do anything, Ehud?" he asked me. I didn't say no outright. But it took me barely a half hour to conclude it was impossible. In order to have any chance of success, we'd need to mount a pinpoint raid and take the terrorists by surprise. But Benghazi was a thousand miles away, and after consulting my team in operational intelligence, it was clear that the sum total of our knowledge about Benina was the Mossad photo Kuti had shown me.

Within a few hours, however, all that was academic. Later Sunday night, Flight 139 took off again. Before leaving Libya, the hijackers freed one of the passengers: a nurse, and a dual national with a British passport as well as her Israeli one. Deliberately making an incision in her stomach, she managed to convince them she was in labor and having a miscarriage. Once she was released, she revealed there were four hijackers: two Arabs and two Europeans. It was a PFLP operation but included members of the far-left West German Baader-Meinhof terror group. They now forced the pilot to head for the East African state of Uganda. On Monday afternoon, it landed at Entebbe Airport, twenty miles outside the Ugandan capital of Kampala and just a couple of hundred yards from the shore of Lake Victoria.

Increasingly alarming radio and television reports focused on the obvious agony of the hundreds of captive passengers. To this day, I've never been able to establish why it took almost another twenty-four hours before we started to seriously consider some way to free them. Prime Minister Rabin was clearly asking himself the same question, however. Initially inclined to leave the response to his defense minister—his longtime Labor colleague and rival, Shimon Peres—he intervened personally on Tuesday afternoon. Turning to his military aide, Rabin said it was now *fifty-three hours* into the hijacking. *What the hell were we doing* to try to come up with a plan? He called an emergency meeting of the government and summoned Motta back from a military exercise in the Negev to attend. When the meeting was over and the chief of staff was on his way back to the kirya, Kuti called me back down to his office. "Motta just told the government that there is a military option," he said with a wry smile. "That means we now have to find one."

I had just begun briefing a few of the analysts in my office when Motta arrived back at the kirya. When I got to his office, Kuti waved both of us across the hallway to the big rectangular conference room where general staff meetings were held. On the side of the room was a globe. Giving it a spin, he said, "*Nu*, Motta. Tell me, when you told the government we had a military option, did you even know where Entebbe *is*?" Motta didn't so much as crack a smile. "We have to find a response," he said. "I've committed us. Ehud, I want you to check what can be done. Take whatever you need, from wherever you want. Bring me suggestions by seven tomorrow morning." Then, he said, we would go brief Defense Minister Peres.

I assembled a team the same way we'd prepared for special operations missions in the sayeret: looking for information, intelligence, and above all experience and insight from whoever I thought was likely to make that always-narrow difference between failure and success. My first calls went to Mookie Betzer and another trusted and experienced sayeret comrade, Amiram Levin. Then I brought in Ido Ambar, the personal aide to air force commander Benny Peled, and Gadi Shefi, the commander of the Shayetet 13 SEALs. Finally, two officers from Dan Shomron's office. Since Dan was katzhar, in overall command of paratroop and infantry forces, it was critical to keep him in the picture. I told them we'd be working through the night, and that I had to tell Motta and Shimon by the morning whether we really could mount a rescue mission.

However daunting the obstacles—not least the fact that Entebbe was 5,000 miles from Israel, across the continent of Africa, *five times* farther away than Benina—I began by pointing out that the core challenge was straightforward. We had to get a commando team to Entebbe, surprise and kill the terrorists, rescue the passengers and crew, and get them out. At this stage, wrongly as it would turn out, we were assuming that whatever Ugandan troops or police might be nearby would not try to stop us. Uganda's increasingly tyrannical president, Idi Amin, had begun to align himself politically with the Palestinians in the past few years—one reason, no doubt, the terrorists had landed there. But he had actually been on a paratroop course in Israel before taking power in 1971. We had sent

Israeli officers on a series of visits to help train his army and air force in the early 1970s. In fact, Mookie himself had been part of one of the training missions.

We began by assuming we would fly the assault team and its equipment in, and the hostages out, on a single aircraft—one of our giant C-130 Hercules military transports. Ido Ambar, the air force aide, said there was no way its fuel capacity would last to Uganda and back. But he assured us that it would be enough to get to Entebbe and, assuming all went well, fly out for refueling in neighboring Kenya, a country with which we had a fairly good military and intelligence relationship. He'd brought a copy of the standard reference book on world airports, which gave us a general idea of the layout of Entebbe. He'd also contacted a reserve pilot who was part of the air force's training program for the Ugandans, and he was on his way to join us.

We talked through the best options for getting the sayeret commandos into the airport, focusing at first on nearby Lake Victoria. We quickly dismissed one idea: having them arrive by boat from across the border in Kenya. There seemed no realistic way to tackle the organization, training, and logistics required in time to make that work. The hijackers had set a deadline—noon on Thursday, July 1, now less than thirty-six hours away. Having moved the passengers off the plane to one of the terminal buildings, they were threatening to start killing them unless we freed fifty-three Palestinians and PLO supporters, forty of them held in Israel and the rest in a number of European countries, and paid a ransom of $5 million.

We considered parachuting a SEALs squad, along with rubber dinghies, onto the lake near Entebbe. While not shelving the idea altogether, we agreed we'd have to run at least a few training exercises, off the coast in Haifa, to determine whether it was really an option. It would turn out not to be, in part because we found out that the amphibious landing team would have to cope not just with the operational challenges, but very likely crocodiles as well.

The more we talked, the clearer it became that a C-130 landing on one of the airport runways, under cover of darkness, would give us by far the best chance of success. The decisive moment came when we focused on how to make sure we retained the element of surprise. For me, and Mookie too, the obvious solution was the one we'd used in Beirut and in our operation against the Sabena hijackers: disguise. In this case, we'd have the C-130 carry in "Ugandan army" Land Rovers. The final part of the plan came together with the arrival of the reserve air force officer who had been on training duty in Entebbe. He brought a reel of 8 mm film from an official ceremony at the airport. At the start, a Ugandan army general could be seen arriving in a black Mercedes. "That's it!" Mookie said. "The Mercedes. Every top Ugandan military officer has one." We decided to swap one of our Land Rovers for a jet-black limousine.

Motta and I went to meet Peres around 8:30 a.m. Shimon had no first-hand military experience, having played a political role alongside Ben-Gurion from Israel's early years, so he was not really interested in the details. But he *was* keen to hear our assurances that a military option did exist. He was even more intrigued when we were joined by the head of the air force, Benny Peled. Rather than using a single Hercules, Peled suggested, why not use four of the transport planes to ferry in a larger force, some 200 men in all, and take over the entire airport? Though I was skeptical, since an operation on that scale seemed to run the risk of sacrificing any chance of surprise, I didn't say so. At least so far, we had no reason to believe Ugandan forces were likely to oppose the sayeret operation, so there seemed no need to expand our plan for a targeted commando attack.

A few hours later, however, the scale of the challenge became abundantly, chillingly, clearer. In a haunting echo of the Nazis' "selection" process during the Holocaust, the terrorists separated out passengers with Israeli passports or Jewish names. They let the rest of them go and allowed them to board a special Air France flight back to Paris. We immediately sent Amiram Levin to debrief the freed passengers. On a scrambled teleprinter line Wednesday night, he came up with far more than we could have hoped for. One of the released passengers was a French woman who had managed to hide the fact she was Jewish. She confirmed reports we had been getting that the hostages were being held in the airport's former terminal building, about a mile from its newer terminal and the main runways. Another passenger revealed that the hijackers had placed explosives around the old terminal building. And that, despite my assumption that Amin would stand aside if we did decide to go in, Ugandan troops were active participants in the ordeal, standing guard over the hostages.

So in addition to taking on the hijackers, we'd have to find a way to deal with the Ugandans. The solution we settled on was an expanded hybrid of the initial plan: Peled's major airborne operation, but spearheaded by an initial landing of the Sayeret Matkal strike force, with its "Ugandan" motorcade. The other three C-130s would begin landing minutes after the initial assault to secure the rest of the airport, deal with any Ugandan army resistance, and help fly out the Israeli force and the hostages.

An operation on that scale naturally meant bringing in Dan Shomron. After I'd taken our final plan to Kuti Adam, he and Mookie briefed Dan, and the three of them, along with Motta, went to see Peres. It was a critical meeting. They did not tell the defense minister that, despite the fact we'd included Dan's aides in all of our planning meetings, his direct involvement had begun less than an hour earlier.

"Do you feel confident that this operation has a high chance of getting the hostages out?" Peres asked him.

"Yes," Dan said without hesitation. Motta was a bit less definitive. No doubt he was still smarting somewhat from Rabin's peremptory summons in the Negev; he also knew that, with Peres's own lack of a military background, his role in signing off on the operational details was especially important. He told Peres we'd still have to test key parts of the plan to be certain. Still, Dan's voice, as commander, mattered most. When he asked Peres whether he could start issuing the orders necessary to prepare for the attack, the defense minister replied. "Yes, you can."

On the way out, he made just one request of Kuti: he wanted me in command of the sayeret force. A few minutes later, Dan phoned me and told me to start putting things in motion.

+ + +

I could understand why Dan wanted me on board. We were about to embark on the most ambitious and difficult commando operation ever attempted. He and I had known each other for well over a decade, and we shared a bond not just of friendship but implicit trust. I'd been in charge of all of the initial preparation for the most critical part of Entebbe: the commando "convoy" that would spearhead the surprise rescue attack. As head of Sayeret Matkal, I'd also commanded the only other remotely similar rescue assault: on the hijacked Sabena jet four years earlier. But— and it was a huge *but*—I knew from the moment Dan phoned me that I would have to be careful to avoid undermining the *current* sayeret commander, Yoni. Dan had clearly been aware of that as well. He'd stressed to Kuti that he meant no disrespect to Yoni. "But I *know* Ehud," he said. "I've worked with him. I want him to lead it."

Yoni was still in the Sinai. I'd phoned him before our first overnight planning session to tell him I was bringing in Mookie and Amiram. Mookie had been giving him daily updates and now arranged for a light aircraft to bring him back to Tel Aviv. But the clock was ticking. Under the initial deadline, the hijackers had threatened to begin "executions" on Thursday. *Today.* The deadline had now been pushed back, but only until Sunday morning—and only after Rabin felt that he had no option but to drop Israel's public refusal to consider negotiating with them.

When Dan called our initial operational briefing for Thursday night, Yoni was on his way back. Dan set out the plan with his customary confidence. The four Hercules would take off on Saturday evening from Sharm el-Sheikh at the southernmost tip of the Sinai to cut the flying distance to Entebbe at least slightly. The first plane would land on the darkened runway, well off from the terminal area of the airport. Inside would be the sayeret strike force, numbering about two dozen men, the pair of Land Rovers, and the black Mercedes, as well as a small team of paratroopers who would place small directional lamps on the edges of the runway for the other transport planes. The next Hercules would arrive seven minutes later: the most critical minutes of the whole operation. That was when our "Ugandan motorcade" would make its way to the old terminal, burst in, and kill the terrorists. The second Hercules would include another Sayeret Matkal team to reinforce the attack unit and secure the perimeter of the old terminal. Hercules Number Three, a minute later, would carry a force to take over the new terminal and the rest of the airport and deal with any Ugandan army resistance. The final plane was a flying medical unit to provide treatment for the hostages and carry them out.

Yoni arrived just as Dan was finishing his presentation. He looked energized and eager to play his part. I realized it was important to explain to him the decision to place me in command. Despite our close relationship, I knew that would be a sensitive task. We spoke only briefly before he and Mookie drove back to the sayeret base to begin more detailed preparations. When I told him that Dan had put me in command, Yoni was insistent that he, as commander of Sayeret Matkal, should be in charge. I told him I understood, and I did. In his position, I would have felt exactly the same way. But Dan had made his decision. That was the reality. I emphasized my determination to do nothing to undercut his authority in the sayeret. Yoni would lead his men in the assault unit. He and Mookie would choose the other officers and soldiers, decide their roles, and take charge of training and logistics. I could tell he was still not satisfied. But I told him and Mookie I'd join them later that night. We could talk further, ahead of the next full briefing, which Dan had set for nine o'clock on Friday morning on the sayeret base.

When they left, I joined Motta and Kuti to go see Prime Minister Rabin. Peres was there too, along with Yitzhak Hofi, the head of the Mossad. Shimon would later say that, as defense minister, he was a crucial voice in pressing to go ahead with the rescue mission. He was right. If he had been skeptical, or opposed the idea of a rescue, it would have made things much more difficult. But his position was far easier than the prime minister's. If the operation failed, or if we decided in the end not to attempt it, it would be Rabin who would bear the responsibility and get most of the blame.

Even under the best of circumstances, Rabin was naturally cautious— part of the meticulousness with which he ran through the fine detail of every military mission. As I remembered from when he was chief of staff, in our slightly surreal conversation about the danger of a booby-trapped device exploding as I defused it, he would focus on everything that might conceivably go wrong with an operation before approving it. Now, he was under huge additional pressure. From the start of the hijacking crisis, there had been calls from the hostages' families to *do something* to end the ordeal. But as I later learned, one of the leading scientific engineers in Israel, Yosef Tulipman, had a daughter among the passengers. Like Yitzhak, he had been a Palmachnik. He had come to see the prime minister and implored him not to attempt an operation that might endanger her or the others. "I demand one thing only," he said. "Don't go on any adventures. Do not play with the lives of these people, with the life of my daughter."

After Entebbe, there would be suggestions that Rabin's readiness to negotiate with the terrorists had been a ploy, designed to buy time. Yet his message to us was that if there *were* a military option with a reasonable chance of success, he would approve it. Otherwise, we could not let dozens of hostages be murdered if by talking, even deal-making, we could have saved them.

After being briefed on the operation we were planning, however, he now told us that he was approving it. *In principle.* He said he still needed answers to two questions, and told Hofi, as Mossad chief, to take charge of getting them. The first was whether it was physically possible to cross from the new terminal area, where we'd be landing, to the old terminal building, where the hostages were being held. He was right to press us. If a retaining wall or a drainage trench had been added during the modernization work on the airport, any element of surprise could be lost. Rabin's second condition was that we find a way to make absolutely sure, by the time the first Hercules landed, that the hostages were still in the old terminal building. I knew why that troubled him, from a remark I'd heard him make a few years earlier when describing an American rescue raid behind enemy lines in North Vietnam. That operation went exactly as planned. Except that the POWs had been moved.

With the hijackers' deadline now just forty-eight hours away, I drove to see Yoni and Mookie at the sayeret base. We focused on the opening few minutes of the operation: the rolling out of the vehicles, the drive to the old terminal, and how to handle the possibility that we might meet Ugandan resistance. Mookie, from his experience on the training missing in Uganda, was adamant. "Their men aren't great fighters, at least at night," he said. Even if we did run into a group of Amin's troops, even if they were armed, even if they were pointing their guns at us, *even if they shouted at us to stop,* they "wouldn't dare open fire on a Mercedes." I trusted his experience. I kept emphasizing that, above all else, we had to retain the element of surprise. We had to go in with the mind-set of *not* engaging Ugandan troops unless there was no choice. If we had to, we would use only small, silenced pistols. But there *was* one threat we had to be aware of. "There will *definitely* be an armed presence in the control tower," I said. We needed to designate a special squad whose sole job would be to train machine guns, rifles, and grenade launchers on the tower. As soon as there was any shooting, the *moment* we lost the element of surprise, "they open fire on the tower."

The next morning, with more than 200 soldiers crowded into the old dining room near Sayeret Matkal headquarters, Dan began his first full, step-by-step briefing on the operation. Just as he was getting to the detail of the motorcade attack, I felt a young sayeret officer tap me on the shoulder. Kuti had phoned to say I was to go see him at the kirya. "He said immediately," the officer added, "and not to discuss it with anyone. Just to tell Dan Shomron that you've been taken out of the operation."

+ + +

To say I was surprised would be an understatement. But I allowed myself to believe the decision to "take me out" could still be reversed. Not only was I ready to command the critical first part of the operation: I believed I was best placed to ensure it succeeded. I felt that was probably best for the sayeret, and Yoni too, due to recent strains within the unit of which both of us were aware.

He had extraordinary strengths as a soldier: in the Six-Day War, in 1973, and afterward when, with my encouragement, he'd taken command of a tank battalion in the north left almost in tatters from the Yom Kippur War. But there was more to him as well. I used to marvel how at the end of sixteen hours of sayeret training, he could spend a further two or three hours reading history, or a novel or poetry. He always struggled between the impulse to devote his life to fighting for the State of Israel and to studying, reading, and living as a more "normal" family man.

His drive to serve, and to excel, was stronger. Tuti Goodman, the young woman he'd met as a teenager and married, understood what drew him to a life in uniform. But that wasn't what she had signed up for. At one point, Yoni asked me to speak to Tuti. Tuti asked me to speak to him. I did my best to explain each to the other. But the gap between what each of them wanted for their lives was too wide. Before the 1973 war, they'd separated. After the war, professionally fulfilled but personally shattered, Yoni heard that I'd found an apartment in Ramat Hasharon, and he asked me if there were other flats in the building. It turned out that the owner of the flat below ours was willing to sell it. Yoni snapped it up.

Over the past year or so, with Yoni leading the sayeret and me in the kirya, we'd seen more of each other. For the first time in years, he seemed to have found a sense of peace, and fulfillment, in his personal life. That was in large part because of Bruria Shaked, his girlfriend, whom he'd met a few years earlier. While Yoni was a thinker and a brooder and in many ways a loner, Bruria was outgoing, playful, funny, and full of life. She sensed *his* need for a shoulder to lean on, a hand to hold at the movies or on a Saturday stroll on the beach. They made their apartment a home. The shelves creaked under the weight of Yoni's books. Often on a Saturday, when Nava and I dropped in to see them, an old 33 rpm record would be playing on the stereo. Yoni would be sitting puffing on his pipe, reading and smiling.

But outside this domestic haven, he still struggled. He had looked forward to leading Sayeret Matkal. But within a few months of his assuming command, there were signs of tension between him and several of the senior officers. Part of this may have been just a matter of personality, a dissonance between these more typically Israeli youngsters and the aloof, reflective, intellectual side of their commander. But in other ways, it went deeper. A number of the officers felt that while Yoni was unflinching in honoring the unit's tradition of critical evaluation and accountability, he was less good about applying it to his own role. Several of them had even gone to Shlomo Gazit, the head of military intelligence, to urge a change in command. Yoni knew this. I tried to reassure him, telling him that every sayeret commander was different, with his own strengths and weaknesses, and I assumed that any tensions within the unit would pass. But we were now in the final countdown for Entebbe. It was a life-or-death mission not just for us but for the hostages, an operation in which even a second's hesitation or tension or uncertainty could prove fatal. I felt that with me in overall command, and Mookie and Yoni leading the assault team, any needless tension, pressure, or uneasiness would be reduced. We'd have a better chance of success.

When I tried to persuade Kuti to stick with the original plan, however, he was insistent. He told me to get ready to fly not into Uganda but to Nairobi instead, within two hours. I'd been reassigned to accompany a

Mossad team to Kenya. Our first task was to get the answers to the questions Rabin had asked. Then, we would be in charge of arranging for the Kenyans to allow us to refuel the C-130s on the way out, and set up a medical facility for any injured soldiers or hostages. During the attempted rescue, I would also be the channel of communications from the Nairobi side of the operation to Kuti, tens of thousands of feet above Entebbe in a command 707. Dan, as overall commander, would be on the ground.

+ + +

The Kenyans were not exactly allies of Israel. But relations between President Jomo Kenyatta's security services and the Mossad had been close for some years. I flew in with three top Mossad men. While one of them called on the aging Kenyatta, our main point of contact was the head of Kenya's security services. Since the secrecy of the mission had to be preserved, we couldn't make overt preparations for refueling the C-130s or the additional 707, which we intended to fly in as a field hospital. But he smoothed the way for us to do both, without anyone asking too many questions.

The Mossad men took the lead in getting Rabin's questions answered. They contacted a pilot they knew and had him fly to Entebbe early on Saturday morning, circle, and, after he was cleared to land, claim mechanical difficulties and fly out again. I had his telephoto pictures by midmorning and phoned Rabin's intelligence officer to let him know we'd confirmed there was a clear path to the old terminal. We still had to make sure the captive passengers were there, however. A woman from Kampala who had been allowed to visit them made three further visits: late Saturday afternoon, then shortly after the first Hercules had taken off from Sharm el-Sheikh, and finally around nine at night. As a result, we were able to reassure Rabin that the answer to his second question was also yes. Although all the C-130s were already airborne, it was only then that he gave the mission the final go-ahead.

As commander of Sayeret Matkal, I'd always found running an operation from a command post hugely frustrating. This was even worse. Once we got word the Israeli force was on the way to Uganda, we put in place the arrangements for refueling. If all went well, the first C-130, with Yoni's assault team and at least some of the hostages, was due to reach

Entebbe and begin the assault at midnight Saturday. Assuming there were no major problems, it would take an hour at most. All *I* could do now, from 300 miles away, was wait.

Around 1:00 a.m. on July 4, Kuti radioed me with a terse message: the first Hercules had left Entebbe for Nairobi, and the command plane was returning to Israel. About forty minutes later, the transport planes began their staggered arrival. When the first Hercules taxied to a halt, I went out to meet it. As its giant rear door lowered, Dan was the first person I saw. I could tell from the awkward silence, the lack of any greeting, something must have gone wrong. "Ehud," he said finally, as we embraced each other. "Yoni's dead. We got the hostages out. But Yoni was killed."

Shocked by the news, I replied, "It was a huge achievement, at a very heavy price." I then sought out two other friends: Mookie and Ephraim Sneh, the Battalion 890 doctor, who had been with us at the Chinese Farm. Both were obviously torn between a sense of accomplishment in having freed the hostages and the blow of losing Yoni. I asked Ephraim to take me to the front of the plane's huge belly to see him. He was on a stretcher, covered with a blanket. I peeled it back. Yoni's face had lost all color. But when I touched his forehead, it seemed slightly warm, almost as if there was still a spark of life inside him.

I couldn't raise Kuti by radio, so I used the landline in the airport director's office to phone Motta. I told him that all the terrorists had apparently been killed. Sadly, at least one of the hostages was as well, and several of them were wounded.

"And Yoni is dead," I said.

"Are you sure?" Motta asked.

I said, "Yes. I've seen him."

Before the transport planes began to leave for Israel, I made another call. It was to Nava. She was asleep. I told her that the operation to free the hostages had succeeded. "But Yoni has been killed." I could hear her gasp. "Listen," I said, "you have to go downstairs. Tell Bruria. Before some army officer shows up at her door. Or worse, because they're not married, no one may come and she'll hear it on the radio. Go. Tell her. Stay with her." At first, she seemed not so much unwilling as unable to do it. "What can I *say*?" I said I knew how hard it would be, but that she needed to make sure Bruria heard the news from a friend. Later, Nava told me she'd waited until daybreak, not wanting to make things worse by waking her. Then, she went downstairs. She told Bruria what had happened, stayed with her, talked with her, and held her during those first few awful hours.

There was a terrible arbitrariness about Yoni's death, as with so many other heroic commanders cut down as they rushed forward with their men. I knew that any one of the others could just as easily have perished—indeed, that I might have lost my life if my command role had not been passed to Yoni. Still, I found his death even more upsetting when I learned the details from Mookie and others. As the sayeret motorcade made its way from the Hercules to the terminal, with Mookie and Yoni in the Mercedes, two Ugandan soldiers had spotted them. One of the Ugandans raised his rifle. Though Mookie held his fire and urged Yoni to ignore the challenge, Yoni and another soldier fired with their silenced pistols. But they'd only wounded the Ugandan. In case he managed to fire back, another soldier in the second Land Rover killed him, with his *unsilenced* machine gun. Now that all surprise was gone, the commandos abandoned their vehicles and began sprinting toward the old terminal. Mookie was at the head of the first squad but had to halt for several seconds to replace his ammunition magazine, causing momentary confusion. Three other soldiers rushed past him, and with Mookie reloaded, the four of them rushed into the terminal. Yoni and his men were still some thirty yards away, and as he urged them forward, he was hit. He'd been shot from the control tower. From my own experience, I knew that unexpected setbacks or slip-ups were inevitable in any operation. But it was still painful to learn that the crucial first stage of the attack had gone wrong in a way so similar to what we'd anticipated in our first planning session at the sayeret base.

I had to remain in Kenya for a few more days. Though we'd rescued 102 passengers and crew, three of the hostages were killed in the crossfire. While most of the injuries to the others were minor, we arranged to have several of the more seriously wounded taken to a Nairobi hospital. So I was unable to join the gathering of hundreds on Mount Herzl in Jerusalem for Yoni's funeral. Or to hear Shimon Peres praise him in terms I knew must have filled his parents, and Bibi, too, with enormous pride. Shimon described him as "one of Israel's finest sons, one of its most courageous warriors, one of its most promising commanders."

The first evening I was back, I visited the Netanyahus at their family home in Jerusalem: Ben-Zion and Tzila, the parents; Ido, the youngest of the three children, who had also served in the sayeret; and Bibi, who had flown back from his studies at MIT. It was a few nights into the shivah, the seven-day period of mourning, and there were dozens of other well-wishers there as well. I spoke to Bibi first, outwardly strong but still obviously overwhelmed by their loss. Hugging him, I said the weeks ahead would be tough, not just because of Yoni's death, but because much of the responsibility of providing emotional support for his parents, both in their sixties, would fall on his twenty-six-year-old shoulders. This was the first time I'd met the father, Ben-Zion, face-to-face, but I was struck by how this balding, professorial figure seemed able to keep inside the pain and loss he must have felt. He did clearly know of me, both from Bibi and the letters Yoni regularly wrote to him at Cornell. Now, after I'd said what I could to comfort him, he asked whether we could meet again. When we did, a few days later, he was clearly conscious of his late, lost son's burgeoning place in Israel's pantheon of national heroes. He asked me to be one of the speakers at Yoni's *shloshim*, a commemorative event in Jerusalem that, in Jewish religious tradition, would mark the end of the first month of mourning. "You knew him well," he said.

I thought about what he wanted, and about Yoni himself, in the days ahead: the tragedy of his death, but also the way all of us now had to draw meaning, value, and ideally something of permanence from the feelings of loss. As I prepared my notes, I also worked out how to square what I felt I needed to say with what many in the audience, and certainly Ben-Zion and Bibi, would *expect* me to say. I did not want to say anything that might dilute or detract from the outpouring of praise for his sacrifice. I recognized Yoni's importance as a symbol of a commando success that, for the first time since the 1973 war, had restored a measure of Israeli self-confidence. A victory, over all logic and all odds. Yet I also wanted to capture Yoni as he really was: a brave man, an extraordinary fighter and officer, but also a man sometimes feeling torn inside, and alone.

I began with words of ancient rabbinic wisdom about the path all of us travel from birth to death, and to whatever comes after. The quotation I chose—from the 2,000-year-old volume known as *Pirkei Avot*, the Ethics of our Fathers—seemed right to me: "Know where you came from: a putrid drop. Know where you are going: to a place of dust, maggots, and worms. And know before whom you are destined to give your final account, the King of Kings." I spoke of the loss of Yoni, and said it was impossible not to think about the meaning of what lay between the "putrid drop" where each of us begins our life and our final reckoning. "I believe that life is not just a sum of the hours and days between the beginning and the end. It is the *content* we pour into the space in between," I said. I'd known people who were given the gift of a long life but who, by that definition, had hardly lived at all. There were also people like Yoni. He'd lived only briefly. But he had learned and loved, fought and trained others to fight, grappled with the most profound puzzles of existence, and yet remained open "to the wonders of a smile. A journey. A flower. A poem." If there was any consolation for a life cut off at age thirty, I said, that was it.

But I wanted to give a more personal, nuanced picture of the life that he, and we, had lost. "Our Yoni . . . We have seen him torn between his passion for knowledge on the one hand, and the sense of mission and of personal fulfillment that he found in uniform. There was the Yoni of history and philosophy books: Plato and Marx. Who saw the history of Israel not just as a compendium of facts, but a source of inspiration, and a call for action. The Yoni who rebuilt a tank battalion reduced to ashes and dust on the Golan. And there was the Yoni at peace. Tranquil. At home. With his pipe and his phonograph records, out of uniform. We saw him in his hours of supreme achievement and satisfaction. We saw him, too, sometimes standing alone, with pain in his heart, grinding his teeth, carrying the heavy, lonely burden of commanding the very fighters who he was leading when he fell.

"We have seen him on the battlefield, engaging the enemy, heading into a test of fire with courage and wisdom and his indomitable spirit—the very essence of the spirit that made possible the operation in which he would lose his life." Because, make no mistake, I said: beyond the weapons used, the people who participated, the training and exercises before the fleet of Hercules had taken off; beyond the fine balance required in the planning, execution, and decision making; it was "this spirit, this essence, that was tested at Entebbe."

When I saw the family afterward, though they thanked me for my remarks, I could see that they were still bleeding inside. I am sure that affected the way they related to Bruria. Even before Yoni met her, he had told me how hard his parents were finding his separation from Tuti. Bruria attended the funeral and the shloshim, but she didn't sit with the family. I think that with the shock of his death, mixed with the pride they felt at his emergence as a national hero, they found it difficult to include her, a woman they hardly knew, in their mourning.

A few weeks later, I got a call from the Netanyahu family's lawyer, Erwin Shimron. It was an odd, rambling conversation. He seemed to insinuate that, as her and Yoni's neighbor and friend, I was encouraging the unwelcome idea that Bruria was part of the immediate circle of the bereaved, that this mere girlfriend was somehow his widow. He wanted me to withdraw whatever mantle I might be providing and help separate her from Yoni and his legacy. He also mentioned wanting to tie up loose ends regarding their apartment, which was in Yoni's name. He even said that one reason he was calling me was because he didn't want to have to take "legal steps." I saw no point in getting into an argument. I sensed that, while it would take time for the grief felt by those closest to Yoni to begin to heal, the issue would gradually resolve itself. But I saw even less point in leading the lawyer to believe I would do what he was suggesting.

"Mr. Shimron," I told him. "I knew Yoni. I know Bruria. I do not know you. But I have a musical ear. I don't like the undertone I hear in what you've been saying. I've seen them close up. Bruria gave Yoni, at a critical time in his life, probably more warmth than he ever received from any other human being."

# The Earth Moves

DESPITE ENTEBBE, THE TRAUMA OF THE YOM KIPPUR WAR AND THE cracks it had shaken loose in Israeli society and politics were yet to play themselves out. The hostage rescue provided a sugar rush, an intoxicating reminder that the army still had the capacity for initiative and precision, audacity and quick-fire victory—like our air strikes in the first hours of the 1967 war. But the *real* reckoning over 1973 was about to come. It would change Israel beyond recognition, with repercussions still being felt today, and would dramatically alter the course of my life in the process.

On the evening of May 17, 1977, as Nava and I watched in our tiny living room in Ramat Hasharon, Chaim Yavin, the anchorman on the country's only TV channel, was handed an exit poll from Israel's latest national election. He began with three words: *Gvirotai verabotai, Mahapakh.* "Ladies and gentlemen, a revolution." For the first time since the state was declared, Israel's government would not be in the hands of David Ben-Gurion or his Labor Zionist heirs. Our next prime minister would be Menachem Begin, who had inherited the mantle of Jabotinsky's Revisionist Zionism. He'd headed its youth wing, Betar, in Eastern Europe, and led the Irgun Zvai Leumi, the main right-wing militia force before 1948. Lacking the intellectual depth and subtlety of Jabotinsky— a liberal intellectual who, among other things, translated Dante into Hebrew—Begin drew his political strength from his powerful oratory, and a refusal to countenance any compromise in securing what he viewed as the ultimate goal: a Jewish state in all of biblical Palestine, from the Mediterranean to the Jordan River and beyond, with whatever military force was necessary to secure and sustain it.

But perhaps Yavin should have used a different metaphor in his dramatic election-night broadcast: *reidat adamah*, an earthquake. Begin's victory, after the loss of eight straight elections over three decades, was the culmination of a series of seismic rumblings. The big, decisive shock was the 1973 war, and not just because of the colossal intelligence failure, or the myriad errors of our military commanders and political leaders. It was the fundamental loss of *trust* in the cozy, self-perpetuating establishment that had dominated Israeli politics, society, and culture from the start: Palmachniks like Rabin and Dado; political players like Golda and Shimon Peres; Haganah veterans like Dayan and Bar-Lev; and, of course, the kibbutznik pioneers. Almost all were of East European background— Ashkenazim—and their prominence and privilege had stoked increasing resentment among Israel's disadvantaged Sephardi majority, with their roots in the Arab world and especially North Africa.

While Menachem Begin had never lost the formal bearing—or the accent—from his childhood in Poland, his long years in Israel's political wilderness mirrored the wider exclusion felt by the Sephardim. The last election he had lost, in December 1973, proved too soon for the earth to part. But he told his supporters: "Even though Labor has won *these* elections, after something like the Yom Kippur War happens to a country, and to a government, they must lose power. They *will* lose power." He was right. Only twice in the four decades that followed would a Labor leader defeat Begin's Likud party: Rabin in 1992, and me, over Bibi Netanyahu, in 1999.

During the first two years of Begin's rule, however, I was 7,000 miles away. Ten days before the election, I'd gone to see Motta, and he agreed that I could return to Stanford to finish what I'd barely begun when the 1973 war broke out. I had been in the army, with the one hiatus as a sayeret reservist at Hebrew University, since the age of seventeen and a half. I did not regret that. But Stanford offered an opportunity to recharge my intellectual batteries and broaden my horizons. It engaged a different kind of intelligence, a different part of who I was: the books, the professors;

a chance to listen to, and at least try to play, beautiful music; and to spend more than a few stolen evenings or weekends with my family.

The timing had nothing to do with the election. Like most other Labor Israelis, and many of Begin's own supporters, I hadn't expected the Likud to win. Rather, I felt I'd reached a natural punctuation mark in my military career. I'd led Sayeret Matkal. I'd commanded a tank company, a battalion in 1973, and, more briefly than I'd hoped, the 401st Brigade after the war. I'd spent the last two years in the kirya. The next step up the command chain would be to lead a full armored division. But at age thirty-five, I was probably too young, and figured I'd have a far better chance in two years' time. I also feared losing the chance to go to Stanford altogether. Motta's term as chief of staff would end the following year. Among those in the frame to succeed him was Raful Eitan. Recalling Raful's dismissive, almost sneering, opposition to my making the Sayeret Matkal into Israel's SAS, I wasn't exactly confident I could count on his support.

I had particularly enjoyed the last year, having been promoted to Shai Tamari's job, in charge of the operations team, when Shai left to command a tank brigade. My office was now in the underground bunker, the bor, and I was part of nearly all high-level planning meetings, often with Motta, sometimes also including Peres. Almost everyone around the table was older than me and outranked me by some distance. Yet with my intelligence brief and my operational background, I was often the one with the most thorough command of the details. Though still just a colonel, I'd risen through Sayeret Matkal. So I was often asked to weigh in on what would work, what wouldn't, and why.

My final year in the kirya also further cemented my relationship with Motta. As chief of staff, he tended to keep a formal distance from all but a few of his fellow officers, but he did seem to enjoy having me around. He even put me in charge of a new department of my own. Not officially. The "department" was strictly ad hoc, as was the name Motta gave it: *Mishugas*. The Yiddish word for craziness.

All army commanders, in all countries, receive their share of unsolicited advice. But I can't imagine any of them gets the number, or sheer range, of wild suggestions that make their way to the kirya. Everything from levitation machines to ideas for making tanks fly. Motta didn't have the time to read all the letters, much less sit down with the self-styled inventors or sages who showed up in person. Still, he couldn't be sure that a jewel of an idea wasn't lurking inside one of them. As an insurance policy, he began sending all the letters, and every supplicant, to me.

The most vivid memory I have is of a visit from a former soldier in Shaked, Israel's Negev reconnaissance and tracking unit. He had taken up meditation and the study of ancient civilizations. Fresh from a period of contemplation in the desert, he arrived in my office with a pamphlet he'd written. It was about special forces strategy and training, as practiced *eight centuries* earlier, in the time of Genghis Khan.

I listened for nearly an hour, enjoying his enthusiasm, the history lesson, and the simple weirdness of it all. I did check his facts afterward. If nothing else, he proved an assiduous student of the Mongols. He explained to me that in their largest battles, involving tens of thousands of troops, they would designate a commando unit of up to a hundred or so men with the sole task of seeking out and killing the enemy's leader. The key to their success was what he called *mind*-training. Over a period of months, sometimes years, the commandos' *self-perception* was altered. They were taught to believe that they had already died. Since their lives on earth were done, all that remained was a formal passage through the turnstile into eternal happiness, and to go out in glory. My visitor suggested that Israel establish exactly this kind of death-cum-suicide unit. What's more, he would train the men himself and lead the first mission. With as straight a face as I could muster, I thanked him for taking the time to see me, but told him his idea was probably not for us.

+ + +

Nava and I, with three-year-old Yael and Michal just turning seven, left for California in the late summer of 1977. The two years that followed were uplifting and reinvigorating—not just because of Stanford, but a further, utterly unexpected transformation back home soon after we'd left.

It too had its roots in the 1973 war, but on the Arab side. Before the war, Egypt's Anwar Sadat had extended feelers about the possibility of peace negotiations, only to see them ignored. Israel won the war in the end. But the Egyptians' surprise attack across the canal—and the panic and huge Israeli losses in the early days of the war—had shattered our aura of invincibility. Politically, Sadat had gone a long way to erasing the humiliation of 1967. That freed him to do something that—after decades of Arab-Israeli conflict—was astonishing. He traveled to Jerusalem, the capital of a country that neither Egypt nor any other Arab country even recognized. He met Begin, and he addressed the Knesset with a call for peace.

It is impossible to convey to Israelis who did not live through the birth of the state and our tumultuous early decades the power of the emotions stirred by Sadat's visit. It was on November 19, 1977. With my arm around Nava, I watched the live American television coverage as Sadat's plane touched down at Ben-Gurion Airport. Begin was at the center of the throng of dignitaries on hand to greet him: a who's who of political and military leaders from his administration, and those who had led Israel in 1967 and 1973. Golda was there. Rabin, too, puffing furiously on his cigarette. When the erect figure of Sadat emerged, there was spontaneous applause and a serenade from Israeli army trumpeters.

Even before Sadat's Knesset address the next day, I understood that his visit, his willingness to make the first, bold move toward a possible peace, marked just the beginning of a difficult negotiating road. But there was one passage in his speech that touched me especially. He ran through the history of how Egypt and other Arab states had fought Israel and denied our right to exist as a state. "We used to brand you as *so-called* Israel," he said. Now, the leader of our most important Arab enemy declared, "You want to live with us in this part of the world. In all sincerity, I tell you that we welcome you among us, with full security and safety."

The formula he proposed was straightforward. Egypt would agree to a full peace, accepting and formally recognizing the State of Israel. But Israel would have to withdraw from all Arab land captured in 1967, including "Arab Jerusalem." We would also have to accept the "rights of the Palestinian people to self-determination, including their right to establish their own state."

Begin's reply was more sensitive than I'd expected from a leader who, through my Labor kibbutznik eyes, I'd always seen as an extremist, unwaveringly committed to a "greater Israel." Though he did make it clear his views on the shape of an eventual peace differed from Sadat's, he proposed further talks with the aim of finding an agreement both sides could live with. Still, like all Israelis, I knew he would never accept at least two of the Egyptian president's demands: a retreat from our control of a united Jerusalem or the creation of a Palestinian state on the West Bank of the Jordan: biblical Judaea and Samaria.

On our territorial dispute with Egypt, I did believe a deal was possible. I didn't expect us to return all of the Sinai, if only because I couldn't see Begin agreeing to it. For security reasons, I also felt we should try to hold on to a pair of air force bases built after 1967, with American help, just a few miles over the Negev border. But as for the rest, I saw no reason not to give it back. As I'd told Motta after the 1973 war, I'd long believed Israel had lost sight of the original reason we'd held on to the Sinai after 1967. It was supposed to be a huge, sandy security buffer. If we did manage to secure a lasting peace with Egypt, there was surely no reason to keep it.

The moment of truth came almost exactly ten months later in September 1978. American president Jimmy Carter hosted a summit with Begin and Sadat at Camp David, in search of a "framework agreement" for final negotiations on a peace treaty. Again, I watched closely, via American TV. But as the summit was winding down, our phone suddenly rang in Palo Alto.

"Ehud, how's it going? Are you following what's happening here? What do you think?"

I recognized the voice immediately: Ezer Weizman, the former fighter pilot Begin had chosen as his defense minister. I'd known Ezer since the early 1960s, when he'd been commander of the air force and Sayeret Matkal was planning its first operations. Still, even though he had a reputation for batting ideas back and forth outside the bounds of hierarchy or chain of command, I was startled to hear from him.

"What do I think about *what*?" I said.

"The solution we've arrived at here. We found there was no way but to give back everything." The only exception was Taba, a sliver of land where the Negev met the eastern edge of the Sinai, across from the Jordanian town of Aqaba.

"Was there no way to convince them, even with some kind of a land swap, to keep the two air bases?" I asked.

"Believe me, we wanted to," Ezer replied. "But no way. Not if we were going to get a peace treaty."

So I said the obvious: if that's what was necessary for peace, I understood.

We were now well into our final year at Stanford. Our home was in Escondito Village, a leafy residential facility off campus mainly for married students from abroad. Our two-story flat was one of a row of cabin-like structures: a bit like a kibbutz, only smaller, American-style, a lot more upmarket. It had a fenced-off play area for the children and, in a common room for all the village residents, an upright piano.

I found the richness of the academic environment—and the time to explore and savor it—enthralling. I'd chosen my master's program at Stanford because it offered the chance to learn across a range of different schools and disciplines. The official home for my degree courses was the School of Engineering, in a department called Engineering-Economic Systems. Its focus was on applying mathematical modeling and analysis to decision-making in "large and complex organizations" such as private companies or government departments. Or the armed forces of Israel. The theorists at Stanford were leaders in the field.

Immediately, I was drawn to other disciplines as well: business, economics, political science, history, sociology, psychology. I studied game theory at the business school, and the evolution of political systems under the sociologist Seymour Martin Lipset. I also went to lectures by James G. March, on how psychological, social, and other factors influenced decision-making. I particularly enjoyed learning from Professor Amos Tversky. Born in Haifa, he was half of an academic partnership with the Israeli psychologist Daniel Kahneman. They were investigating the effect of human bias and other subjective factors on how we perceive reality, and thus make decisions. Tversky's work especially fascinated me, because it questioned a basic assumption in the kind of predictive formulas my own department was advancing: that we make choices rationally, calculating the outcomes of competing alternatives. Tversky had found that the human brain didn't always work that way. For choices with a fairly obvious outcome—90 percent of cases, say—the assumption did hold. But at the margins, the brain didn't, or couldn't, always gauge the implications of a decision accurately. Years before it became widely accepted, he would go on to demonstrate that an individual's choice could vary significantly depending on the way the options were presented.

My home faculty's prevailing orthodoxy was that by using specifically designed interview techniques, alongside mathematical modeling of the predicted outcomes, we could isolate the effect of human agency on how, and what, decisions were made. The wider my studies ranged, and the more deeply I reflected on my own experiences, the more skeptical I became that the complexities of human decision making could be accommodated by such models. I also saw problems in the methodology we used. Since it was based partly on interviews with participants in the decision-making process, it seemed to me that this added a subjective bias into our ostensibly objective conclusions.

My department obviously didn't share my skepticism. But one of the things I most valued about my time in Stanford was that, far from discouraging my excursions into other departments, my professors combined a confidence in their own approach with a genuine open-mindedness to other ideas: the hallmark of true intellectuals, and of great universities.

As I completed my master's degree, it was impossible to be unaware of the new political and security context in which I'd be returning home, and to active service. While I was at Stanford, our negotiators and the Egyptians had been thrashing out the terms of a peace agreement. Sadat was being denounced as a traitor in the Arab world. Begin was seen by most in the outside world, and by many Israelis, as dragging his feet on the negotiations and risking the chance for peace altogether. If we *did* manage to sign a peace treaty, however, we would be withdrawing for the first time from land captured in 1967. That would mean finding a new approach to security in the south, as well as a new focus on the majority of our Arab neighbors who were railing against Sadat and seemed less interested than ever in making peace.

In some ways, it was hard to leave our mini-kibbutz in Palo Alto. Michal, now nearly nine, had thrived, quickly learning English and ending up with a perfectly American accent that has never left her. Yael has less vivid memories of our time there. But we'd had the nearest thing to a normal family life since our first, war-truncated time at Stanford. During the university holidays, we'd also traveled: to Canada, Mexico, Lake Tahoe, even Las Vegas, where, thankfully, we lacked the money to chance our luck, but where my years in the sayeret suddenly came in handy. We spent the day at Circus Circus, a joint casino and theme park tailored for families with kids. At a shooting gallery in the amusement area, I had no trouble landing dead-center hits on a passing procession of metal geese, to the consternation of the guy behind the counter but the delight of my two young daughters. In probably the single greatest moment of parental accomplishment I'd experienced since their birth, I bagged a huge fluffy teddy bear for each of them.

+ + +

I returned to Israel with the expectation that I would command one of Israel's two regular armored divisions: the 252nd, which was responsible for defending the south and, at least for now, was based in the Sinai. Dan Shomron was now head of the southern command and had told me before we headed back from California that he'd recommended me for the post. It was an especially exciting prospect because the US-backed negotiations with Egypt finally appeared to be nearing an agreement. As commander of the 252nd Division, I'd be coordinating and implementing Israel's Sinai withdrawal.

But I didn't get the job, at least not on my return. Raful Eitan had indeed succeeded Motta as chief of staff, and I'd evidently been right to assume I would figure no higher in his estimation than I had as sayeret commander. To be fair, however, he did agree to my becoming commander of Dan's *reserve* division in the south: the same 611th that Arik Sharon had led across the canal in 1973. When I took up that post in April 1979—just days after the formal Israeli-Egyptian peace treaty was signed—I was also promoted to one-star general. And eighteen months later, when the regular division post came open again, I got the nod to command the 252nd.

Even then, it was a close-run thing. Raful called me in to see him and said he wanted me to return to the kirya instead, in the one-star general's post inside military intelligence. He said he had more than enough candidates for division commander, but that my previous experience meant I was the best choice for the intelligence post. I was determined to remain in the field, especially with signs that Begin, and certainly his more right-wing supporters in the Likud, were already having second thoughts about the peace deal with Egypt. In part, they feared that a withdrawal from *any* of the land taken in the 1967 war might create a precedent and invite pressure for more withdrawals. But the real buyer's remorse centered on the fact that, as part of the initial agreement at Camp David, Begin had needed to accept a parallel framework for negotiations toward a broader peace that would include the West Bank and Gaza Palestinians.

In any case, with Raful balking a second time at giving me the division command, I figured I had little to lose by confronting him head-on. "Look, I realize that you're chief of staff," I told him. "But don't forget we're *both* just temporarily in whatever role we hold. I'm not here as a draftee. I'm in the army by choice. It's your decision to tell me what position you want me to take. But you can't *impose* anything. I can always leave. Or I can bide my time until *you* leave." He apparently concluded he couldn't actually force me to take the intelligence job. With Dan having made his preference clear, he didn't press the point.

My major twin responsibilities as commander of the 252nd were to make sure the division remained battle ready and to implement our withdrawal from the Sinai. Israel had committed itself to bring all of our forces behind the 1967 border within next two years, and along with Dan, I threw my energy into planning and implementing the terms of the treaty. But Begin was facing a reelection campaign against Labor, now led by Shimon Peres, and was keen to play to the opponents of any further negotiating concessions. He was positioning himself as the voice of military strength and painting Peres as someone who would risk our security by going further than the separate peace with Sadat.

Begin had no more experience or knowledge of military details than Shimon. But from his days in the pre-state Irgun, he'd been an unapologetic admirer of men of military action. After his victory in the 1977 election, he'd formed a government stocked with some of Israel's best-known former generals. Not just Ezer Weizman. He'd brought back Moshe Dayan, as foreign minister, and as agriculture minister, the country's most swashbucklingly self-confident, and controversial, battlefield commander: Arik Sharon. Begin had recently lost both Ezer and Dayan, who accused him of deliberately torpedoing chances of building on the peace with Egypt. But Arik was still there, foursquare behind a more forceful military posture on Israel's other fronts. He also had been a driving force in a plan to establish groups of new settlements throughout Judaea and Samaria, intended to encircle the main Arab towns and cities on the West Bank and foreclose any realistic prospect of a Palestinian state.

After Begin's second election victory in June 1981, some commentators, and many in Labor, insisted that he'd won because of a dramatic surprise air strike, a few weeks before election day, against a French-built nuclear reactor outside Baghdad. I never believed that, in part because I knew from intelligence friends that the attack had been set for earlier, and was pushed back because of fears the plan might become public. But mostly because of what I witnessed in the heart of Tel Aviv the night before the election, when I joined one of my top officers, a Likudnik, at Begin's final campaign rally.

Peres still had a narrow lead in the polls. I hadn't been at his closing rally the previous evening. But like the rest of Israel, I'd heard and read about it, in particular the warm-up act: a popular, solidly pro-Labor comedian and actor named Dudu Topaz. Greeting the crowd, he'd said what a pleasure it was that it was not full of *chachachim*—sneering Israeli slang for uncouth, uncultured Sephardim. In a single sentence, he'd managed to sum up everything the Sephardim resented about the Ashkenazi, Labor Zionist establishment. Begin, at his rally, played it like a virtuoso. "Did you *hear* what they called you?" he cried. *Chachachim*. He slightly mispronounced the word, as if he'd never heard, much less used, it before, and that even having to repeat it made his blood curdle. "Is *that* what you are?" There was pandemonium. Maybe Begin would have won anyway. It was close, just one Knesset seat between the two major parties. But win he did.

I became increasingly convinced in the weeks that followed that Begin's second government, with Arik now moved to defense minister, would further put the brakes on any follow-up negotiations for a deal with the Palestinians. I did not yet know that Arik, in particular, had a far more ambitious military plan to try to bury the possibility of a Palestinian state once and for all. But I did know he had his eyes on a possible thrust across our northern border into Lebanon, where Arafat and the PLO were based.

There was no public mention of any of this. But several times in 1981, I was ordered to move a large part of my division onto the Golan Heights for weeks at a time: two brigades, 200 tanks, and dozens of APCs in a massive motorcade from the bottom to the top of the country and back again. We dubbed it Cinerama, from the Hebrew words for Sinai and the Heights, *Ramah*. If there was an escalation of hostilities, the northern command's regular division would cross into Lebanon. Our role would be to take their place in defending the Golan, and possibly follow them in.

When I returned from my final episode of Cinerama in the late summer of 1981, the Sinai withdrawal was entering its final stage. I organized a major live-fire military exercise on the roughly one-third of the Egyptian desert we still held, knowing that we'd no longer have the room to do so after the final withdrawal. It was the largest exercise I'd ever commanded. The advances and tactical retreats, the flanking maneuvers and ambushes and fighter jet attacks were like a very big war in a very small place.

But a war game was not a real war. The Sinai was not like the Golan, or the cramped, hilly confines of Lebanon. And it was in Lebanon, the following year, that the next war came. It was different from any in Israel's history. Arik was in charge. And I became involved in ways that began to change the way I saw not only Arik, but the political and military direction of our country.

# Israel's Vietnam

My own part in the Lebanon War would change dramatically as a result of that last military exercise in the Sinai. Arik Sharon was now minister of defense, and he came for the final afternoon. From his experience as a frontline commander, he knew the dunes and wadis and sprawling expanses of sand as well as any general in Israel. Watching our enormous, intricately waged mini-war draw to its close, he made no effort to hide his enthusiasm for the kind of quick, assertive battlefield maneuvers he'd long championed. But more than that, two of his closest aides soon began sounding me out on my views about the long-term organization, force balance, and funding for the Israeli military. A few weeks later, Arik offered me a promotion: a return to the kirya, as a two-star general, to become head of planning for the armed forces.

I don't know why he chose me: the Sinai exercise perhaps, the fact he knew I'd studied "large and complex organizations" at Stanford, or maybe just the fact our paths had first crossed when I was in Sayeret Matkal. But even though it meant leaving my division command, especially tough since the final Sinai withdrawal was approaching, it was an offer I never contemplated turning down, and not just because of a second star on my uniform. Ever since the 1973 war, along with a few other senior officers including Dan Shomron, I had been making the case for a shift to more mobile and less vulnerable forces and weapons systems. I saw the new role as a chance to help encourage that critically important change.

There was just one hitch: all senior military assignments required the formal recommendation of the chief of staff, my old friend Raful Eitan. Raful managed to delay things for several weeks. At one point, with his familiar sardonic humor, he told Sharon: "OK, I'll agree to promote Barak," only to say the following day that he'd meant *Eitan* Barak—a very good commander, by the way, who had been one of my instructors in officers' school. Arik insisted, however, and the appointment went through.

My new posting came as momentum was building toward Arik's toweringly ambitious, ill-planned, and ultimately disastrous war in Lebanon. It followed on the heels of a major new crisis in our peace with Egypt. Only weeks before I gave up my Sinai command, an extremist Muslim officer shot and killed President Anwar Sadat at the annual Cairo military parade to mark the anniversary of the 1973 war.

Like many Israelis, I felt an almost familial sense of bereavement. Sadat was the first Arab leader to make peace with Israel. He seemed to *understand* us: people who were ready, willing, and able to fight, but who wanted above all to live unmolested and accepted by our neighbors. Yet for Begin and the Likud, I knew the assassination would cast the whole peace process into doubt. Sadat's successor, Vice President Hosni Mubarak, made it clear he would abide by the peace treaty, defusing calls on the Israeli right for us to cancel our final withdrawal from the Sinai. But after Sadat's killing, Begin and those around him seemed more determined than ever to hold the line against the wider peace negotiations agreed with President Carter and Sadat at Camp David. At Begin's insistence, Camp David had not proposed giving the Palestinians a state, but instead "autonomy" and a locally elected "self-governing authority." Yet that was defined as a transitional period. The elected Palestinians were to be included in negotiations for a yet-unspecified "final status" arrangement for the West Bank and Gaza. That, Begin feared, left the door ajar for something *more* than autonomy. Shutting that door, I soon discovered, was a big part of Arik's ornate reasoning for invading Lebanon.

My new job was a promotion, but I also had a personal reason for welcoming the move back to Tel Aviv. Ten days after Sadat's assassination, I had endured a frightening few days surrounding the birth of our third daughter, Anat. The crisis was another reminder that the demands of frontline command rested not just on my shoulders, but my family's. We had moved house again early in Nava's pregnancy, to the suburb of Ra'anana, about ten miles north of Tel Aviv and a few miles in from the coast. We bought one of a newly built row of small, semidetached townhouses that, best of all, had a backyard. It was tiny by American standards, but was still a place for the girls to play. Once again, however, I wasn't there when my daughter was born. I was rushing north as Nava went into labor.

The birth itself went smoothly. By the time I got to the hospital, both baby and mother seemed happy and healthy. A few days later, however, when they were back in the townhouse and I'd returned to my division, Nava felt suddenly, desperately unwell. I shudder to think what might have happened were it not for one of our new neighbors, who was a friend from my first military intelligence stint in the kirya. In almost paralyzing pain, Nava phoned him, and he rushed her to the hospital. It turned out that the doctor who delivered Anat had left part of the placenta inside. Once the mistake was discovered—as I was again speeding north—he went back in and rectified it. When I arrived, I was relieved, to put it mildly, to find Nava smiling bravely and on her way back to full health. Still, doctor friends of mine said that if the problem had not been diagnosed and addressed quickly, she could have suffered shock, serious infection, even death.

+ + +

In my new role, I was nominally accountable to both the defense minister and the chief of staff, but Arik made it clear to both me and Raful that he was boss. And though my official brief was longer-term planning, almost from day one the issue of Lebanon overshadowed all other issues. I knew, from Cinerama, that preparations for a possible military operation in Lebanon were under way. Yet from my first meeting with Arik and Raful, it became clear it was more than just a possibility. "Why the hell is Arafat still alive?" Arik snapped at us. When he'd been commander of Unit 101, he said, he'd *never* waited for the government to ask him to plan an operation. He'd plan it and go to the ministers for approval. When I told him I'd done just that when I was commander of the sayeret, only to be told Arafat was "not a target," Arik replied: well, he is *now*. The PLO leader's current residence was on the southern edge of Beirut.

To anyone looking from the outside, there was no pressing reason to expect a war. It is true that the potential for conflict was always there. The PLO had nearly 20,000 fighters in Lebanon and hundreds of rockets capable of reaching our northern towns and settlements. The Syrians were there, too. As part of an Arab League agreement in 1976 to quell two years of civil war between Lebanon's traditionally dominant Maronite Christians and an alliance of PLO and Lebanese Muslim forces, some 30,000 Syrian troops had been brought in as the core of a peacekeeping force. But in the summer of 1981, new US president Ronald Reagan's Mideast envoy, Undersecretary of State Philip Habib, had brokered a cease-fire to halt Palestinian Katyusha rocket fire into Israel. It was generally holding.

But fundamentally, Arik's war plan was not a response to the Katyushas. It was a way of using military force to achieve a political aim that she shared with Prime Minister Begin: stopping the Camp David peace process in its tracks and ensuring it did not go beyond the peace treaty with Egypt. Nor, like past Israeli governments, did Begin seem to feel constrained by a need to ensure at least some measure of support from key foreign allies, especially the United States. He had already ordered the bombing of Saddam Hussein's nuclear reactor, an action unarguably in Israel's vital security interest but also taken without informing the Americans beforehand. Shortly after I returned to the kirya, he provoked further anger in Washington by announcing the de facto annexation of the Golan—in effect "balancing" our Sinai withdrawal with a dramatic reassertion of Israeli control over other land captured in the 1967 war. Part of Arik's plan in Lebanon was to deliver an even more forceful riposte to any suggestion that we would give up control of the West Bank and Gaza.

Yet these political aims, which I gradually grasped in their full form through my discussions with Arik, were only part of the reason I was deeply uneasy about the plans for our Lebanon invasion. Having now spent more than two decades in the military, I recognized that the security challenge north of the border was real. I did not believe it was inherently wrong for Begin's government to order a preemptive military operation with the aim of ending it. My view, as an army officer, was that the decision on how, when, whether, and against whom to go to war was a matter for our elected government. But for that principle to work, I believed that government ministers had to have a clear understanding of the military action they were being asked to approve, and of its potential consequences. The more we geared up for an invasion, the less certain I became that Begin's cabinet understood the full implications of what we were planning to do.

Arik's original plan was codenamed Oranim: Hebrew for "pine trees." It involved pushing deep into Lebanon, all the way up to the strategically critical road that ran between Beirut and Damascus. We would link up in Beirut with the main Maronite Christian force, the Phalangists, whom we had been supporting and training for several years. When that plan was presented to Begin's cabinet at the end of 1981, however, a number of key ministers opposed it. Thus was born Arik's Plan B, so-called Little Pines. Its stated aim was a lot more modest. We would create a "security zone"—a twenty-five-mile-wide strip running north of the border with Lebanon.

I could see that Little Pines was a kind of fiction. All you had to do was take a map and draw in the twenty-five-mile line. In the areas nearer to the Mediterranean, in the western and central parts of the border area, it indeed covered territory controlled by armed PLO groups. But in the eastern sector, there were *Syrian* positions a mere six to eight miles up from the border, well inside the "security zone." Not much further north were two full Syrian divisions. That meant we'd be fighting not just the Palestinians, the ostensible aim of Little Pines; we would have to take on Syria too. As soon as *those* hostilities began, we would have to destroy radar and SAM sites in the Syrian-controlled Bekaa Valley further north into Lebanon. After the first costly days of the 1973 war in the Sinai, we were not about to enter a major conflict without ensuring air superiority. Unless the Syrians retreated or surrendered, the inevitable result would be a wider conflict, paving the way for Arik to go ahead with his original plan and push all the way to Beirut.

This wasn't mere supposition on my part. In early February 1982, working from detailed military maps of the area, we ran a simulation exercise based on Plan B. The result: Little Pines became Big Pines. A clash with the Syrians proved inevitable. Any idea of a quick, limited strike to establish a security zone was fantasy. A few days later, Raful chaired a wide-ranging discussion on Lebanon. Near the end of the session, I asked him directly whether government ministers were aware that our war plan "will inevitably lead to a clash with the Syrians." Raful hesitated for a second, but then answered briskly: "Yes."

Raful's assurance would turn out to be untrue. But my wider concern, as the weeks passed, was Arik's *political* plan, of which I was getting an ever-clearer idea from both him and his senior aides. It struck me as not just grand, but grandiose. Part of it was to obliterate Arafat and the PLO as a political force, if not by killing him then by forcing him and every one of his fighters from Lebanon, a country Arik wanted to place under the unchallenged control of the most prominent of the younger generation of Christian Phalangist politicians, Bashir Gemayel. All that would be challenging enough. But in Arik's eyes, this was only part of a complete reordering of our conflict with the Arabs. He expected *Gemayel's* Lebanon to openly align itself with Israel and expel all Syrian troops. As for the expelled Palestinians, they would go back to Jordan, where they would resume—and, this time, win—their civil war with King Hussein. The result, with Hussein deposed, would be a "Palestinian state" in Jordan, which would free Israel to retain open-ended, unchallenged control of the West Bank.

I could see how, on its face, it was an alluring scenario. Even the Labor party, fifteen years into Israel's occupation of the West Bank, was still speaking about a "Jordanian option" for an eventual political settlement with the Palestinians who lived there—though this meant a kind of confederation with Jordan under Hussein's rule. Very few Israelis began seriously to engage with the Palestinians' own separate identity or national aspirations until later in the 1980s—when I, too, would do so, amid the widespread Palestinian unrest known as the intifada. But even without a fully thought-out view on these issues, I was taken aback by Arik's almost godlike supposition that he could use fire and brimstone, or the modern military equivalent, to remake the Middle East. If only because it rested on a tacit assumption that the rest of the region, the outside world, and especially the Americans would sit by and let the whole drama play out as scripted, I simply could not see how he believed it would actually work.

There was also the matter of Arik's vision of a "new" Lebanon under Bashir Gemayel's Phalangists. Unlike the other generals in the kirya, I'd never actually met any of our "Lebanese Christian allies." Yet a few weeks after taking up my new post, I was invited to a lunchtime discussion with a group of Phalangist officers on a training course in Israel. They were obviously politically astute. They bandied around military vocabulary proficiently enough. But they were a bit like teenagers playing with guns: big on political rhetoric, yet full of machismo and too much aftershave. Hardly the kind of "army" I could see as a lynchpin in Arik's plan to redraw the geopolitical map of the Middle East.

+ + +

By June 1982, Arik's invasion was a war simply waiting for a trigger. On the evening of June 3, Palestinian terrorists shot and critically wounded Israel's ambassador in London, Shlomo Argov. Appalling though the attack was, it seemed unlikely to be viewed by the Reagan administration as a credible catalyst for a full-scale invasion. Habib's cease-fire terms did not include terror attacks like the one in London. It was meant to keep the PLO from firing across our northern border. Even to some Israelis, the attack on Ambassador Argov seemed more a rationale than a reason for war. But Begin summoned an emergency cabinet meeting the next day. Gideon Machanaimi, his adviser on terrorism, was someone I knew well. When the cabinet convened, he pointed out to the ministers that the London terrorists were from a fringe Palestinian group led by Abu Nidal. Far from being an ally of Arafat, he had been sentenced to death by Fatah. According to Gideon, Begin wasn't interested in the distinction. Even less so were the two leading military figures in attendance: Arik and Raful. They said all Palestinian terror was the responsibility of Arafat, and that now was the time to hit back hard. The cabinet was informed that our initial response would be limited: aerial and artillery bombardment of PLO targets in and around Beirut. Yet Raful told the cabinet that the Palestinians would almost certainly respond with shell and rocket fire into northern Israel. Then, he said, we could strike more forcefully. In other words, the invasion would begin.

It did. Dubbed Operation Peace for Galilee to convey the aim of protecting northern Israel from shell and rocket fire, it got under way at around 11:00 a.m. on Sunday, June 6. The publicly declared aim was *Little Pines*: the establishment of our twenty-five-mile security zone. Both Israelis and the Americans were led to believe it would be a relatively short operation aimed at destroying the PLO's military capacity in the border area. We also said that we wouldn't attack Syrian forces as long as they didn't attack us.

That last public pledge had particular relevance to my role on the ground. I was deputy commander of the largest of Israel's three invasion forces under Yanoush Ben-Gal, head of the northern command until shortly before the war. We had 30,000 troops and 600 tanks and were responsible for the "eastern sector"—from the edge of the Golan Heights north through the Bekaa Valley along Lebanon's border with Syria. At first, we deliberately stopped short of Syrian forces. We deployed our main reserve division about six miles across the border, below the first Syrian positions at the bottom of the Bekaa. From day one, our part of the invasion force began a pincer movement around the area of eastern Lebanon where large numbers of Syrian soldiers were based. Still within the twenty-five-mile line, we hoped, simply by being there, armed and ready, we could convince the Syrians to pull back their forces. My former Sinai division, the 252nd, came down from the Golan and started making its way up alongside the Syrian border. Our other units, further inland, also began pushing northward. But the Syrians stayed put.

For the first couple of days, we avoided a confrontation with them. Yet on June 8, day three of the war, the morphing of Little Pines into Big Pines began.

The two other Israeli invasion forces had crossed the border parallel to us, one pushing up through the steep hills and twisting valleys of central Lebanon, and the other along the Mediterranean coast. The central force was now ordered to mount an attack that would bring them within striking distance of the Beirut-Damascus road. The first skirmish came in the hilltop town of Jezzin, still barely within the twenty-five-mile zone. The Syrians had a commando force and tanks in the town. An Israeli battalion was ordered in, and it took Jezzin by the evening of June 8. But it came under assault from Syrian units with grenades, RPGs, and Saggers, as well as shell fire from a nearby ridge. Shortly before midnight, another unit of Israeli tanks and infantry passed through the central Lebanese village of Ayn Zhalta, to the north of Jezzin and beyond the twenty-five-mile line, and began to wind its way through a valley toward the Beirut-Damascus road. They waded into a Syrian ambush, and for hours found themselves in a fierce battle with Syrian units.

I don't believe Arik specifically planned to confront the Syrians in Jezzin and Ayn Zhalta. But he could not have doubted that, given the enormous scale and range of our invasion, a clash with Syrian forces *would* happen at some point. Now that it had, all that remained was for him to tell the cabinet that Israeli forces had come under Syrian fire and insist, as defense minister, that the imperative for our forces on the ground was to strike back.

On the afternoon of June 9, the fourth day of the war, we got the order to go on the offensive against the Syrians in the Bekaa. As our artillery pounded the southernmost SAM sites, nearly one hundred Israeli jets swarmed into the Bekaa Valley and attacked Syria's air defenses in eastern Lebanon. When a second wave screamed in an hour later, the Syrians sent up their Soviet-made MiGs to intercept them. Forty-one Syrian planes were shot down. Seventeen of the nineteen SAM batteries were destroyed by the end of the day. The other two were taken out the next morning, and another forty-three Syrian jets shot down.

There was no longer any pretense about our war aim: to fight our way through any resistance and reach the Beirut-Damascus road. But after the Bekaa air battle, and the most serious air losses for an Arab state since 1967, Yanoush and I knew that international pressure for a cease-fire would quickly escalate.

Aware we were racing against the clock, we began a coordinated push toward the Beirut-Damascus road. The left arm of our pincer was ordered to make its way toward a town called Joub Jannine. Though still some distance from the Damascus road, it was an important way station: Syrian headquarters on the western side of the Bekaa Valley. The eastern part of our pincer, the 252nd Division, advanced up the Bekaa alongside the Syrian border toward the town of Yanta, across from Joub Jannine.

But as it made its way there, we got word a cease-fire had been agreed. It was set for noon the next day, Friday, June 11. The main focus of our advance shifted to a crossroads a few miles east of Joub Jannine. It was a flat, open area surrounded by hills, codenamed the Tovlano Triangle on our maps. We knew we would meet some resistance. On the way up the valley, we'd seen signs of reinforcements from inside Syria. But we had overwhelming superiority in tanks, artillery, and infantry in the area, as well as full control of the air. In our command post, about five miles back from our frontline forces, Yanoush set in motion the plan for a pre-cease-fire advance to take the hills overlooking the Tovlano Triangle. It was still about eight miles short of the Beirut-Damascus road. But the idea was to establish a more secure defensive position by the time the truce took effect, and to put us in position to advance further if the cease-fire was delayed, or collapsed.

Shortly before sunset, Yanoush left by helicopter for a field commanders' meeting with Raful in northern Israel. That left me in charge, alongside Yanoush's de facto chief of staff, Amram Mitzna. A decorated veteran of 1967 and 1973 whom I knew well, Amram had the added distinction of being disliked by Raful almost as much as I was. Our main reserve division had been ordered to take control over the hills south of the Tovlano Triangle. One of its brigades, led by a former Sayeret Matkal soldier named Nachman Rifkind, was sent to take up a position immediately south of the triangle. Soon after nightfall, Rifkind radioed in that he was there and the area seemed clear of enemy forces. The divisional command post then ordered a second brigade to move toward the hills dominating the crossroads.

The first sign of trouble came around midnight. From our overall command post, we were listening in on all radio traffic and heard the second brigade report that it had come under fire while moving toward the crossroads. At first, we assumed it must be from the remnants of a retreating Syrian unit. But Rifkind, who had reported the area was clear, now said that *he* could see flashes of shell fire two or three miles to his north. Only the following morning did it become clear that he had not deployed immediately south of the triangle as planned. He had mistakenly halted at a hill about two miles short of there.

By the time Yanoush returned to the command post a little after midnight, we were facing another problem. The battalion nearest to the south of the triangle had spotted a dozen large vehicles armed with missiles a few hundred yards ahead. The missiles seemed to be pointed north, away from them. But the battalion commander was asking us for permission to open fire.

"Do not open fire," I was saying as Yanoush arrived. "I repeat: do *not* open fire." When Yanoush asked me what was going on, I told him the lead unit had reported unknown vehicles with missiles and wanted to know whether it could attack. "Tell them *yes*," Yanoush said. I looked first at him, then at Mitzna. "We can't," I said. "It's dark. The situation is confused. We don't know whose missiles these are. It doesn't make sense they'd be Syrian, just sitting there, pointed north. At least give it a few minutes." I think Yanoush would have grabbed the microphone and told the unit to fire had Amram not been there as well. Together, we convinced him to hold off. I ordered the brigade commander to get one of the battalion's APC crews to go out on foot and get as near as possible to the missiles. They returned nearly fifteen minutes later. They said they'd never seen this kind of missile vehicle, but that the soldiers manning them seemed to be speaking *Hebrew*. It turned out to be a new ground-to-ground missile, not yet formally in service, that had been sent into Lebanon without our knowledge by the northern command.

While that catastrophe was averted, worse lay ahead. Yanoush asked to be brought up to date on our progress in taking control of the area around the Tovlano Triangle. We briefed him on the situation as we understood it: Rifkind had reported the triangle was clear, but the second brigade had still not reached it. Yanoush tried to radio the divisional commanders. When he couldn't raise them, he ordered the brigade and battalion commanders to pick up their pace and move forward.

With Yanoush back and the advance resumed, I tried to grab at least a few hours' sleep. But around 3:45 a.m., a junior officer shook me awake. When I rejoined Yanoush and Amram, they told me the lead battalion—under Ira Ephron, one of Dan Shomron's best company commanders during the 1973 war—was in deep trouble. For reasons I've never been able to establish, his orders were not to take the hills south of the triangle as we'd planned, but to go through it to a point two miles or so north. Minutes after crossing the triangle, his tanks came under heavy fire. Hoping to escape, he kept going, only to find himself surrounded by a Syrian force near a village called Sultan Yacoub, nearly three miles north of Tovlano. It would be light soon, and his predicament could only get worse.

At dawn, he reported he was under heavy artillery, anti-tank missile, RPG, and close-range rifle fire. The only realistic hope was to retreat. We were unable to get air support, but the commander of our artillery force called in all available units, and they drew a kind of protective box of shell fire around Ira Ephron's men as they moved back. We sent our other reserve division toward the crossroads to provide support, and Amram went with them to coordinate the operation. But Ephron still had to fight his way out. It was fifteen minutes of hell. By the time he reached safety at around nine in the morning, he'd lost ten tanks and nearly twenty men, four of them during the final, frantic retreat. Five more were missing. The reserve division also found itself in a fierce firefight with the Syrians and lost eleven men.

We were now just three hours from the cease-fire. We advanced nearer to the Beirut-Damascus road. An hour before noon, our dedicated anti-tank unit destroyed twenty of Assad's top-tier tanks, Soviet-made T-72s. Under different circumstances, those successes might have been a cause for consolation. Yet it was hard to dwell on them given what had happened north of Tovlano. After the war, Sultan Yacoub created fertile ground for conspiracy theories, half truths, and finger-pointing. Clearly there had been many oversights and errors, though there was never a full and formal debriefing process to identify in detail what went wrong. I found it deeply frustrating that, unlike in 1973, I was now several steps removed from what was happening on the ground. But *everyone* involved had a part of the responsibility for the failures, including the overall commanders: me and Yanoush as well.

That weight felt even heavier because the tragedy occurred only hours before our own force's involvement in the Lebanon War was over.

+ + +

It was not, however, the end of the war. The cease-fire held only intermittently in the rest of Lebanon, barely at all in some areas. Freed from fighting in our sector, Yanoush, Amram, and I began spending time with units elsewhere. A couple of days after the cease-fire, I found myself alongside a pair of generals, Uri Simchoni and Yossi Ben-Hannan, south of Beirut. In front of us, troops from the Golani Brigade were completing their takeover of the Beirut airport. "You were right," I told Uri and Yossi. They had been in charge of the simulation exercise in the kirya and predicted how Arik's ostensibly more limited invasion plan would inevitably develop into Big Pines. Even as we were talking, another Israeli unit broke through to the Beirut-Damascus road. On the far side of Lebanon's capital city, they linked up with Bashir Gemayel's Phalangists.

I remember a mix of feelings at the time. First, amazement that through sheer determination and political maneuvering, Arik seemed to have pulled off his grand plan—or at least the Lebanon part of it. Yes, we'd ended up fighting a kind of half war against the Syrians that, though we'd won it, still left 30,000 of Assad's men in Lebanon. They showed no signs of leaving. Our main strategic threat north of the border was not, in fact, the Palestinians: Syria was in military control of Lebanon and, after the peace with Egypt, our most powerful adversary. And no matter what Big Pines might have achieved, it was clear to me that the Syrians would be free simply to replace the weaponry we'd destroyed; stung by the humiliation we'd inflicted on their air forces and air defenses, they would have every incentive to fight another day.

In Arik's mind, Bashir Gemayel would soon be in a position to fix that. But beyond my skepticism from having met some of Gemayel's boy officers in Tel Aviv, I couldn't see how that would work. I strained to imagine Gemayel daring to form what would amount to a formal alliance with Israel and ordering the Syrian troops to leave. And given what would be at stake strategically for Damascus, I certainly couldn't see the Phalangists being able to drive them out by force.

The more immediate, open question involved Arafat and the Palestinians. Our other two invasion forces had driven almost all the PLO fighters out of south Lebanon, if not without costs and casualties. Most of the Palestinians, however, had retreated north to their de facto capital, the southwestern neighborhoods of Beirut. The idea of a ground assault—street-to-street battles in an area packed with fighters, weapons, and tens of thousands of civilians—was obviously fraught with difficulty and risk. After the war, some of the officers around Beirut said Arik seemed to hope that the Phalangist militia would go into the overwhelmingly Muslim western side of Beirut. At one point, he even considered an Israeli attack. Fortunately, given the Phalangists' record of violence bordering on savagery during the Lebanese civil war, Bashir Gemayel wasn't willing to send them in. As for an Israeli assault, Begin's ministers weren't ready to sign off on it, and the Americans let it be known, repeatedly, that they were vehemently opposed to the idea.

Arik again turned to a fallback plan. He knew that Begin *did* share his determination to get Arafat and the PLO out of Lebanon. Even the

Americans were ready to support such an arrangement, assuming it could be negotiated and implemented in a way that would bring the fighting to an end. Whether by intent or political fortune, the mere prospect of Arik further expanding the invasion had the effect of persuading Washington to send Philip Habib back into the diplomatic fray. With no early sign, however, of Arafat agreeing to leave, Arik now steadily tightened what amounted to a siege on west Beirut. For seven weeks in July and August, our forces pounded the PLO-controlled neighborhoods from land, air, and sea; intermittently cut water and electricity supplies; and hoped that the accumulated pressure, and casualties, would force Arafat and his men to agree to Habib's terms for a wholesale evacuation.

By this point, I was spending most of my time in the kirya, with periodic visits north, sometimes with Arik or Raful, to our positions on the eastern, Phalangist-controlled side of Beirut. On several occasions, I helicoptered back with Habib or his deputy, Morris Draper. In one instance, I accompanied Draper into a meeting with Arik. In what I imagine had become a familiar, and frustrating, part of the US mediation mission, he pressed Arik to rein in our bombardments, arguing that we were in danger of ruining the chances of negotiating Arafat's departure. Arik argued straight back. His view was that unless the PLO felt squeezed into submission, they would stay put.

On that, I thought Arik was probably right. Other Israeli generals with far more experience, and weight, also seemed to agree—notably, Yitzhak Rabin. He was no longer in government, nor even in charge of Labor. But he had always had a soft spot for Arik, as did Sharon for him. With uneasiness, questions, and outright criticism of the siege building both internationally and inside Israel, Arik got Rabin to helicopter north with him to Beirut. Yitzhak spent six or seven hours there. His verdict on the siege, at least as reported in the Israeli press, was more than Arik could have hoped for. *Lehadek*, he said. "Tighten it." In the end, I'm convinced the siege did have a critical effect on getting the evacuation deal. But unleashing our single most relentless series of air attacks, on August 12, when the deal was basically done, seemed to many both perverse and excessive. Habib and President Reagan himself were furious. So were a lot of Begin's own ministers, with the result, unprecedented in Israeli military annals, that they formally removed Arik's authority to decide on future air force missions. That turned out not to matter, however, because August 12 effectively marked the end of the siege.

On the afternoon of Saturday, August 21, the first shipload of an eventual total of nearly 10,000 Palestinian fighters left Beirut harbor for Cyprus, and then for a variety of new host countries. On this score at least, Arik's grand design had proven beyond him: the Palestinians were not bound for Jordan. By far most of them headed for the PLO's new political base, the North African state of Tunisia. Arafat himself left on August 30.

Still, as the evacuation proceeded, another of Arik's central aims in Big Pines was also achieved. On August 23, the Lebanese parliament elected Bashir Gemayel as the country's new president.

+ + +

During the several weeks that followed, Arik and his inner circle in the kirya projected confidence. To the extent that he and Raful saw any cloud on the horizon, it was their concern about "several thousand" Palestinian fighters that they were certain had stayed on in Beirut. True, Bashir Gemayel hadn't been formally inaugurated as president, and there had been reports he was privately reassuring Lebanese Muslim leaders that he would be conciliatory once he took office, and would not consider a formal peace with Israel. He had also resisted Israeli efforts to get him to make an early, public show of friendship, like an official visit to meet Prime Minister Begin. Still, there was an undisguised hope that this was just a brief political hiatus, for appearance's sake, and that before long Lebanon would become the second Arab country to make peace with Israel. Not just peace, but something almost like an alliance.

Though I still looked through the eyes of an army officer, not a politician and certainly not an experienced diplomat, I had doubts this would happen. Simple logic suggested that, since Gemayel knew Israel had no realistic option of turning its back on him, his interests were best served by keeping his distance from us and trying to build bridges at home. But a huge explosion in Beirut on the early evening of September 14, nine days before his scheduled inauguration, suddenly made all this academic. I was at my desk on the third floor of the kirya, getting ready to go home, when the news broke: a bomb had gone off at the Phalangist Party

headquarters as Gemayel was beginning to address hundreds of his supporters. For a while, the reports from Beirut suggested he had survived
the blast, but shortly before eleven at night, the confirmation came: the
president-elect was dead.

Though no one claimed responsibility, there was no shortage of sus-
pects. During and since the civil war, Gemayel had at various times been
at odds with a whole array of enemies or rivals: Muslim militias, the PLO,
other Maronite factions, and, of course, the Syrians. But I think for all of
us, even Arik, the issue of who was behind the bombing was hardly the
most urgent concern. The immediate danger was a revival of the kind of
rampant, sectarian bloodletting Lebanon had endured during the civil
war. All sides were part of it. But especially at the height of the fighting,
in 1976, Gemayel's militia had been at the center of brutal attacks in which
at least several thousand Palestinian civilians were massacred.

The day after the assassination, I joined a half dozen other members
of the general staff and helicoptered up to the Lebanese capital. Arik, ignoring weeks of strong US pressure not to do so, had already ordered Israeli troops into west Beirut—not to fight, but to take control of key
junctions and vantage points and keep basic order. It was early afternoon
when we reached an Israeli command post in the largely Palestinian
southwest part of the city set up by Amos Yaron, a leading paratroop
commander whose division had landed by sea at the start of the invasion
and played a key part in the push north to the capital. At his side was
Amir Drori, the head of the northern command. They had established a
rooftop observation post just a few hundred yards in from where I had
landed with my Sayeret Matkal team a decade earlier for the Rue Verdun
operation. It overlooked a pair of densely populated Palestinian refugee
camps: Sabra and, a couple of hundred yards closer to us, Shatila.

Raful was with us, as were Moshe Levy, the deputy chief of staff, and
Uri Saguy, the head of the operations branch in the kirya. I listened rather
than spoke. All I could gather from the other generals' conversation was
that they were trying to figure out how to handle the Palestinian camps,
apparently concerned that in the confusion and instability after Gemayel's
assassination, whatever PLO fighters might remain there would rejoin
the battle. No one explicitly mentioned the idea of Israeli troops going in,
presumably because they realized that, far from helping ensure order, it

might well inflame things further. Even Raful, at least in my earshot, made no reference to the "several thousand" PLO fighters he and Arik still wanted out of Beirut. There was, however, a general agreement that the Phalangists had not been carrying their load of the fighting during the war. One comment stuck with me. I can't remember which general said it, only that everyone seemed to agree: "Why the hell do *we* have to do their fighting for them?"

It was not until the next morning back in Tel Aviv that the alarm bells rang for me, and by then it turned out to be too late. It was Friday, the eve of the Jewish New Year. Yet in the wake of Gemayel's assassination, the kirya was crowded. I heard the first rumors from a staff officer in military intelligence, though neither he nor anyone else I asked was sure if they were true. But it seemed the Phalangists had been allowed into Sabra and Shatila. And that they had begun killing people.

Even in retrospect, I can't honestly say that, in Arik's or Raful's place, I'd have been sufficiently wise not to have let the Phalangists enter the camps in the first place. If the decision was to send *someone* in, I certainly wouldn't have sent in Israeli troops. But unlike other Israeli generals, my firsthand knowledge of the Phalangists was limited to a single lunchtime encounter in Tel Aviv. My impression from that meeting was that they were overblown, postadolescent thugs, not murderers. I did, of course, know the militia's reputation for untrammeled violence in the Lebanese civil war. Still, I might conceivably have agreed to have the Phalangists go in—under strict orders to limit themselves to keeping order—knowing that our own troops were stationed in the area immediately around the camps.

Yet from the moment of the first rumors—as soon as I heard even the *hint* that killings were under way—I had not a second's doubt about what had to happen next: get the Phalangists out. Immediately. I tried to reach Arik but couldn't get through to him. Then I called Tsila Drori, Amir Drori's wife. I asked whether she'd spoken to him that morning. She said no. He'd called her the day before, however, and she was sure he'd be in touch before the New Year. "Please, swear to me, Tsila, you'll give him a message," I said. "I was there yesterday. Tell him *please* do whatever he can to stop this action. It will end very, very badly." I told her he would know what I meant.

It was too late to stop it altogether. The slaughter—the roundups and the beatings and the killings of Palestinians in the two camps—had indeed begun the night before. I'm not certain what could have been done at that stage to get them out. But the atrocities went on. It would be another twenty hours before the Phalangists finally withdrew.

One night's massacre would have been enough to produce the outcry that resulted once the first news reports, photos, and TV video were sent around the world. That the bloodletting continued, after we basically knew what was going on, made it even worse. In Israel, the response was unlike anything ever seen. There had been some opposition to the war: from parts of Labor, from political groups further to the left, and particularly the pressure group Peace Now, formed in 1978 to protest the Begin government's obvious desire to use the peace with Egypt as a means to limit, rather than actively explore, prospects for a wider agreement with the Palestinians.

After Sabra and Shatila, Peace Now was the driving force behind demands for an inquiry into the Israeli role in what had happened in the camps. But the trauma went deeper. Israelis of all political stripes jammed shoulder-to-shoulder into the Kings of Israel Square in the heart of Tel Aviv a week after the massacre. The crowd included soldiers, twenty-somethings back from the fighting, and reservists a decade or more older. The protest was nominally aimed at forcing the government to empower a commission of inquiry, which it did a couple of days later. But the mood in the square was more like an outpouring of shock and shame. While the catalyst was the massacre in the camps, it tapped into a rumble of growing questions and doubts about the war itself, which had been building ever since the prolonged siege of west Beirut: what the invasion was for, how it had been planned and prosecuted, and what it said about our country, our government, and our armed forces.

I was at home with Nava watching the coverage of the demonstration on television. I shared the protesters' view that an inquiry was needed. In the days since my phone call to Tsila Drori, I'd remained troubled not just by our failure to stop the killings, but by the response from Begin, Arik, and some other ministers to the massacre. Determined to shift the blame and responsibility elsewhere, they kept driving home the point that it was Phalangists, not Israelis, who had carried out the killings. That was true.

But it could not erase the failures of judgment and control on our part. We were the ones who had allowed them into the camps. Our forces were deployed around the perimeter. And the killers were our "Lebanese Christian allies."

The formal picking-apart of Israel's share of responsibility would be the job of the inquiry commission. I took some heart that such large numbers of Israelis, and ultimately the government, had ensured a truly independent probe would now go ahead.

But other ways in which the war had gone wrong were already glaringly apparent. Some were operational. It is true we ended up overcoming Palestinian and Syrian resistance. Given the numerical balance of forces, that was a foregone conclusion. But with all the attention paid to the *political* aims of the invasion, we'd never sufficiently planned for operating against a wholly different kind of enemy than in our previous wars, and on a wholly different kind of terrain. Huge columns of Israeli armor had found themselves stuck on the winding roads of central Lebanon, running low on diesel fuel, vulnerable to relatively small ambush squads. In some instances, a dozen Palestinian fighters or Syrian commandos had halted the best-armed, best-trained tank forces in the Middle East for hours on end. Overall, the pattern of past wars had been broken. Even in 1973, once the surprise attacks had been turned back, Israeli forces had advanced, attacked, and, within days, broken enemy resistance. That hadn't happened here.

There was a deeper problem too. At the start of the conflict, Begin had declared, boastfully almost, that this was Israel's first "war of choice." That wasn't true. Both 1956 and 1967 were wars of choice. Yet those preemptive attacks, especially in the Six-Day War, were in response to a sense of strategic threat that was commonly understood by almost all Israelis. There was a sense not just of consensus, but national unity. This war *was* different. It had been launched in pursuit of a specific political vision: a marriage of Begin's political credo and Arik's determination to use overwhelming force to bulldoze a new political reality in Lebanon and the wider Middle East.

The findings of the inquiry commission were published in February 1983. They were all the more powerful for the forensic language used. The inquiry did concede Begin's point: it was Gemayel's men who had actually done the killing. But it said that the Israeli decision to allow the Phalangists into the refugee camps "was taken without consideration of the danger—which the makers and executors of the decision were obligated to foresee as probable—that the Phalangists would commit massacres." The commission added that "when the reports began to arrive about the actions of the Phalangists in the camps, no proper heed was taken. The correct conclusions were not drawn. No energetic and immediate action was taken to restrain the Phalangists and put a stop to their actions."

Arik bore personal responsibility for this, the report said. So did Raful, and the head of military intelligence, Yehoshua Saguy. The commission recommended that Begin fire Sharon and Saguy. They left Raful in place, but only because his term as chief of staff was due to end in a matter of weeks. Arik at first refused to go, and Begin refused to fire him. Yet in the end, popular pressure forced the issue. When another demonstration was called in protest at Sharon's continuing as defense minister, a right-wing political activist tossed a grenade into the crowd, killing a young member of the Peace Now movement. Even Arik was evidently shaken by the specter of one of his presumed political admirers murdering a fellow Israeli for peacefully protesting. Or at least shaken enough to step down as defense minister. He did remain in the government as a minister without portfolio. Begin himself would quit as prime minister and retire into virtual seclusion about half a year later.

Like the rest of the senior officer corps, I tried with difficulty to get on with my own job. I imagined the contribution I could best make for now would be, as head of planning, to ensure the mix of forces and weaponry deployed in any future conflict were better suited to the task than in the Lebanon War. But I didn't believe that such technical failings or planning lapses, however seriously they contributed to the more than 650 Israeli lives lost, were what had mainly caused the war to go wrong. The central mistake was what had bothered me all along: the invasion was not a considered response to a particular security threat. It was an overreaching exercise in geopolitics, with sleight of hand used to evade the need to make and win support from government ministers and, critically, the public. Even with questions still to be resolved about when and how to withdraw the thousands of Israeli troops that were still inside Lebanon, I remember wondering aloud to a few army friends, and to

Nava as well, whether we would look back in a decade's time and see the war as "our Vietnam." In fact, Israeli troops would still be in south Lebanon nearly *two* decades later, after I had left the military and was about to become Israeli prime minister.

Even as a two-star general in the kirya, I doubted I would be in a position to help fix the deeper issues raised by the war. Any real influence would be in positions like the chief of staff and his deputy; the head of operations; the head of military intelligence. They were the core of the armed forces' leadership and had the most regular dealings with senior figures in government.

But I'd failed to factor in the effect of the inquiry recommendations. Within days of the report, Israel had a new defense minister: Moshe Arens, who returned from his post as ambassador in Washington. Among *his* first orders of business was to act on the inquiry's verdict on Raful and Yehoshua Saguy. As chief of staff, Arens settled on a choice I suspect most senior officers saw as the right man for the moment: Raful's deputy, Moshe Levy. Well over six feet tall, he was known as *Moshe Vechetzi*: "Moshe and a Half." He was reserved and soft-spoken, a safe pair of hands after the trauma of the war.

But Arens also had to name a successor to Saguy as head of military intelligence. And for that job, he nominated me.

# Chain of Command

I WAS SUDDENLY IN CHARGE OF AN INTELLIGENCE APPARATUS RANG-
ing from Unit 8200, our sophisticated signals collection and decryption
unit, to the operational unit: Sayeret Matkal. At stake was success or failure in war, and the life or death of thousands of men on the battlefield.
We'd paid the price of intelligence failures painfully in 1973, and again
in Lebanon.

Conveniently placed on my new office wall were the photographs of
my nine predecessors since 1948 as head of the intelligence directorate, or
Rosh Aman in Hebrew. All had come to the role with talent and dedication. All but three had either left under a shadow or been fired. Sometimes this was because of ultimately nonfatal lapses, like a botched
mobilization of our reserves in 1959, or the Rotem crisis a few months
later. Sometimes, it was lethal failures, like the Yom Kippur War and
Lebanon.

I went to see all seven former directors who were still alive. "You know,
I used to read the newspapers and listen to the BBC in the car to work,"
Shlomo Gazit told me. He was the director I'd worked for in operational
intelligence, the one who'd so memorably made the point that we might
endanger Israeli security by missing not only the signs of a war, but an
opportunity for peace. He was also one of the few to have left office without a blemish. "By the time I got to the kirya, I already knew 80 percent of
what I could about what was going on," he said. "Then I'd spend six or

seven hours reading intelligence material, to fill in at least *part* of the remaining 20 percent." His message, echoed by my other predecessors, was that the job wasn't mainly about the raw information. It was what you *concluded* from the information, what you *did* with it. It was about judgment.

The intelligence did matter, of course. For all of Israel's strengths in that area, I knew from my own experience at Sultan Yacoub that there was room to get more, better, and timelier information about our enemies, and make sure it got to the commanders and field units that needed it. While the details of many operations I approved as military intelligence chief remain classified, we did succeed in doing that.

Above all, I set out to apply the lessons of the 1973 and 1982 wars. The intelligence failings had been different in each. In the Yom Kippur War, the problem was not only Eli Zeira's failure to activate the "special sources" in Egypt, deeply damaging though that had been. It was, indeed, also *judgment*. Inside Aman, a kind of groupthink had taken hold, rooted in a confident, costly misconception that went unchallenged. It was that Egypt would never risk another war without an air force capable of breaching our defenses and striking towns and cities deep inside Israel. No one pressed the alternative scenario: that Sadat might strike with the full force of his military to achieve more limited territorial objectives and, under cover of his SAM batteries on the other side of the Suez Canal, advance into the Sinai.

In the Lebanon War, the inquiry suggested, Yehoshua Saguy *did* try to warn the generals, and the government, about major risks. But individual ministers testified that they hadn't heard, hadn't been there, or hadn't understood, leading the inquiry to stress the responsibility of a Rosh Aman to ensure not just that his message was conveyed, but that it was received as well.

I set out to address both problems. I insisted on making all preconceptions within the department open to challenge. I strengthened the role of a unit whose sole function was to play devil's advocate when a consensus was reached. It began with the opposite conclusion and, through a competing analysis of the data and logical argument, tried to prove it. I also wanted to be challenged on *my* preconceptions. I assigned a bright young major as my personal intelligence-and-analysis aide. He read everything that crossed my desk and could access any material in the department. "You have no responsibility to agree with any of the analysts, or with me," I said. "Part of your job is to *dis*agree."

In the Lebanon War, Saguy had been excluded from some government meetings at which crucial decisions were made. That was out of his control. I didn't want it to be out of mine. I raised the issue with Begin in our first meeting. "If you want to get the maximum value from your head of intelligence," I said, "you should make sure he's there not just after, but *when* decisions are made." But he was now only months from leaving office, exhausted by the war and its aftermath. He waved his hand weakly in response, as if to say none of it mattered. His successor, in October 1983, was Foreign Minister Yitzhak Shamir. Ideologically, he was cut from the same cloth: an advocate from the 1940s of securing a Jewish state in all of Palestine, by whatever force necessary. He'd broken with Begin's pre-state Irgun militia to set up a group called Lehi, which went further and carried out political assassinations: the 1944 killing of Lord Moyne, Britain's minister for Middle East affairs, and four years later the United Nations envoy, Count Folke Bernadotte.

"Why are you so *strident*," Shamir asked me, only half-jokingly, after I'd insisted on joining a government discussion and pressing several intelligence matters. "It's because I've read the Lebanon inquiry," I replied. "I saw what happened when a message isn't delivered assertively. I'm not going to be in the position of making the same mistakes." He nodded, and didn't raise it again.

In fact, it was under Shamir that I began to get more involved with political and policy issues beyond the armed forces. Part of this came with the job of Rosh Aman. There was hardly a major domestic or foreign challenge that did not have some security component, and no security matter in which intelligence was not critical. I also found myself working more closely with leading politicians: mainly Shamir and Misha Arens, who as defense minister was my main point of contact. Since I came from a Labor kibbutz, we made an odd threesome. Arens was also a lifelong Jabotinsky Zionist. He had been in the movement's Betar youth organization in America before going to Palestine in 1948 and joining the Irgun. It was with Misha's personal backing that one of my former Sayeret Matkal officers—the son of a Jabotinsky acolyte—had recently taken his first steps into the political limelight: after a two-year stint as Israel's number two diplomat in Washington, Bibi Netanyahu had become our ambassador to the United Nations.

I built a solid relationship with both Arens and Shamir, and it would deepen further when I moved on to a wider role in the kirya a few years later. They were straight talkers. While resolute about decisions once they'd taken them, they were genuinely open to discussion and debate. I also sometimes found a surprising degree of nuance behind their tough exteriors.

The toughness was there, however. One of the first major security crises we faced after Shamir became prime minister was known as the Kav 300 affair, named for the bus route between the southern port city of Ashdod and Tel Aviv. On the evening of April 12, 1984, four Palestinians from Gaza boarded the bus and hijacked it back toward the border with Egypt. They told the passengers they were armed with knives, as well as a suitcase containing unexploded anti-tank shells. After a high-speed chase, an Israeli army unit managed to shoot out the tires and disable the vehicle about ten miles short of Gaza. One of the passengers had been severely injured at the start. A number of others managed to escape when the bus was stopped. But several dozen remained inside.

I was in Europe at the time, on one of my periodic trips to discuss Middle East issues with a fellow intelligence chief. When an aide called me with the news, I knew there was every possibility Sayeret Matkal might be called in, and my instincts told me we should proceed with caution. The situation we were facing felt nothing like Sabena, much less Entebbe. Here, we had a single bus. Our troops, and in fact everyone from ministers and officials to reporters and photographers, were in a loose cordon a couple of dozen yards away. That said to me there was no sense that the hijackers posed an immediate danger. Nor did they seem to have come equipped for a major confrontation. In place of the AK-47s and grenades we'd seen in previous terror attacks, these guys had knives and, if they were to be believed, a couple of shells with no obvious way to detonate them.

I phoned a friend in the command post set up near the stranded bus.

He told me that both Misha Arens and Moshe Vechetzi, the chief of staff, were there. There was a standoff with the terrorists and, for now, it was quiet. The defense minister and the chief of staff, of course, did not need my presence, much less my agreement, to order the sayeret into action. But I said, why not wait? Though the last flights back to Israel had already left, I could be at the command post by midmorning. Beyond wanting to be present if the sayeret was ordered in, I believed the crisis might even be brought to an end without another shot being fired. "I'll tell them what you said," my friend replied. "But I doubt it'll be allowed to drag on much past daybreak."

He was right. With my Chinese Farm comrade Yitzhik Mordechai in overall command, Sayeret Matkal stormed the bus at about seven in the morning. They shot and killed two of the hijackers immediately, through the vehicle's windows. Sadly one of the passengers, a young woman soldier, died in the assault, but the rest of the hostages were freed, none with serious injuries.

A controversy soon erupted over what came next. The sayeret commandos had captured the other two terrorists alive and uninjured. Yet barely a week later, first in an American newspaper and then the Israeli media, reports emerged that the two surviving Palestinians had been killed after the hijacking was over. A year later, Yitzhik Mordechai was—wrongly—put on trial for his alleged part in what had amounted to a summary execution. And, rightly, exonerated. Though the full details never became public, the people responsible turned out to be from the Shin Bet, our equivalent of the FBI.

Weeks later, Misha Arens mentioned Kav 300 in one of our regular meetings. It was not so much a statement of what should or shouldn't have happened, but a show of genuine puzzlement. "How can it be," he asked, "when there is a real fight, an operation in which our soldiers are shooting, that terrorists come out *alive*?" The answer, to me, was simple: the norms that governed Sayeret Matkal. From our earliest days, there was an understanding that you used whatever force necessary in order to make an operation successful, including a readiness to kill without hesitation if you had to. Yet once the aim had been achieved—in this case, eliminating the danger to the passengers—it was over. I am convinced that Misha wouldn't have contemplated actually ordering the sayeret, or any Israeli army unit, to kill all the terrorists, even at a point when they no longer posed a risk. I'm equally convinced there was a tacit assumption on the ground that Misha's view, and Shamir's as well, was that if that happened, it would be no bad thing. Nor were they alone in feeling that way. At least some senior officers seemed similarly minded.

+ + +

By the summer of 1984, Shamir and Arens appeared in danger of losing their jobs. Israel's next election, the first since the Lebanon War, was due in July. Just as the trauma of the 1973 war had helped Begin end Likud's three decades in opposition, the polls and the pundits were now suggesting that Shimon Peres might bring Labor back to power. There was no prospect he'd win an outright majority in the 120-seat Knesset. Nor would the Likud do so. No one ever had, not even Ben-Gurion in his political heyday. From 1948, Israel's political landscape had been populated by at least a dozen or so parties, mostly a reflection of the various Zionist and religious groups before the state was established. The dominant party always needed to make deals with some of the smaller ones to get the required sixty-one-vote parliamentary majority and form a government.

But the Likud's position as the largest Knesset party now looked vulnerable. It was partly domestic concerns that were eroding its support. Under Begin's turbocharged version of Milton Friedman economics, an economic boom had given way to runaway inflation and a stock market crash. Lebanon, however, was the main issue, and it remained a running political sore. Bashir Gemayel's brother, Amin Gemayel, had become president. But Israel still had large numbers of troops there. And while most of the PLO fighters had gone, we faced a new and potentially even more intractable enemy in the south of the country. When our invasion began, the area's historically disadvantaged Shi'ite Muslim majority had been the one group besides the Christians that might benefit. The PLO rocket and artillery bases had disrupted their lives and, worse, placed them in the line of our retaliatory fire. Some of the Shi'ite villages in the south even greeted our invading units with their traditional welcome, showering them with perfumed grains of rice. But for a new Shi'ite militia calling itself Hizbollah—formed after the invasion and inspired by the Ayatollah Khomeini's revolution in Iran—our continuing military presence was anathema. In November 1983, Hizbollah signaled its intentions when a truck bomber drove into a building being used as our military headquarters in the south Lebanese city of Tyre, killing more than sixty people.

In spite of Labor's seeming advantage, the election ended up as a near tie. Peres did lead Labor back into top spot for the first time since Begin's victory in 1977. But he got only forty-four seats, to the Likud's forty-one. After weeks of horse-trading with smaller parties, he could not form a government. Neither could Shamir. The result, for the first time in peacetime, was a national-unity coalition, including both main parties. Peres would be prime minister for the first two years, and Shamir the final two. But the stipulation of most relevance to me was the one man who would be the defense minister throughout the four years: Yitzhak Rabin.

My relationship with Rabin went back much further than with Misha. I'd first met him when I was a sayeret soldier. I'd interacted with him more as a young sayeret officer, and of course during Entebbe. Now, we began to work even more closely, and the main challenge in his early months as defense minister was what to do about our troops in Lebanon. We had been pulling back gradually and were now more or less on the twenty-five-mile line that Sharon had claimed was the point of the invasion. But even this was costing us lives, with no obvious benefit from controlling a large slab of territory on which nearly half a million Lebanese lived. A decision was now reached to shrink our "security zone" further and pull back to a border area ranging from about three to six miles, south of the Litani River.

I argued strongly in favor of getting out altogether. I accepted that the security zone might help impede cross-border raids. But the remaining Palestinian fighters and Hizbollah were acquiring newer Katyushas, with a range of up to twelve miles, and they could fire rockets over the security zone. My deeper concern was that we intended to hold the area with between 1,000 and 1,500 Israeli troops in open alliance with a local Maronite Christian–led militia called the South Lebanon Army. That was a recipe for conflict with the *non*-Christian majority in the south. I tried to persuade Rabin we should withdraw all the Israeli soldiers and coordinate security arrangements with the equivalent of a local civil-defense guard. I suggested four separate militias drawn from the local population—Christian, Shi'ite Muslim, Druse, and ethnically mixed—with the aim of reflecting the balance in each part of the south.

Israeli troops might still have to cross into Lebanon, but only for brief, targeted operations to preempt preparations for a terror attack. "We need to remember what we're there for," I said. "We have no territorial claims. It's to protect the north of Israel. But it will end up being about protecting our own troops inside the security zone. It will be like the Bar-Lev Line in 1973, fighting for fortifications we don't need." I couldn't persuade him. When a terrorist unit launched a raid across the border, or Katyushas next fell on northern Israel, he as minister of defense, not I, would be the one in the political firing line.

Far from straining our relations, our frank exchanges on Lebanon seemed to build further trust between us. We worked closely on a range of issues. When Sayeret Matkal planned an operation across our borders, both of us would present the action to the cabinet. During the operations, I'd be either in the kirya or a forward command post. Since nearly all of them happened after nightfall, Yitzhak would usually be back home, asleep, by the time they ended. I would phone him. The trademark voice—slow, gravelly, deep even when he was wide awake—would answer. I'd tell him the mission was over and—with only one exception during my period as head of intelligence—successful. "*Todah*," he would say. "*Lehitraot*." Thanks. Bye. He was never a man to waste words.

For one of the very few times I can remember, *he* phoned me one morning in October 1985 to discuss our strategy in response to Palestinian terror. It was a couple of days after an especially gruesome Palestinian terror attack. Even with Arafat now more than a thousand miles away in Tunis, much of Rabin's focus was taken up in responding to, or trying to preempt, Palestinian terrorism. The issue was especially sensitive politically in the wake of the Lebanon War, which was supposed to have eliminated that threat. For Rabin, moreover, it had become personal. He'd had to sanction an unprecedented exchange of 1,150 Palestinian security prisoners earlier in the year to secure the freedom of three Israeli soldiers, including one of our men from Sultan Yacoub, who had ended up in the hands of the radical Popular Front for the Liberation of Palestine–General Command after the Lebanon War. Now a group from another of the radical factions, the Palestine Liberation Front, had hijacked an Italian cruise ship called the *Achille Lauro* en route from Egypt to Israel. They had murdered one of the passengers, a wheelchair-bound, sixty-nine-year-old Jewish American named Leon Klinghoffer, and dumped his body overboard.

Rabin's closest aide, Eitan Haber, whom I knew well, was aware that Unit 8200 had intercepts that laid bare the details, and left no doubt the murderers were from a PLO group. He called me the next day and asked me to appear on a weekly television interview program called *Moked*. It was hosted by Nissim Mishal: brash, incisive, and one of Israel's best-known broadcast journalists. I pointed out to Haber that I'd never done anything like this before, but he insisted it would go well. We talked through the questions I could expect, not just about the *Achille Lauro* but the wider issue of Palestinian attacks, as well as Syrian president Hafez al-Assad's efforts to reequip his air force after his losses in Lebanon. So I came to the interview well prepared. I brought audio tapes of the hijackers and a large photograph of MiG-25s, which the Syrians were seeking to acquire.

My appearance will not go down in the annals of great moments in television. But at the time, very few Israelis even knew who I was, and I felt I'd done OK. I was surprised, however, when Rabin phoned the next day. "Ehud, I didn't see it. I was attending some event," he said. But his wife, Leah, had recorded the program. "I just watched it. I should tell you, I think it was exceptional. You did a great job. It was highly important for us, for the army, and, I dare say, for you."

+ + +

I was not sure what he meant by saying it might be good for me as well. It is true that there was some politics at the upper reaches of the military, especially around the choice of chief of staff, and Moshe Vechetzi's term had only a year and a half to go. But I didn't view myself as a serious candidate at this stage. Moshe's own preference seemed to be Amir Drori, the head of the northern command during the Lebanon War. My own view was that the nod should go to Dan Shomron.

I had first got to know Dan well in the late sixties after Karameh, Israel's costly standoff with Arafat, when Fatah's influence was in its infancy. We'd exchanged impressions on what had gone wrong, and why. When I became commander of Sayeret Matkal, we remained in touch, and he took a close interest in all of our operations. We also crossed paths in the Sinai in 1973: Dan's division was key in stanching the Egyptian advance in the first days of the war, later inflicted heavy losses on one of Sadat's armored forces, and was part of the final push on the other side of the canal. And, of course, during Entebbe. Dan had sharp tactical instincts, a belief in the importance of using new technology to gain and sustain an edge, and an openness to unconventional approaches. Faced with a challenge in planning or executing an operation, he looked at it from all sides, determined to come up with the *right* approach, not always the expected one. In a lot of these ways, we were similar, which was no doubt one reason our relationship had grown closer as he and I—six years younger, and a step or two behind—rose up the ranks.

In fact, Dan was the reason I'd made one of my rare forays into kirya politics not long after Moshe Vechetzi took over as chief of staff, when Misha Arens was still defense minister. I acted to derail what seemed to me a blatant attempt by Moshe to advance Drori's prospects for eventual succession as chief of staff, and to take Dan out of the contest altogether.

I was sitting at my desk on the third floor when the chief of internal army security, a colonel named Ben-Dor, walked into my office. "Listen," he said, "the chief of staff has a right to give me a direct order in cases where he thinks there is a need for a special investigation. But you're my commander, so I wanted to let you know."

"What is it?" I asked.

He replied that he had been ordered to "check out rumors that Dan Shomron is a homosexual."

I was appalled. The whole thing stank, on every level, and not just because I thought the "rumors" were nonsense. "Look," I said, "I have no idea whether some sub-clause in army regulations allows the chief of staff to give you orders over my head. But even if it does, I'm ordering you to do nothing until I talk to Moshe." He nodded in agreement. In fact, he seemed relieved. He also let me know that the source of the rumors was a number of senior officers, including a couple of generals.

I went straight downstairs and into the chief of staff's office. Moshe was at his desk, smoking a cigarette. One of the advantages he had in being nearly a foot taller than most of us was that I found myself looking not into his eyes, but up at them. "Moshe," I said, "Ben-Dor told me you've ordered him to investigate a rumor that Dan Shomron is a homosexual." He said nothing, so I went on. "I've told him not to do it. And I've come *here* to convince you that it's improper." This was more than thirty years ago, at a time when being gay, and certainly being gay in the armed forces, was a much bigger deal than now. But I still believed this amounted to a witch hunt.

Moshe still said nothing. "I have no idea whether Dan is or is not a homosexual. After knowing him for years, I have no reason at all to believe that he is. But let's assume, for a moment, that he is," I said. "He's not some junior lieutenant . . . This is a man who has *risked his life* for Israel. Repeatedly. Under fire." Then, I got to the real issue. "I hesitate to mention this, but if you order this, the very fact of doing so might be interpreted as being a result of some other motives on your part. I'm doing my best to convince you to think again. But I want you to know that if I can't, I'm going from here to Misha's office. I'll try to convince him of the damage from what you're contemplating to the whole fabric of trust in the general staff and the army." Still, he said nothing, only nodding occasionally as he puffed on his cigarette, put it out, and lit another one. It was clear he had no intention of rescinding his order.

Within twenty minutes, I was in the minister of defense's office. I spoke to him for about ten minutes. Misha listened. At the end, he said only, "I understand what you've told me." I never discovered what exactly he said to Moshe Vechetzi. But the investigation never happened. I never spoke a word about any of it to Dan until years later, after both of us had left the army.

The result, however, was that Dan became deputy chief of staff under Moshe, the latest step in what was beginning to look like a steady rise to the top. But Misha did make a few concessions to Moshe's preferred candidates, and that now turned out to have major implications for me. It was a long-accepted practice that chiefs of staff had more than one deputy during their period in charge. In the homestretch of Moshe's tenure, he was able to bring in Amir Drori for a spell as his number two. Early in 1986, he also brought Amnon Lipkin back to the kirya. Amnon was given *my* job, as director of intelligence. But I got the post that Amnon was leaving: head of the central command. This meant that, for the first time, I would be in charge of one of Israel's three regional military commands, and we were based on the edge of Jerusalem, with security responsibility for the West Bank.

This was my first direct exposure to the combustible mix of restive Palestinians and the growing number of Jewish settlers. Our main brief was to prevent terror attacks, violence, or unrest from the roughly 850,000 West Bank Palestinians toward the 50,000 Israelis who were then living in the settlements. It was now two decades since our capture of the territory in the Six-Day War. By far most of the Palestinians were not involved in any violence. They were mainly interested in getting on with their lives. Yet there were signs of trouble. The PLO leaders' relocation to Tunis had reduced their direct influence, but the briefings I got from Shin Bet officers made it clear that some young West Bankers had begun trying to organize attacks against police, soldiers, and Israeli civilians. The settlements were also growing in number, and an ideologically driven minority of their residents were not above acts of violence against Palestinians.

Further complicating the situation was the fact that the settlement enterprise enjoyed the support of key Likud members in the cabinet: Shamir, who was about to take his turn as prime minister in October 1986; Misha, now a minister without portfolio; and most of all Arik Sharon. In a demonstration of resilience, Arik had remained as a minister without portfolio when Shamir succeeded Menachem Begin. In the unity government, he had become minister of trade and industry. As agriculture minister under Begin, Sharon had been a major force in plans to expand Jewish settlement on the West Bank. There had been some settlements before then, in the decade of Labor government following the 1967 war, but on a fairly limited scale. Almost all of them were planned for areas away from major Palestinians towns. The two exceptions were Kiryat Arba, near Hebron, and Gush Etzion, not far from Bethlehem. Both were acts with deliberate symbolic significance. Hebron had been the site of a massacre of its Jewish residents in 1929. And nearly 130 of the Jews of Gush Etzion were killed in May 1948. Both were also areas where Jews had lived, owned property, and flourished before 1948. Arik's settlement vision was the polar opposite of Labor's. After the peace agreement with Sadat, he, like Begin, was determined to prevent the envisaged "Palestinian autonomy" on the West Bank from ever becoming a Palestinian state. So he proceeded to encircle all of the main Arab towns with new rings of settlements.

I had a responsibility to protect the settlers, and I did my best to fulfill it. Yet it was essential they understood that they were subject to the authority of the State of Israel and, like other Israeli citizens, had to operate within the law. This was no mere theoretical problem. A Jewish underground had been established by members of Gush Emunim, the Orthodox Jewish movement set up in the 1970s to advance what they saw as a divinely mandated mission to settle the West Bank. It had carried out car bombings and other attacks in the early 1980s, leaving two Palestinian mayors crippled for life. The terror campaign had ended only when the Shin Bet caught the cell placing explosives under Arab-owned buses in Jerusalem.

Hopeful of preventing misunderstandings, and ideally building a relationship of trust, I visited many of the settlements during the early weeks in my new post and spoke with their leaders, a few of whom remain friends to this day. But in the spring of 1986, we faced our first major test on the ground. In a pre-Passover event organized by Gush Emunim, some 10,000 settlers streamed into Hebron, a city sacred to both Jews and Muslims, as well as the burial place of Hebrew patriarchs and matriarchs. Peace Now activists had planned a counterprotest, but Rabin denied them permission. Still, antisettlement members of the Knesset and other Israeli peace activists did get clearance to march from Jerusalem to Hebron.

My job was to ensure the security not just of the Gush Emunim march but of the counterdemonstrators and, of course, the local Palestinian population. As the rival marches by the Israelis proceeded, I personally delivered warnings against any violence, both to the settlement leaders and to a pair of the most prominent counterprotesters, the peace activist Uri Avneri and Knesset member Yossi Sarid. The event went off without major incident. But the next day, *Davar*, the venerable Labor newspaper I'd first read as a child in Mishmar Hasharon, let rip against me. Under a photo of me with Avneri and Sarid—my arm raised, ostensibly in some kind of threat but actually in the time-honored Jewish practice of talking with my hands—the article accused me of siding with the settlers. If blood was spilled in the weeks and months ahead, the newspaper said, "it will be on Barak's hands."

Ordinarily, I would have ignored it. But never in my military career had I been similarly attacked on an issue of any importance. I was especially angry because not only was the insinuation unfounded, it was diametrically opposite to the stance I was determined to take in this, my first regional command. Yes, I was committed to providing security for the settlers. But I was determined to ensure they remained within the boundaries of the law.

A few days later, I called Eitan Haber and asked to see the defense minister. I was told to come see him after Saturday lunch at his home. When I arrived, Rabin got right down to business. "Ehud, you wanted to see me?"

"You've probably seen *Davar*," I replied. "It was a pretty nasty piece. It distorted things."

Yet as he asked for details, it seemed he had no idea what I was talking about. "Ehud, I never read it," he said. "If you hadn't told me, I'd never have known there was an issue." I assumed this was a white lie, told to reassure me. But years later, when I was minister of defense, and then prime minister, I sometimes found myself on the other side of such meetings. An officer or official would come see me because of something said about them in the media, or remarks they were quoted as having made. When I told them I'd been unaware of it, I could see the disbelief in their eyes. By then, however, I realized that under the multiple demands of a senior role in government, you really could fail to notice events that others viewed as crucial to their reputations. To reassure them I truly hadn't noticed, I'd tell them the story of my meeting with Rabin.

✢ ✢ ✢

There was another, slightly less noble, reason I wanted to set the record straight with Rabin. Though only gradually did I admit this even to myself, I realized that my experience in a regional command had ticked the one missing box in the CV of our top generals, meaning that I might indeed be a candidate to succeed Moshe Vechetzi as chief of staff. At first, I resisted taking the prospect too seriously. The job of ramatkal carried responsibility for overall command of the armed forces. Since our country still faced multiple security threats, the chief of staff was, along with prime minister and defense minister, among the most important, influential, and visible positions in Israeli public life. As the April 1987 date for the changeover drew nearer, Israeli media reports, and officers' small talk, suggested that Rabin had whittled down the possibilities to two: Dan Shomron, and me.

It was only when Rabin phoned me early in 1987 that I knew this was true—and that I would not be getting the job. "Ehud," he said, "I wanted you to know I've decided on Dan to be the next ramatkal. I want you to be his deputy." I can't say I was surprised. Dan was more experienced. He was also older; missing out on the top job this time would surely mean missing out for good. Yitzhak had always valued Dan's directness and honesty, his courage and record of service. Above all, I'd long sensed that he felt a special debt to Dan: for Entebbe. At a time when so much could have gone wrong, it was Dan who had taken a firm, confident, successful hold on the operation.

Still, I was now forty-five, and there was no guarantee I'd be chosen as chief of staff the next time around. "I respect your decision," I told Rabin. "And I have no doubt Dan will be a good—a *very* good—chief of staff." But I had to consider my own future. "Even though I'm grateful for the offer of deputy," I said. "I think it's better for me to leave. To open up a new chapter, and do something else in life."

Rabin said he couldn't accept that. "Come see me," he said. "Now." When I got to Jerusalem, I emphasized again that I had no doubt Dan would lead the armed forces well. But I said my decision to leave the military wasn't a mere whim. I had been thinking about my own future and my family's. We had three young daughters. A few months earlier, we had moved home again, into a wide, one-story rambler with a big yard out back. It was in a new town called Kochav Yair, just inside Israel's pre-1967 border with the West Bank, and it struck me as a good time to settle down in a way that would be impossible if I stayed on in the upper reaches of the military. Perhaps I'd do something more academic, in a university or a policy think tank, or explore the idea of getting involved in business.

For the first time, politics had some appeal, too, though I didn't say this to him. At that point, I had no idea how, or even whether, I might get involved. But since my appearance on *Moked*, others seemed to assume it might happen at some stage. Out of nowhere, a leading political journalist, Hanan Kristal, had written a story in the newspaper *Hadashot* in 1986 purporting to predict the successors to Israel's political old guard: Peres and Rabin in Labor, Begin and Shamir in the Likud. The paper ran side-by-side photos of the ostensible future leaders, doctored to look older, who Hanan predicted would go head-to-head in the election of 1996, a decade away. One was Israel's ambassador to the UN and a protégé of Misha Arens: Bibi Netanyahu. The other was me.

Rabin listened with patience but remained firm that I should stay and become Dan's deputy. In the end, I agreed I'd think things over and that we'd talk in a week's time. In the meantime, I went to see two veteran generals who had found themselves in a similar situation, mentioned as possible chiefs of staff but never chosen: Arik and Ezer Weizman. I visited Arik on his farm and found him, and his expanding girth, settled on a sofa in the living room. I filled him in on my conversation with Rabin. "I'm considering leaving," I said. "It just seems like a long time to wait, even if I do get the job after Dan. There's a lot else I want to do in life."

Arik was probably the general most experienced in being denied the chief of staff's office. On at least two occasions, he might reasonably have been considered. But in a career littered with tense encounters with his superiors, it never happened. "You should stay on," he said. "You're not that old. It'll probably be good for you, and the army, to be deputy and *then* chief." The only further advice he gave me was to do all I could formally to commit Yitzhak to making me Dan's successor after his term ended.

I visited Ezer at his home in the seaside town of Caesarea. We sat on the terrace, with Ezer's gangly frame stretched out in one of the cane chairs. "Ehud, if you stay, do you think you have a good chance of being the next ramatkal?" he asked. I said that while nothing could be certain, I thought there was a good chance. He replied without hesitation: "Then stay." He'd come close to the top job, he told me. On the eve of the Six-Day War, when Rabin had collapsed physically from the weeks of tension, Yitzhak had asked him to take over. He'd said no. But he said he'd always believed he could and should have been chief of staff—and that if he hadn't left to go into politics, he still might have got the job. Then, suddenly, he shouted, "Reuma!" When his wife appeared, he said, "Tell Barak the missing piece in my life, the one I've never stopped regretting." She smiled and said, "It's the fact you did not become ramatkal."

I saw Rabin a couple of days later. Though I'd pretty much decided to take the deputy's job, I was still bothered by the prospect of serving as deputy for the next four years only to find someone else being named chief of staff. I knew that no matter what assurances Yitzhak gave me, there was no way of being sure. He did say he viewed me as the natural next-in-line. But I still felt hesitant. "I want you to consider two things," I said. The first was a formal decision that Dan would have only a single deputy during his time as chief of staff. He said yes to that. Yet the second request was going to be even more difficult. Heartening though it was to hear I was Dan's "natural successor," I asked him to put it in writing. It was not that I doubted his word. But if the surprise result of the last election was any indication, there was no way of predicting which party would be in power when Dan's term ended. I wanted him to keep a record for himself of our understanding in his desk and pass it on if someone else was defense minister by that time. Without a moment's hesitation, he took out a piece of paper and wrote down exactly what he'd told me about the succession. He shook my hand as I left. "You've made the right decision," he said.

And I had, even though Dan and I—and Rabin too—would soon face by far the most difficult challenge in Israel's conflict with the Palestinians since our capture of the West Bank and Gaza in the 1967 war.

# Intifada

It began with an accident. On Tuesday, December 8, 1987, an Israeli tank transporter crashed into a minibus carrying Palestinians from the Jabalya refugee camp near the main crossing from Gaza into Israel. Four passengers were killed.

By the time of the funerals the next day, a rumor had spread, no less incendiary for being absurd, that the crash had been deliberate—retaliation for the fatal stabbing of an Israeli man a few days earlier. Crowds of Palestinians leaving the burials began shouting "Death to Israel!" They hurled rocks and bottles at Israeli security patrols and blocked streets with burning tires. By the following day, the violence started spreading to the West Bank, and then to parts of east Jerusalem. The headline writers moved from the word "disturbances" to "unrest" and finally to the Palestinians' own name for the most serious outbreak of violence since 1967: the "intifada." The uprising.

At least for the first week or two, we assumed its ferocity and scale would subside. Our immediate aim was to contain it and limit the human cost on both sides. Yet when Dan and I began visiting units on the front line of this new conflict, we realized that if it kept escalating, we'd have to find new tools and strategies to bring it under control. We were in charge of an army trained to equip and fight enemy *soldiers*. Now, we were asking teenage recruits to operate as riot police against stone-throwing mobs. Before long, it wasn't just stones, or even bottles. In one incident in Gaza, a young soldier was surrounded by a crowd of Palestinians and stabbed. He opened fire, wounding two of the attackers. Yitzhik Morde-chai, now the head of the southern command, told reporters that his troops were under "strict orders to open fire only if their lives are under threat." That was true. But I couldn't help wondering how long the other part of his statement would hold: that we remained "in control of the situation."

We did *feel* in control for the first few days. Defense Minister Rabin was away in Washington on an official visit. When his office asked us whether he should fly back, we said there was no need. But on his return, we quickly agreed that as a first priority we needed to find an alternative to live am-munition in quelling the attacks. Otherwise, we'd be left with two equally bad options: either simply stand aside in order to avoid killing or injuring demonstrators; or intervene with the inevitable fatalities, which might fuel further violence.

One of our most important early discussions was about the broader aspects of the violence, to get a hold not just on how to respond to the situation on the ground but to address the longer-term implications. The meeting, held outside the kirya in a facility just north of Tel Aviv, was Rabin's idea. In addition to Dan and me, he included key members of the general staff and senior Defense Ministry officials. A half dozen academ-ics and other specialists would weigh in on the political aspects of the sudden eruption of Palestinian violence.

Though he spoke for barely ten minutes, the last speaker left the deepest impression on me. Shimon Shamir, a historian at Tel Aviv University, began by emphasizing he was not an expert on riot control. Finding a response to the violence was something we were far better equipped to do. He then paused, looked intently at Rabin, Dan, and me, and said, "What I *can* do is draw on history." One by one, he cited examples of more than a dozen similar rebellions over the past century, in the Middle East and beyond. "If we were dealing with simple rioting, things might be dif-ferent." But the Palestinians were, fundamentally, acting out of a shared sense of grievance and national identity. Both were in large part the result of Israel having controlled their daily lives now for more than two decades. "I'm afraid I can find no historical precedent for the successful suppression of the national will of a people," he said. Even when those in power used unimaginably punitive tools: like expulsion, or forced starvation. "Even, as we know well as a Jewish people, extermination."

I glanced at Yitzhak and at Dan. Both of them looked like I felt: no doubt the professor was right, but in the short term, we still had to find a way of keeping the situation from getting irretrievably out of control.

It wasn't as if I'd been unaware of the sense of the anger building among many West Bank and Gaza Palestinians, or of their wish to see an end to Israel's military administration and the growing number of Jewish settlements. From my time as head of the central command, I also knew there was a young activist core intensifying efforts to organize attacks on troops and settlers. But none of us had any inkling that something of the scale, longevity, and political complexity of the intifada lay ahead.

Partly, this was a failure of specific intelligence warnings. But it went deeper than that. Sobering though it was, I had to accept that—no less so than before the Yom Kippur War in 1973—I and many others had for too long been comforting ourselves with a fundamental misconception about our military occupation and civilian settlement in the areas captured in 1967. The roots of the myopia went back to the immediate aftermath of the Six-Day War, to the generally civil, and often friendly, contacts Israelis had with Palestinians at the time. The local population had, after all, been under *other* occupation powers before 1967: Jordan in the West Bank, and Egypt in Gaza. Our administration was in many ways less onerous, at least in the early years. Most Israelis believed a way to coexist could be found and that, sooner or later, there would be a land-for-peace agreement under which we would withdraw from a major part of the territory. But as the years passed, with no sign of a willingness by the PLO to consider any kind of peace talks, we made the cardinal error of assuming the occupation was sustainable. Yes, there might be periods of violence, but nothing that a combination of political resolve, arrests, detention, and, where necessary, military force could not hold in check. For us, and certainly for me, the Palestinians became essentially a security issue. As one of Israel's finest novelists, David Grossman, would lay bare in a bestselling book of reportage called *The Yellow Wind*, about a year into the intifada, we had ceased to see the *human* effects of twenty years of occupation, not only on the Palestinians, in whom it helped forge an ever-greater sense of national identity, but on Israeli society as well.

The power of Professor Shamir's presentation lay not so much in its novelty as its succinctness, its clarity, and above all its timing. The rioting had already gone on for several weeks, longer than any of us had expected. It seemed to be gathering strength. But until our meeting, we were still looking at it essentially as a civil disturbance. *That* was what began to change, for all of us.

What didn't change was the need to try to bring the violence to an end. Dan immediately put me in charge of looking for alternatives to live ammunition. I began with our own research and development engineers. We also asked military attachés in our embassies to talk to law enforcement agencies, academics, or anyone else with knowledge of nonlethal methods of crowd control. Some of the more far-flung examples seemed promising, at least until further investigation. South Korea had years of experience in confronting student protests—generally, though not always, managing to avoid fatalities. But it turned out this typically involved sending in serried rows of up to 25,000 riot police against a few thousand campus protesters. Besides the fact we'd have needed an army the size of the Americans' to field enough soldiers, it was absurd to imagine dealing with dozens of disparate confrontations on any given day with parade-ground formations of troops.

We looked at anything that seemed it might work. In the early stages, most of the attacks involved rocks and bottles. Our R&D engineers developed a jeep-mounted "gravel gun" that fired stones at a distance of up to 250 feet. They could cause injuries but weren't lethal. We acquired launchers for pepper spray and tear gas. We even looked at the possibility of dropping nets over crowds of attackers. Very early on, we shifted to using plastic bullets. But even that presented problems. At a distance of a hundred feet or so, they could drastically reduce deaths. However, when a young recruit saw hundreds of Palestinians closing in on him, he wasn't about to take out a tape measure. Over time, we began to rely wherever possible on rubber bullets and, in extreme cases, snipers to target the legs of the organizers or ringleaders.

If all of this sounds soul-destroying, that's because to a certain extent it was. Especially with daily television coverage of the clashes amplifying overseas support for the Palestinians, morale among our soldiers also took a battering. In visits to units on the West Bank and in Gaza, Dan and I, and Rabin too, heard two opposite responses. Some of the young soldiers wanted us to use maximum force. *We are the army*, they argued. We have the weapons. Why the hell don't we *use* them? But we also heard another view, if less often: *why are we here at all?*

We imposed closures and curfews. We made thousands of arrests. Still, hundreds of soldiers and settlers were being injured, a number of them disfigured or disabled. By the end of 1988, the Palestinian death toll was above 300. In February 1989, an Israeli officer was killed by a cement block tossed from a rooftop in Nablus. A month later, a Palestinian knifed several people in Tel Aviv, killing one of them. And in July, in the first attempt inside Israel at a suicide attack, a Palestinian passenger grabbed the wheel of a bus on its way from Tel Aviv to Jerusalem and drove it off the road, killing sixteen people.

+ + +

By the summer of 1990, although the violence had begun to flag slightly, I was drained and exhausted. I even briefly thought of leaving the army after Dan's term ended the following year. But then the intifada gradually began to subside, and an entirely new crisis suddenly intervened.

On August 2, against a background of long-standing financial and territorial disputes, Iraq's Saddam Hussein sent in tens of thousands of his troops and occupied the neighboring state of Kuwait. He then tried to divert attention from US-led international condemnation of his invasion by threatening Israel. He said "all issues of occupation" were on the table—the West Bank and Gaza, the Golan Heights, and Lebanon—and vowed to "let our fire eat half of Israel" in a future war. We could not assume this was mere rhetoric. Iraq had an arsenal of Soviet-made ballistic missiles. Called Scuds, they were not always accurate at long range, but they could reach Israeli towns and cities and carry not just conventional explosives but chemical warheads. Moreover, Saddam had *used* chemical weapons: during the Iran-Iraq War, and to kill thousands of his own Kurdish population in the town of Halabja in the spring of 1988.

Even the prospect of American military action seemed not to faze him. Hours into the invasion, he moved an armored force toward Kuwait's border with Saudi Arabia, a key US regional ally, immediately prompting President George H. W. Bush's administration to respond. With Saudi agreement, Washington dispatched a squadron of F-15s to the kingdom—the first step in what would become a huge American land, sea, and air force to face down Saddam and force him out of Kuwait.

Given the credible threat of Scud missile attacks, Dan immediately assigned me to coordinate our assessment and evaluation of what Saddam was likely to do in the event of a US-led attack, and what defense arrangements or Israeli military response would be necessary. We knew we'd be under strong pressure from the Americans to stay out of any war. Israeli involvement would be a political gift to Saddam, allowing him to convert a conflict over his aggression against an Arab neighbor into a "defense" against "Israeli occupation." But our primary responsibility was to protect our citizens.

I was now working with a new Israeli government. After Shimon Peres tried and failed to topple the unity coalition in the spring of 1990, Shamir had formed a Likud-led government shorn of both Peres and Rabin. Misha Arens was again minister of defense. I began preparing regular, fortnightly reports for him, Dan, and Prime Minister Shamir. Within days of the invasion, I produced my initial assessment. The bottom line was that we had to assume there would be a war. It was impossible to imagine the Americans would commit hundreds of thousands of troops and simply bring them home again, unless Saddam succumbed and retreated. I was equally certain Saddam would use his Scuds against us. He'd figure the benefits of trying to bring Israel into the conflict far outweighed the risk of retaliation. But I was "nearly 100 percent sure" he wouldn't use chemical warheads, since that would almost guarantee an Israeli military response, or an American one, on an incomparably greater scale. It would also totally isolate Saddam internationally and end any chance of peeling off Arab support for the Americans.

It was my *nearly* 100 percent caveat that prompted a tense debate within the inner security cabinet. Even if the probability of a chemical attack was microscopic, *any* risk of civilians being subjected to terror, panic, and very possibly agonizing death meant that the government had to take precautions. The obvious first step would be to distribute gas masks. But in a series of meetings with Misha and Dan, I emphasized this was not a decision that could be taken in isolation. By handing out gas masks, we might actually raise the probability of a chemical attack. We all agreed to make sure as a matter of urgency that we had a workable *military* option to attack Iraq's Scud launchers.

By early November, I was dealing both with plans for distributing the gas masks and preparations for a possible military operation. So when I got a call asking me to report to Shamir's office in Jerusalem, I assumed he wanted to talk about Iraq. "How are things?" he asked. But when I began by filling him in on the plans to distribute the gas masks, he interrupted me. "I called you here," he said, "because I wanted you to know that we've decided that when Dan leaves next April, we want you to replace him as chief of staff." Briefly and unusually tongue-tied, I said, "Thank you, Prime Minister." The news was made public the next morning. A few days later, it was ratified by the government. There was only one vote against, from a *former* chief of staff who was now Shamir's agriculture minister: Raful Eitan.

It was one of the rare instances in all my years in the army when I took a step back to appreciate a moment that felt special. It was not only, or even mainly, a matter of a personal ambition fulfilled, but more a sense that I was being given the opportunity to apply everything I'd experienced and learned in the army, from the day I first joined Sayeret Matkal as an eighteen-year-old, to improve the security and safeguard the future of Israel. I know that sounds corny. But, while the momentum toward war in Iraq almost immediately crowded out everything else, that was truly how I felt.

+ + +

By mid-December 1990, war was virtually certain. Misha and I had been to Washington in September. With the assurance that the American military would take care of Iraq's Scud missile launchers, we agreed that, unless attacks by Saddam left us with no alternative but to respond, we would stay out of it. Yet with hostilities obviously getting closer, Misha phoned Defense Secretary Dick Cheney a few days later to remind him of the quid pro quo: we would be kept fully in the loop about the details and timing of the initial American air strikes. At around five o'clock in the afternoon on January 16, 1991, Misha got a call from Cheney. He said "H-hour" would be at seven that evening Washington time. Three a.m. in Israel.

Though we hoped to stay out, I'd now spent months coordinating and overseeing preparations to ensure we could attack Saddam's Scuds if necessary. By far most of the missiles were mounted on mobile launching vehicles, and Saddam was almost certainly going to be firing them from the vastness of Iraq's western desert. That meant an Israeli air strike alone wouldn't work. We decided on a joint air and ground operation, built around a newly created air-mobile combat team and other special units. A force of 500 to 600 soldiers would take control of key areas and road junctions in western Iraq and start hunting and destroying, or at least impeding, the Scud launchers.

We also engaged in secret diplomacy in the hopes of reducing one of the obvious risks in such an attack: a conflict with Jordan, which we'd have to overfly to reach Iraq. The Mossad had a unit called Tevel, a kind of shadow foreign ministry for states with which we had no formal relations but with which, in both sides' interests, we had a channel of backdoor communications. It was headed by Ephraim Halevy, a London-born Israeli who had come to Palestine in 1948 as a teenager. He had built up a personal relationship with King Hussein, and now arranged for us to meet him at a country residence the king had in Britain.

A few weeks before the war, I boarded a private jet to London along with Halevy; Elyakim Rubinstein, a veteran diplomat and senior cabinet official; and Prime Minister Shamir. Shamir had never met the king before, nor, of course, had I. But we didn't talk about the forthcoming meeting on the five-hour flight. Instead, Shamir opened up in a way I'd never seen: about his childhood as part of a relatively well-off family in Poland; his love of literature, and of the Bible. In a way, it reminded me of how my father had spoken to me when I was growing up—minus the "well-off family" part.

When we got to Hussein's country home, we were greeted by an impressively self-assured man in his late twenties who, like Hussein, had studied at Britain's military academy in Sandhurst, before going to spend a year at Oxford. It was Abdullah, the king's son and later his successor, and he explained that he would be in charge of handling security for the talks. For a few hours in the afternoon, we held preliminary discussions, and I presented our assessment of the challenges and options facing all the different players in the crisis. Then we retired to a dinner at which the

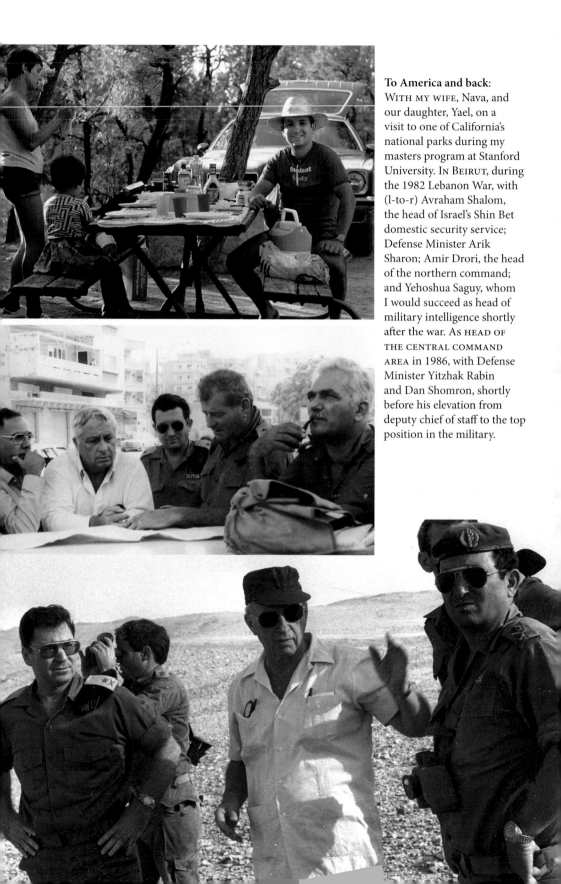

**To America and back:** WITH MY WIFE, Nava, and our daughter, Yael, on a visit to one of California's national parks during my masters program at Stanford University. IN BEIRUT, during the 1982 Lebanon War, with (l-to-r) Avraham Shalom, the head of Israel's Shin Bet domestic security service; Defense Minister Arik Sharon; Amir Drori, the head of the northern command; and Yehoshua Saguy, whom I would succeed as head of military intelligence shortly after the war. As HEAD OF THE CENTRAL COMMAND AREA in 1986, with Defense Minister Yitzhak Rabin and Dan Shomron, shortly before his elevation from deputy chief of staff to the top position in the military.

**Up the ladder:** As DEPUTY CHIEF OF STAFF, with Dan Shomron, minutes before a special police unit frees hostages from a Palestinian bus hijacking in southern Israel in 1988. In direct command, walkie-talkie in hand, is the head of the southern command, Yitzhak Mordechai, whose paratroopers my battalion was sent into rescue at the Chinese farm in the 1973 Yom Kippur War war.

**Chief of staff:** FORMALLY RECEIVING THE EMBLEM of office as head of the Israeli military in April 1991 from Defense Minister Misha Arens (left) and Prime Minister Yitzhak Shamir (right).

**Defense and democracy:** CASTING MY VOTE in Israel's 1992 elections for Yitzhak Rabin's Labor Party during a visit to an armored unit on the Golan Heights.

**Citizen army:** Watching a live-fire military exercise in the Jordan Valley. Consoling soldiers in the Golani Brigade after Hizbollah attacks, using remotely detonated roadside bombs, killed eight of their men in southern Lebanon in the summer of 1993. Discussing troop deployments in Gaza several months later.

**At the negotiating table**: WITH DEFENSE MINISTER MISHA ARENS and Israel's ambassador to the United States, Zalman Shoval, shortly after becoming chief of staff, in talks with Secretary of State James Baker and Middle East peace negotiator Dennis Ross. RECEIVING AMERICA'S LEGION OF MERIT medal at the Pentagon in 1993 from my fellow general and friend Colin Powell, chairman of the Joint Chiefs of Staff. WITH JORDAN'S KING HUSSEIN in 1994 during talks in Amman on the military aspects of the Israeli-Jordanian peace treaty.

**Partners in peace:** SHAKING HANDS with my counterpart, the Jordanian chief of staff, at the signing of the peace treaty in October 1994, as (l-to-r) Crown Prince Hassan, Prime Minister Yitzhak Rabin, US President Bill Clinton, and King Hussein look on.

**At home and abroad:** (from top left) WITH PRIME MINISTER RABIN and Foreign Minister Shimon Peres, longtime Labor partners and rivals, on a military transport plane a few days after the treaty signing. CONFERRING WITH ISRAELI PRESIDENT and former air force chief Ezer Weizman. REVIEWING THE GUARD OF HONOR during a visit to London in the autumn of 1994. TALKING WITH DIRECTOR Steven Spielberg at the Israeli premiere of his powerful Holocaust film *Schindler's List*.

**Prime minister:** TENS OF THOUSANDS throng in central Tel Aviv to celebrate my victory over Prime Minister Bibi Netanyahu in the 1999 election. The raw energy of the crowd was electric, but I remember thinking to myself at the time: *They think that, with Bibi gone, peace is around the corner—that it's going to be easy.* As I REFLECTED during the new prime minister's traditional visit to the Western Wall of the ancient Jewish temple in Jerusalem the following day, I knew it would be anything but easy, and that a breakthrough would require historically tough, even painful, decisions not just on our side but from Syrian and Palestinian leaders.

**Tide of emotion**: MOMENTS BEFORE my formal swearing-in at the Knesset as successor to a pensive Bibi Netanyahu (foreground), with my parents and children looking on from the parliamentary gallery.

atmosphere—despite the royal china, crystal, and silverware—was sur-prisingly informal.

The main meeting came the next morning. Both sides recognized the seriousness of the issues we had to discuss. Shamir began with the one we assumed would be the least difficult. Israel was on a heightened state of military alert, prompted by Iraqi reconnaissance flights over Jordan. The king's forces were also on high alert. It was important to ensure this didn't lead to an unintended conflict between us and the Jordanians. While the king was careful to steer clear of any detailed comment on the Iraqi moves, he made it clear that he understood our concern about stum-bling into an Israeli-Jordanian conflict and seemed to agree that we had to avoid doing so.

Yet the issue of *our* overflights, if we needed to attack the Scuds, was more sensitive. We said that if we did have to cross into Jordanian air-space, we would find whatever way the king suggested to make it as unobtrusive as possible. We raised the possibility of using a narrow air corridor. His response was firm. This was an issue of Jordanian sover-eignty. He could not, and would not, collaborate in any way with an Is-raeli attack on another Arab state. Ephraim tried to find a way around the apparent stalemate. He suggested Shamir and the king withdraw to speak alone, and they met for nearly an hour. When Shamir emerged, clasping the king's hand and thanking him for his hospitality, he turned to us and said, "OK. We're going home."

He didn't tell us exactly what Hussein said. In the few sentences with which he described the talks on the flight back, he said that, as a sovereign, Hussein was compelled to protect his kingdom and would not order his forces to ignore Israeli planes if we overflew his territory. But Shamir added: "I assume there will be no war with Jordan."

+ + +

The Israeli public's concern over a possible Iraqi attack was growing by the day—in part because we had handed out gas masks to the whole country. Though I'd been concerned this action might raise the prospect of a chemical attack, I still thought a chemical strike was highly unlikely. The government, however, understandably decided that *not* distributing the masks would betray a fundamental responsibility to our citizens' safety. We'd also issued instructions about how to equip a room, usually the shelter included in nearly every Israeli home, as a *cheder atum*, or "sealed room" to keep gas from getting in. The Israeli media was full of speculation about the likely effects of a chemical attack. Many families had begun panic-buying of food and other necessities to prepare for the possibility of days and nights in their sealed shelters.

In my report for Dan, Misha, and Shamir a few weeks before the war, I drew on systematic analysis by a team of experts in the Israeli air force and made my most specific estimate yet of the damage conventionally armed Scuds might cause. We had gone back into historical accounts of the closest equivalent: the Nazis' use of V-1 and V-2 rockets against London in the Second World War. Given Saddam's primary need to fight Americans, and the likelihood either they or we would take military action against the launchers, we concluded we'd be hit by roughly forty missiles and, based on Britain's wartime experience, up to 120 Israelis might lose their lives.

The first air-raid sirens wailed at about 2:00 a.m. on January 18, 1991, almost exactly twenty-four hours after the Americans began their bombing raids over Baghdad. I was home in Kochav Yair. Though I felt a bit silly doing it, having assured the government Saddam was highly unlikely to use chemical warheads, we woke up the kids and Nava took them inside our sealed shelter. I put on my own gas mask, but when I ran out to my car I removed it and put it on the passenger's seat before heading into the kirya. I wanted to get there quickly enough so that the *bor*, the underground command bunker, wouldn't have to be reopened when I arrived.

I took a shortcut through the West Bank town of Qalqilya. That was, to put it mildly, stupid. Although the intifada had become steadily less intense during the buildup to the war, it wasn't completely over. Within seconds, my black sedan was pelted with stones by a half dozen Palestinian youths. I thought to myself: this is nuts. One of Saddam's Scuds might well be about to hit Israel, and I've got myself stuck in the middle of a West Bank town. To the obvious shock of the Palestinians, I floored the accelerator and raced toward Tel Aviv. It still took half an hour. Misha and Dan, who lived closer to the kirya, were already in the bunker.

Ten Scuds hit near Tel Aviv and Haifa that night. It was not until shortly before dawn that our tracker units got back to us with formal con-firmation that there had been no chemical warheads. The rockets caused a half dozen injuries, though thankfully none of them was serious. Still, the very fact Saddam had proven he could hit Israel with ballistic mis-siles provoked widespread alarm. Well into the next morning, the streets were almost empty. Misha phoned Cheney and strongly implied we were going to have to attack the Scud sites. I know that was Misha's own view, and it only hardened after another four missiles hit the Tel Aviv area the next morning. Again, no one was killed, but several dozen people were injured from debris, shards of glass, and blast concussion. I visited sev-eral of the areas that had been hit and was surprised by the scale of the damage. One four-story apartment building had been virtually destroyed, and there was blast damage to other buildings hundreds of yards away.

The Americans were determined, in both word and deed, to persuade us not to take military action. They rushed the Patriot anti-missile sys-tem to Israel. Cheney provided frequent updates on American air strikes against suspected Scud launch sites. And fortunately, the Israeli public seemed to grasp the serious implications for the US-led coalition if we took unilateral military action. Opinion polls suggested most Israelis were giving Shamir credit for the way he was handling the crisis.

Still, it wasn't easy for Shamir to hold the line. This was the first time since 1948 that enemy munitions had landed on Israeli homes, provok-ing not just fear but a feeling of helplessness. That inevitably led to calls for the army and the government to *do something*. I saw his dilemma first-hand at an emergency cabinet meeting after the first two Scud attacks. For Arik and Raful, the political effects on the US coalition were irrelevant. The issue, for them, was simple: Israeli cities had been attacked, and we should respond with any and all force necessary. Our air force commander, Avihu Ben-Nun, favored going ahead with the joint air and ground attack we'd prepared, and Misha agreed with him. So did Dan Shomron. The key voices of caution were Foreign Minister David Levy; Arye Deri, the leader of the Sephardi Orthodox party Shas; and two young Likud politicians, Dan Meridor and Ehud Olmert, with whom I had become friendly. They, like me, were concerned about undermining America's military and diplomatic coalition.

Shamir mostly listened, until very near the end. He then asked Dan

Meridor, Misha, and me to join him in a separate room. He asked each of us for our views. Misha, even more strongly than in front of the full cabinet, argued that we could not allow night after night of missile attacks without responding. Meridor reiterated his opposition, stressing the damage we'd risk doing to the Americans' war effort by possibly weakening Arab support for their attack on Saddam. When Shamir turned to me, I said that if the government did decide on military action, we were ready. From a purely military and security point of view, I said, an attack made absolute sense. Even if we didn't succeed in destroying all of the mobile launchers, putting a military force on the ground would almost surely lead to a dramatic reduction in the number of Scud launches. But, echoing Meridor, I added that a military response would risk undermining the US-led coalition and carry a *price* in our relationship with the Americans. My view was that, at least for now, we should hold off.

When we rejoined the meeting, Shamir rapped his hand on the table. In the startled silence that followed, he said he shared many ministers' urge to hit back against the Scuds. But he said, "*At this stage*, we're not going to do anything. We bite our lips and wait."

Three nights later, his resolve was stretched almost to its breaking point. Missiles landed in the Tel Aviv suburb of Ramat Gan, and nearly forty homes were damaged. A three-story house was flattened. In all, nearly one hundred people were injured, and three elderly residents died of heart attacks. On the night of January 25, another seven Scuds hit. Nearly 150 apartments were badly damaged, and a fifty-one-year-old man was killed. The pressure on Shamir was all the greater because the Ramat Gan attack had come within range of one of the Americans' Patriot batteries. The Patriots had been originally designed not as anti-missile weapons, but to shoot down aircraft, and they seemed to have been ineffective. Nor were American air strikes in Iraq stopping the Scuds. Though American jets had taken out a few fixed launch sites, they were having no luck with finding and destroying any mobile launch vehicles.

Even Shamir now felt that unless the Americans got the mobile launchers, we would have to take military action. I was sent to Washington along with Misha and David Ivri, a former air force commander, to deliver that message to the Bush administration. From the first days after Saddam's attack on Kuwait, I'd been impressed by President Bush's political acumen in assembling an international coalition including the key Arab countries: first the Saudis and the other Gulf states, then Morocco and eventually even the Syrians. The picture that emerged was of a president deftly able to stake out common ground, and common interests, with each of the Americans' growing number of anti-Saddam allies.

When we entered the Oval Office on the evening of February 11, Bush was flanked by Secretary of State James Baker, Defense Secretary Dick Cheney, and National Security Adviser Brent Scowcroft. Also there was Colin Powell, whom I had got to know well, and to like, over the past few years and who was now head of the joint chiefs of staff. Given the seriousness of our mission, the start of the meeting was almost surreal. The Americans had obviously been told that I was born on February 12. Since it was just past midnight in Israel, they began by wishing me a happy forty-ninth birthday.

Pleasing though that was, it also highlighted the jarring disconnect between the tension among Israeli government ministers and ordinary Israelis back home and the relaxed, self-assured, at times even jovial mood of the president and his inner circle. Their primary focus was not Israel, but the overwhelming success of their air attacks on Iraq and the approach of a ground offensive that they were confident would finish the job. That didn't seem to change even after a truly extraordinary interruption to our meeting, when one of Misha's aides passed on the news that a Scud had struck the Tel Aviv suburb of Savyon, where Misha himself lived. He immediately excused himself and phoned his wife, Muriel, to confirm she was fine. When he returned, despite their pro forma words of empathy, it seemed almost as if the Americans thought we had cooked up the entire thing for political effect.

Bush said the right things as the discussion turned to the missile attacks on Israel. He told us he understood our frustration, and the pain the Scud launches were inflicting. He appreciated our restraint. I have no doubt all of that was true. But the message we'd been sent to deliver clearly wasn't hitting home. As politely but as clearly as I could, I told him that while we didn't want to do anything to undermine the coalition, unless someone else took care of the Scuds, we would have no choice but to act.

The president responded by suggesting we go to the Pentagon and talk in greater detail about how that could be avoided. When we convened in

Secretary Cheney's office, I delivered the same message, but more force-fully. It was essential not only to make it clear we were serious about taking action, but that we had the military capability to do so. So I told Cheney and Colin Powell what we were planning. We intended to launch a com-bined air and ground assault by an air-mobile force and our best para-troop units. At that point, Colin, who was clearly worried, suggested the two of us withdraw to speak "soldier to soldier." We retreated to his office. Spreading out a map of western Iraq, I went into greater detail, explaining how we would remain in the Iraqi desert on a search-and-destroy mission against the mobile launchers. Colin stressed the efforts the Americans were making from the air, and the commitment they'd shown to Israel. Not only had they delivered the Patriots: they had allo-cated their best fighter jets, F-15Es, to the task of taking out the Scuds. It helped that he and I knew and respected each other, so it wasn't an all-out argument. But I reiterated that if the Scud attacks kept up, we would have to act. "We *will* act," I said. For a few seconds, he said nothing. But as we headed back to join the others, he told me that only a few hours ago, he had briefed American commanders on an anti-Scud operation by "allied forces" like the one we were planning. "It will happen," he assured me. "Within forty-eight hours."

That task fell to Britain's SAS, and its operation was almost exactly what we'd planned. A force of nearly 700 commandos was helicoptered in to Iraq's western desert. They were equipped with Land Rovers, and armed with anti-tank missiles and laser targeting capability. They could also call in attack helicopters and F-15 jets if necessary. Still, the opera-tion did not prove easy, quick, or entirely successful. The British troops blocked the main roads and patrolled them, but did not find or destroy a single mobile launcher. They ended up in gun battles with Iraqi troops and lost two dozen men. Five were part of a group that got separated from the others and ended up freezing to death in the February cold. One of the commandos survived only by walking one hundred miles into Syria. All of the men risked their lives, with incredible determination and brav-ery, in an operation to secure the safety of Israel's civilian population. I have no doubt that the outcome, like the plan, would have been almost identical if we had done it ourselves.

But it *did* have an effect. As I'd told Prime Minister Shamir when briefing him on our attack plan, the very fact of a military presence on the ground made a dramatic difference. The number, accuracy, and impact of the Scuds dropped off steeply. A few missiles kept coming, however. Since we did not yet have a fully detailed picture of the progress of the SAS action, skeptics and hawks in the cabinet were inclined to see a glass half empty. They continued to press for Israeli military action.

In a rare public statement, I tried to reassure the country that we did have a military option, but also urged restraint. I pointed out that the number of Scuds was decreasing. Though the threat had not been eliminated altogether, we had "very good operational plans" that would be "carried out when and if the Israeli government instructs us to implement them." Yet I added a caveat: "On the political level, fingers are itching to carry out operations which, in our opinion, can remove the threat. But in the complex situation created by this war, neither anger, hurt, nor itchy fingers can replace rational thinking."

The American ground invasion did turn out to be swift and decisive. In Israel, Scud attacks continued for a few more days. But the last two missiles fell in the Negev before dawn on February 25, among the very few to cause neither casualties nor damage. We turned out to have been right in our prewar assessment about the number of missiles: around forty. Fortunately, the casualties were far fewer than we'd anticipated. Not 120 dead, but 15, only one of whom died directly because of a missile blast. The other deaths were the result of understandable panic: the misuse of gas masks or the gas antidote drug atropine, or from respiratory and cardiac failure. The physical damage, however, was far greater than I'd anticipated. Buildings were destroyed. Cars were crushed. Glass and debris flew everywhere. The cost ran to hundreds of millions of dollars. The true impact was greater on families who saw the destruction of not only their homes but a lifetime of prized possessions. For Holocaust survivors in particular, there was the unimaginable terror of having to huddle in sealed rooms for fear of gas. And all Israelis had experienced a new sense of vulnerability to a faraway enemy they could neither see nor, apparently, stop.

+ + +

I was due to become Israel's fourteenth chief of staff at the start of April, barely a month after the last Scud attack. As the handover drew nearer, I felt fortunate, in a way, to have missed out on the job four years earlier. Dan excelled as ramatkal, and I'd benefited from his range of experience, his judgment, and his trust as well. We had worked together truly as a team.

I was grateful not only to Shamir for naming me chief of staff, but to Rabin and Misha Arens. Both had honored the assurance Yitzhak had given me that I'd be Dan's successor. I also discovered Misha had played an even greater role than I'd assumed. I knew there had been other candidates for the job, the strongest among them Yossi Peled, the head of the northern command. He, too, possessed the undoubted credentials to be an excellent chief of staff. What I hadn't been aware of was the sentiment among some in the Likud that I was the wrong choice *politically*. Not only had I been born on a Labor kibbutz, but there was the small matter of the article in *Hadashot* several years earlier, imagining me as a Labor leader going head-to-head in a future election against Bibi Netanyahu for the Likud.

Yossi was assumed to be more of a Likudnik, and a few weeks before Dan left office, I learned how Misha had rebutted the suggestion that I was politically unfit to lead the armed forces. He was visiting the north and was taken aside by a group of Likud activists who asked how he could possibly be thinking of supporting *Barak*—a Labor guy—for chief of staff. At first, Misha didn't reply. But one woman kept pressing him.

"Do you have children in the army?" he asked.

"Yes. I have a son in the Golani Brigade," she replied proudly.

"So let's assume your son is going on a raid across the border. Would you want his company to be led by the best commander in the battalion? Or by a commander who's Likud?"

"The best commander, of course," she said.

To which Misha said, "Well, we do, too."

# Chief of Staff

O<small>N THE MORNING OF</small> A<small>PRIL</small> 1, 1991, I <small>GOT UP EVEN EARLIER THAN</small>
usual, to visit the graves of the men who had lost their lives in my battalion
in the Yom Kippur War. I also went to pay my respects to Uzi Yairi, killed
when he'd rushed from his desk in the kirya to join Sayeret Matkal's
response to the terror attack at the Savoy Hotel. Then Nava and I drove
to Jerusalem. At Israel's national military cemetery on Mount Herzl, we
stood before the resting place of Nechemia Cohen, Yoni Netanyahu, Dado
Elazar, and Avraham Arnan. From there, we went to the prime minister's
office. With Dan Shomron and his wife looking on, Shamir presented
me with my third star and formally made me chief of staff.

For years, I'd developed the habit of carrying around a notebook in
which I'd jot down thoughts on things I thought that the Israeli military,
and I as an officer, could have done better: errors, oversights, and how we
might fix them. In the weeks before becoming ramatkal, I'd filled dozens
of pages on issues large and small I hoped to address as the commander
of the armed forces. A lot of them dealt with what I sensed was an ero-
sion of cohesiveness in the army and, since ours was a citizen military, a
fraying of the relationship between the army and Israeli society. To some
degree, this was inevitable in a country now nearly forty-five years old:
we were developed economically and free of the kind of existential threat
we'd faced in the state's early years. But the political divisions over the

war in Lebanon and the morale-sapping effort to quell the violence on the West Bank and in Gaza had further strained our unity of purpose.

Militarily, we were indisputably strong enough to defeat any of the Arab armies, even if they launched a joint attack as in 1973. Our most important overseas ally, the United States, was committed to helping us retain that position—what both we and they called Israel's "qualitative military edge"—in the interest of our security and their own. But we were facing a series of new, *unconventional* challenges. One of them, which had shown up on Dan Shomron's and my radar over the past year, was Iran. Though geographically distant, it was potentially the most serious in the longer run, as Dan himself warned Israelis in his final interview as chief of staff. Iran was likely to become even more assertive regionally now that the Gulf War had weakened its neighbor and rival, Iraq. We also knew, from our intelligence sources, that the Iranians were making preliminary efforts to develop a nuclear weapon.

Yet the most immediate security concerns were right next door. In Lebanon, Hizbollah fighters were being armed and financed by the Iranians and by Syria as well. They were mounting increasingly effective operations against the Israeli troops we'd left in the security zone. Even closer to home, Palestinian attacks on both troops and civilians, though on nowhere near the scale of the first months of the intifada, showed no sign of ending. I had my own views on both. In Lebanon, I still believed we should pull out all our troops and focus our security arrangements on what really mattered: protecting the citizens of northern Israel. As for the lessons to be learned from the intifada, my view that we needed a political dialogue had inadvertently become public from remarks I made in Moshe Dayan's honor at a memorial event a few months before becoming chief of staff. "We are currently in a struggle with the Palestinians— a long, bitter, and continuing struggle," I said. "A people cannot choose its neighbors. But we will have to talk to the Palestinians about matters, especially about issues that are vital to them."

Still, I was the commander of the armed forces, not a politician. Though all chiefs of staff had political influence, if only as part of the decision-making process on all major security questions, making *policy* was for our elected government. My main focus was on how to improve the military's fitness to respond. I'd lived through all, and fought in most, of

Israel's wars. I felt we had yet to apply some of the critical lessons from those conflicts. Leading tanks into battle against the Egyptians' deadly Sagger missiles in 1973, and a decade later watching whole Israeli armored columns stalled and attacked by small bands of PLO fighters or Syrian commandos in Lebanon, had hardened my conviction that Israel needed a leaner, more mobile army, with more specialized strike units as well as more easily targeted, less vulnerable weapons systems. I wanted to shift the emphasis to weaponry that relied on Israel's strengths in new technology, invention, and engineering. In a sense, this was the macroscopic equivalent of one of the guiding principles of Sayeret Matkal: brains, not just brawn.

While cost-saving wasn't the catalyst, I did realize that a change in strategy would mean a change in how we allocated our resources. When Israel bought its first Mirage jets from France in the 1960s, they cost about a million dollars apiece. The price tag of an F-16 was now closer to *fifty* million dollars. The cost of a tank had increased tenfold. I wasn't going to deprive the air force of state-of-the-art aircraft, key to our ability to fight and win a war. But while we still needed a strong armored corps, it was important to realize that units like the new air-mobile division we'd planned to use against Saddam's Scud launchers were likely to be a lot more important than expanding the number of our tank units in future conflicts.

Six days into the job, I called together every officer in the army from the rank of lieutenant colonel up. I said we needed to remind ourselves of the army's purpose: to protect Israel's security, and if a war came, to win it. My budgetary rule of thumb over the next four years would be simple: anything that didn't directly contribute to that mission was expendable. In fact, I put it a bit more bluntly: "We need to cut anything that doesn't shoot."

My first attempt failed utterly. I proposed to close, or sell off, the army's radio station, Galei Tzahal. Running it cost serious money. If we were going to cut everything that didn't shoot, it was an obvious candidate. But what I failed to take into account was its popularity with the listening public. Although other radio stations had opened recently, for many years it had been the only major alternative to the state-funded Kol Yisrael. It also provided a training ground and employment feeder for future journalists. Galei Tzahal's alumni included some of the country's top media figures, and more than a few members of the Knesset. Within weeks, a lobbying effort was under way to "save" the station. I went to see Misha. He agreed that from a military and budgetary standpoint, closing it was the right thing to do. But in an early lesson in how different politics were from the army, he told me that *politically*, it simply wasn't going to fly. "Drop it, Ehud," he said. So I did.

Still, I did end up fundamentally retooling the armed forces during my time as chief of staff. We developed agile new strike forces and high-precision, high-tech weapons systems with "stand-off" munitions designed to be fired from many miles away. In the 1973 war, and for the decade or two that followed, Saggers, and the US-made TOW missiles that Israel acquired after the war, had the capability to transform a battlefield. Now, Israeli developers came up with small, ground-launched missiles that could take out a tank from five to ten miles away, even without a direct line of sight to the target. Of even more long-term military significance, I pushed ahead with developing pilotless drones—so-called unmanned aerial vehicles, or UAVs—making us the first army in the world to produce and deploy them.

Yet these were of little use in dealing with a security challenge like the intifada. The latest stage in the violence involved knife attacks by Palestinians against Israeli civilians, both on West Bank settlers and inside Israel. Days after I took over, a twenty-six-year-old from Gaza, wielding a butcher's knife and shouting *Alahu Akhbar*, killed four people, including a kindergarten teacher, in Jerusalem. On the morning of May 24, 1992, a fifteen-year-old Israeli schoolgirl named Helena Rapp was on her way to catch the bus to school south of Tel Aviv, when another Gazan stabbed her to death. To the extent Israelis were looking for someone to blame, there were obvious candidates. The army, the primary defense against the intifada, was one. The police even more so, since many of the attacks were now taking place inside Israel. And in ugly rioting after Helena Rapp's murder, bands of Israelis took to the streets, some of them yelling, "Death to the Arabs." Still, most people understood that criticizing the army or the police, or going on a rampage against "the Arabs"—hundreds of thousands of whom were Israeli citizens and had lived among us since the birth of the state—would not help. Most, in fact, placed the blame on, and lodged their hopes with, the government.

By the time of the next election, in June 1992, the combination of Palestinian violence and the still-traumatic memories of Saddam's Scuds left Israelis doubtful that Shamir could fulfill the most basic responsibility of government: ensuring their day-to-day security. Labor had once again placed its electoral fortunes in the hands of Yitzhak Rabin, following Peres's several failed attempts to lead the party back into power. Knowing that Rabin had a record of military command unmatched in Israeli politics, Labor strategists did not so much need to convince voters as to reinforce their fears and frustrations. One of the campaign slogans, a direct appeal to the anger over the stabbing of Helena Rapp, was "Get Gaza out of Tel Aviv!" Labor ended up gaining five Knesset seats, and now had forty-four. The Likud lost eight and was left with only thirty-two.

That meant that my last three years as chief of staff would be with Rabin as prime minister—an especially important relationship because Rabin, like Ben-Gurion before him, was defense minister as well. He and I had been in touch only occasionally since his departure from the unity-coalition government two years earlier. But I had, of course, spoken with him after my appointment as ramatkal. Though he was twenty years older than me, our relationship had become steadily closer over the years, especially when I'd worked with him in his role as defense minister. In some ways, we were alike. We'd both been forged by Labor Zionism. We were career military officers and less comfortable in the political arena. In large groups especially, both of us tended to be men of a few words. Over the next few years, we would become even closer, speaking not only in the kirya or at his office in Jerusalem, but also, with Nava and Leah, around the dinner table at the Rabins' apartment in Tel Aviv.

+ + +

But there were times of crisis and high tension, as well. Only five months after the election, we faced one of the most painful periods during my tenure as chief of staff. It began with the gruesome deaths of five Sayeret Matkal soldiers during a training exercise in the Negev Desert. I'd made preventing such accidents a top priority. By the end of the 1980s, they were claiming nearly eighty lives a year. During Dan's tenure, we'd brought the number down to about thirty-five. But I knew we had to do more. When I addressed the officers after becoming chief of staff, I told them: "Parents are giving us their children in order to allow us to protect the country. They know there is risk involved. But they expect their children not to be brought home in coffins because of our own negligence, or stupidity." What happened at the military base of Tze'elim in the Negev on November 5, 1992, was not only a reminder of how far we still had to go. It occurred during a dry run for an operation unlike any Israel had ever considered. For that and other reasons, it would erupt into a major political controversy.

Though the exercise was meant to have remained a closely guarded secret, foreign newspaper reports in the weeks after the training accident made secrecy impossible, and it became known that we were considering an operation to infiltrate a Sayeret Matkal team into Iraq and kill Saddam Hussein.

The Gulf War had blunted any immediate threat from Iraq. But Saddam had proven he could launch missiles into the heart of Israel. We knew from our intelligence reports that, in addition to his unabated desire to acquire nuclear arms, he retained facilities to produce chemical weapons. He was trying to acquire and develop new biological weapons. In fact, the Iraqis had actually acknowledged a biological weapons program to UN inspectors, claiming it was for "defensive purposes."

The idea for an attack on Saddam had first been raised a year earlier, when my former Sayeret Matkal comrade, Amiram Levin, asked to see me. He was between military postings but had come up with the outline of a plan he felt would allow us to isolate Saddam during a public appearance and kill him. With my approval, he and a small group of officers began working further on the idea, with the initial aim of seeing whether it was really workable. Since Misha was still defense minister, I briefed him on what we were doing. I also briefed Rabin after the election. At that stage, there was no discussion of whether we actually would, or should, target Saddam. I asked Misha, and then Yitzhak, only whether such an operation might seriously be considered by the government. If not, I said, we'd drop it. Both replied that we should go ahead with the planning and preparation. The November 1992 exercise was intended as a final test of its viability.

A few weeks earlier, Rabin and I, along with a dozen other officers from the military and the Defense Ministry, had talked through the arguments for and against. The arguments *against* it were obvious. Yes, in the past we had abducted, or even killed, leaders of groups involved in terror attacks. But we'd never contemplated targeting a head of state. That would be crossing a line: breaching long-accepted norms of international relations and possibly running the risk of encouraging similar attacks on Israeli leaders. The arguments in favor began with the fact that Saddam was a megalomaniacally ambitious dictator. In addition to his record of ruthlessness and murder at home, he had fired missiles on Israeli towns and cities only two years earlier. He retained the capability to arm them with chemical warheads, possibly biological agents, and even conceivably a nuclear warhead in the future. Both Rabin and I agreed there were two key tests of whether an attack could be justified: Was it the only realistic way of confronting the threat from Iraq, and would killing him end, or at least exponentially reduce, that threat?

Though there was no final decision at our meeting, Rabin was clearly inclined to go ahead. An Israeli TV program two decades later unearthed a summary of the discussion, written by his military aide. "The Prime Minister approves the target. This is an operation we should go for when the probability of success is very high," it said. "Thus, we have to build the operational capability in the best possible way, and continue preparations." In another part of the record, Rabin is quoted as having defined the elimination of Saddam as a "meaningful objective" with implications for "the very security of Israel." He added, in what was at the time a simple statement of fact: "I do not see anyone similar to him in the Arab world."

On balance, I too was persuaded we should do it. In the years since, I've sometimes reflected on what happened with Saddam still in place: the 2003 invasion of Iraq, led by the younger President Bush, the tens of thousands of lives lost, the trillions of dollars spent on a war without any clear end, and the near disintegration of Iraq. But with the complexities of Iraq then and now, there can be no simple answer to how the situation would have changed if we'd killed Saddam. Our view, based on detailed intelligence analyses, was that the likely result would have been a fairly rapid takeover by a few top security and Baath Party figures and that, while the new Iraqi leadership might try to retaliate with terror attacks, a major military response was highly unlikely. Saddam's successors were never going to be Zionists. But we were persuaded that his uniquely central role meant the threat to Israel would be dramatically reduced.

I'm much less sure whether the elder President Bush, whose election defeat to Bill Clinton came just two days before our final exercise in the Negev, would have agreed with the attack. After the victory in the Gulf War, Bush had deliberately stopped short of sending American forces on to Baghdad. He was also vice president under Reagan when Israel had bombed Saddam's nuclear reactor—an attack publicly condemned by Washington. I asked him, nearly a decade after he'd left the presidency, whether the Gulf War might have been handled differently if Israel *hadn't* taken out Saddam's nuclear program a decade earlier. "What if he'd had a couple of crude nuclear devices?" I suggested. He smiled in response, saying that he never dealt with "hypotheticals."

Yet any idea of an Israeli attack on Saddam became instantly irrelevant once foreign media reports had disclosed the reason for our ill-fated military exercise in the Negev. And inside Israel, the focus, and the controversy, shifted to the accident itself.

The foreign media reports of the operation we were planning proved remarkably accurate. Some of the details still remain classified, but we were going to use one of our new "stand-off" weapons systems: a camera-guided missile that could be fired from a considerable distance and, in coordination with a Sayeret Matkal squad closer to where we would be targeting Saddam, maneuvered in for the strike. After months of planning and intelligence work, we were confident that we'd found a way to get the sayeret unit into Iraq, target Saddam at an event we knew he would be attending, isolate and kill him with minimal danger of any other casualties, and get our unit out safely again. The Negev exercise was a run-through of the entire operation. It lasted nearly forty-eight hours and culminated in a simulation of the missile attack on Saddam.

I was there as an observer along with Amnon Lipkin, my deputy chief of staff, as well as the head of military intelligence, the head of operations, and Amiram Levin. We assembled at dawn and watched from a few hundred yards away as a group of young Israeli soldiers walked into a wide area in front of us: posing as Saddam and his entourage. We—and they—knew this was just the first part of the exercise. More than five miles away, a member of the sayeret strike unit would confirm coordinates and, in rapid succession, "fire" two of the precision missiles. But this was just to confirm the targeting system had worked perfectly. No missiles would actually be shot. This stage was for the telemetry and coordination. Once that was done, the soldier-actors would be replaced with wooden targets and the real munitions would be tested.

The young soldiers started chatting with one another and milling about, simulating as best we could the circumstances in which we expected to target Saddam if the operation got final approval. In theory, within a minute, two minutes at most, we would get word that the preliminary mock-firing sequence had gone perfectly—at which point the wooden-framed targets would be brought in for the live test. But suddenly, there was an explosion. A split second of silence. Then pandemonium. There was no need to know, and no time to wonder, what exactly had gone wrong, or how it had been allowed to happen. It was obvious to all of us that the *live* missiles had been fired. We rushed forward. When we got to the group of soldiers, we could see that four of the young men were beyond help. Another was fighting for his life. Several others were also wounded.

A sayeret medic and several senior officers were fighting to save the most badly injured man, but I knew I needed to get military doctors and medevac helicopters in immediately if we were to save the lives of the injured soldiers. I had a mobile phone but couldn't get a signal. I climbed toward a slightly higher area a few dozen yards away and managed to issue orders for the nearby training base in Tze'elim and an air force base near Beersheva to dispatch helicopters to treat and evacuate the wounded.

We heard the first chopper about twenty minutes later, but it initially didn't see us, flying past us before returning and landing two minutes later. By that time, a medical team from the base in Tze'elim had arrived. Ten minutes later, two other medevac choppers landed. But the soldier who had been the worst wounded could not be saved. After the doctors had been there about twenty minutes, I again retreated to the area where I could get a mobile signal and phoned Rabin to tell him what had happened.

We agreed I should come back to brief him in detail. It was now about fifty minutes since the missiles had hit. The wounded were all being treated. One of the helicopters had taken off for Beersheva Hospital. Another two, including a heavier Sikorsky transport helicopter, were preparing to leave. I arranged for Amnon, military operations chief Shmuel Arad, and me to return to the kirya. I told Amiram to stay until he had confirmed all the injured had been evacuated, and to talk to everyone involved to get a preliminary idea of what had happened.

When I got back, we immediately met with Rabin and agreed on the need to launch a formal investigation. Rabin then asked me to brief the "editors club," a group of about fifteen media figures that operated on a gentleman's agreement that there would be no publicity or leaks. We agreed we should not make public the fact that I and other generals were there when the accident occurred. At this stage, we still hoped to hide the purpose of the exercise if possible, something Rabin knew would be harder if it was known the top military leadership had observed the exercise. When I delivered my detailed briefing to the editors club, I did tell them in confidence that I'd been there. Though not specifying the reason for the exercise, I told them it was for a major operation. The time-honored understanding was that this information would go no further. But it did, presumably at first because of leaks by Israeli journalists, then in a series of detailed reports in the foreign press. Even more frustrating on a personal level, some of the Israeli reports insinuated that, far from giving the editors the full story of who had been at the Negev exercise, I'd tried to *hide* my presence in order to protect my reputation or shirk responsibility.

Two official inquiries followed: the one we'd agreed to with Rabin, which was completed within a matter of days, and a standard army legal investigation, which took more than a year. They found the cause of the tragedy to be a mix of fatigue after some of the soldiers had spent nearly forty-eight hours awake plus pressure, confusion, and negligence. Astonishingly, it turned out the code word for the mock-firing of the missiles in the first stage of the exercise was the same as for the live missiles. Formal charges were brought against two Sayeret Matkal officers, and reprimands issued to Uri Saguy and Amiram Levin. I was also subject to criticism because due to the unique complexity of the plan, although Sayeret Matkal fell under the formal authority of Saguy as head of intelligence, I had placed Amiram and senior sayeret officers in charge of different aspects of the preparations. This was viewed as possibly reducing the clarity over who was ultimately responsible for each aspect of the exercise. Yet neither I nor Rabin had played a direct role in what went wrong in the exercise itself, and my own involvement was to make sure the medical teams were helicoptered in and that the injured soldiers were cared for and evacuated as soon as possible. Neither of us could have anticipated that the tragedy at Tze'elim would dramatically resurface several years later—shortly after I'd left the military and was on the verge of becoming a minister in Rabin's government.

I was getting to know Yitzhak much better. His office in the kirya, as defense minister, was just down the hall from mine. Almost without fail on Friday afternoons, he'd ask me in to chat before going home. We would sit around a low table in the corner of the room, each of us sipping coffee, or sometimes beer, and Rabin invariably puffing on a cigarette. He never raised questions of party politics. But we talked at length about Israel's immediate security concerns, as well as the country's longer-term challenges in finding its place in a more stable, peaceful Middle East. How, over time, we might manage to extricate ourselves from the escalating violence with Hizbollah; reach a land-for-peace deal with the enigmatic President Hafez al-Assad in Syria; and find some form of coexistence with the Palestinians.

He also spoke about international politics. I remember one afternoon in the summer of 1992 when he mentioned the then US presidential candidate Bill Clinton. He'd met Clinton for the first time in Washington after two days of talks with President Bush at his summer home in Maine. Rabin was naturally more comfortable dealing with Republicans. Almost all his experience in public life—as a military officer, ambassador to Washington, defense minister, and prime minister—had coincided with Republican administrations. The irony was that he would go on to forge a much closer relationship with President Clinton than between any previous Israeli leader and US leader. But his first impression was more cautious. "Clearly, Clinton is very intelligent," he said. "He is surprisingly sharp politically for someone his age." But Rabin said one couldn't be sure how these qualities would transfer to the presidency if Clinton won.

+ + +

We did not have long to focus on the lessons and implications of Tze'elim. For weeks before the training accident, a crisis had been building in south Lebanon, with a sharp escalation of the now-familiar mix of clashes inside our "security zone" and cross-border rocket attacks. Hizbollah was now armed not just with Katyushas but American-made TOW anti-tank missiles and an increasingly sophisticated array of roadside bombs. A combination of Hizbollah attacks and "friendly fire" incidents or firearms accidents involving our troops meant that Israelis were still dying in Lebanon a decade after the formal end of the war. It was demoralizing for the Israeli public, for the soldiers we rotated into the security zone, and for the government as well. The difficulty was that it was also a situation that perfectly suited Hizbollah.

In late October, a Katyusha rocket had claimed the life of a fourteen-year-old boy in the northern Israeli town of Kiryat Shmona. Hizbollah fired more missiles in the days that followed, forcing tens of thousands of residents into their shelters. Predictably, there was pressure from Likud politicians to hit back hard. Raful Eitan, who had founded a small right-wing party called Tsomet, went further. He called the attacks "an act of war" and said we should "respond in kind." We did move troops and tanks to the border. But my view, which Rabin shared, was that a major ground operation would risk miring ourselves more deeply without fundamentally improving the situation. Hizbollah was the kind of nonconventional enemy I had in mind when I'd taken stock of Israel's changing security imperatives on becoming chief of staff. It was a small force, entrenched and well armed, increasingly supported by Iran and Syria. Its tactics rested on quick-hit attacks on our soldiers in south Lebanon. Far from fearing military retaliation, Hizbollah knew that short of a 1982-scale war—and maybe even then—it would survive. It also didn't care whether Lebanese civilians died in the cross fire. In fact, like the PLO fighters who had controlled the area before 1982, Hizbollah deliberately fired into Israel from civilian areas.

Neither Rabin nor I had abandoned the idea of a large-scale military operation at some point, particularly if the cross-border rocket fire didn't subside, which for a while it did. But we were determined that if and when we did decide to strike, we would avoid anything on the scale of the 1982 war. It would have to be with a clear, finite, and achievable goal.

That point finally arrived in the summer of 1993. In addition to re-newed Katyusha strikes, there was a series of deadly Hizbollah attacks in the first two weeks of July inside the security zone. Each used what was becoming the tactic of choice: a remotely detonated bomb by the side of the road on which our military vehicles were traveling, followed by an ambush of soldiers who survived the blast. Six Israelis had been killed in all, making it the largest monthly toll in three years. When I went to see Rabin with our plan for a military response, I recognized the risks. It would be the largest military operation in Lebanon since the war. But I believed we could limit civilian casualties, and that it was the only ap-proach that might lead to a significant reduction in the missile attacks on northern Israel. I began with the assumption that, left to its own devices, Hizbollah would have no incentive to stop firing. Since the two Arab gov-ernments with the potential to rein in the attacks—Lebanon and above all Syria—were showing no interest in doing so, we had to find a way to hold them to account.

The operation I proposed was intended to send a message to Beirut and Damascus. It would not be a ground invasion as in 1982. Most of the attacks would be from the air, in two stages. The first would target Hiz-bollah, both in southern Lebanon and in the Bekaa Valley further north, near the border with Syria. We could halt at that stage, in the unlikely event Hizbollah showed signs of de-escalation. But if it didn't, the air strikes would intensify. The aim was not to target the nearly 250,000 Leb-anese civilians who lived in the immediate border area. It was to use our attacks, along with leaflet drops and radio messages, to encourage them to flee north. My assessment was that this would bring pressure on the Lebanese government and, through the Lebanese, on the real power in Lebanon, the Syrians. I doubted Damascus would respond directly by telling Hizbollah to cease fire. I did believe they'd be ready to engage with American efforts to stop the fighting, and that Rabin and the government could then secure terms we were prepared to accept.

On July 25, we began our heaviest air strikes since 1982. Far from pro-ducing a sign of a de-escalation by Hizbollah, they were met with inten-sified rocket fire. We escalated over the following twenty-four hours, but still with no indication of any change from Hizbollah. So as planned, we expanded our bombing to wider areas of south Lebanon. Sadly, some Lebanese civilians were killed; thankfully, the majority fled north. In south Lebanon, this meant that our jets and artillery had much greater freedom of operation against Hizbollah, which had now lost its human shields. In Beirut, a government suddenly overwhelmed with the need to provide shelter for tens of thousands of refugees from the fighting did press Syrian president Assad to help bring it to an end. Critically, the new Clinton administration, especially Secretary of State Warren Christopher, reinforced that message.

Our military operation lasted just a week. We took out a lot of Hizbollah's infrastructure in the border area, destroying some 150 Katyushas and killing sixty-five of its fighters, with the loss of two Israeli lives. It did *not* bring an end to Hizbollah attacks on Israeli troops in the security zone, something I think even most Israelis were coming to realize was impossible as long as our soldiers remained in Lebanon. But the rocket attacks on northern Israel did stop, with very few exceptions, for a period lasting nearly two years.

The intifada, however, had not stopped. Nor, as I knew from my increasingly frequent meetings with Rabin, had the search for a way to both control the violence and seek out any realistic prospect of a *political* path to resolving our conflict with our Arab neighbors.

---

# Prospects and Perils
# of Peace

RABIN HAD INHERITED A PEACE PROCESS, PUT IN MOTION BY THE Bush administration after the Gulf War. But since both Prime Minister Shamir and Arab leaders had reasons of procedure, politics, or principle to resist the talks, merely getting them off the ground had required the same combination of deftness and determination President Bush had brought to assembling his wartime coalition against Saddam. After a formal opening session in Madrid at the end of October 1991, the "bilateral tracks"—between Israel and negotiators from Syria, Lebanon, Jordan, and the Palestinians—had stalemated and stalled.

Yitzhak came to my office saying he was not interested in a peace *process*, which seemed to him a license for endless talk with no set endpoint, but in *peacemaking*. Since I had the good fortune to be part of the informal inner circle with which he discussed the potential opportunities, pitfalls, and frustrations along the way, I know that he didn't assume we would succeed in achieving a peace agreement with any of our neighbors. But after the twin shocks of the Lebanon War and the Scud missiles, he was concerned that Israel would retreat into a mix of inward-looking political caution and military deterrence that he believed was understandable, important as far as it went, but shortsighted. He was convinced that we needed at least to try to seize a "window of opportunity" with those enemies who were at least open to compromise, if only because we were facing new threats from enemies for whom talk was not even an option. An increasingly assertive Iran, with nuclear ambitions, was one. But the intifada had also thrown up new Palestinian groups grounded not in nationalism, but fundamentalist Islam: Hamas in Gaza, which opposed Israel's presence on any part of "Muslim Palestine," and Islamic Jihad on the West Bank. And in Lebanon, we were confronting the Iranian-backed Shi'ite militia fighters of Hizbollah.

Each of us in the small group on whom Rabin relied for input on the peace talks brought something different to the mix. In addition to me, there were four other generals: Uri Saguy, the head of military intelligence; Gadi Zohar, in charge of civil administration for the West Bank; my deputy chief of staff, Amnon Lipkin; and my former sayeret deputy, Danny Yatom, who was now head of the central command. Also included were longtime political and media aide Eitan Haber, and another trusted political adviser thousands of miles away: Itamar Rabinovich, our ambassador in Washington and Israel's leading Syria expert. But I'm sure we weren't chosen just for our insights. It was because we were people with whom Rabin felt *comfortable*—a counterpoint, I suspect, to the old Labor Party rival whom he had made foreign minister, Shimon Peres. Though the two men had grown to respect each other over the years, Rabin neither trusted, nor much liked, Shimon. In fact, though Peres's support inside Labor had secured him the Foreign Ministry, Rabin had stipulated that all peace talks would remain under his control.

As I would discover nearly a decade later, even the most carefully planned negotiating strategies were subject to setbacks, diversions, or simply what former British prime minister Harold Macmillan once called "events, dear boy, events." Rabin's initial plan was to start not with the Palestinians, but with Syria. President Assad was obstinate, and publicly opposed to the idea of making peace with Israel. But he had been in power for more than two decades and, crucially for Rabin, had lived up to the few, indirect agreements Israel had made with him. The *substance* in any agreement, though politically difficult, was also more straightforward. We knew what Assad wanted: the recovery of the Golan Heights, in return for the absolute minimum level of political normalization with Israel. We knew what we needed in such an agreement: security guarantees and assurances regarding water resources, and a full and final peace treaty. For Rabin, there was an additional attraction in beginning with Syria: if

we *did* reach a deal with our main Arab enemy, the pressure would intensify on the Palestinians to follow suit. It might well also open the way
to peace with Lebanon.

In one respect, the prospects for a deal with the Palestinians looked
slightly better than before. Yasir Arafat's political position had been
weakened: first by an intifada, which was driven as much by local insurgents as by the PLO in faraway Tunis; then by his ill-judged decision to
break with his longtime Arab Gulf financial supporters and side with
Saddam Hussein in the Gulf War. In 1988, as the entry price for a formal
dialogue with the Bush administration, he had also agreed to a statement
in which he renounced terrorism and accepted the principle of a two-state
peace agreement with Israel. Still, there remained a yawning gap between
the "self-rule" envisaged in the Camp David accords of 1978 and the
Madrid conference on one hand, and the independent state the Palestinians
wanted. Rabin's inclination to focus first on Syria was because he assumed
that negotiations with the Palestinians were likely to be fraught and long.

+ + +

The dramatic turn of events that ultimately forced him to change tack
got under way in January 1993 in the sitting room of a villa outside Oslo,
at an ostensible "academic seminar" convened by the Norwegian diplomat Terje Rød-Larsen. It included two Israeli academics: Yair Hirschfeld
and the historian and former *Haaretz* journalist Ron Pundak. Three
PLO officials were there, led by Arafat's closest economic and political
aide, Abu Ala'a. Though both of the Israelis were friends of Yossi Beilin, a
protégé of Peres and our deputy foreign minister, even Peres didn't know
about the meeting until Yossi told him the following day. Rabin knew an
hour later. I first learned of it from Uri Saguy. At first, even Peres was
skeptical that the paper agreed on at the "seminar"—calling for international aid to the West Bank and Gaza along the lines of the Marshall Plan,
and an initial Israeli withdrawal limited to Gaza—would lead to serious
negotiations. But Rabin authorized follow-up sessions in mid-February,
late March, and again in April. Our intelligence teams continued to provide
detail and occasional color. The burly, bearded Yair Hirschfeld was "the
Bear." The slighter Ron Pundak was "the Mouse." Yet the main *political*
impetus in driving the process forward came from two men who were not

there: on our side, Yossi Beilin, and for the Palestinians, Arafat's trusted diplomatic adviser and eventual successor, Mahmoud Abbas, also known as Abu Mazen.

Since Rabin knew I was following the ostensibly secret talks, we discussed them often. For quite a while, he remained dismissive. He believed the chances of a breakthrough were remote. He was also suspicious of the involvement of Peres and Beilin, whom he called "Shimon's poodle." And he deeply distrusted Arafat. The PLO had been founded with the aim of "liberating" every inch of Palestine. The fact that Arafat had agreed to the Bush administration's demand to accept the principle of land for peace struck Rabin as mere sleight of hand.

By the third Oslo meeting, it was clear that the Palestinians were in fact open to an agreement that would fall well short of "liberating Palestine." Still, Rabin was leery. He tried briefly to return the focus to the stalemated Madrid-track talks with the Palestinians. Yet when, with obvious PLO encouragement, the Palestinian negotiators stood their ground there, he seemed almost resigned to supporting Oslo. When we discussed it, he used a battlefield metaphor. "When you have to break through, you don't necessarily know where you'll succeed. You try several places along the enemy's lines. In the sector of the front where you *do* succeed, you send in your other forces." It was a matter of "reinforcing success."

"It's the *opposite* in this case," I replied. "In a battle, the enemy is doing everything it can to stop you. When you break through, it's against their resistance. Here, the other side will choose to make it easiest for us in the place *it* prefers. If Arafat thinks he'll get more from the Bear and the Mouse than from the other talks, it's hardly a surprise we're finding that only Oslo seems to offer a way forward."

Rabin made one more move, not so much in a bid to end the talks in Oslo as to slow them down and create a context more favorable for the kind of agreement he wanted. He reverted to his original peacemaking priority: the Syrians. In an effort to remove a roadblock to even beginning serious talks, he offered the Americans what they would later call his "pocket deposit." He authorized Secretary of State Warren Christopher to tell Assad that *Washington's* understanding of our position was that, assuming all our own negotiating concerns were met, we accepted that peace with Syria would include withdrawing from the Golan. Rabin didn't tell Peres or other ministers about it, though Itamar Rabinovich knew. I did as well. Since acceptance of the need for a withdrawal had security implications, Rabin and I discussed the issues in detail, and formulated the "deposit" together. We used an English acronym: IAMNAM, "if all my needs are met." The point was to convey to the Syrian president that if he addressed our requirements for a demilitarized zone and early-warning facilities; noninterference with our critically important water sources; and a full peace including embassies, open borders, and joint economic projects, we knew the trade-off would be to return the Golan.

It was by diplomatic accident that the Syrian overture went nowhere. The reason even the Americans had called our proposal a "pocket deposit" was that it was to be kept in Christopher's pocket, to be pulled out as *an American understanding* of our position if he felt it might lead to a breakthrough. But Christopher ended up presenting it as a straight message from Rabin to the Syrian president, giving it the status of Israel's new, formal opening position in negotiations.

The distinction may seem minor. But for Israel, it mattered greatly. In any agreement with Syria—or, indeed, the Palestinians—there was bound to be an imbalance. Both parts of a land-for-peace exchange were important. But land was not just the more tangible asset. Once given up, short of resorting to all-out war, there was no claiming it back. The "peace" part of the equation was more difficult. Genuine peace, and trust, would inevitably take years to reach fruition. That was no mere academic problem in a conflict in which, for decades, our enemies had defined Israel's mere existence as illegitimate. The reason for Rabin's reluctance to have his "deposit" presented as a set negotiating position was that it meant dealing away our only card—territory—before the hard questions about security and peace had been answered. It was a problem I'd face as prime minister as well, both with Assad and Arafat.

When Rabin phoned Christopher, I don't think I'd ever heard him as angry. That was *not* what we agreed, he told the secretary of state. He said it had spoiled any prospect of serious negotiations on the *peace* side of the balance. Christopher didn't agree there had been any real damage, nor that Assad had failed to understand the context.

It might not have mattered anyway, since by this stage, the Oslo talks were nearing a draft agreement. In mid-August, Rabin gave Peres the go-ahead to initial this "Declaration of Principles." It provided for a period of interim Palestinian self-government; the start of a phased Israeli withdrawal from Gaza and the West Bank with the creation of a Palestinian police force to deal with internal security; and a commitment to reach a full peace agreement within five years. In early September, ahead of the formal signing of the Oslo declaration, there was an exchange of "letters of recognition" between Arafat and Rabin. Arafat's letter also renounced "terrorism and other acts of violence" and declared invalid "those articles of the Palestinian Covenant which deny Israel's right to exist." A few days later, President Clinton hosted a signing ceremony in Washington. Thus emerged the famous photo of Rabin and Arafat shaking hands, on either side of Clinton, who was beaming, arms outstretched in conciliation. They say a picture is worth a thousand words. In this case, you needed barely a dozen. Rabin's demeanor, his posture, the look on his face, all seemed to say: "I would rather be shaking the hand of anyone on earth than Arafat." Still, the image was on front pages worldwide. The news stories spoke of a new spirit of hope. Now that these old enemies had grasped hands, surely a full peace agreement was within reach.

My feeling, as I watched it on TV in the kirya, was more guarded. I hoped for peace, of course. I also recognized that the signing on the White House lawn was just a beginning, and that my role would be to ensure that Israel's security needs were met under whatever formal peace agreement might eventually be reached. The security omens were hardly encouraging. Despite Oslo, Palestinian attacks continued. Hamas, Islamic Jihad, and other dissident factions saw Arafat's concessions as treachery, and they drove home that point with violence.

+ + +

As I approached my final year as chief of staff in early 1994, we were suddenly confronted by an appalling act of *Israeli* violence: mass murder, committed by a West Bank settler. It was terrorism, no less so than the worst Arab attacks on Israeli civilians. The settler, a physician named Baruch Goldstein, was a member of the stridently right-wing, anti-Arab Kach movement founded by the Brooklyn-born rabbi Meir Kahane. Goldstein lived in Kiryat Arba, one of the first post-1967 Jewish settlements, located on a hill outside the West Bank town of Hebron. At the heart of Hebron lay the burial place of the patriarchs and matriarchs of the Jewish faith: Abraham and Sarah; Isaac and Rebecca; Jacob and Leah. Since Abraham is also revered as a prophet in Islam and a mosque had stood on the site for nearly a thousand years, our post-1967 arrangements set out separate times of worship for Muslims and Jews. Goldstein chose to attack during a holiday period for both faiths: Purim for the Jews and the Muslim holy month of Ramadan. He arrived shortly after the Muslims' Friday prayers began on the morning of February 25. Dressed in his reserve army uniform and carrying an automatic rifle, he opened fire on a group of nearly 800 Palestinian worshipers. He killed 29 and wounded 125 others before several of his intended victims knocked him unconscious and beat him to death.

I rushed to Sde Dov Airport in north Tel Aviv, a few minutes from the kirya, and boarded a helicopter for the old British fort near Hebron, used by the Jordanians until 1967 and now Israeli headquarters. After visiting the scene of the killings, I sought out local Palestinian leaders to voice my condolences and the sense of outrage I shared over what had happened, and to urge them to do all they could to maintain calm. I then went to Kiryat Arba and conveyed the same message.

Our immediate task was to prevent more deaths, on either side. It was a frustrating, and violent, week. Protests reminiscent of the first days of the intifada erupted around the West Bank, in Gaza, in east Jerusalem, and in several Arab neighborhoods and towns inside Israel. While I had no trouble understanding the Palestinians' anger, I also had a responsibility to prevent the violence from spiraling out of control. We turned to the same tools we'd used at the beginning of the uprising—though with even greater emphasis on the need for soldiers to use only the necessary force to restore order, and to avoid causing fatalities wherever possible. We closed off the West Bank. We imposed curfews on the main West Bank and Gaza towns and refugee camps. We also imposed a curfew on Kiryat Arba and for the first time were given the authority to use administrative detention orders not just against Palestinians, but specific Jewish settlers. We arrested about a half dozen Kach leaders. Still, there were repeated clashes—and a number of deaths and injuries as a result—before things finally began to subside a week or so later.

The massacre had made me feel more strongly than ever that our responsibility to protect the security of the settlers could not extend to allowing them to defy the government or the law. The principle would be put to the test within a few weeks. Tel Rumeida, a settlement near Hebron, had been set up without Israeli government approval in 1984. As part of the response to the Goldstein killings, Rabin considered closing it down. That prompted a number of right-wing rabbis to issue a formal religious ruling against any such action. Rabin called me in to ask whether it would be operationally possible to dismantle Tel Rumeida and remove the settlers. I said yes, by sending in a Sayeret Matkal force after midnight, as long as news of the operation did not leak. "We'll take over the area, close it off, and get control." Given the tensions in the wake of the massacre, I added that I couldn't promise that our soldiers would hold fire. "There are people in there with weapons," I said. "If someone shoots at *them*, they will shoot back."

"*Should* I do it?" he asked me. Maybe I should have given him an answer. But I didn't feel it was my place to add to the pressures around what was clearly a finely balanced call, especially since my inclination would have been to tell him to go ahead. I said it was something only he could decide. "What I *can* tell you is that we can do it." When I left, my sense was that he was sufficiently angry over what had happened in Hebron that he felt it essential to draw a line—the line of law—over what settlers were allowed to do. But the Passover holiday was now a couple of days away. I believe he realized the operation would not be possible until after the holiday period; by then, he was probably concerned he would have lost the clear political logic for moving against Tel Rumeida. The settlement has remained in place, a flashpoint in the conflict between settlers and Palestinians in the area around Hebron.

The repercussions, and the controversy, from the massacre reverberated widely. Rabin and his cabinet immediately decided to establish an inquiry, under Supreme Court chief justice Meir Shamgar. It would look into every aspect of the killings—including any failings by the army, the Shin Bet, the police, or other authorities that might have allowed the tragedy to happen. The commission interviewed dozens of witnesses, Israeli and Palestinian, in thirty-one separate sessions. I knew early on that the inquiry would throw up difficult issues. I was especially upset to learn that two soldiers and three border guards scheduled for guard duty at the mosque had shown up late on the morning of the killings. By the time I testified in late March, the inquiry had heard from a range of senior and local commanders and individual soldiers. A picture had emerged of a series of security breakdowns, equipment malfunctions, oversights, and confusion.

The security lapses around the Cave of the Patriarchs that day had contributed to what happened. In addition to the fact that the guard unit was not at full strength until after the murders took place, several of the security cameras weren't working. I acknowledged that if the cameras and the guards had done their job, at the very least some lives might have been saved. Yet I also made the point that this specific act of *mass murder* was something the army could not have anticipated. I reminded the commissioners that they were judging things after the fact. They *knew* how the tragedy had ended. In the context in which we were operating, the prospect of an Israeli settler, a reserve officer, walking into a place of worship and deliberately killing defenseless Palestinians had come as a bolt from the blue.

The commission's report did not apportion blame to any of the army officers or commanders. But an inescapable conclusion from the testimony of the many witnesses was that the way in which we'd become conditioned to view the settlers had blinded us to the possibility of the kind of crime Goldstein had committed. Even before I testified, I'd been disturbed to hear soldiers saying that even if they had *seen* him shooting a Palestinian, their orders were not to open fire on a settler, so they wouldn't have intervened. When asked about this by the commission, I said that this was a fundamental misunderstanding of our rules of engagement. "In no case is there, nor can there be, an army order that says it is forbidden to shoot at a settler even if he is shooting at others. A massacre is a massacre. You don't need special orders to know what to do."

I also knew that the soldiers' "misunderstanding" was all too understandable. As I acknowledged in the inquiry, the army on the West Bank and Gaza was predisposed to see Palestinians who were carrying weapons as potential terrorists, especially since the outbreak of the intifada. The settlers, even overtly anti-Arab Kach militants like Goldstein, were assumed to be carrying arms in self-defense. One lesson I took from the massacre was that the mix of Jewish settlers—particularly those who believed themselves on a messianic mission to resettle all of biblical Israel—and restive Palestinians who wanted sovereignty and control over their own lives was potentially toxic, for both sides. Ideally, the process, which had begun with Oslo, might start to disentangle it, though I remained far from confident that anything resembling full peace would come anytime soon.

+ + +

Rabin, and even more acutely Shimon Peres, believed it was important to press ahead with the opening phase of the handover of Israeli authority mapped out by Oslo. In May 1994, a draft of the so-called Gaza and Jericho First agreement was completed. Once it was ratified, the five-year interim period would begin, with further withdrawals and parallel negotiations on the "permanent status" of the territories, addressing core issues like settlements, refugees, final borders, and the status of Jerusalem. During this first stage, Israel would transfer civil authority in the Gaza Strip and the Jordan Valley town of Jericho to the Palestinians, and local security would be in the hands of a newly created Palestinian police force.

My primary concern, and my responsibility, was the security provisions in the agreement, since the Israeli army retained its role in charge of overall security. When I went to see Rabin a few days before the cabinet meeting to approve the Gaza-Jericho agreement, I told him I was worried that it left room for potentially serious misunderstandings, friction, and even clashes. There was no clear definition of how our soldiers would operate alongside the new local police in the event of a terror attack, violence by Hamas or Islamic Jihad, or, for that matter, a car crash involving an Israeli and a Palestinian. He agreed this needed to be addressed, although it was clear he intended to do so with Arafat, via the Americans, not by reopening and delaying the formal agreement.

But I had a deeper concern about the entire Oslo agreement, which I also now raised with Rabin. I did not doubt the importance of reaching a political agreement, and ideally a peace treaty, with the Palestinians. But I'd read the Oslo Declaration in greater detail and discussed it with lawyer friends of mine. I'd also reread the 1978 Camp David framework on which the self-rule provisions were based. The endpoint was pretty clear, just as it had been at Camp David: Palestinian authority over the West Bank and Gaza, defined as a "single territorial unit" under Oslo. In essence, and very probably in name, this meant a Palestinian state. I wasn't opposed to that in principle, if it was in return for a full and final peace. But the Oslo *process* meant that we would be handing back land, and control over security, in an ever-larger portion of territory *before* we'd reached any so-called permanent-status agreement—in fact, before we even knew whether that would prove possible. It wasn't "land for peace." It was land for the promise, or maybe only the hope, of peace. It was the same problem Yitzhak had faced over the Americans' misuse of our "pocket deposit" on the Golan. I realized that, having come this far with Oslo, neither he nor the government was likely to back away from approving the Gaza-Jericho accord. But he did say he thought the points I'd raised were important, which I took as meaning he was comfortable with my raising it with the cabinet.

I spoke near the end of the four-hour cabinet meeting to ratify the Gaza-Jericho plan. The ministers seemed attentive as I ran through my security concerns, even nodding when I compared the agreement's security provisions to "a piece of Swiss cheese, only with more holes." But then I said a few words that I recognized were beyond my responsibility as chief of staff. "I'm speaking just as an Israeli citizen," I told the cabinet, "and as a former head of military intelligence." Referring to specific provisions in Oslo, and in the Camp David framework agreed to by Begin and Sadat fifteen years earlier, I said it was important for ministers to realize that, even though permanent-status issues were yet to be resolved, "you will be taking us nearly the whole way toward creating a Palestinian state, based on the internationally accepted reading of Camp David." They reacted with a mix of defensiveness and hostility. In the latter camp were ministers from Rabin's left-wing coalition partners, Meretz, who seemed especially angry when I quoted from Camp David. The prime minister motioned them for calm. "Ehud had a responsibility to talk about security questions, and we had a responsibility to listen. As for his additional remarks, they are not a surprise to me," he said. "He made these points to me, and I said he could repeat them here. It is right that he should raise them." He said there was no need for ministers to agree with me, but that it was proper that the points I'd raised be heard.

Many clearly *didn't* agree with me, or simply believed that, whatever the potential complications, the Gaza-Jericho agreement still had to be ratified, which it was. But my remarks did lay the groundwork for my objection to the next, more far-reaching stage in the Oslo process barely a year later. By then, I was no longer chief of staff. I was a member of Rabin's cabinet.

+ + +

It was still my responsibility to ensure Gaza-Jericho's implementation, and that the initial withdrawals and redeployments went ahead smoothly. And they did. But I also was soon playing a part in Rabin's renewed effort to use the momentum of Oslo to achieve peace agreements with our other Arab neighbors: the Syrians, although he knew that would be tough, but first the Jordanians. I would always have had some role by virtue of the need for a chief of staff to weigh in on security issues. But as Yitzhak had done from the start, he involved me and others in his inner political circle in wider discussions on the whole range of negotiating issues. He remained determined to keep Peres's role to an absolute minimum.

No peace talks are ever completely straightforward, but the process with Jordan was very close to that. The main issues on the Jordanian side involved ensuring a proper share of scarce water supplies and dealing with Israel's de facto control of a fairly large area near the southern end of our border. A number of kibbutzim and moshavim were farming the land there. But under the post-1948 armistice, that area had been allocated to Jordan. Israel's priorities were to put in place a fully open relationship of peace and cooperation, and to get assurances Jordan would not allow its territory to be used by Palestinian groups to launch terror attacks.

I was struck by how much more easily compromises can be found if you truly trust the other side. At our meeting with Hussein before the Gulf War, I'd been impressed by the king's thoughtful and measured, yet warm and open, demeanor. That, in itself, inspired trust. Since 1967, even in times of high tension, both Israel and Jordan had generally demonstrated a shared desire, and ability, to steer clear of conflict. The main trade-off in the search for a formal peace turned out to be not too difficult. We agreed to ensure water provision, while the king allowed the Israelis who had been working the land in the 1949 armistice area to stay in place as lessees. On the final Wednesday of October 1994, near our border crossing in the Arava desert, I watched as Rabin, King Hussein, and President Clinton formally sealed the full "Treaty of Peace Between the State of Israel and the Hashemite Kingdom of Jordan."

Syria was always going to be harder. But Rabin moved past his anger over the pocket deposit, and we began a new effort via the Americans. Our aim was to lay out a comprehensive, staged proposal to trade nearly the entire Golan for peace. With Rabin, Itamar Rabinovich, and the rest of the team, we put together a framework limiting Syria's military presence on the Heights. We envisaged phasing out the restrictions as Syria took steps toward the kind of peace that had proved possible with Egypt and Jordan. But indirect exchanges in the autumn of 1994 produced little progress. In December, Rabin proposed to the Americans that I meet with a Syrian representative, and President Assad agreed. Later that month, I went to Washington for talks with Syria's ambassador, Walid Muallem. With the Americans' Mideast envoy, Dennis Ross, as host, we met in Blair House across the street from the White House.

I began by explaining the security provisions we envisaged for the Golan, which included early-warning provisions, force limitations, and other means of safeguarding Israel against any surprise attack. Muallem's response was formulaic, almost icy, with no indication he was ready to discuss any of the specifics, much less offer ideas of his own. But then Dennis led us out into the garden, where the atmosphere, if sadly not the weather, was a bit warmer. I told Ambassador Muallem I believed Israel's issues with Syria ought to be resolvable. Both sides understood the broad terms of an eventual peace, but we needed a context of *trust* in which to negotiate. President Assad, and we as well, were always going to be reluctant to formally commit to a position until *each side was satisfied that the other understood its core needs*. Politically, both sides also faced constraints. "In formal meetings, a record is taken and negotiators have to explain and justify every last word back home," I said. "I think our negotiators can get further in conversations like the one we're having now." Though Muallem nodded agreement, he did not explicitly say he believed that informal exchanges were the way forward. Still, he obviously passed on a broadly positive message to Damascus. Before the Blair House discussion, our understanding had been there would probably be a kind of mirror arrangement for a follow-up meeting: between *our* ambassador in Washington, Itamar Rabinovich, and a high-ranking army officer from the Syrian side. Instead, we received word that Assad wanted me to meet directly with General Hikmat Shihabi, my counterpart as Syrian chief of staff and Assad's oldest and closest political ally—the effective number-two man in the regime.

General Shihabi and I met over a period of two days at Blair House. He had greater authority, and thus a greater sense of self-assurance, than the ambassador. But not for the last time in negotiations with Syria, any real progress was blocked by an apparent combination of misunderstanding and miscommunication. The discussions were lively. Shihabi had served as Syria's liaison officer with the UN force set up along the cease-fire line after the 1948 war. "Go check with the UN," he said at our first meeting. "You'll see almost all the exchanges of fire in the late 1950s were provoked by Israel." I didn't respond directly, though I did note it was the Syrians who had tried to divert water from the Jordan River in the early fifties. "You did it first," he retorted. So it continued, yet without any real sign that Shihabi was ready to engage on any of the issues of substance. After a phone call with Rabin after our first day of talks, I became equally cautious. He agreed that we wanted to avoid a repeat of our experience with the Golan "deposit." We did not want to put concessions on the record before we got an indication that the Syrians were genuinely ready for peace talks.

Still, establishing the precedent of a "chief of staff channel" was a step forward. My successor as ramatkal, Amnon Lipkin, would meet again with Shihabi in early 1995.

+ + +

I was confident Amnon was inheriting an army stronger, better prepared, and better equipped than at any time since the Six-Day War. We also had peace treaties with Egypt and Jordan, and none of the substantive issues with the Syrians seemed insurmountable.

But the main security challenges continued to be the unconventional ones. In the long term, a resurgent Iraq, and very likely Iran, might make strides toward getting nuclear weapons. There was every sign that Hizbollah in Lebanon—and Hamas, Islamic Jihad, and their supporters in Gaza and the West Bank—would escalate violence and terror. As the negotiations with Jordan were entering their final phase in early October, a further Hamas attack—this one, a kidnapping—had brought home that threat. On Sunday, October 9, men dressed as Orthodox Jews abducted an off-duty soldier named Nahshon Wachsman near Lod. Two days later, Israeli television received a videotape showing the nineteen-year-old, hands and feet bound, pleading for his life in return for the release of the founder of Hamas, whom we had arrested and jailed in 1989. "The group from Hamas kidnapped me," he said. "They are demanding the release of Sheikh Ahmed Yassin and another two hundred people from Israeli prison. If their demands are not met, they will execute me on Friday at eight p.m."

As soon as we got word he was missing, I met with Rabin. Since we assumed he was being held in Gaza, I ordered a unit from Sayeret Matkal to head south and coordinate efforts with the Shin Bet and the southern command to locate him. But it gradually became clear he might be much closer to where he'd been seized. The Shin Bet got a description of the kidnappers' car and found it was a rental that had been picked up and returned in east Jerusalem. They tracked down the man who rented it. A little before dawn the morning of October 14, barely twelve hours before the Hamas deadline, Shin Bet established that Wachsman was being held in a village on the road to Ramallah, north of Jerusalem, in a house owned by a Palestinian living abroad.

The hostage soldier's ordeal was made even worse by the fact his mother, Esther, was a Holocaust survivor, born in a displaced-persons camp in Germany at the end of the war. Rabin had been ready to approve a rescue attempt from the outset, assuming we could locate Wachsman and come up with a plan that might work. But as with Entebbe, he said that if we couldn't be reasonably confident of success, we would negotiate. Now that we knew where Wachsman was being held, I ordered Shaul Mofaz, the commander with responsibility for the West Bank, to prepare for a possible rescue.

Before briefing Rabin, I arranged for another commando unit to begin visible preparations for an operation in Gaza, in the hope of reassuring Hamas that we still believed he was being held there. Assuming we could retain the element of surprise, several things worked in our favor. The house was relatively isolated. It was in an area where Israel, not the incipient Palestinian authorities, still had control. And Sayeret Matkal had expertise and experience in this kind of mission. Still, no plan could be foolproof. I told Rabin that the fact Hamas was holding a single hostage meant that if our assault teams were delayed for any reason at all, the kidnappers might kill him before we got in. But we had to weigh the risks of *not* acting. We were no longer trying to find a missing soldier. We knew where he was. We had a unit ready. Unless Hamas relented, he was facing death within hours. In those circumstances, the precedent of doing nothing would, in my view, be a serious betrayal of our responsibility to do whatever we could to try to save him. I recommended that he approve the operation, and Rabin agreed.

I attended the final briefing shortly afterward. I was impressed by the determined faces of the men in the two sayeret teams. I remembered one of the officers, a twenty-three-year-old named Nir Poraz, from operational briefings before previous sayeret missions. Wachsman was being held in a room on the first floor. The commandos would simultaneously detonate explosives on three doors: at the front, on the side, and a third one leading through a kitchen to the room where the kidnappers had their hostage. The attack began fifteen minutes before the Hamas deadline. The explosive charges went off, but only the one in the front blew open the door. Poraz and his team rushed in, but one of the kidnappers opened fire, killing him and wounding six others. The other team had by now made it to the first floor. But despite firing at the metal lock, they had trouble getting the door to open. By the time they got in, Wachsman had been killed, shot in the neck and chest.

I was in the command post a few hundred yards away. I called Rabin and then went to see him in the kirya. The head of personnel for the army had gone to see the Wachsman family and break the news. Now, we had to tell the country. Rabin and I appeared on television together. Rabin insisted—wrongly—on saying he bore full responsibility. What had gone wrong, I emphasized to him, was not the *decision* to attempt the rescue. It was the rescue itself. That was not his responsibility. It was mine.

The next day, I visited Wachsman's parents and tried to convey how painful the failed rescue was to me, Rabin, and everyone else involved. I was inspired and humbled by their response. His father had told a reporter he wanted to convey his condolences to the parents of Nir Poraz. "This added loss has shaken me terribly," he said. He told me he also believed that the prime minister had approved the rescue using his best judgment on the information that he had available. I spent time separately speaking to Mrs. Wachsman. I tried to explain that in fighting an enemy like Hamas, people who not just threatened to kill but had proven they had no hesitation in doing so, I'd felt there was no choice but to attempt the rescue. I admitted we'd known the risks. But we'd tried to do the right thing, both for the country and her son. I think she understood, though I knew that nothing could alter the terrible sadness of her loss. The pain would take years to heal. Some part of it never would. Still, I felt it was important she and her husband know that we, too, felt their loss. For years afterward, Nava and I continued to visit them.

By then, however, I was no longer chief of staff. Handing over to Amnon Lipkin, I left the kirya proud of all that I had sought to accomplish during my thirty-six years in uniform. I realized there had been failures and setbacks, none more painfully fresh in my mind than our inability to rescue Nahshon Wachsman. But I was about to find that the area of Israeli life I now chose to enter—national politics—was a battlefield of sorts as well. And that when trouble hit, even your allies sometimes ducked for cover.

# Hate versus Hope

THE AMBUSH CAME IN JULY 1995, SIX MONTHS AFTER I'D LEFT THE ARMY and only days before I was expected to be named interior minister in Yitzhak Rabin's government. The effect was to threaten my political career before it had even begun—by reviving, and lying about, the tragic training accident at the Negev army base of Tze'elim, during our preparations for the operation against Saddam Hussein.

When the "story" broke, I was nearly 5,000 miles away. I was accompanying Nava's brother, Doron Cohen, on a business trip to China—and savoring my last few days as a private citizen. I'd received a hint of the storm that was about to engulf me a few days before we left for the Far East, in the form of a letter from a reporter at *Yediot Achronot*, Israel's largest-selling newspaper, with a list of questions about Tze'elim. Their thrust made clear the story *Yediot* seemed intent on telling: that after the live missile strike that killed the Sayeret Matkal men, I had abandoned the injured and "fled" to Tel Aviv. I probably should have answered the letter. But I assumed even rudimentary checks would reveal the story to be false. I'd had similar questions from a TV journalist a few months earlier. I did phone him to explain the true details of what had happened and suggested he talk to others who were there, like Amnon Lipkin, the current chief of staff and my former deputy, to confirm my account. The story was dropped.

But *Yediot* evidently decided not to let the facts get in the way of the "exclusive" it ran in its weekend edition on July 7. Under a banner headline—an undeniably clever Hebrew pun, "EHUD BARAKH" ("EHUD RAN AWAY")—it accused me of having stood by, paralyzed with shock, when the missiles struck and then, as other officers tended to the wounded, rushed away by helicopter.

Doron and I were having dinner in Beijing when Nava phoned. She'd just seen the newspaper story and read it to me. I'd never been angrier. As best I could work out, it had been concocted from a patchwork of accounts long after the fact. To the extent the notion of my "fleeing" had been raised, I could only imagine that *Yediot*'s "sources" had misunderstood the arrival of the first medical helicopter, when the pilot was unable to see us and flew on before returning a couple of minutes later. But in every single detail about my actions after the tragedy occurred, it was simply untrue.

Doron and I immediately made arrangements to return to Israel, which, since there was no direct air connection, meant finding the first flight out through London. But before we left, Nava phoned again, almost sputtering in fury. She told me she'd just received a call from Aliza Goren, Rabin's media spokesperson. "Does Ehud know about the *Yediot* story?" she'd asked. When Nava said yes, Aliza told her: "It is important that Ehud knows that we are not going to get involved in getting him out of this."

*Welcome to politics*, I thought. Rabin knew the story was untrue. I had still been in Tze'elim when I'd phoned him about what had happened. He knew I'd remained there to order in the medical helicopters and arrange for the evacuation of the wounded before returning to brief him. But as the controversy continued to gather force, he was clearly not going to weigh in to set the record straight. I, meanwhile, was on the other side of the world.

During our stopover in London, I sat with Doron and talked through how to get my voice heard. I telephoned Yoni Koren, the officer who'd been my top aide in the kirya and whom I'd asked to work for me in the Interior Ministry, assuming I now actually got there. I told him to phone Amnon Lipkin and say that I had expected him to answer the fabrications. Not only had he and I been at the site of the tragedy together, we'd *left* together, on the same helicopter. Amnon did issue a statement saying that he knew *Yediot*'s allegations were wrong, but his rebuttal caused barely a ripple.

As I read the latest Israeli newspapers before landing in Tel Aviv, I found that at least I wasn't totally on my own. Reporters had been phoning politicians for comment. Most responded like weathervanes, going with the prevailing wind, which was gusting against me. But three Knesset members dissented. One was Ori Orr, a friend even before we'd both gone into the army and who had now joined Labor. The other two were leading members of Likud: Dan Meridor and Benny Begin, Menachem Begin's son. All three said they were sure the allegations were false. Did they know the details about the accident, they were asked. No, they replied, they didn't need to. They knew *me*.

Now all I had to do was convince the rest of the country. It had been nearly a week since *Yediot*'s "exposé." Yoni Koren passed on a request from Channel 1 television, our equivalent of the BBC, that I appear with Nissim Mishal, the journalist who had interviewed me ten years earlier, at the urging of Rabin's political aide, in my first appearance on Israeli TV. For Mishal, the interview would be a journalistic coup. For me, it was a risk. He was a famously combative questioner, a bit like Sam Donaldson at White House briefings, or Jeremy Paxman and John Humphrys in Britain.

On the night of July 13, I drove to the television studio in Tel Aviv. Mishal confronted me with *Yediot*'s version of events. I was angry, and showed it. "This report was not some night editor's mishap," I said. "It was authorized by the highest levels of a mass-circulation newspaper which is power-drunk, corrupted by power, and manipulative. The so-called story was an amateurish and distorted depiction of a chief of staff who sees wounded soldiers, turns his back, deserts them, and flies away. That is an evil, vain falsehood." As Mishal pressed me about the allegation that I had fled, I cited, by name, other officers who had been there with me and had confirmed precisely the opposite. I had left Tze'elim, along with Amnon Lipkin, a full fifty *minutes* after the missiles struck—and only *after* the helicopters had arrived, the injuries had been treated, and the choppers were evacuating the wounded. "A chief of staff's job is not to treat the wounded, when others are doing that already," I added. My responsibility was "to keep my head, and ensure a safe and speedy medical evacuation." That was what I'd done. "I've given years of my life to serving this country," I said. "I have been shot at. I have shot men dead from as close as I am to you now. How did the hand that wrote these things against me not tremble?"

It was certainly high drama. But it was not an act. The way I'd gone after *Yediot* prompted some pundits to suggest I was too thin-skinned. Yet what mattered most to me was what the *rest* of Israel felt, and opinion polls the next day showed something like 80 percent of Israelis believed what I'd said.

Almost as soon as I'd got home from the interview, the phone rang. It was Rabin. "Ehud," he said, "you did well. Let's move forward."

+ + +

It was rumored that at least two influential Labor politicians had played a part in steering *Yediot* toward the story and urging the newspaper to run with it: Haim Ramon, a veteran party figure and cabinet minister, though he'd quit the government the year before over the party's failure to follow through on health-policy reform; and Shimon Shevess, one of Rabin's top advisers. An Israeli magazine article that delved into the detail of the political controversy said the aim had not been to "*kill* Barak" as a new cabinet minister: "Just fire some bullets at this legs, so he'll enter politics with a limp." In other words, it was a way of cutting me down to size.

I suppose that was understandable. I was by no means the only former general to enter Israeli politics. Other chiefs of staff had gone on to play prominent roles in government: Dayan, Motta Gur, and of course Rabin. But the fact that I was going directly into the cabinet, and so soon after leaving the army, was seen by the Israeli media—and a number of Labor politicians, who had worked their way up through Labor politics in the more traditional way—as a reflection of a close, maybe even privileged, relationship with Rabin.

It was true Rabin had personally urged me to join his government, starting with a lighthearted remark only days after I'd ended my term as chief of staff. It was at a farewell organized by my staff. The event began with film clips from my years in the army and a series of entertaining cameos from men I'd served with and led. Rabin spoke at the end. He said he'd recently been on an official visit to South Korea. He'd met the president, who told Rabin he was the first Korean leader not to have been an army general. Rabin said he'd replied that *he* was the first Israeli prime minister who *was* a general. Then, smiling and looking straight at me, he added: "*Nu*, Ehud?"

I did want to join his government. But I had been in the army since the age of seventeen and was now in my early fifties. For my family's sake, as well as my own, I had figured on taking a year or two to explore other things. Two options appealed to me especially. One was business. My brother-in-law, in addition to having a successful law practice, was involved in a number of business ventures, and we'd discussed areas we might jointly explore. I had also received offers from think tanks in the United States.

Despite Rabin's quip about ex-generals and prime ministers, I was surprised when, a couple of days later, he asked me to come see him. He smiled as I entered his office. Then he said, "Ehud, now that you are out of uniform, I would be glad to see you come into politics, together with us, and be a member of the government." He said he'd discussed it with Peres. "It's a joint invitation." Though I did, of course, say yes, I said that I'd been hoping to take some time off, probably at first with a think tank in the United States. Though I wasn't sure about the legal provisions for officers leaving the army, I also reminded him that there was a set period of time during which they could not enter politics. He replied, a bit enigmatically, that he would be sending an "operative" to talk to me further about the timing.

The operative was Giora Eini, a uniquely important figure in Labor because he was trusted both by Rabin and Peres. I liked him immediately, and throughout my years in politics, I would come to rely on him for his experience, good humor, and judgment. He knew the rules for former army people going into politics: there was a hundred-day moratorium. "Rabin wants you immediately," he said. "I guess we'll tell him that 'immediately' will have to mean sometime in April." In fact, I told Giora that I'd hoped it would be longer. So we agreed that in order to give me at least a few months in the United States, he'd tell Rabin he could get in touch at any time from March 1996 with his invitation to join the cabinet. As soon as he did so, I would formally cut my ties with the military, meaning that the hundred-day countdown would begin and I could join the government sometime in the summer.

Nava, the girls, and I left for Washington in January. I joined the Center for Strategic and International Studies and was given the overwrought title of Distinguished Visiting Statesman and Senior Associate. The CSIS had invited me to write and speak on the Middle East. About two months in, I presented a paper outlining my view of developments in the region. I began by welcoming the constellation of changes that seemed to offer at least an *opportunity* for stability, security, and peace: the unraveling of the Soviet Union, the Oslo agreement, the peace treaty with Jordan, and the continuing talks with the Syrians. As long as we had partners committed to reaching an agreement, I believed Israel would be ready "to consider major compromise and to take upon ourselves significant calculated risks." But I also delivered much the same message that I had given to ministers on the potential risks inherent in the Oslo process.

I pointed out that Arafat had made no move to rein in groups like Hamas, and that more Israelis had actually been killed by terror since Oslo than in the year before. "We signed a three-phase contract with Arafat," I said. "Try to imagine one of you selling me three pieces of property. If I fail to pay for the first one on time, you might not immediately cancel the contract. You might even be ready to help me collect the necessary money. But you would never proceed to deliver the second property before I paid for the first one, unless you were a fool." I also warned of longer-term dangers: "terrorism, radical Islamic fundamentalism, the proliferation of surface-to-surface missiles and weapons of mass destruction, and threats to the long-term stability of the more pragmatic Arab regimes." I singled out Iran because it was determined to export its brand of fundamentalist Islam, sponsor terror, and develop a nuclear weapon.

I also accompanied CSIS colleagues on speaking engagements to other American cities. I was about to board a flight to Seattle in April when I got a message saying Rabin wanted to talk. After we took off, I used the onboard phone facility and, with a swipe of a credit card, was soon on the line to the prime minister. "I need you to come back as soon as possible," Rabin said. I already knew, from Giora, that he was anxious to find a long-term replacement as minister of interior. The leading light in the

Sephardi religious party Shas, Arye Deri, had been forced to leave the post amid allegations of bribe-taking. After Rabin had taken on the portfolio himself for eighteen months, he had placed Labor's Uzi Baram there, but only as a temporary arrangement. I didn't feel I could refuse outright. But I reminded him that under army rules for retiring senior officers, "as soon as possible" still meant another one hundred days. Ideally, I said, I wanted to finish the best part of a year in Washington, so I asked him whether it would be possible to join the cabinet in the middle of November instead. "What difference will a few more months make?"

Rabin said mid-November would be too late. "Ehud, in politics, you can never predict what will happen by then." Neither of us could have known how terribly prophetic his words would turn out to be.

+ + +

Not only was I new to cabinet politics, I still wasn't even a member of the Knesset. Yet in addition to naming me as head of a major ministry—in charge of everything from citizenship and immigration to planning, zoning, and the funding of local government—Rabin made me a member of his "inner cabinet" on security and foreign affairs. Barely three weeks after I joined the government, we had to decide on the most important agreement with the Palestinians since Oslo. Dubbed Oslo II, it involved a major transfer of authority and territory. The process would begin with our pulling out from more than a quarter of the West Bank, including the major Palestinian towns and some 450 smaller towns and villages. After that, there would be two further redeployment phases, at six-month intervals, in so-called Area C of the West Bank—a mix of unpopulated land, settlements, and a number of points we'd designated as strategically important. Under Oslo, and its parent agreement Camp David, it was all part of ensuring the Palestinians could exercise their "legitimate rights" in the "single territorial entity" of the West Bank and Gaza—in other words, a path to statehood. But the final three phases of redeployment might be *complete* before we'd addressed the permanent-status issues like final borders, Israeli settlements, the future of Jerusalem: the *real* core of a peace agreement.

By the time I joined the discussions on Oslo II in August 1995, the main points had already been agreed. Rabin was in favor, as were virtually all the cabinet ministers. Whatever scant influence I might exercise would have to come at the decisive cabinet meeting, set for August 13. Rabin knew I'd be concerned not only to ensure the security provisions avoided potential misunderstandings on the ground, but about the longer-term implications, especially since the scale of the Israeli withdrawals was much larger this time. In fact, the agreement could be interpreted as requiring us to cede Palestinian control of the great majority of Gaza and the West Bank by the end of the third redeployment phase—quite possibly before talks on the permanent-status questions had even begun.

I went to see Rabin a few days before the cabinet vote. I argued we should either delay some of our redeployments or bring the permanent-status negotiations forward. He listened patiently. But he barely spoke, and made no effort to rebut the case I was making. He already knew that I would be against Oslo II, if only from the concerns I'd raised about the "Gaza and Jericho First" agreement a year earlier, when I was still chief of staff. But having now been brought into government by Rabin, it was obvious that I would be expected, on a vote of this importance, to be in his corner.

The cabinet vote wasn't happening in a political vacuum. Likud's defeat in 1992 had meant the end of Yitzhak Shamir's leadership. The new Likud leader was the former Sayeret Matkal officer with whom I'd shared a newspaper cover in 1986 predicting that he and I would end up facing each other at the ballot box: Bibi Netanyahu. Positioning himself as the fresh young face of Israeli politics and vowing to defeat Labor, Bibi had seized on Oslo II to accuse Rabin of "surrendering" to Arafat, and by extension to Hamas terrorism.

I couldn't sleep the night before the cabinet meeting. I didn't want to be disloyal to Yitzhak, and still less to lend any further impetus to Bibi's rhetorical onslaughts against him. But the more I thought of it, the less I could see the point of entering politics if I wasn't going to vote my beliefs. The cabinet meeting lasted for hours. It was near the end that I spoke, calmly and in detail, about my reservations. Many of the ministers seemed barely to be listening. They'd long since made up their minds. But when I'd finished, two ministers passed me notes. Both said the same thing: *Ehud, don't do anything crazy. Don't vote against it.* So I didn't. But I abstained.

Rabin was bitterly upset. He didn't tell me directly. But when the meeting broke up, his longtime political aide, Eitan Haber, took me aside to tell me that what I'd done was "terrible." Giora Eini came to see me the next day, after Rabin had phoned him in a mix of anger and disbelief. "What *is* this?" he'd asked Giora. "The first big vote, and Barak *abstains*?"

It wasn't until a few weeks later that Rabin and I spoke alone, over a beer in his office. He didn't raise the question of the vote. So I did. "Yitzhak, I understand it's caused you pain," I said. "But I think you understand I was acting out of what is genuinely my belief and my position." I asked him why, unlike the other ministers, he hadn't passed me a note before we'd cast our votes.

"Ehud," he said, "I never write requests or orders on how to vote. Ministers must vote according to their conscience." He meant that my conscience should have told me, given the importance of the issue, to vote yes.

The tension between us eased somewhat in the weeks ahead. But the tension *around* us escalated. Opinion polls showed the country split down the middle. Settlement leaders and extremist rabbis launched a campaign impugning the legitimacy of Rabin and the government. Right-wing religious leaders issued a decree rejecting the planned redeployments on the West Bank—"the evacuation of bases and their transfer to the Gentiles"—as biblically prohibited. A new group called Zu Artzenu organized a campaign of civil disobedience to try to bring the government down.

The sheer venom hit home during a pair of events I attended with Rabin, to award the status of "city" to towns that had crossed the required threshold in population and economic activity. By tradition, this was marked by a ceremony with both the interior minister and the prime minister present. The first was in Ofakim, near where I'd worked in the fields with Yigal Garber in the 1950s. Shortly after we arrived, a group of protesters started shouting at Rabin. *Manyac*, they yelled: "maniac." *Boged*: "traitor." At the second event, near Haifa, busloads of protesters from right-wing religious schools shouted abuse at Rabin when he rose to speak.

As the Knesset vote on Oslo II approached, the hatred reached new levels. The day before, thousands of protesters packed into Jerusalem's

Zion Square. Some shouted "Death to Rabin!" Others burned pictures of him or passed out photos of him dressed in an Arab keffiyeh, or even a Nazi uniform. Bibi had publicly declared that opposition to the agreement must remain within the bounds of the law. Yet as he addressed the baying mob from a hotel balcony, he uttered not a single word of reproach. In fact, he called Rabin's government "illegitimate," because it relied in part on the votes of Israeli Arab Knesset members.

The day of the vote, the mob descended on the Knesset. Rabin had called a government meeting beforehand, and when I got there, the crowd was so large that I was taken in through a special security entrance away from the front of the building. But the housing minister, Binyamin "Fuad" Ben-Eliezer, arrived late and tried to drive through the main gate. Protesters pounded furiously on his car and tried to break the windows. He had spent nearly as long as I had in the army, but when he joined the meeting, he was shaken. Interrupting Rabin, he banged his fist on the table. "I've been on battlefields," he said. "I've been shot at. I know how to read a situation. I *saw* their faces. It's insane! It is beyond anything rational, this kind of hatred." Pounding the table again, he shouted: "I warn you. It will end with a murder! It will end with a murder!" Rabin motioned for calm. He too was concerned by the rhetorical violence, even more so now that it was becoming physical violence. But as he would tell an interviewer a few weeks later, he simply didn't believe that "a Jew will kill a Jew." Nor, at that point, did I.

After the Knesset vote, which passed by a margin of 61–59, plans got under way for a rally in defense of the peace process and against the tide of hatred on the right. It was the idea of two people: Shlomo Lahat, a Likud mayor of Tel Aviv who now backed Oslo, and a French Jewish businessman named Jean Frydman, a friend of Shimon Peres whom I had got to know and like. But in several of the early planning discussions in which I was involved, Rabin opposed the rally, which was to be held in the huge Kings of Israel Square in the heart of Tel Aviv. He was worried that not enough people would show up, and that those who did would be from the left: Meretz, not Labor, people who would be there mainly to *criticize* him for not going far enough, or quickly enough, in pulling out of the West Bank.

In the end, he was persuaded it should go ahead. In fact, by the time the date approached—Saturday evening, November 4—he seemed to be feeling more energized and upbeat. I wouldn't be there because I was going to New York as the government's representative at a fund-raising dinner that same night for the Yad Vashem Holocaust memorial. A few hours before leaving, however, I met with Rabin. We'd found a fifteen-minute window in his schedule, but ended up talking for an hour. He said he knew that, in some ways, the difficulties surrounding the peace talks were likely to get worse. Hamas would not abandon terror. The kind of intolerance we were seeing from the right wing was not going to go away. He was furious at Bibi, who in his view was hypocritically going through the motions of calling for restraint and pretending to be unaware that the mobs were full of Likud voters. "They're his people," he said, "and he knows it."

But he was relishing the idea of taking on Bibi in the next election, due in about a year's time. Though Rabin was trailing in the polls, he was confident of turning that around once the campaign began. "The main thing is that the party isn't focused. We have to get serious about preparing," he said. He was worried about the effect of inevitable tensions between his supporters and Peres's over how to run the campaign. "Bring back Haim Ramon," I suggested. I knew by now of the rumors that Haim may have helped orchestrate the false story *Yediot* had run about Tze'elim. But I also realized he was a Labor heavyweight and that, although he'd left the government, he remained personally close to Yitzhak. "Yes," Yitzhak replied, nodding, suggesting that we talk through the idea in detail when I returned from New York.

I was in my room at the Regency Hotel, on New York's Upper East Side, when the phone rang on Saturday afternoon. I was dimly aware that the Tel Aviv rally had been going on back home, but was more focused on preparing my speech for the Yad Vashem event. "Ehud, *Ehud!*" It was Nava, her voice barely understandable through the sobs. "Rabin has been shot!"

+ + +

Danny Yatom called me a couple of minutes later. He said Rabin was still alive. But from the details he gave me, I knew it would take a miracle for him to pull through. "Three shots, from close range," Danny said. "From an *Israeli*, a *Jew*." Like Rabin, like me too until this had actually happened, it was something Danny was struggling to believe. He said that he'd call me back when he knew anything more. But I had the TV on in the room. Before he did, I watched Eitan Haber announce that Yitzhak Rabin was dead.

Although I hadn't known it until I'd arrived, Yossi Beilin, one of the main forces behind the Oslo negotiations and now minister of economic planning, was also in New York for meetings and a speech of his own. Though he was a Peres protégé, and I was seen as closer to Rabin, the two of us had become friends. We immediately made plans to get the next flight home. But before leaving for the airport, I phoned Leah Rabin. However inadequate I knew it would be in helping her even begin to cope with the loss, I told her that my, and Nava's, thoughts were with her. That Yitzhak's death would leave a tremendous hole, in all of us, in every single Israeli. "They shot him," she kept murmuring. "They shot him. They shot him. They shot him." I called Peres, too. "Shimon, you have a mountain on your shoulders," I said. "But your task is to carry on. All of us will be with you, supporting, helping however we can."

It was the saddest flight I'd ever taken. Yossi and I barely spoke. Each of us was deep in thought. I found myself lost in memories of Rabin— from the very first time I'd met him, in the sayeret, to that last, long talk we'd had in his office a couple of days earlier. For some reason, I kept wondering whether, when the shots had been fired, he'd been turning to look behind him. It was an idiosyncrasy he had, whenever he was leaving a meeting or an event—even, as I now recalled vividly, when the two of us were leaving the municipal ceremony in Ofakim. I was behind him as we left. "Ehud," he said, turning back, "are you there?" It was a senseless detail. It wouldn't change anything. But I still felt torn up inside thinking about it.

After we landed at Ben-Gurion, I went with Nava to the Rabins' apartment in Ramat Aviv. There were hundreds of people outside, and nearly a hundred crowded inside the flat. Leah looked exhausted, her face ashen. "They shot him," she said over and over as Nava and I hugged her. "Three shots. In the back. *Why?*" I said there was no sane answer, but that with Yitzhak's death, Israel seemed different, the world seemed different, emptier. Before we left, we added our candles to the forest of flickering memorial lights outside the apartment block. Then, we drove to the Kings of Israel Square. Thousands of people were huddled in small groups throughout the plaza, sitting around thickets of candles and chanting, almost prayerlike, anthems of mourning and of peace.

I felt the need to see the place, near the front of the square, where Rabin had been assassinated, by a twenty-five-year-old Orthodox Jew and settlement activist named Yigal Amir. Standing there with Nava, I felt even more strongly what I'd told Leah on the phone from New York: his murder would leave a huge hole—in me, in all Israelis. He was an extraordinary mix of qualities: a brave officer, first in the pre-state Palmach and then the new Israeli army; a chief of staff and defense minister at critical periods in our history. Shy, even at times uncertain or hesitant, and naturally cautious. Decisive, when he felt that he, and Israel, needed to be: whether on Entebbe or the prospect, with all its risks, of launching an operation to kill Saddam Hussein. Humane, too: ready to negotiate with terrorists to save the lives of those they were planning to kill, unless he was confident our soldiers could save them first. Underpinning it all was a dedication to fighting and defeating Israel's enemies, yet a mindfulness that the real victory, if and when it was possible, would be an end to the conflict with our neighbors. I never doubted that we were fortunate to have him leading us on the inevitably difficult road to a negotiated peace. I never ceased to believe there was no politician more suited to the role, and that he would do everything he could to achieve it, except put Israel's security at risk.

On Sunday evening, Peres called a cabinet meeting in the kirya. He said our task was to continue what Rabin had begun, and that at least for now he would fill Rabin's shoes not just as prime minister but defense minister as well. The whole country stood still, shocked, until the state funeral two days after the assassination. It was attended by dozens of leaders from around the world. My role was to escort King Hussein and Queen Noor. On our drive into Jerusalem, we passed the Old City walls. We were barely a mile from the stone terrace above the Western Wall of our ancient temple where the golden Dome of the Rock and the Al-Aqsa Mosque stand. I knew Hussein had been there as a boy when his grandfather, King Abdullah, was shot and killed by a Palestinian amid rumors he was contemplating peace with Israel. "To me, this is like the closing of a circle," Hussein said. "Those who are murdered because they are not extreme enough. Because they look for normalcy, and peace."

Yitzhak's murder acted like a kind of lightning strike, freezing Israelis in a mix of disgust over what had occurred and awareness of the dangers this brand of hatred and extremism posed. I was concerned the moment would pass. I hoped that we could seize the opportunity to bring together all those Israelis—on left and right, secular and Orthodox, Ashkenazi and Sephardi—who were prepared to stand up against the fanaticism, the violent messianism, of which Yigal Amir was just a part. That was the main reason I wanted Peres to call an early election, to present the country with a choice: not just between those for and against specific compromises being contemplated in pursuit of peace, but between those who wanted a tolerant, functioning democracy and those who were ready to use demagoguery and violence to get their way.

Peres's first order of business was to put in place a new cabinet. He did, briefly, consider giving up the Defense Ministry and putting me there. But instead, he made me foreign minister. Like Rabin before him, Shimon stipulated that he, as prime minister, would retain authority over the peace negotiations. But I would be involved in all the discussions around the peace talks, and in meeting many of the Arab leaders we'd have to negotiate with if we were to find a lasting resolution of the Arab-Israeli conflict. Just a few weeks after the assassination, I represented Israel at a Euro-Mediterranean Partnership conference in Barcelona. Its only real diplomatic work consisted of ironing out the wording of the communiqué. The real value was in exchanges outside the formal sessions, and at the dinner held at one of King Juan Carlos's palatial estates; it was my first opportunity to meet not only Arab foreign ministers but Yasir Arafat.

My first encounter with Arafat was our meeting at the Barcelona summit, beginning with my embarrassing failure to realize he was behind me as I played the piano, lost in the beauty of a Chopin waltz. In the half hour or so we spent speaking, without aides, later that night, I was struck initially by his apparent frailty. His skin seemed almost translucent in places. His hands shook slightly. He spoke softly. Yet despite this ostensibly vulnerable exterior, I could see how daunting, and frustrating, he must be as a negotiating partner. Henry Kissinger has described how Mao Tse-Tung, rather than engage directly in discussion or debate, tended to wrap his remarks in parables. Without stretching the parallel too far, Arafat was like that. While I tried to engage him on how each of us might help cement the Oslo process and ensure that the interim agreement indeed led to a full peace, he responded with stories, or off-topic remarks, that I was left to unwrap and decipher.

He began our discussion by saying that now that I was foreign minister, he was glad to meet me, implying that were it not for my new post, he would have seen little point. He said he'd heard "reports" from his intelligence people that when I was chief of staff, I had organized a dissident band of generals who were working to torpedo the Oslo agreements. He compared this to the OAS, the military cabal in France that had opposed de Gaulle. I could only laugh. I told him I'd actually spent two months with OAS men years earlier, in Mont Louis, but that Israel was different. Even at times of the toughest of disagreements, we were a family. An "Israeli OAS" would never work, even if I had been crazy enough to contemplate such a thing. Which, I hastened to add, I was not.

Another idiosyncrasy I found in Arafat was that he was constantly writing notes as we spoke. Maybe he did it just as a kind of aide-memoire. But in later meetings that I had with him, it had the added effect, if not the intention, of making me choose my words more carefully. That, I believed, reduced the prospect of exploring more creatively the boundaries of each of our official positions. It also helped Arafat to argue, as he did on more than one occasion, that Rabin, or Peres, or whatever Israeli interlocutor he chose to name, had promised him such and such. He always implied this was based on his written record, though he never produced any evidence to that effect. He also never seemed to have recorded anything that *he* had promised Israelis.

I tried, with only partial success, to engage some of the other Arab foreign ministers when we'd arrived in the banqueting hall. I did have a good talk with Egypt's Amr Moussa, and the foreign ministers of Morocco and Tunisia. When I tried to start a conversation with Syria's Farouk al-Sharaa, however, he pointedly, though politely, said he felt that would not be appropriate. President Assad had broken off talks with us earlier in the year, insisting that we first commit explicitly to honor Rabin's pocket deposit on the Golan Heights. Still, in my formal remarks at the dinner, I urged both sides to resume our effort to negotiate an

Israeli-Syrian agreement. Sharaa's response was, again, unencouraging. But I did notice, and take heart from, the fact that it was neither polemic nor overtly hostile toward Israel.

When I returned to Israel, I found that Peres, too, wanted to restart the negotiating process with the Syrians. The effort took on fresh momentum after a meeting at Peres's home in Jerusalem in early December, ahead of his visit to Washington for talks with President Clinton. Itamar Rabinovich and I had each met with him separately a few weeks earlier to brief him on how the talks with the Syrians had gone under Rabin, and why they'd reached an impasse. We emphasized Assad's insistence on a preemptive agreement on our leaving the Golan. Peres now came forward with a plan. It was the diplomatic equivalent of what the Americans, a few years later in the Second Gulf War, would call "shock and awe." This was "dazzle and befuddle." As Peres explained it, we would flood Assad with proposals: not just on land or security, but everything from water and electricity to tourism and industrial zones. Assad was in personal control of the Syrian side of the talks. The mere volume, range, and complexity of the simultaneous engagement Peres had in mind would, he hoped, dilute his focus on the Golan. "The best results are extracted from confusion," he said. Having watched President Assad operate for years when I was head of intelligence and chief of staff, I said I was skeptical. I used the image of a bulldog. "It comes into your living room with one aim: to lock on to your ankle. You can throw fireworks, cookies, balloons, a tasty bone. But it's a bulldog. It's still going to move another step toward your ankle." For Assad, the ankle was the Golan.

I understood why Peres wanted to make a new effort to get peace with Syria. Obviously, it was something to be desired in itself. It would transform the terms of our conflict with the Arabs, and maybe even bring within reach the hope of ending it altogether. But there was a political consideration as well. For all his other accomplishments, Peres had a record of repeated electoral defeat as head of Labor. This next election would be the first held under a new set of rules. Instead of merely choosing lists of Knesset candidates, Israelis would cast two votes: one for a party list and one for a directly elected prime minister. This would be a *personal* test, an opportunity for Shimon to build on the still-tenuous achievement of Oslo and finally secure the endorsement of the Israeli people.

It seemed, for a while, I might even have a role. A few days later, Peres and I met again. In Israeli elections, the campaign manager is called head of *hasbarah*—media and public-information planning. He told me he still didn't know exactly when he would call the election. But he asked me to take on that role.

+ + +

Both Peres and I proved to be right about the Syrians. The negotiations did resume, and two rounds of talks were held at Wye River, on Maryland's eastern shore, in December 1995 and January 1996. They focused on the whole range of issues in an eventual peace, just as Peres had hoped, and some progress was made in identifying areas of potential agreement. But the bulldog never took its eyes off our ankle. There was no escaping the fact that without addressing the question of our withdrawal from the Golan Heights, we weren't going to get to the next stage. So we had to make a decision.

Peres, no less than Rabin, knew what the trade-off would be. Israel needed a series of ironclad security arrangements, and a *genuine* peace, rather than just agreement to a cessation of hostilities. Syria would demand to get back all, or at least virtually all, of the Golan. Peres now focused on clarifying, in his own mind, whether we should be willing to agree to trade the Golan for a peace treaty. Our key meeting took place in early February in the underground bunker in the kirya. Peres asked Amnon Lipkin, as chief of staff, and our other top generals for a presentation on their view of the security arrangements required with Syria under a peace deal. They recommended that Israel insist on keeping a sizeable part of the Golan, as well as a range of demilitarization provisions, which reached pretty much to the edge of Damascus. I'd been asked for my view by Rabin when I was chief of staff. Obviously, from a purely military standpoint, the ideal situation would be to keep the whole of the Golan Heights. No chief of staff was going to recommend pulling out. But I'd always added a rider: to withdraw as part of a peace agreement, with all its other likely benefits, was not a *military* question. It was a decision for the government. The relevant question for a *chief of staff* was whether we could ensure the security of Israel if the government decided on a withdrawal, to which I answered yes.

I suspect Amnon would have said much the same thing. But that wasn't the question he'd been asked. As the proceedings wound down, Peres looked glum. Maybe he was anticipating the potential leaks of army concerns about a Golan withdrawal if we did get closer to a deal, and the venomous political attacks he could expect from the right. Bibi's stated view on a deal with Syria at the time was that we could get peace *and* keep the Golan. It was classic Bibi, spoken with verve and conviction as if simply saying it would make it true.

When the presentation was over, Peres called us into a small room in the bunker reserved for use by the defense minister. As foreign minister, I was the only cabinet member with him—along with Uri Savir, Peres's senior deputy for peace negotiations, and several other Peres aides. If there had been a discussion, I would have told him that as long as he felt the talks were progressing, he could ignore Amnon's presentation. If we didn't get a deal, it would be irrelevant. If we did, the military could find ways to deal with the security issues. But he just looked at us and said, "We're going for elections."

A few days later, the date was set for May 29, 1996. That would not be the end of Peres's doubts or difficulties, however. It was only the beginning.

# Labor Pains

THE FIRST OF A WAVE OF HAMAS SUICIDE BOMBINGS DESTROYED A Jerusalem bus at 6:42 a.m. on February 25, 1996. It left twenty-six people dead, and nearly eighty injured from nails and shrapnel packed into the explosive charge. Less than an hour later, near Ashkelon, a terrorist disguised in an Israeli army uniform joined a group of young soldiers waiting to hitch rides back home and blew himself up, killing one of them. A week later, a third suicide attack blasted the roof off a bus on the same Jerusalem commuter route, leaving nineteen more dead. And on March 4, a twenty-four-year-old Palestinian walked up to the entrance of Tel Aviv's busiest shopping center, on Dizengoff Street, and detonated thirty pounds of explosives, killing thirteen people. At the bomb scenes, bloodied survivors and crowds of pedestrians surveyed a hellscape of twisted metal, shards of glass, and mangled body parts. While most Israelis were too shaken to worry about the immediate political repercussions—and Bibi, to his credit, avoided any immediate move to make political capital—they were shaken and afraid. Peres's embryonic reelection campaign, not to mention the peace process, seemed to lie in tatters.

The attacks were not a surprise. The peace promise of Oslo had been assailed from the start by a new alliance of Islamist Palestinian violence: mainly Hamas, and Islamic Jihad on the West Bank. They saw Arafat as a traitor who had sold out to Israel. For them, the issue wasn't just Israel's capture of the West Bank and Gaza in the 1967 war. It was *1948*: they op-

posed any Jewish state, anywhere in Palestine. During the two years following Oslo, they'd mounted ten suicide attacks, leaving nearly eighty
Israelis dead. The attacks had actually stopped since the summer of 1995.
But when the election date was announced—with Peres holding a roughly
15 percent lead in the polls—political commentators both in Israel and
abroad began speculating about a resumption of terror. For Hamas, the
election presented not just an opportunity to kill innocent Israelis but, by
helping defeat Peres and Labor, perhaps to kill Oslo as well.

Even before the bombings, our campaign was struggling for focus, energy, and even purpose, beyond the aim of ending up with more votes
than Bibi Netanyahu. Despite Peres's assurance that I'd be the campaign
manager, that hadn't happened. I wasn't really surprised. When he offered
me the job, I wondered how he'd managed to clear it with much more
established Labor politicians. It turned out he hadn't. Haim Ramon, the
veteran whom I'd urged Rabin to bring back into the government, was
given the role. Shimon put me in charge of a small advisory team reporting directly to him, but the key campaign decisions were taken at weekly
strategy sessions chaired jointly by him and Ramon. I hoped to make the
campaign a referendum on Rabin's murder, and on the need to recommit
Israel to democracy and dialogue over vitriol and violence. But Haim began
with the assumption that, given Peres's lead in the polls, we should play it
safe, ignore the issue of the assassination, and try to ignore Bibi too. He
described it as a soccer match. We were leading by two goals, he told our
first strategy meeting. The other side was never going to score unless
we screwed up. "To win, we do what all good teams do. We play for time. We
kick the ball around. We kick the ball into the stands. We wait for the final
whistle." I tried, without success, to argue that we were underestimating
Bibi. "He may be young and inexperienced in national politics. But I
know him from when he was even younger. He knows how to analyze a
task, break it down, work out a plan, and execute it systematically and
tenaciously. If we play it safe and don't *define* the campaign, he'll seize
on every error we make and *he* will define it."

I wanted us at least to connect with Yitzhak's legacy. I argued to both
Peres and Ramon that we should promote Shimon as the leader with the
background, experience, and vision to take forward what he and Rabin
had begun. I also wanted us to echo a core assumption in all that Rabin

did as a military and political leader: that peace was achievable only if Israel and its citizens felt secure. Even before the renewed terror attacks, I argued that we had to recognize that as much as Israelis yearned for peace, many were conflicted and fearful about the Oslo process. Our central campaign message should be *bitachon ve shalom*: security and peace. "In that order," I added. "We should tell voters openly that we expect groups like Hamas to try to launch attacks. But they don't *want* a secure Israel. They don't want peace. *Don't play their game.*"

The scale and intensity of the bombings threw everything into crisis. After the bomb in the Dizengoff shopping mall, Peres called an emergency cabinet meeting at the kirya. We had to find a way to reassure the public that we were getting the situation under control. We had got a start in our regular Sunday cabinet meeting the day before, by reviving an idea, proposed by Internal Security Minister Moshe Shahal, which I'd supported when Rabin was prime minister: to build a security fence all along the edge of the West Bank, with a series of controlled crossing points for people and goods. Rabin had rejected it, because he was worried it would be seen as a de facto border and undermine the scope for future negotiations. My view was that we would never be able to begin final peace negotiations with the Palestinians unless we could stop at least most of the terror attacks. Peres too had been worried that a security fence would undermine coexistence. But now, he and the rest of the cabinet were so shaken by the carnage Hamas had left that they approved it.

At our kirya meeting, hours after the latest bomb had exploded less than a mile away, Peres recognized we had to go further. Under Oslo, we had begun giving the Palestinians control over internal security in Gaza and parts of the West Bank. Since the new Hamas attacks, Arafat had been *saying* the right things. After the first bomb in Jerusalem, he'd phoned Shimon to offer condolences, telling reporters afterward that this was "a terrorist operation. I condemn it completely. It is not only against civilians, but against the whole peace process." Yet when it came to *action*, we saw no sign that he was willing, ready, or perhaps able to crack down on the Islamist terror attacks. So Peres now announced that, if necessary in order to detain known terrorists, we would for the first time send Israeli troops back into areas where control had been handed back. If Arafat couldn't act, we would.

On the political front, Peres got help from President Clinton, who was anxious to preserve the progress he'd worked so closely with Yitzhak to achieve and organized an unprecedented show of international condemnation of the terror attacks. With Egypt's Hosni Mubarak, he cochaired a "Summit of Peacemakers" in Sharm el-Sheikh with the participation not just of an equally concerned King Hussein, and of course Arafat, but also German chancellor Helmut Kohl, Russia's Boris Yeltsin, and leaders of Arab states from North Africa to Saudi Arabia and the Gulf. The only significant holdout was Syria's Hafez al-Assad, who objected because he said the conference was too focused on Israel. As foreign minister, I accompanied Shimon to the summit. A single day's meeting was never going to end terror. But it was unprecedented in the breadth of Arab engagement in an initiative that, as Assad had anticipated, condemned terror in general and specifically denounced the attacks being launched inside Israel.

I'd met President Clinton briefly once before, when he received Syrian chief of staff Hikmat Shehabi and me after our Blair House talks in 1994. But the Sharm conference provided my first opportunity to spend time with him face-to-face. When Peres and our delegation were about to leave, a Clinton aide approached and said the president had asked whether I'd like to join him on the flight back to Israel. As surprised as I was, Shimon nodded at me to signal it was OK, so I headed off for Air Force One. I spent most of the brief flight talking to the president in the office space carved into the middle of the plane. I would later discover that he quite often tried to engage with foreign leaders' colleagues or advisers on overseas trips. It was part of his voracious appetite for information, aimed at getting a rounded understanding of the complexities of the issues he was trying to address. I got my first real look at Clinton's natural gift for person-to-person politics, as well as his mastery of both the detail and nuance of Israel's predicament and of the wider conflict in the Middle East. Looking straight at me, almost never breaking eye contact, he encouraged me to feel I had something of value and importance to share with him. In fact, he created the impression that I was the first sentient, intelligent human being he'd ever met, a quality I later saw him bring to bear in meetings with a range of other political figures. He made no grand policy statements. Mostly, he asked me questions: What were the prospects of Arafat reining in Hamas and Islamic Jihad? How were our relations going with King Hussein? What was my view of the chances of concluding a peace with Hafez al-Assad, despite his boycott of Sharm el-Sheikh? If Shimon did go on to win the election, what new diplomatic opportunities could he as president, and we, exploit in the search for peace? And, finally, what if *Bibi* won?

+ + +

The summit restored a small lead for Peres in the polls, which was taken as a vindication of Haim Ramon's soccer strategy. Haim still wanted to ignore Bibi, but I pointed out that we were never going to be able to do that completely. Near the end of the campaign, there was going be a head-to-head television debate between the two candidates for prime minister. In the meantime, Bibi was telling voters that while Peres had been busy making deals with Arafat, ordinary Israelis were being left to wonder where the next terrorist would strike. He was sure to ramp up the accusations that Peres was "weak on security," especially if there was more violence. Yet when I mentioned to Shimon that a couple of our internal polls still actually had Bibi slightly ahead, he just laughed. "I have good polls," he said. "Why should I believe the bad ones?"

Violence intervened again, though it was not Hamas this time. Beginning on March 30 and escalating sharply ten days later, Hizbollah rained Katyusha rockets onto towns and settlements in northern Israel—the first sustained attack since the cease-fire in 1994. It was pretty obvious that, like Hamas, the Iranian-backed Shi'ite militia in Lebanon was targeting Israeli civilians as well as Oslo, and Peres's chances of winning the election. The last thing Shimon wanted was for tens of thousands of people in the north of Israel to be cowering in shelters during the final stretch of the campaign. So on April 11, he ordered a major military operation in Lebanon.

I wasn't party to the discussions about the operation, but the model chosen was similar to the one we'd used in 1994: a large-scale air and artillery assault designed to hit Hizbollah hard, force civilians to flee, and persuade the Lebanese and Syrian governments to commit to a US-mediated end to the rocket attacks. All of that happened, but not before a tragic accident brought a storm of international criticism that hastened the end of the operation. An Israeli special forces team was ambushed while providing laser targeting support for an air force strike. When it called in artillery support, four of the shells accidentally fell on a UN compound near the Lebanese village of Qana, killing more than one hundred civilians seeking shelter inside.

Peres phoned me a few hours later, distraught not just because the wayward artillery strike had laid us open to charges of "targeting" civilians in an operation designed to try to avoid doing so, but because the accident seemed likely to deal a further blow to his efforts to convince Israel's voters that he, rather than Bibi, was best placed to lead the country. "We're in trouble," he said. Yet within days, it became clear that our basic campaign strategy—ignore Bibi and "kick the ball into the stands"—was not going to change. I made one last attempt to put us on the political offensive after I was asked to record one of Labor's TV campaign messages. I knew what I wanted to say. Rather than ignore Bibi, I used my position as his former commander in Sayeret Matkal, someone who knew him well, to explain why *Peres* should lead Israel.

"How many of us can really understand what it means to be a prime minister?" I began. "As head of intelligence, and chief of staff, I have seen, close-up, what it takes to be a prime minister. It is not a game. We've had good prime ministers: Ben-Gurion, Peres, Rabin, Begin. Bibi, we know each other well, from the days when you were an officer under my command. A young officer, and a good one. Prime minister is the most important and serious role in this country. Bibi, it's not yet you. We need an experienced leader, who will know how to guide us with wisdom, strength, and sensitivity. Shimon Peres is that man."

The face-to-face television debate between the two candidates was set for May 27, two days before the election. By American standards, the format was fairly tame. No direct exchanges were permitted, only a series of questions directed at each candidate by a leading political journalist, Dan Margalit. Still, it would place Shimon and Bibi side by side. We spent two days prepping Peres, with Avraham Burg—an early Peace Now supporter, former Peres aide, and Knesset member—standing in for Bibi. Avraham played the role well, anticipating the lines of attack Shimon would face. But as I watched, I worried that even he couldn't replicate one of Bibi's key advantages. During his time at the embassy in Washington, and especially as UN ambassador, Bibi had become a frequent presence on American television interview shows. Always articulate, he was now also an experienced, and completely comfortable, television performer. In our debate rehearsals, Peres sounded well versed on all the issues. Yet he seemed a bit distant, unengaged, almost as if the TV debate was something he knew he had to go through, but which he thought slightly sullied the proper purpose of politics. The problem wasn't the message, but the medium.

In the real debate, Shimon conveyed a sense that merely being in the same studio with a pretender as raw and untested as Bibi was offensive. When each of the candidates was given the opportunity at the end to ask a single question of the other, Peres didn't even bother. He did come off as the man with much more experience, gravitas, substance. He also had what was probably the best line in the debate, saying that if Israeli voters were choosing a male model and not a prime minister, Bibi might indeed be their man. Yet Bibi was the more polished performer, and more focused. No matter what question Margalit asked him, he almost invariably answered with the driving message of his campaign: that because of Peres, Israeli citizens were living in fear, wondering where the next suicide bomber would strike or the next Katyusha would land. Unavoidably, there was another contrast as well: Bibi was twenty-six years younger and projected greater youth, energy, and confidence. When it was over and Peres asked us how he'd done, we all hemmed and hawed. Only Avraham Burg offered a clear verdict: Bibi had won.

It still remained possible Ramon's strategy might work. Though Peres's poll lead had been narrowing by the day, he was—just—ahead. With a large number of voters undecided, however, Bibi pulled one final trick out of his campaign bag. Under Israeli law, election spending is tightly regulated and nearly all campaigning is barred during the last forty-eight hours before election day. Yet with the backing of wealthy overseas supporters, the Netanyahu campaign suddenly flooded Israel with blue-and-white banners under the slogan: *Bibi, Tov la Yehudim*—"Bibi is good for the Jews." The aim was to galvanize support among Orthodox, and pro-settlement, voters, while also leaving the clear implication that Peres was not on their side.

I had worried for some time we might lose. That was why Nava and I had persuaded Michal, our eldest daughter, to move up her wedding to her teenage boyfriend, a wonderful young man named Ziv Lotenberg. They had originally planned it for a week later, but we did not want to risk having it overshadowed by an election defeat. The wedding took place in a beautiful area of lawns and gardens called Ronit Farm, north of Herzliya. It was how weddings are meant to be, full of smiles, good food, and dancing. Near the end, Shimon showed up. As he walked over to greet us, one guest after another shook his hand, patted him on the back, hugged him, wished him luck. It was as if all the pressure and tension of the campaign were suddenly gone. He smiled, returned the embraces, even joined in the dancing. When he left, I told him that he'd done all he could to secure victory, and that I hoped the voters would make the right choice.

The first exit polls suggested he was going to win. But our internal polling was less clear. As more and more votes were counted, Shimon's margin inexorably narrowed. It wasn't until the next morning that the final result was clear: Bibi Netanyahu had won. By 29,000 votes. If a mere 15,000 of the 3 million ballots cast had gone in our column instead of his, Shimon Peres would have remained prime minister.

I knew he'd be crushed. This latest electoral defeat was a direct, head-to-head vote for prime minister. He, like all of us who had campaigned for him, knew what was at stake. Barely six months had passed since Rabin was gunned down in Tel Aviv's main square by a fellow Israeli riding a tide of hatred so blind that it could paint Yitzhak—who worked all his life to create, defend, and develop the Jewish state—as a traitor, even a Nazi. All because he tried to make peace with the Palestinians, at the price of ceding control of part of the biblical land of Israel. Bibi had gone through the motions of urging restraint, but politically, he rode their wave. It was hard not to see his victory over Peres as a triumph for the ugly intolerance and the venom that had claimed Yitzhak's life. In policy terms, it was in large part a rejection of both men's vision of an Israel that, while still ready to fight if necessary, could explore compromise in the search for the ultimate prize of peace. The last time Yitzhak and I had talked, he'd been confident of defeating Bibi at the polls, and I do believe he might well have won. But despite his differences with Peres, I'm equally certain he would have wanted *Shimon* to win, not just for his sake but for Israel's.

I had got to know Shimon during my years in the kirya. In fact, he was the Labor leader who first spoke to me openly about one day moving into politics, something Yitzhak was always assiduous in not broaching before I'd left the army. Shimon had also taken to including me—usually along with Yossi Beilin and Shlomo Ben-Ami, a bright young historian who would become our ambassador to Spain before entering politics himself—in a coterie of "youngsters" he would bring along to meet visiting dignitaries from abroad. He occasionally invited me to chat about military and security issues in his and Sonia's flat in Ramat Aviv. My personal ties to Rabin were stronger, of course. After I joined the government, Shimon's and my relationship became slightly more circumspect. But since the assassination, some of the old warmth had returned. As his foreign minister, as well as in discussions on wider questions of security, we worked closely together.

Within days of the election, however, there was a new source of potential friction between us: Shimon's future, and possibly mine, in leading our opposition to Bibi and bringing a Labor government back to power.

+ + +

The question of whether Peres would stay on as party leader was unavoidable. Labor's constitution mandated a vote for party chairman within fourteen months of an election defeat. A little before midnight on election day, with the returns beginning to show we might lose, I was invited to a morning-after breakfast by two senior Labor ministers: Fuad Ben-Eliezer, who had delivered the table-thumping warning that the hatred on the far right would lead to a murder, and Avraham Shochat, finance minister under both Rabin and Peres. Both had been in the Knesset since the 1980s. They had taken part in two of Peres's earlier, failed election campaigns, and both now said they weren't prepared to see him lead us into electoral battle the next time around. "Everyone in the party understands the meaning of this defeat. Shimon is done," Shochat said, as Fuad nodded his agreement. "You will have to go for the leadership."

Though their endorsement was a surprise, it would be disingenuous to pretend I hadn't thought about the possibility of running for the party leadership at some stage in the future. The point of politics for me, no less than my long military career, was to make a contribution to the path my country took. Yet my election campaign differences with Ramon and Peres had not been just for the sake of intellectual argument. I had badly wanted Shimon to win—both for his sake and Israel's. Despite my misgivings about some aspects of the Oslo process, I believed there was a possibility of achieving peace with the Palestinians, and a compelling case to do all we could to reach that goal. From my involvement in the talks with the Syrians, I also knew that the outline of a possible agreement with Assad was in place. I wasn't confident that Bibi Netanyahu was the man to lead our country forward on either front. Yes, Bibi was smart. He was organizationally astute. He'd been a good Sayeret Matkal officer. Yet as I'd said in my TV campaign spot, being prime minister required more than that.

Our election defeat, and the morning-after message of support from two Labor heavyweights, meant that the question of Labor leadership had come much earlier than I'd hoped or expected. I believed that if Peres decided to step aside, I could help ensure that we held Bibi to account on the key issues of security and peace and if he faltered, lead a reinvigorated party back into government. But I had no appetite for rushing into a challenge to Peres. Bibi was about to begin his negotiations with other political parties to form a government that could command a Knesset majority. That process was likely to take at least a few weeks. Shimon had yet to give any sign of whether he intended to stay on.

Still, when he invited me for a late-night chat at his apartment a week after the election, I was concerned that *he* might raise the leadership issue; if he did, I would have to be honest and open with him. The conversation went very differently than I'd expected. After he'd poured each of us a glass of Armagnac and offered me a plate of Sonia's cakes, he spoke for a while about Bibi, though he could not even bring himself to utter the name. *This man*, he said, knew nothing about leadership, much less about running the country. He would be outmaneuvered, overshadowed, and ultimately controlled by the "real strongman" in the Likud: Arik Sharon. I said I thought we were again underestimating Bibi's strength, as well as the effect of the country's new electoral system. In the past, the voters had cast a single ballot for their preferred party. Now, on the model of an American presidential election, they'd separately chosen their candidate for prime minister. This meant that Bibi had a personal mandate to govern, turning upside down the balance of power and influence in the negotiations to form his government. As he assembled his coalition, any of the political parties that hoped to be included would have to deal with him on his terms. The same would apply with potential rivals like Arik inside Bibi's own party, the Likud.

As we talked, Shimon seemed to have come to terms with the election defeat. He struck me as more relaxed, at ease with himself, than at any time since the start of the grueling campaign. Then, abruptly, he said, "Ehud, I understand the meaning of the election result. You will have to take on the leadership, and lead the party." He said he didn't plan to spend the rest of his years hanging around the apartment. He would remain active—"working for peace"—but no longer in the party political arena. "I understand the meaning of what has happened," he repeated. "I will pass the Labor leadership torch to you. We should find a way to do it quickly, and in the right way."

It was nearly three in the morning when I left. I was touched by Shimon's magnanimity. He was now nearly seventy-three. His life in our country's politics, and in Labor, stretched back to before the state, when he'd been a favored protégé of Ben-Gurion. Walking away was going to be hard. I was touched as well by the fact that he had decided to "pass the torch" to me, even though I'd been closer to his rival, Rabin. But I remained cautious, too. When I got back home, Nava, knowing where I'd been, was still awake. I told her everything that Shimon had said. I told her how extraordinary it felt to have the prospect, at least, of leading Labor in opposition to Bibi, without the need to confront, or to inflict personal hurt, on Shimon. But I added, "It seems a bit too good to be true."

It was. The next morning, I joined other ministers and party officials with Peres in his office. It was as if our conversation a few hours before had never happened. Shimon set out his strategy for Labor going forward. And the first thing he said was that the party needed to push back any leadership election beyond the mandated fourteen months. "It's too early," he said. He said we needed to focus on the challenge of rebuilding the party, and also had to address the question of joining a possible "unity" government with Bibi.

Though Bibi went on to form his government without us, in alliance with a number of smaller Orthodox parties, the idea of a Labor leadership change seemed off the agenda, at least for now. In early August, I was standing next to Giora Eini—the "political operative" Yitzhak had sent to help bring me into his government, and a friend of Peres as well—when Shimon rose to speak to the dozens of well-wishers at his seventy-third birthday celebration in Tel Aviv. He was at his old, self-confident best. With just a few thousand extra votes, we would have won the election, he said. He was sure Bibi's coalition—"a coalition against peace"—would not survive for long. Giora, smiling, turned to me and said, "It doesn't sound like a farewell speech."

Another of Peres's old friends, a few weeks later, urged me to press him on the need to step aside. I'd become closer to the French Jewish businessman Jean Frydman during the election campaign. Since he had helped organize the fateful peace rally at which Rabin was shot, he felt—wrongly, but powerfully—a sense of responsibility for what had happened. He wanted to do everything possible to ensure that Rabin's political legacy, and Shimon's, survived. He invited Nava and me to visit him. When he asked about the birthday celebration, I told him what Peres had said. "He's making a huge mistake," Jean told me. "After every election, he goes through the same process. Always, he's convinced that next time he will win." I told Jean that I dreaded the prospect of being part of an effort to *force* Shimon out. He replied that he believed I was the only potential Labor leader who could defeat Bibi in an election and "bring back sanity to Israel, lead it to peace." He said he was convinced that Peres's time had passed. "I can say that. I'm from his generation. And as a very close friend of Shimon, I will be the first in line to help you."

Early in September, having let Shimon know through Giora and then phoning him directly, I declared publicly that I would be running for the Labor leadership. Though he'd thanked me for telling him beforehand, Shimon said he thought I was making a mistake. He was still against having a leadership election at all, all of which made his public response to my announcement puzzling. He went on Israeli TV and said he would *not* be a candidate for prime minister in four years' time. "The time has come for a change," he said. But while everyone took that to mean he was reconciled to a change of party leadership as well, it turned out that we had jumped the gun. He intended to stay on as chairman.

During the early months of 1997, Shimon and I held a series of late-night meetings at his apartment to thrash out an agreed course. The process was hard for both of us, and hurtful for him. He was now at least reconciled to the inevitability of an election for a new party leader, if only because his protégé Yossi Beilin had also put his name forward. But he kept proposing to push back the vote. I insisted that since the deadline under party rules was June 3, it was only right that all of us abide by that. I do remember a particularly poignant moment from one of our sessions. Peres had left the room for a minute, and Sonia came in. "Ehud," she said to me, "keep your nerve. You're the only one who can talk to him this way. He should have retired from politics years ago. You're the only one around him who tells him the truth."

We ended up with a compromise. Shimon accepted that the leadership election would be held on June 3. I agreed that in the unlikely event Bibi decided to invite us into his coalition during the three months after the leadership vote, Peres would select the Labor ministers. Our last discussion ended at nearly four in the morning. He told me he'd arranged a meeting for the party leadership at 10:00 a.m., in barely six hours' time.

He was relaxed and gracious when I arrived. We went through the details of what we'd agreed, and worked out what each of us would say to reporters. What came next, as the party faithful filed in, was simple human nature, I suppose. Seeing some of his oldest supporters, he again had second thoughts. His comments to reporters afterward were more hedged than what we'd discussed. Giora told me that after all of us had left, Peres turned to him and said, "Look what Barak is doing to me. What have *you* been doing?" Giora, who had been a conduit between us at the very beginning of our discussions, replied, "You *asked* me to bring Barak to you." At which point Shimon said, "OK. So probably I made a mistake."

At a convention of 3,000 party activists in mid-May, a few weeks before the leadership election, he made a final attempt to mitigate that "mistake." Nissim Zvili, the secretary-general of the party and a longtime Peres ally, introduced a motion to vote him into a new post of party president. A couple of Shimon's friends urged me to back the idea, describing it essentially as a ceremonial role. But I feared it was a recipe for prolonging the agony. Whatever powers "President Peres" would have, the idea of two captains on a ship would almost certainly mean trouble. Labor needed to steer a calm, decisive course toward the next election if we were going to defeat Bibi.

What followed was one of the most painful spectacles I've ever witnessed. When Peres rose to make his case for becoming party president, he said, "I don't want powers. I don't want honors. But I also don't want insults. I *announced* my decision to resign from the position of party chairman. Did someone push me into it? Am I trying to hold on to my job?"

"Yes!" many of the several thousand delegates shouted back at him.

Stung, he reminded the meeting that it was he who had led Labor back from the battering it took in the 1977 election against Begin. In 1981, he'd helped us recover a dozen of our lost seats. Even so, because he hadn't succeeded in forming a Labor government, people had called him a loser! "*Mah? Ani* loser?" he asked, using the English word. "Am I a *loser?*"

"Yes! Yes!" came the shouts.

Yet the saddest note came at the end. "I apologize for being healthy, for not getting old according to plan," he said, adding that even *without* the title of president, he would keep working for peace.

There were three other candidates for party chairman: Yossi Beilin, whom I'd found invaluable in helping me to understand the world of politics after I left the army; Ephraim Sneh, the friend who'd been the paratroopers' chief medic when we'd fought at the Chinese Farm in 1973, and at Entebbe too; and Shlomo Ben-Ami, the gifted academic whom Shimon had often taken along with Yossi and me to meet visiting foreign politicians when I was still in uniform, and who was now also a newly elected member of the Knesset. When the vote came, it was assumed by most political commentators that I was going to win. The only question was whether I'd get the 50 percent of votes needed to avoid a run-off. But I got 57 percent against Yossi Beilin's 28, with the remaining 15 percent split between Ephraim and Shlomo.

+ + +

Now, we had to put ourselves in a position to defeat Bibi and the Likud. The policy message would matter most: strong and credible steps to confront terror and safeguard our security, allied with the leadership and will to try to negotiate a peace with Syria and the Palestinians. But in at least one important way, I approached my new role as if it were one of our operations in Sayeret Matkal. My first priority was to put in place the *practical* foundations for a successful election challenge against Bibi. Through Jean Frydman and other business supporters with the means and the desire to help, my brother-in-law, Doron Cohen, assembled sufficient funding for us to begin engaging with the strategists who had helped deliver electoral success for a trio of other center-left political leaders overseas: Bill Clinton, Tony Blair in Britain, and later Gerhard Schröder in Germany.

My main early political focus was on holding Bibi and the government to account in the Knesset, above all on the tortuous process of ensuring our security while implementing the West Bank redeployments agreed in Oslo II. We'd made a small start under Rabin and Peres, but the two major withdrawal phases due in the five-year interim period had yet to begin. In one respect, I had some sympathy for Bibi's predicament. The reason I'd tried to get Yitzhak to alter the terms of Oslo II was that it required us to hand back control before we knew what a permanent-status peace deal would look like. But where my sympathy ended was in how Bibi handled the situation. Despite my concerns about the way the Oslo process had been designed, I never doubted that killing it off would be by far a worse alternative. Bibi had been elected to *lead* Israel. Instead, he acted as if he were playing some sort of pinball match, flipping the ball first one way, then the other, with no obvious aim beyond keeping it in play—and where Oslo was concerned, simply stalling for time. Rather than setting out any vision of where he hoped to move the negotiating process, he seemed more concerned with keeping the right wing of Likud and the smaller, even more extreme parties from turning against him.

In late September 1996, Bibi and the Likud mayor of Jerusalem, Ehud Olmert, decided to go ahead with the festive opening of an archeological tunnel that provided access to a larger portion of the Western Wall of the ancient Jewish temple. It was a decision that, under both Rabin and Peres, we'd delayed out of concern about inflaming tensions with the Palestinians. As Shimon said publicly after the three days of violence that followed, we understood that, at a minimum, it would need to be coordinated beforehand with Arafat. As the unrest spread into the West Bank and Gaza, there were media warnings of a "new intifada," the difference this time being that the Palestinians' newly established police had entered the fray. By the time urgent US diplomacy, Israel's efforts, and Arafat brought it to a close, seventeen Israeli soldiers and nearly one hundred Palestinians had been killed. Bibi did not slam on the brakes altogether on the American-led efforts to move ahead with Oslo. In early 1997, in fact, he and Arafat reached a separate agreement on the critically important question, and potential flashpoint, of Hebron. It stipulated that about 80 percent of the area would be under Palestinian authority, with Israel retaining control and responsibility for nearby settlements and key security points. Despite right-wing and settler opposition, it was approved by a wide margin in the Knesset, with Labor's backing. But a few months later, in the spring of 1997, Hamas launched a new campaign of suicide bombings in shopping areas of Jerusalem and Tel Aviv, leaving twenty-four people dead, and Bibi moved to slow the pace of further US-mediated talks on the details of implementing the Oslo II redeployments.

By November, his foreign minister, David Levy, was making noises about quitting. He said it would be a waste of time to stay in the cabinet if it was going to bring the peace process to a halt. I warned Bibi, both in the Knesset and in a series of speeches, about the alternative on the Palestinian side if those who *wanted* a negotiated peace had nothing but a stalemate to show for it. I was convinced that the result would be a second, much more deadly, intifada. Not with Molotov cocktails, but guns and suicide bombs.

But I also offered help: I announced that if Bibi *did* go ahead and finalize the terms for Israel's redeployment, Labor would once again provide the extra Knesset votes needed for him to get it approved. Early in 1998, he sent word that he wanted to talk. The message came through Yaakov Ne'eman, his finance minister. He and I held an exploratory meeting at which he proposed talks with Bibi on the prospect of a unity government that would help move the peace process forward. I said I'd talk, with one proviso: the discussions would be genuinely secret, with no leaks. In May, Bibi sent an assurance of confidentiality through Ne'eman. The first of about a half dozen meetings came a few days later at the prime minister's residence in Jerusalem. Then we shifted venue, meeting at a Mossad-owned villa north of Tel Aviv. I brought along Bougie Herzog, a bright young lawyer and Labor Party member, who was working in the same law firm as Ne'eman. To my amusement, if not altogether to my surprise, I got word that Bibi was putting out separate political feelers to Shimon Peres. But before long, it became clear there was a specific political motivation behind his approaching me. It was indeed the peace process. But it wasn't the *Palestinian* peace process, something Bibi still clearly wanted to avoid as much as humanly possible. It was an attempt to engage with Syria.

He asked me about the talks under Rabin and Peres, and my views on the possibility of a deal with President Assad. He also wanted my assessment about whether the army could work out arrangements to safeguard the country's security if we handed back most, if not all, of the Golan Heights. What kind of security arrangements would we need, with what timeline? We met through the summer, as the talks with the Americans on the further West Bank redeployments meandered ahead. We also discussed in detail how a unity government would work. We agreed it would be presented, like the Shamir-Peres partnership in 1984, as a cross-party response to an important challenge for the country: in this case, security and the peace process. I would be both defense minister and "vice–prime minister," with the understanding that Bibi and I would jointly talk through all major issues before jointly bringing them to the full cabinet.

In August, the talks ended after news of our talks leaked. I immediately phoned Ne'eman and reminded him that at the outset, I'd said that would mean the discussions were over. Ne'eman speculated that the source might have been my old comrade from the Chinese Farm, Yitzhik Mordechai. He had presumably heard that Bibi was ready to make me defense minister as part of a unity government. There was, of course, already a defense minister in place: Yitzhik.

Bibi's idea to reopen efforts to get peace with Syria didn't last either. Although I'd learn of this only a few years later, he'd approved a series of visits to Damascus by the American businessman Ronald Lauder to meet President Assad, culminating in a ten-point document outlining the shape of a peace deal, including an Israeli withdrawal from virtually the whole Golan Heights, with the border based on the "June 4" line before the 1967 Six-Day War. But the initiative foundered when Assad insisted that the American go-between get a detailed map from Bibi setting out his precise idea of the final border. Though no one in the cabinet knew the initiative was under way, Bibi realized that before sending back the map Assad wanted, he would need to tell the two senior ministers directly affected: Arik Sharon, who had replaced David Levy as foreign minister, and Yitzhik Mordechai as defense minister. Both said no, with Yitzhik in particular warning that any map signed by the prime minister would become a formal part of the negotiating record. It was a step that, in any future negotiations with the Syrians, could not be undone.

Bibi's coalition was now creaking. The Syrian option was off. David Levy had already jumped ship. Yitzhik, increasingly concerned about Bibi's delay and drift on Oslo II, seemed to be thinking of leaving as well. Right-wing ministers and Knesset members were no happier: they opposed even the slightest prospect of movement on Oslo. In October, Bibi finally tried to seize the initiative, wrapping up the redeployment details in a summit with Arafat and Clinton in Wye River. But as soon as he got back home, he backtracked rather than risk facing down his right-wing critics in the cabinet. Implementation of the deal was due to begin in early November, but he kept putting off a vote in the cabinet. When the vote came, on November 11, Bibi squeaked through by a margin of 8–4, but with five abstentions. Fewer than half of his ministers had voted for it.

The easy part for him was Knesset ratification, since I had committed Labor to supporting him on any move toward continuing the peace process. The day after the Knesset's vote, Bibi won the cabinet's clearance for actual implementation of the redeployments to begin. But with hard-line ministers threatening to bring down the government, Bibi again stalled. That was the turning point. I'd made it clear our parliamentary support would remain for as long as Bibi moved ahead with what had been agreed at Wye River. It was not intended as a blank check, or an offer to prop up a prime minister who now seemed to be looking for any possible way *not* to implement the agreement.

My key ally in what came next was Haim Ramon. Despite our differences over the direction of the Peres election campaign, we had become effective parliamentary partners. Ramon had a depth of political experience I still lacked. While I found the details of how the Knesset operated arcane and often tiresome, Haim knew all of it instinctively. When it came to the need for discreet discussions or bargaining with other parties, he could draw on his personal relationships with Knesset members across the party divide. He had the additional advantage of being able to avoid the scrutiny that would follow a direct approach from me. Before Bibi had gone to Wye, Haim and I discussed how we might move to force early elections. The peace process, and the country, were drifting. There seemed no point in waiting, if we could be confident of lining up the necessary votes among the growing number of others who were also convinced Bibi should go. After the Wye summit agreement, I put all that on hold. But now that Bibi had shifted into reverse, I told Haim to resume his efforts.

In early December, he told me he had enough votes for a no-confidence motion, under his name, to dissolve the Knesset and pave the way for early elections. The axe fell on December 20. Bibi had lost the support of the right wing, who wanted Oslo ended altogether. He had now lost me, too. His approach to the peace process was leaving Israel rudderless. The way we were heading, we would not just forfeit any potential benefits from Oslo: we would be leaving a political and diplomatic vacuum at a time when a serious new explosion of Palestinian violence was becoming ever more likely. In the Knesset debate, Bibi made one final bid to save himself: by suggesting a delay of seventy-two hours for talks on a "unity" government. I said that I was all for unity. But I reminded him that time after time, we'd saved his government in order to continue the peace process. As tension rose around the chamber, I said we could no longer help out a "government that is not interested in upholding the Wye agreement, but only in its political survival."

The vote of no-confidence went against him by the yawning margin of 81–30, with nine Knesset members abstaining or staying away. A few days later, the date for the election was announced: May 17, 1999.

# One Israel

A FEW HOURS BEFORE HAIM RAMON INTRODUCED HIS NO-CONFIDENCE resolution, he came to see me in my office in the Knesset. Our political partnership was still fairly new. He also realized, of course, that only once, since Menachem Begin's victory in 1977, had Labor won a national election. So he was understandably worried—not about the Knesset vote, but about what would come after. "Ehud, I'm sure that we can topple the government," he said. "But only you know whether we're ready—whether *you're* ready—to defeat Bibi."

"I'm ready," I said. "We are going to win."

Few agreed. In fact, there had been times during my first year and a half as Labor leader when I wondered if I'd be able to hang on to the job. I was in charge of a party whose grassroots were on the left. I was, by intellect and instinct, a pragmatist and a centrist, but I did share Labor's vision of a socially just and democratic Israel.

After seeing far-right rabbis egg on the fanaticism that ultimately killed Yitzhak Rabin, I felt strongly that we needed to separate organized religion from our day-to-day politics. But I'd been raised with a deeper respect for our Jewish traditions than many on the left. Right after Yitzhak's murder, I'd gone to see Zevulun Hammer, the leader of the National Religious Party. The NRP had been part of both Labor and Likud governments ever since 1948, though not Rabin's. It, too, had been drifting steadily rightward. But it still basically subscribed to the idea of a strong, democratic Israel under the rule of law. I wanted to bring the NRP back into the government under Peres, as part of the widest-possible political alliance against the assassination and the campaign of hatred that had fostered it. Sadly that didn't happen, in part because of the anger against all Orthodox politicians after Rabin's murder. Yet in my readiness to engage politically with Orthodox leaders who did not reject the very idea of peace negotiations—whether in the NRP, or the increasingly influential Sephardi religious party, Shas—I was outside Labor's mainstream, and its comfort zone.

On my approach to peace as well, I differed from many on the left. Though I was determined to pursue any realistic avenue to negotiations, I was convinced that security considerations had to be paramount in what we were prepared to give up or accept in negotiations. I was cautious about ceding too much too soon, in case the Palestinians or the Syrians proved either unequal to, or uninterested in, making the hard decisions required for peace. That approach provoked more left-wing parties like Meretz to suggest—as they sometimes did when Rabin was prime minister—that if I *really* wanted peace, I'd be ready to give away more, and more quickly.

My position wasn't helped by the way I had come across in the media during my first months as Labor leader. A number of newspaper commentators wrote that while they found talking with me stimulating, I seemed to be operating in a world of my own, either unable or unwilling to give straight answers and a single, clear message. They were right about that. My instincts went toward nuance, not sound bites. The difficulties that could result hit home in an interview with a leading Israeli journalist in the spring of 1998. He asked how my life might have turned out if I'd been born and raised not as a kibbutznik, but a Palestinian. I answered, "At some stage, I would have entered one of the terror organizations and fought from there, and later would certainly have tried to influence from within the political system." I did hasten to add that I abhorred terrorists, describing their actions as "abominable" and "villainous." But that was lost in the political storm that followed. I'd simply answered as honestly as I could, trying to imagine I'd been one of the Palestinian babies in Wadi Khawaret, yet with the same mind and approach to life that had defined me as an Israeli. Still, as even my brother-in-law told me when he phoned a couple of hours later, it was not the most astute thing to say as a potential candidate for prime minister.

None of this might have mattered if I'd been able to show I was bringing Labor nearer to defeating Bibi. But the only measure of progress that mattered for the media was the opinion polls. Briefly, in late 1997, I did pull ahead, during the period leading up to Bibi's agreement to pull out of most of Hebron. But for much of 1998, I ran behind, and questions about my leadership surfaced publicly by the summer. The media commentators spoke of the need for a Labor "liftoff." Why, after a full year as leader, had I failed to deliver it?

+ + +

There *was* a part of politics for which I was naturally suited after my life in the army: to plan an operation, prepare, and execute it. To get the lay of the land, assess your own and your rivals' strengths and vulnerabilities, and to win. And the "lay of the land" struck me as more encouraging than many Israeli commentators believed. When I became Labor leader, I didn't expect Bibi to fall anytime soon. But I believed it was inevitable that at some point he'd have to make tough choices about the peace process, and I doubted his coalition with the more right-wing Orthodox parties would survive. I also took encouragement from the fact that the political winds in other developed democracies seemed to be blowing in our direction. Bill Clinton had won in the United States. In Britain, which had a parliamentary system much closer to Israel's, Tony Blair, as leader of a party renamed as New Labour, had ended eighteen years of Conservative rule and swept to victory.

Within weeks of my election as Labor chairman, I used my acquaintance with a British Jewish businessman named Michael Levy to see what lessons our Labor party might learn from Tony Blair's. Levy had been an early supporter of Blair and persuaded the prime minister to welcome me through the famous black door of Number 10 Downing Street. After chatting in the front hallway, he led me into the back garden to discuss how he had refashioned his party and brought it back into government. In addition to modifying or abandoning rigidly left-wing positions that most British voters had rejected, he had created a formidable campaigning team under an ally and adviser named Peter Mandelson. When I asked Blair whether it would be possible to meet Mandelson, he said he couldn't "give me Peter." But he did put me in touch with Philip Gould, the polling expert and strategist who had partnered with Mandelson in designing and running the election campaign.

We met at Labour headquarters in Millbank Tower so Philip could show me the "war room"—modeled, in part, on Bill Clinton's campaign operation—from which the victory had been planned and executed. It was a large, open-plan space, nothing like the warren of offices and tiny conference rooms in which we operated. Pride of place went to an advanced computer system, the heart of a "rebuttal unit" that charted every statement from the Conservative Party so it could be answered, neutralized, or used to adjust Labour's own campaign. I was struck by how different the approach was from our campaign for Peres. As I filled my notebook with the details, Philip added a final bit of advice. "If you want to win, have it run by the best *professionals* you can find. Not politicians. They always have personal agendas. Focus is everything. Distractions and arguments and infighting can be fatal."

Philip recommended one professional, in particular, to get us started: Stanley Greenberg, the pollster who had advised Blair's and Clinton's campaigns. We used our contacts in New York to put us in touch not only with Greenberg but the strategist behind the Clinton victory, James Carville, and another leading Democratic Party consultant and speechwriter, Bob Shrum. We began working with all of them well before the no-confidence vote in the Knesset. Philip had a wonderfully British understatement and reserve. Stanley, with his eyeglasses and demeanor, came over as slightly professorial. With Bob, it didn't take long to understand why he was such a gifted speechwriter. He loved words, especially the way they could be used to inspire a connection with important campaign themes: above all with the idea of hope, and new beginnings. Carville was the human equivalent of a volcano. If he hadn't been a campaign strategist, he could have made a living as a hybrid of a cowboy and a stand-up comedian. But they all shared the easy, infectious self-confidence of people who were very good at what they did and knew it.

When I went to New York with Doron to meet Carville in February 1998, my confidence as Labor leader was taking some fairly hard knocks. But from the moment he walked through our hotel-room door, it was impossible not to like him. He showed up in a T-shirt and tennis sneakers, walked straight across the room, slouched into a chair, and didn't hold back. "General Barak, I don't get it. You're a known public figure, with a great mind and a great military record. It's already been a year and a half since Israel got Netanyahu. What have you done to *go after* him? Why haven't you gone on the attack?" He said it was time for me to wake up and change tack. "Can you run through your stump speech for me?" he asked, motioning me toward the center of the room like a film director.

"I don't have one," I replied, to which he replied briskly that I should have had one *months* ago.

When Stanley and Philip Gould paid a preliminary visit to Israel, they too urged me to sharpen my message and pay more attention to my public image. Stanley was worried by polling data that suggested most Israelis saw Bibi as "strong." I argued that strength was one area where we wouldn't have to worry. "No way, in a campaign, he'll end up coming over looking stronger than me." Stanley did not seem entirely convinced.

Both in "strength" and other ways, I think my background did prove an advantage. The years I'd spent in the military had given me a focused, disciplined determination to set goals, follow through, and achieve them. Still, my military background was not always an asset as I found my feet as party leader and prepared to take on Bibi in the election campaign. In searching for the tools, the structure, and the people that would give us the best chance to win, I sometimes failed to pay due attention to the party's existing apparatus and institutions. This alienated a number of established Labor politicians, eventually including Haim himself. So as the campaign approached I tried to shore up my ties with the party establishment. I drafted in Bougie Herzog to act as my regular liaison with leading figures in the party. I was careful to include a number of Labor politicians in our campaign team as well, though, as Philip had recommended, I made sure they didn't actually run it.

The closest equivalent to the role Haim had played as manager of Peres's election campaign went to a young businessman, PR professional, and Labor supporter named Moshe Gaon. For spokeswoman, we brought in someone who—though she'd been a messenger of doom during the

Tze'elim controversy that engulfed me before joining Rabin's government—had undeniable experience and ability, which I valued and respected: Yitzhak's former media aide Aliza Goren. For campaign coordinator, I chose Tal Silberstein, who at the time was in charge of a citizens' group called Dor Shalem Doresh Shalom: "A Whole Generation Demands Peace." I relied on frequent, less formal input from political friends whose judgment I had learned to trust, like Eitan Haber and Giora Eini, and from a few journalist friends as well, including Ido Disenchik and Dan Margalit. Also crucial was a group of four women, led by Orna Angel, a successful architect and a former soldier in Sayeret Matkal. She built from scratch an army of nearly 20,000 volunteers who helped organize events and contact voters during the campaign. We outfitted our own war room in an open-plan floor of offices on the edge of Tel Aviv. Philip called it "Millbank South." For organizational head of the campaign, I chose Chagai Shalom. An industrial engineer by training, he was a reserve army general who, when I was chief of staff, had been in charge of the logistics branch of the military. I gave him Sayeret Matkal backup as well, in the person of Danny Yatom, my longtime friend and former sayeret deputy.

+ + +

But all that was process. Important though it was, winning or losing would come down to the strength of our message, our ability to forge alliances, and how my own personal and political appeal measured up against Bibi's.

The system of separate elections for party and prime minister meant that in order to win a majority, I would need the support of voters outside Labor. I set out to establish a broader movement, a big tent under which a majority of Israelis could coexist politically. I wanted to convey to voters that I was reaching out beyond my core party constituency: to "soft" right-wingers nearer the political center; to the Sephardim who since 1977 had overwhelmingly voted Likud; to the growing number of Russian immigrants who had helped Bibi defeat Peres; and to those among the Orthodox who still subscribed to tolerance and moderation in the mold of the old-style National Religious Party in the first few decades of the state. Though almost all the candidates on our Knesset election list would be from Labor, I ran the prime ministerial campaign under the broader banner of Yisrael Ahat—One Israel. I envisaged it as an alliance of at least several different parties with Labor at its center.

I began with Bibi's jettisoned foreign minister, David Levy. A Moroccan-born 1950s immigrant, he had begun his political career at the grassroots, in the northern town of Beit She'an, and gone on to play an important role in Begin's victory in 1977. The leading Sephardi figure in the Likud, he was at one point mentioned as a future leader. His star had waned over the years, however, and many Israelis, especially on the left, increasingly portrayed him as a figure of ridicule. I'd always had a high opinion of him. During the 1982 Lebanon War, with two sons fighting on the ground, he'd been a rare voice of common sense, and caution, in the Begin cabinet. I'd also seen him operate in Shamir's inner security cabinet when, as deputy chief of staff, I would present military operations for approval. I remember one occasion when an air force general laid out the details of a planned heliborne mission into Lebanon. I added a few remarks in summary. Raful Eitan and Arik Sharon, who were both ministers, immediately began peppering the general and me with questions. Why were the attack helicopters taking one route north instead of another? Why not closer to Mount Hermon? Shouldn't they fly lower? Levy interrupted. "Gentlemen," he said, "we are not in a company commanders' course. We're in the inner cabinet of the government of Israel. We have a chief of staff and other generals and military professionals. It's their job to decide the operational details. *Our* job is to balance the reasons for doing an operation against the risks as presented to us."

I met with Levy in the Knesset cafeteria before Bibi went off to the Wye River summit, by which time he headed a small breakaway faction from Likud called Gesher, Hebrew for "bridge." Without explicitly suggesting we join forces, I explained my hope to run my eventual campaign for prime minister in alliance with a few other parties. I told him I wanted to make my candidacy a legitimate choice for voters from the center-right and the Orthodox as well as the Russian communities. I took a napkin and drew a big umbrella to illustrate what I had in mind. He said he understood—though he did tell me to make sure I tore up the napkin. There came a point at the end of November when it looked like my overture had failed. Scampering for a way to shore up his coalition, Bibi tried to lure Levy back into the fold by offering him the Finance Ministry. But with resistance from other ministers, Bibi broke off the talks with Levy, leaving him humiliated and furious. I met with him several more times, and we brought in Gesher as our first "One Israel" partner. The second to join us, early in the new year, was a small, moderate religious party called Meimad, inspired by an openly pro-peace Orthodox rabbi named Yehuda Amital and including a former chief rabbi of Norway, Michael Melchior.

By the end of January 1999, several months before the real campaign, I was feeling better about where we stood, in part because of a series of hits Bibi was taking from former friends and allies. The first salvo was fired by Misha Arens, who had helped engineer his move into national politics. Arens announced that he was going to put himself forward for the Likud leadership before the election, saying that he and others were convinced Bibi couldn't win. A couple of weeks later, Yitzhik Mordechai appeared to be on the verge of resigning, openly flirting with the idea of joining a new centrist party formed by Likud's Dan Meridor. Bibi struck back with a mixture of subtlety and venom. He fired Mordechai, accusing him of being driven by personal ambition. Then he offered the defense minister's job to Misha Arens.

Yitzhik Mordechai did join the Center Party, as did Amnon Lipkin, who had ended his term as chief of staff and, with initial opinion poll numbers suggesting he'd do well, even briefly entered the race for prime minister. Now, he endorsed Mordechai instead: a man with strong military credentials, of Sephardi background and religiously observant, and a proven politician and cabinet minister. It was clear that he and I would be going after many of the same votes.

That situation wasn't ideal, to put it mildly. But all I could do at this stage was ensure that we ran the strongest campaign possible.

+ + +

At the start of April, the final list of candidates was set. There were five. In addition to Bibi, Yitzhik, and me, Benny Begin, the late prime minister's son, had decided to run on the right. Also in the contest was Knesset member Azmi Bishara, the first Israeli Arab citizen to seek national office.

One Israel was not meant just as a catchy name. Though now a half century old, the country had rarely seemed so diverse, and in many ways divided. It was not just the old fault line between Labor and Revisionist Zionism that defined our politics, or even the Ashkenazi-Sephardi gulf that had predominated since the late 1970s. There were new, younger, more assertive, more right-wing, and more pro-settlement voices among the Orthodox. There was the contrast between the overwhelmingly secular, politically and socially liberal, and culturally Western Tel Aviv, with its lively cafés and restaurants, and the constellation of wealthy suburbs to the north; and smaller Israeli towns and cities in the interior, Jerusalem as well, not to mention the settlements in Judaea and Samaria. Since the fall of the Soviet Union, about a million Russians had also flowed into Israel. Most of them identified as Jews more in terms of culture and history than religious observance. But they were instinctively inclined to support candidates—like Rabin in 1992, and Bibi the last time around—who they felt were likely to take a tough line on security issues and in any peace negotiations with the Arabs.

I was never going to get the backing of many West Bank settlers, or of core supporters of the Likud and parties even further to the right. But I would need to make at least some dent in Bibi's hold on the Russian voters who had supported him by a wide margin in 1996. I focused first on Yisrael Ba'Aliyah, the main Russian immigrant political party. It had been set up by the iconic Soviet-era refusenik Natan Sharansky—or, as he was then known, Anatoly Sharansky. He'd been an ally of Andrei Sakharov, an outspoken human rights advocate and, until he was finally released and allowed to leave in 1986, a political prisoner in the gulag. Though Natan's party was not going to offer a formal endorsement for any candidate, I met with him to press the case for "security and peace," the message I'd tried to advance with Shimon three years earlier, and to emphasize the need to bring back unity and shared purpose. Though I think he would have been receptive anyway, it didn't hurt that he, like me, was a mathematics graduate—from Moscow's Physics and Technology Institute. He was also a chess aficionado. When I was rash enough to face him across the board, it took him all of five minutes, and seven moves, to checkmate me.

I also made dozens of visits to Russian community groups and met with individual families whenever I could. I often found myself talking to older men and women among the immigrants about the military details of the Great Patriotic War, as the Russians called World War II. On a number of occasions, I accepted the invitation to sit down and play on a sitting-room piano. I think the first time I got a sense that any of this might be having an impact was in a quote from a Yisrael Ba'Aliyah official in an Israeli newspaper. Though still stopping short of a formal endorsement, the official was quoted as saying: "A month ago, young Russians thought Barak was a boring, left-wing socialist party leader who doesn't look good on TV and mumbles a lot. Today, they see him as a high-ranking Israeli general who knows how to play the piano. The Russian immigrants like strong, cultured people." Except for the bit about mumbling, I couldn't have wished for more.

The next key moment in the campaign involved something I did *not* do. This time, the Israeli television debate came earlier in the campaign, a month before the election. Bibi, Yitzhik, Mordechai, and I were all invited as the three main candidates. But I told the TV people I had a conflicting personal engagement. In reality, I figured I had nothing to gain by going. To join a three-way debate risked creating the impression this was a genuine three-man race, and I still held out hope it would come down to just me and Bibi. Besides, a debate between the other two would help me. Yitzhik knew Bibi well. He had served in Bibi's government. Though not a natural orator, he was always forthright, and often pugnacious, in making his points. And he couldn't stand Bibi.

Unlike the 1996 debate, this time there was a knockout blow, and Bibi was the one left on the canvas. It was a bit like Senator Lloyd Bentsen's killer riposte when Republican vice presidential candidate Dan Quayle compared himself to John F. Kennedy in their debate, a few months earlier: "Jack Kennedy was a friend of mine. Senator, you're no Jack Kennedy." Bibi entered his television showdown with Yitzhik Mordechai with much the same strategy he'd used against Peres. He went on the offensive. He tried to portray himself as an indispensable bulwark against those, like Mordechai or me, who he said would cozy up to Arafat and Assad and endanger Israel's security. But Yitzhik was up for the fight. He also knew that only months earlier, Bibi himself had been exploring the idea of giving up the Golan Heights to the same President Assad. He didn't actually refer to the secret mission by Ronald Lauder, or explicitly accuse Bibi of hypocrisy. But his reply—and Bibi's visible discomfort—were just as effective. Smiling sardonically, he said, "I know your outbursts, and they won't do you any good." He challenged Bibi to just "look me in the eye" and admit what he really thought about the future of the Golan. The media verdict was unanimous. Mordechai had won. Which meant I had won.

Though my American and British brain trusts had little input into our day-to-day campaign, they did play a role in the thrust and strategy. I tried to drive home two things as we entered the two-week homestretch in May. My first, broad message was an echo of James Carville's central theme in the Clinton presidential campaign: "change, versus more of the same." It had resonated with large numbers of American voters, and I sensed from the start of the campaign that this would be true of Israelis as well. Different groups had different gripes, and different ideas of what they hoped I would provide as prime minister. But fewer and fewer Israelis were enthusiastic about four more years of Bibi. I also was keen to convey the *substance* of what my premiership would be about. Domestically, I spoke of the need to narrow gaps in education and opportunity— particularly, though not only, the continuing disadvantage of many in the Sephardi communities who had arrived in the early years of the state. I wanted to try to build bridges between the secular and religious as well.

In terms of policy, I believed my primary job would be to deliver security and peace—in that order. I declared my commitment to continue, and build on, Oslo and to make a new push in negotiations with Syria. Deliberately following the model Philip Gould had used in Tony Blair's election campaign, we also distributed nearly a million copies of a six-point policy "pledge card." It included a promise to hold a referendum on any peace deal we reached with Syria or the Palestinians, as well as several domestic policy pledges, including an end to discrimination against Russian immigrants whose Jewish religious status had been called into question.

Yet the most widely reported promise was that I would pull out all Israeli troops from Lebanon within a year. I realized that even among those who knew that made sense, voices would be raised both in the Knesset and the kirya against withdrawing. As with the Bar-Lev Line before the 1973 war, the longer the "security zone" was in place, the more difficult it was for politicians to say it was a mistake. Yet it had now been there for nearly two decades. The main argument for keeping it—that it protected the security of northern Israel—was undermined by the fact that thousands of Katyusha rockets had been fired over it. And in the low-grade war we were fighting against Hizbollah inside the security zone, around twenty Israeli soldiers died each and every year. When I'd first visited our positions in south Lebanon in the early 1980s, chatted with the troops, and asked them how they were doing, the invariable response was: we're OK, we're just worried about our young kids back home. Now, those *children* were manning the same outposts, facing the same danger, in a sliver of land on which we had no claim, no desire to hold, and was, at best, of questionable security value.

+ + +

I tried not to pay too much attention to newspaper polls during the campaign, perhaps because even the "good" ones, to use Shimon's phrase, gave me only a narrow lead, with Mordechai's 10 or 11 percent still likely to prevent me from getting the required 50 percent needed to avoid a second-round runoff with Bibi. But our internal polling showed things were moving in our direction. In mid-May, they had me above 40 percent. A final batch of internal polls, on the Friday before election day, had me just short of 50 percent. But I made sure our pollsters didn't share the results with anyone on the campaign team. This wasn't just because I wanted to guard against complacency. Deep down, I still didn't trust the numbers.

I retreated to Kochav Yair on Friday evening. On Saturday, two days before the election, I had a surprise visitor, someone I knew from Yitzhik Mordecai's team. He said he had a letter for me, with terms of a proposal under which Yitzhik would announce an eleventh-hour withdrawal from the race. I still could not be absolutely confident I'd win, at least in the first round. Yitzhik's pulling out would help. But if I *did* win, I wanted to start the process of assembling a coalition with a blank slate and an open mind. Doing a deal was not the way to begin. I didn't accept or open the envelope. "Go back to Yitzhik," I said. "Tell him, as he knows, that I have a lot of respect for him. But this is a decision that he has to make on his own."

The next day, less than twenty-four hours before the polls opened, the other three candidates announced they were pulling out. Benny Begin and Azmi Bishara were never going to affect the outcome. But Yitzhik's withdrawal very possibly would. When he spoke to reporters, he said it had been one of the most difficult decisions he'd had to make, but that he'd concluded he wouldn't get enough votes to reach his "primary goal" of defeating Bibi. "The prime minister was given a chance and he failed," he said. "We must give Barak a chance."

I got up early on May 17, confident we'd done everything we could to put ourselves in a position to win, but also aware, from Shimon's defeat, that the smallest of details, and the narrowest of margins, might determine the outcome. After the 1996 election, I'd learned of cases where Peres volunteers outside polling stations in the Negev or the north of the country had left early, in order to make sure they'd be back to Tel Aviv in time for the "moment of victory." Now, I sent out word that all our volunteers should stay in place until the polls had closed. After Nava and I voted, we attended an event for Labor supporters north of Tel Aviv, then flew to Beersheva to spend the final hours in the Negev. I'd arranged for Shlomo Ben-Ami to go to Kiryat Shmona in the north to emphasize, as throughout the campaign, our determination to broaden our support beyond Labor's heartland. The polls closed at ten o'clock. I knew Bibi would be staring at the same Channel 1 newscast as I was, equally prepared to put the best spin on things if there was no clear sign who had won.

The exit poll findings came as a shock: Barak, of One Israel, 58.5 percent; Netanyahu, Likud, 41.5 percent. A landslide.

The full impact hit me only when I got to our election-night headquarters, in a fifth-floor suite at the Dan Hotel in Tel Aviv. My three brothers, and Nava and our daughters, were waiting for me. Leah Rabin, too. Our eyes teared up as we embraced. My parents were by now too frail to come. But I'd promised to phone them. "We did it," I told my father, who said *mazaltov* with a depth of feeling that had become rare as his health began to fail. My mother had always been a bit conflicted about my going into politics, despite her lifelong belief that the *issues* of politics mattered, especially after Yitzhak had been killed for following the path on which I hoped to continue. Still, I could hear the pride, and relief, in her voice when I said, "Remember, *ima*. I did promise you that if I ran, at least I'd make sure to win."

When we'd finished speaking, Bibi called. He had conceded publicly as soon as the exit poll was released. He had also stunned the Likud crowd by immediately resigning as party leader. "Congratulations," he said, sounding tired more than anything. "I accept that the voters have spoken." I thanked him for taking the trouble to call. I said I appreciated the contribution he'd made to the country, and that we'd meet in the next few days to discuss how best to handle the political transition. "Thanks," Bibi said. "And again, mazaltov."

By the time I got off the phone with Bibi, the TV was showing pictures of tens of thousands of people celebrating the results in the central Tel Aviv square, now renamed in Rabin's memory, where he had been murdered nearly four years earlier. Before leaving to join them, I fielded a stream of calls: from friends, other Israeli party leaders, and leaders from abroad, including Tony Blair and Bill Clinton, both of whom not only offered warm congratulations but said they looked forward to working with me as I tried to move Israel forward and to finish the work Yitzhak had begun.

At the start of my brief remarks at the hotel podium before going to Rabin Square, I had to call for quiet when I mentioned the phone call from Bibi. "No," I said, raising my voice to be heard above the boos, "we will not boo an incumbent prime minister of Israel . . . A short time ago, I spoke with Prime Minister Netanyahu and thanked him for his service to the State of Israel." Then—with both Leah and Shimon Peres at my side—I paid tribute to that one special person who had a unique role in our reaching this moment—somebody who was my commander and guide, and the person who led me into politics: Yitzhak Rabin. I pledged to fulfill his legacy and complete the work he'd started. And I extended a hand to "secular and religious, the ultra-Orthodox and the residents of the settlements, to Israelis of Middle Eastern origin and Ashkenazi extraction, to immigrants from Ethiopia and the former Soviet Union, to the Arabs, the Druze, the Circassians, the Bedouin. All, all of them, are part of the Israeli people."

It was almost sunrise when I reached the square. As the crowd shouted and sang, I began with a line borrowed from Bob Shrum. It seemed particularly apt: "It is the breaking of a new dawn," I said.

But was it? As I paid tribute to Rabin—"in this place where our hearts broke"—and dedicated myself to completing the work he'd begun, I could feel the thousands in the square willing me on. But some in the crowd were carrying posters saying "No to the *charedim*"—the strictly Orthodox. Others were chanting, in anticipation of the negotiations needed to put together a coalition: *Rak lo Shas!* Anyone but Shas! It was a reference to the Sephardi Orthodox party, which in addition to being more nuanced and flexible than other religious parties on the issue of peace talks, had been the big winner in the election. It had gained seven additional seats and, with seventeen, now had only two fewer than the Likud.

I did not specifically mention Shas. But I said, "I tell you here that the time has come to end divisions. The time has come to make peace among ourselves, whether we are traditionalists or secularists . . . We must not be enemies of each other." Paying tribute to all those in the square who had worked for our election victory, I added, "I know it would not have been possible without your support. But I also know it would not have been possible without the support of many in the Likud. I appreciate that as well. And I undertake to be *rosh hasmemshalah shel kulam*: prime minister for *all* Israelis."

As fervently as I hoped to be able to deliver on that pledge, I knew even as I spoke the words that fulfilling it was going to be much, much tougher.

# Struggle for Peace

As Israel's prime minister and minister of defense after the election, I was sometimes described as emotionally buttoned-up, even stoic, and there is some truth in that. But while it may not have shown, I felt a churn of emotions when formally presenting my government in July 1999 as Nava, our three daughters, her parents, and mine looked on proudly from the gallery of the Knesset. Even more when I entered the prime minister's office, I was powerfully conscious of both the honor and weighty responsibility of becoming just the tenth person to hold that position. I'd been in the office before: as head of military intelligence, chief of staff, and a cabinet minister. Yet to sit behind the vast wooden desk and to know that the buck now truly stopped with me was very different.

Israel faced two deepening crises. The first was domestic. Though Rabin's assassin was now in jail, the divisiveness and hatred of which he was a product and symbol had not gone away. Nor had other rifts: between the privileged and disadvantaged, Ashkenazim and Sephardim, and, perhaps most of all, secular and religious. The second, more immediate challenge was the stalled peace process. If we were going to revive it, we were running against the clock. President Clinton, key to any hope of our redeeming Yitzhak's legacy and turning the promise of Oslo into real peace, had only eighteen months remaining in office. In terms of Israel's security, the timetable was even less forgiving. From my very first intelligence briefings as prime minister, I saw strong evidence of what I'd been warning Bibi about for months: without a political breakthrough, a new, much more deadly intifada was only a matter of time.

That would have been reason enough to make peace efforts my first priority. But even as I addressed the victory rally in Rabin Square, I sensed that the simple arithmetic of the election results would leave me no other choice. I was entering office with the largest electoral mandate in our history. But that was because of Israel's new voting system, with separate ballots cast for prime minister and party. That system had exerted precisely the opposite effect on party voting. In previous elections, most Israelis had chosen one of the two main parties, knowing that only they had a realistic chance of forming a government. Now they could directly choose the prime minister, giving them the luxury to vote in much greater numbers for an array of smaller, issue-specific parties. The result: though I'd won by a landslide, and One Israel had the largest number of Knesset seats, even with our natural left-of-center ally, Meretz, we would have only thirty-six Knesset seats—well short of the sixty-one needed for a majority. Even if we included a few smaller parties, there was no choice but to bring in one of the two larger ones: the Sephardi Orthodox Shas, with seventeen seats; or Likud, which, after Bibi's sudden resignation, was now led by Arik Sharon, and had nineteen.

It wasn't just a math problem. It had a critical policy implication. If I wanted to tackle the *domestic* challenge—to reassert the values of secular-led democratic government over increasingly assertive religious involvement in our day-to-day politics—that would mean choosing Likud over Shas. But it would also signal the effective end of the peace process. Even though Arik assured me privately that he understood my determination to reopen peace efforts with Arafat and Hafez al-Assad, I *knew* Arik. The path toward peace agreements, assuming they were even possible, would be tough. Sooner or later, I was certain he would begin acting as a kind of opposition from within. That was why, over the angry opposition of Meretz leader Yossi Sarid, I decided to go with the Sephardi Orthodox party. I realized that even Shas might walk out if the scale of any land-for-peace concessions proved too high. But it was the least extreme of the major religious parties on the question of peace with the Palestinians. My conversations with the party's spiritual leader and guide, the seventy-nine-year-old rabbi and Talmudic scholar Ovadia Yosef, revealed a man of intelligence, erudition, and subtlety of thought. He believed in the core Jewish principle of sanctifying human life. When it came to detailed aspects of peace negotiations, like the specifics of any Oslo redeployments, he was inclined to trust the judgment of those in government and the military with the experience to evaluate the security implications and decide the best way forward.

To Meretz's additional consternation, I included two smaller, right-of-center Orthodox parties in the coalition. It was not just to make good on my pledge to be prime minister for *all* Israelis. To put top priority on the peace process, I wanted to avoid an undiluted left-of-center, secular thrust to the government. When I'd stood in front of the tens of thousands of cheering supporters in Rabin Square after the election, I thought to myself: *they think that with Bibi gone, peace is around the corner.* I wanted a coalition broad enough to keep Meretz, and Labor ministers as well, from forgetting a crucial fact: the compromises that we might have to contemplate during peace negotiations were still anathema to many other Israelis.

+ + +

Syria was my first negotiating priority, as it had been for Rabin and, for a brief period, Bibi too. This was not just because the shape of a final agreement with the Syrians was clearer than with the Palestinians. It was also because I was determined to make good on the main specific policy pledge of my campaign: to bring our troops home from Lebanon. No matter what the increasingly emboldened fighters of Hizbollah said publicly, our withdrawal would be bad news for them. It would deprive them of their "anti-occupation" rationale for firing Katyushas into towns and settlements in northern Israel, and free us politically to strike back hard if necessary. It was clear to me that Hizbollah would try to make the withdrawal as difficult as possible. But the real power in Lebanon rested with the Syrians, who, along with Iran, were Hizbollah's main backers. If we could get a peace agreement with Assad, there seemed every reason to hope he would rein in Hizbollah, and perhaps open the way to a peace treaty with Lebanon.

There was an additional reason for trying to get a deal with Syria first: it would increase our negotiating leverage with the Palestinians. That would certainly not be lost on Yasir Arafat, which was one reason it was important to have an early meeting with him: to convey my commitment to keeping the Oslo process alive and achieving, if possible, a full and final Israeli-Palestinian peace.

+ + +

I went to see Arafat a few days after taking office. We met for well over an hour at Erez, the main crossing point into Gaza. It was swelteringly hot inside. At least I was in an ordinary business suit. I couldn't help wondering how Arafat was coping in his trademark military uniform. Still, the political atmosphere going into the meeting was encouraging. After the election, Arafat had tried to use his ties with the ayatollahs in Iran to get them to release thirteen members of the tiny Jewish community in Shiraz who had been jailed on patently absurd accusations of spying for the "Zionist regime." Iran had told him no, hardly a surprise given the Iranian regime's support for Hizbollah and its serial diatribes about destroying the State of Israel. But I appreciated Arafat's gesture nonetheless, and I told him so. I also arrived with a gift: a leather-bound volume with both the Hebrew Bible and Koran. I began our meeting with what I felt I most needed him to hear: that both of us were trying to achieve something hugely important, nothing less than a new relationship between Israelis and Palestinians based on trust. As I would discover in the months ahead—as Yitzhak had found as well—Arafat responded warmly to such general appeals of principle. He replied, as he had often said to Rabin, that he viewed me as a partner, and a friend. But the key issue of substance— the difference between how I envisaged taking Oslo forward and what he wanted—was impossible to avoid.

I emphasized that I was committed to the further Wye River summit redeployments, which Bibi hadn't yet implemented, and to a release of Palestinian prisoners that was also agreed on at Wye. Then came the more difficult part: explaining my view of how we could best move toward a full peace agreement. I said I was convinced the prospects would be much better if we delayed the redeployments and brought forward the start of the real negotiations: on the permanent-status issues, including final borders, settlements, Jerusalem, refugees. In any case, I'd need a few months to reach a settled view with my coalition partners and our negotiating team on how to proceed. Arafat seemed to accept the idea of a pause for reflection and planning. But he held firm in his opposition to any further delay in the Wye redeployments. More worryingly for the longer-term prospects of an agreement, he ignored altogether my suggestion that we move ahead toward the permanent-status talks.

Speaking to reporters, I accentuated the positive. I said I'd come to see Arafat so soon because of the importance I attached to his role in "shaping peace in the Middle East." I said I would not waver in continuing on the path that Rabin and he had begun. And while the security of Israel would be my paramount concern in negotiations, "I also want each Palestinian to feel secure." Both sides, I said, had suffered enough. The open question, however, was whether *I* had done enough to persuade Arafat that his exclusive focus on redeployments—on only the *land* part of a land-for-peace deal—meant we risked ignoring the core issues that would determine whether a full peace agreement was achievable.

More urgently, I knew from our diplomats in the United States that the Americans would not necessarily be receptive to a further delay in moving ahead with Oslo, even if it meant focusing on trying to make peace with Syria. That made my first visit to see President Clinton as prime minister especially important.

+ + +

It was billed as a "working visit," and work we did. After a gala dinner for Nava and me in the White House, we left to spend the weekend at the presidential retreat in Camp David. There, President Clinton and I spent more than ten hours discussing shared security challenges in the Middle East, especially terrorist groups and states like Iran that were backing them, and, of course, how best to move forward our efforts to negotiate peace. These face-to-face meetings set a pattern that would last throughout the time he and I were in office. On almost all key issues, my preference was to deal directly with the president, something I know sometimes frustrated other senior US negotiators like Secretary of State Madeleine Albright and Mideast envoy Dennis Ross. This was not out of any disrespect for them, both of whom I found to be extraordinarily gifted and dedicated diplomats. It was because the decisions on which negotiations would succeed or fail would have to be made at the top, just as President

Clinton and I would ultimately carry the responsibility, or the blame, for errors, missteps, or missed opportunities.

Our first meeting ran until three in the morning. When the president asked me how I saw the peace process going forward, he smiled, in obvious relief, at my answer: I wanted to move quickly. He had only a limited time left in office, and I was determined that we not waste it. Much is often made about the personal "chemistry" in political relationships. Too much, I think, because the core issues and the trade-offs of substance are what truly matter when negotiating matters of the weight, and long-term implications, of Middle East peace. Still, chemistry does help when moments of tension or crisis arise, as they inevitably do. My first few days with President Clinton laid a foundation that allowed us to work together even when things got tough. I benefited, I'm sure, simply by not being Bibi. The president and his negotiating team had spent the previous few, frustrating years trying alternately to urge, nudge, and cajole him—and Arafat—toward implementing Oslo. Clinton did finally succeed in getting the Wye River agreement. But it, too, remained to be implemented.

Nava's presence, and Hillary Clinton's, contributed to an informal, familial atmosphere. Before my first round of talks with the president, we joined Bill and Hillary for dinner. Though I would work more closely with Hillary in later years, when she was secretary of state under President Barack Obama, this was the first time I'd had the opportunity to engage her in anything more than small talk. She was less naturally outgoing than her husband. Yet in addition to being obviously bright and articulate, she was barely less informed on the ins and outs of Middle East peace negotiations than the president. She and Bill spoke with us about things well beyond the diplomacy of the Middle East: science, music, and our shared interest in history. What most struck Nava and me, however, was the way the Clintons interacted with each other. The scandal surrounding Monica Lewinsky was still fresh, with the president having survived an impeachment vote in the Senate only five months earlier. I suppose we expected to see signs of tension between the two of them. Whether the tension was there, we had no way of knowing. But they *did* obviously have a respect for each other's intelligence, insight, and creativity in looking for solutions where so many others saw only problems. It was impressive.

At the outset of my long discussions with the president, I set out to convey in detail what I hoped we could accomplish in the months ahead and how, in my view, we were most likely to get there. I wasn't trying to impose "ground rules" on the president of the United States, something I neither would nor could do. But I was clear with him about how I would approach the negotiations. I would be prepared to be flexible, but I would rely on two critical assumptions. First, when we and the Americans agreed to a position on a specific issue, there would be no unilateral "surprises"—by which I meant, though didn't say, things like the unfortunate American redefinition of Yitzhak's "pocket deposit" assurance regarding the Golan. The second assumption may seem overly legalistic: until and unless we reached a full and final agreement with either Syria or the Palestinians, any Israeli negotiating ideas or proposals would *not* be binding. If no agreement was reached, they would become null and void. I wanted to avoid a situation, as had happened so often in past negotiations, where an Israeli proposal was rejected by the Arab side but then treated as the opening position in the expectation of further concessions in later talks.

I realized that we might discover that Assad, and certainly Arafat, were unwilling, or unready, to make peace. Initially at least, we might have to settle for a more incremental step. "Right here in Camp David, Begin, Sadat, and Carter couldn't complete the process," I pointed out. "They signed a 'framework agreement' and it took months of further diplomacy to reach a peace treaty. Maybe we'll end up doing the same." But I told the president I was convinced that if we didn't *try* to get agreements, we risked heading toward a new period of instability and almost certainly violence. Assad, I suspected, was the more likely to be receptive to a diplomatic initiative. That was a major reason I wanted to start our efforts with him. But so far, his true intentions had never been tested, beyond his obvious determination to get back the whole of the Golan. Nor had Arafat's, beyond his focus on the detail and extent of West Bank redeployments.

President Clinton did not object to an early effort to reopen our efforts with the Syrians. But he was worried about the effects of ignoring the already-creaking prospects of fulfilling the promise of Oslo. If we were going to delay focusing on that, Clinton told me, he needed to be able to assure Arafat the wait would be worth his while. What could we give the PLO leader in return for putting off the Wye redeployments further? And then, the real question on his mind: "Ehud, when we get to the final redeployment and a peace deal, how much of the West Bank are you prepared to hand back?"

I simply didn't know. Much would depend on whether we could be sure Arafat could or would deliver a final peace. But even if I had known, I would have been reluctant to name a precise percentage. Though I had full trust in President Clinton, I knew that everything he and I said would be shared with at least a few of his closest policy aides and negotiators. Sooner or later, word would get to Arafat. When we did begin negotiations, he'd take whatever number I gave as a mere starting point. Still, I knew I had to signal to the president that I was serious about negotiating with Arafat when the time came. I also knew the main source of his concern. In order to get the agreement at Wye, the president had signed on to a provision that the dimension of the third and final redeployment phase would be determined by Israel alone. By that stage, when we got there, Arafat would have control of something like 40 percent of the West Bank. That meant—at least in theory—that Israel could limit phase three to a mere token pullout, leaving the Palestinians with less than half of the territory.

"I don't know what percentage, exactly," I replied. "But one of my cabinet ministers thinks that a formula of 70-10-20 would work, meaning 70 percent for the Palestinians, 10 percent to allow us to retain and secure the largest of the settlement blocs, and the rest to be worked out in further talks." When he nodded, I added: "Peres thinks it could end up at 80-20, and says he thinks Arafat would find it hard to walk away from getting control of four-fifths of the West Bank. But it's not about the number. It's about the area needed for the major settlement blocs, and whatever further area is required to safeguard Israel's security. Beyond that, we don't need a single inch of the West Bank, and we won't ask for a single inch."

I replied in much the same vein when President Clinton urged me to help kick-start new talks with Assad by formally reaffirming Yitzhak's pocket deposit on the Golan Heights. As with the Palestinians, I was not going to cede a major negotiating card—our only real negotiating card—before we had any indication Assad was serious about making peace. But I did feel it was necessary to reassure Clinton that *I* was serious. I told him that if and when the Syrians showed real signs of readiness to address *our* needs in a peace agreement, I would reaffirm the pocket deposit.

I'd come to Washington hoping that President Clinton would be with me on the main issues, and especially my intention to try to engage with Syria first, and shift the emphasis with the Palestinians toward focusing on the critical permanent-status issues. What emerged from our first meetings was essentially a trade-off. He knew that I would be ready to make concessions in pursuit of genuine peace. I was confident that, on the route I was proposing to take in hope of getting there, he would have my back.

But would my own government have my back? On paper, we had a comfortable Knesset majority: 75 out of the 120 seats. But I knew it was inherently vulnerable, due both to friction between the Orthodox parties and assertively secular members of the Knesset (MKs) from Meretz and inside Labor, and to possible defections over the concessions we might have to consider in peace negotiations. The first stirrings of discontent had begun even before I went to see Clinton. On the basis of my commitment merely to *try* for peace, Arik Sharon had presented a no-confidence motion in the Knesset. It was never going to pass. But only days after I'd made him interior minister, Natan Sharansky let it be known he was going to vote against us. He didn't. He stayed away from the chamber, in effect abstaining. But I'd been put on notice.

I lost my first coalition partner in September: the small United Torah Judaism party, with five Knesset seats. It wasn't over land for peace. In an echo of a similar crisis that had brought down the government during Rabin's first spell as prime minister in the 1970s, it was over a violation of the Jewish Sabbath. Israel's state electric company had been transporting a huge steam-condensation machine from the manufacturing site near Haifa to a power plant in Ashdod. The unit was the size of a small apartment and weighed about one hundred tons. It couldn't be driven across the country without bringing weekday traffic to a standstill. The obvious solution was to do it when road use was lightest, on Shabbat. Precisely the same procedure had been followed—*twenty-four times*—under Bibi. But when I asked a United Torah Judaism leader why he'd seemed happy when Likud had waved it through, he replied: "Past sins cannot pardon future ones." Most other ministers agreed with me that we should stand firm. So I did. But UTJ walked out of the government.

In the midst of the Sharanksy rebellion, Haim Ramon, who was the minister in charge of liaising with the Knesset, insisted I "punish" him for his political grandstanding. "You should fire Sharansky. Act like a leader!" I just laughed. "The coalition doesn't need a leader," I replied. "It needs therapy." In truth, I suspected that if we ever got near to a peace agreement with Assad or Arafat, even therapy might not help protect the coalition from splits and resignations. That was a major reason I'd promised a referendum on any final peace deals. I believed that in the balance between the need for concessions, even painful ones, and the achievement of a genuine peace deal with Syria or the Palestinians, most of the Israeli public would choose peace.

I relied on a strong, close team around me, people I knew well and who shared my determination to stay focused on the central goal: to put Israel in a position where its citizens could be given that choice. I made Danny Yatom, my former sayeret deputy, my chief of staff. The negotiating team also included Uri Saguy; Gilead Sher, a gifted lawyer I'd known for a quarter of a century and who had been a company commander in my armored brigade in the 1970s; and Amnon Lipkin. Also, Shlomo Ben-Ami, the Moroccan-born, Oxford-educated historian and diplomat who had run against me for the Labor leadership. Shlomo had a gift for systematic analysis and reasoned judgment, especially on security issues, that I highly valued.

It did not escape the attention of Israeli commentators, or other politicians, that almost all of them were former soldiers whom I'd known from my time in uniform. But that observation missed a more important point: we were all members of the "generation of 1967 and 1973." We had been soldiers during the Six-Day War. In the years immediately after it, like almost all Israelis, we had allowed ourselves to believe that our victory had been so comprehensive, and so quick, that any threat from the defeated Arab states was gone for good. We assumed that inevitably, inexorably, they would realize they needed to sue for peace, and that there was no particular urgency on our part to do anything more than wait.

Then, on Yom Kippur 1973, all of that had been turned on its head. We had not only learned the lessons of 1973, we had internalized them. Even had we not known of the danger of a new Palestinian campaign of terror, the option of simply watching and waiting—and assuming that our military strength, which was now even greater, could make events around us stand still—would not have made sense to us. Besides, as I remarked to Danny and others, to do so would run against the founding purpose of Zionism: to establish a state where Jews would no longer be victims of events, but would take control of their destiny and try to shape them.

+ + +

Yet making peace, like making love, takes two. Much as I'd wanted to begin with Syria, until well into the autumn of 1999 President Assad held firm on his insistence that without our "deposit," without a prior agreement that he'd get back the entire Golan, there could be no substantive progress. This was particularly frustrating because I was getting reports from our intelligence services, and Western envoys who had seen the Syrian president, that Assad's many years of health problems had left him almost skeletally frail, even at times disoriented.

Even my own negotiating team urged me to concentrate on the Palestinians instead. President Clinton kept stressing the importance of showing Arafat at least some movement on the Oslo front. In September 1999, I took a first, significant step in that direction, agreeing to a timetable that would deliver the Wye redeployments by the end of January 2000, while also committing us to negotiating a framework agreement, on the model of the Begin-Sadat Camp David accords, on the permanent-status peace issues. In early November, I joined Clinton and Arafat for talks around an event in Oslo—a deliberate echo of the optimism with which the peace process had begun, held on the fourth anniversary of Rabin's assassination. Both Leah Rabin and Peres came with me. Its centerpiece was a memorial service, at which Leah spoke very movingly of the need for both sides to finish the work Yitzhak had begun, a responsibility I pledged that we would do everything in our power to fulfill. Only Arafat struck a discordant note. He paired a tribute to Rabin with a polemic call for an end to "occupation, exile, and settlements."

After the ceremony, he, President Clinton, and I met at the American ambassador's residence. I was still struck by Arafat's public comments: by his apparent desire, or need, to play to hard-liners back home in what was supposed to be a time to remember and honor Yitzhak. I didn't raise his remarks directly, but I told him that each of us was approaching a moment of truth for the future of our people. The decisions required wouldn't be reached in heaven, but down here on earth, by human beings. By us. "And if we don't have the courage to make them, we'll be burying thousands of our people, probably more Palestinians than Israelis." Worse, I said, those deaths would not advance his people's position or mine by a single inch. When future Palestinian and Israeli leaders did finally prove equal to the challenge of making peace, they'd be looking at the same conflict, requiring the same compromises. "The only difference will be the size of our cemeteries." Arafat nodded occasionally. But he said little, beyond that he considered Rabin to have been a friend, and repeating his now-familiar, nonspecific pledge to "do what is necessary" for peace.

"The hardest part won't be the tough decisions in negotiations," I continued. "It won't be facing each other. It will be facing our *own* people." We would need to make the case openly, honestly, strongly that the peace agreement we might reach was in the interest of both Israelis and Palestinians. And in this, each of us had a responsibility to support the other. With President Clinton looking on, I steered Arafat toward the window of the ambassador's fifth-floor apartment. "Look down," I said. "Imagine that we each have parachutes, and we're going to jump together. But I have my hand on *your* ripcord, and you are holding *mine*. To land safely we have to help each other . . . And if we don't jump, many, many innocent people who are now walking the streets of Gaza and Ramallah and Hebron, Tel Aviv and Jerusalem, will die." Arafat again just nodded, leaving me and the president unsure whether anything I'd said had struck home.

The true test of that would come only when we got to the stage of negotiations when the "difficult decisions" could not be evaded. Yet only weeks after I returned from Oslo, the focus finally shifted to the Syrians. President Assad suddenly signaled his willingness to resume talks without any preconditions—a message he delivered first to my British Labour Party friend Michael Levy, who was visiting Damascus as Tony Blair's roving Mideast envoy, and then to Secretary of State Madeleine Albright.

Assad said he would send Syrian foreign minister Farouk al-Sharaa to meet me for initial talks in Washington in December, ahead of a full-scale, US-mediated attempt to negotiate peace at the start of the new year.

+ + +

The broad terms of a potential deal had long been clear, both to us and the Syrians. The danger was always that the process would get derailed, or never really get started, due to an inability to take key decisions, in part as a result of domestic political considerations on both sides. Syria had a tightly state-controlled media and an intelligence service dedicated mainly to crushing any signs of dissidence. That meant Assad's main concern was to ensure broad support, or at least acquiescence, from top military and party figures. In Israel, however, every sign of a concession risked igniting charges that we were "selling out" to Syria. The Likud and the political right would denounce the idea of giving up the Golan Heights, even though Bibi had been ready to do just that when he was prime minister. But even on the left, there was little enthusiasm for returning the Golan. There were far fewer Israeli settlers there than on the West Bank, not even 20,000. But most of them, far from being religiously motivated ideologues, were Labor supporters. And almost no Israeli, of any political stripe, viewed Hafez al-Assad as a natural partner for peace. For years, he'd been a constant, sneering presence on our northern border, denouncing any Arab leader who'd shown willingness to engage or negotiate with Israel. Amos Oz, one of our finest writers and a cultural icon for Labor Zionists, probably put it best. He said the Syrians seemed to think that "we will give them the Golan, and they'll send us a receipt by fax." The consensus was: forget Assad, keep the Golan. Before I left for the United States, the Knesset voted on whether it supported my attempt to negotiate an agreement with Syria. We could muster only forty-seven votes, fourteen short of a majority. An opinion poll found only 13 percent of Israelis favored a full withdrawal from the Golan.

The message I drew from this was *not* that we should give up on the chances of a peace agreement. After all, before Begin and Sadat went to Camp David in 1978, only a small minority of Israelis had been in favor of withdrawing from the Sinai. Yet once they had seen the other side of the equation—full, formal peace with our most powerful neighbor—the opposition all but evaporated. The problem I saw was that if we and the Syrians couldn't find a way to insulate our negotiations from leaks, speculation, and a swirl of opposition to our efforts at home, we'd never *get* to the key issues of substance.

I'd been making that point to the Americans for weeks. At first, I tried to persuade them to hold the talks at Camp David, ensuring the same media-free isolation that had yielded the historic Israeli-Egypt agreement. But Dennis Ross replied that the very association of Camp David with that breakthrough meant it would be a nonstarter for President Assad. I then suggested we consider sites outside the United States: NATO's Incirlik air base in Turkey, for instance, a British base in Cyprus, an American naval ship in the Mediterranean. Even, half-jokingly, an abandoned missile silo in South Dakota. Yet my point was serious, in fact critical, if the talks were going to have a chance.

In the end, the Americans settled on a beautiful, and undeniably remote, town in West Virginia called Shepherdstown. But from the outset, I was worried it couldn't provide the kind of environment we needed. As our plane was descending toward Andrews Air Force Base outside Washington, I got a call from the head of our advance team. He told me the news media were already there and that reporters—Israeli, Arab, American, and European—could be seen chatting with American, Israeli, and Syrian officials in the town's coffee shops. I knew the press would have to publish *something* about potential concessions as the negotiations proceeded. Whether the stories were true wouldn't matter. They would still make the real bargaining necessary for peace far more difficult, perhaps even impossible, not just for us but for Assad as well.

I also had doubts whether he was ready for real peace: embassies, open borders, personal contact between Syrians and Israelis, and ideally an internationally backed free-trade manufacturing zone on the Golan to give Syria a tangible stake in ensuring the peace lasted. In earlier talks, under Shimon Peres, Syrian negotiators had at one stage brought a message from Assad. What did we *mean*, he wanted to know, with all this emphasis on peace, peace, peace? Syria had peace with *El Salvador*, but without any of the trappings we were insisting on. Peace, in Assad's mind, seemed to mean merely an absence of war.

I did, however, come ready to negotiate. Though I was still not pre-pared to reconfirm Rabin's pocket deposit as a mere ticket of admission, my position remained essentially the one I had worked out with Yitzhak in formulating the deposit: IAMNAM, "if all my needs are met." Mean-ing that if Assad showed a readiness to deal with all of *Israel's* require-ments, I recognized that as part of a formal peace agreement we would have to give up the Golan Heights. In addition to early-warning facilities, we envisaged an open border with a demilitarized area on either side, as well as guarantees that important sources of water for Israel would not be blocked or diverted. As Assad knew, despite his presumably feigned puzzlement about Syria's arrangements with El Salvador, we also needed the agreement to embody a mutual commitment to real peace: through elements like an exchange of ambassadors and the establishment of the free-trade zone. As with the Begin-Sadat peace, we assumed that our Go-lan withdrawal would come in phases, parallel to the implementation of the other provisions of the treaty.

In our initial meetings in Shepherdstown, Foreign Minister Sharaa showed no inclination even to talk about these other issues. So on the second afternoon we were there, I suggested to President Clinton the Americans try to break the logjam by addressing the negotiating issues in a draft paper of their own. It would detail all the issues in an eventual agreement, with parenthetical references to those on which we and the Syrians still differed. Then each side could respond with a view toward narrowing the gaps. The president liked the idea. So did Sharaa. Three days later, the president presented the eight-page American draft. With his customary eloquence, he emphasized the need for us to use it as a springboard for peace, not to score political points, and each side agreed to take a couple of days to look through it. It seemed to me we might fi-nally be on a path to substantive negotiations. There was obviously not going to be a deal at this round of talks, but I agreed with President Clin-ton that if Sharaa engaged seriously with the points in the US paper, after this round ended, he could phone Assad and tell him I had confirmed Rabin's pocket deposit.

Yet by the time we left for home, the prospects suddenly looked much worse—for the reason I'd feared from the moment we arrived. There were two major leaks. The first came in an Arabic-language newspaper in London. Given the thrust of the story, it had presumably come from the Syrians. But it was more annoying than truly damaging. The second leak, however, was in the Israeli newspaper *Haaretz*, which published the entire US negotiating paper. This was unwelcome for us, since it confirmed how far, in the Americans' assessment, we were ready to go in return for peace. But for the Syrians, the fact the final-border section was still a work in progress, with the parentheses to prove it, created the impression that they'd decided to negotiate the details of a full peace without first nailing down the return of the Golan Heights. Assad's image as a strongman, implacably tough on Israel, had been built and burnished over his three decades in power. The embarrassment of being seen as amenable to talking about a Syrian embassy in Israel *without* an agreement on the Golan struck me as a potentially fatal blow to the prospects for a deal, since it dramatically narrowed the scope for the flexibility needed by both sides to negotiate. I wasn't surprised when Clinton phoned me after we got back to Israel to say that Assad had refused to send Sharaa back, as planned, for further talks in ten days' time.

I didn't give up, however, and neither did President Clinton. In February, at the Americans' request, I sat down with Danny Yatom and US ambassador Martin Indyk in Jerusalem to draw up a "bottom line" proposal on a withdrawal from the Golan Heights. If only because of Assad's failing health, I believed it was the only way we could know whether an agreement was possible. We worked on a large satellite map of the Golan and the valley below, and drew our proposed border in red. It made it clear we were prepared to consider pulling out of the entirety of the Heights, reserving only a strip of several hundred meters in the valley below, on the far side of the Sea of Galilee. This area came close to the remains of a handful of Syrian villages that had been there before 1967, but we compensated for this by bending the border slightly westward to give the Syrians part of the slope overlooking the lake, in what was now Israel. We also included the hot springs at al-Hama, which we knew Assad had insisted were part of Syria during talks held under Rabin.

But the details turned out not to matter. President Clinton agreed to present the map to Assad in what we both hoped would be a step to reopening the negotiating path for peace. The two of them met in Geneva in late March. Though the president also came with full details of our positions on the other negotiating issues, he began by telling Assad that I had agreed to the Syrians' long-standing point of principle on our future border: it would be "based on the June 4, 1967 line" before the Six-Day War. Then, the president unfurled the map.

It was shortly after five in the afternoon in Israel when Clinton phoned me. He sounded as if he'd been punched in the stomach. "Ehud, it's not going to work," he said. "The moment I started, he tuned out. He just said, 'Do I get my land?' I tried to get him to listen, but he just kept repeating: 'Do I get all my land?'" According to the president, Assad reiterated his insistence that he would countenance nothing less than being able to sit on the shore of the Sea of Galilee and "dip his feet in the water." Clinton said he'd done his best, and that was true. "I understand the effort is over," I replied. "Probably, he's too frail and ill by now." Assad would die of leukemia barely two months later. His immediate focus was on ensuring an uncontested succession to his son, Bashar.

When Dennis Ross came to see me in Jerusalem, I think he expected to find me distraught. Of course, I was disappointed. But I told him I was grateful that Clinton had stayed with a negotiating effort that had been frustrating for all of us. When I became prime minister, I'd assured the Americans that as long as our vital security interests were protected, I was ready to go further than any previous Israeli leader to get peace with Syria, and with Arafat too. We might fail to get an agreement, but not for lack of trying. I believed even a "failure" would tell us something: whether the other side was truly ready for peace. With Syria, I told Dennis, "It's not what we hoped for. But at least now we know."

+ + +

My own negotiating team, not to mention the Americans, assumed I would now turn my attention to the Palestinians. Arafat was pressing for us to go ahead with phase two of the Wye redeployments. In fact, he now wanted us to add the transfer of three Arab villages on the edge of east Jerusalem: Eizaria, El-Ram, and most importantly Abu Dis, since it was the seat of the Palestinians' parliament and also afforded a view of the golden dome of the mosque above the Western Wall in the Old City. I understood why the villages were politically important for him. But in practical terms, I also knew I'd have to secure the support of the cabinet and the Knesset for what the Likud, and the main religious parties too, would interpret as a first step toward "handing back Jerusalem."

For me, this underscored the problem at the heart of Oslo. We were transferring land to Arafat, yet still without any serious engagement from the Palestinians on the permanent-status questions, like the future of Jerusalem, critical to reaching even a framework agreement, or a declaration of principles, as a basis for a final treaty. I probably should have seen the crisis-ridden spring of 2000 as a harbinger of the difficulties we'd face when we finally got to that stage. I did make a first major effort to find compromise ground on the main issues. I sent Gilead Sher and Shlomo Ben-Ami to begin back-channel talks with a Palestinian team led by Abu Ala'a and Hassan Asfour, the Palestinian negotiators in Oslo. But as I prepared to seek Knesset approval for returning the three additional villages, my main Orthodox coalition partners—Shas and the National Religious Party, as well as Sharansky's Yisrael Ba'Aliyah—all threatened to walk out of the government. I managed to keep them on board, but only by getting the Knesset vote classified as a no-confidence motion. That meant that if we lost, the government would fall and there would be new elections. That was something none of them wanted. They feared that Arik and the Likud would do better this time around and they would end up with fewer seats.

Still, even that didn't avert a different kind of crisis. The vote was on May 15. For the Palestinians, this was also Al-Naqba Day, the annual marking of the 1948 "catastrophe" of the founding of the State of Israel. Danny Yatom told me the night before that there were intelligence reports of large protests planned for the West Bank and in Gaza. President Clinton immediately got the American consul to deliver a message to Arafat, saying that the president expected him to intervene against any sign of violence. But Arafat's reply was that, while he'd do what he could, he couldn't guarantee anything. In the months ahead I would come to understand what that meant, because it would happen again. I don't think Arafat himself orchestrated the violence. Maybe he couldn't have stopped it completely. But I have no doubt—nor did President Clinton—that he stood aside and let it happen.

Even worse—since he *did* have control over them—his security forces, with arms that Israel had agreed to as part of Oslo, fired on our troops as they tried to keep order. All of this, while I stood in the Knesset battling to get approval to give him the villages. As news arrived in the chamber of gunfire just a couple of miles away, it was not just Likud or other right-wing MKs who were furious. I certainly was. Yet I also knew that the price of losing the vote would be the fall of the government. We did win the vote, by a margin of eight, meaning that I now had full authority to return the three villages. Fuming over what had happened, however, I called President Clinton and told him I was going to delay the handover. I was not about to return the villages under gunfire, or reward Arafat for breaking even his existing security commitments.

Prospects for serious negotiations with the Palestinians were again on hold. But another, immutable, priority probably would have delayed any new initiative anyway: my pledge to get our soldiers out of Lebanon within a year of the election. I was determined to go ahead with it because I knew from experience that without setting a deadline and sticking to it, it wouldn't happen. I'd thought it was a mistake to keep the security zone from the start. Over the years, many Israelis, both inside the military and beyond, had come to accept that we would be better off pulling out. It wasn't just the attritional loss of Israeli soldiers' lives, but the fact that there was no obvious point, and no obvious end, to our mission. Especially when major tragedies occurred—like the collision of two Israeli helicopters a couple of years earlier, leaving scores of young soldiers dead—there was *talk* about a withdrawal. Yet there was always a reason to put it off: a Hizbollah attack in the security zone, accusations of weakness from right-wing politicians, or simple caution in the kirya. The only way to get it done was to decide, and to do it.

My self-imposed deadline for the pullout was now eight weeks away. Hizbollah had already begun escalating pressure on our military positions in south Lebanon with the obvious aim of making the withdrawal as difficult as possible. They were also targeting our local surrogates, the Maronite-led South Lebanon Army militia. I'd been meeting regularly with Shaul Mofaz, the former paratroop officer who was now chief of staff, to work out a plan to get our troops out within a single night once the order was given. But complex though the operational issues were, that was not the most difficult part. The withdrawal had a critical political aim as well: to denude Hizbollah, with full international support, of its "occupation" fig leaf for targeting and terrorizing the towns and villages of northern Israel. Mofaz and a number of other generals, including the head of the northern command, were against the pullout. They argued that our withdrawal would give Hizbollah positions a direct line of fire onto Israeli border settlements. Several cabinet ministers, including Meretz leader Yossi Sarid, were also opposed, convinced that Hizbollah fire would continue, or even escalate, after we pulled out. I strongly doubted that, but in any case was convinced that a complete, internationally verified withdrawal of all Israeli forces from Lebanon represented a long-overdue end to a situation that was needlessly costing Israeli lives and hadn't prevented periods of intense rocket attacks either. I insisted that not a single Israeli soldier or emplacement remain on Lebanese soil. Throughout the spring, we had been coordinating the details of our pullout line with UN cartographers on the ground, to ensure that they, too, recognized it would be a *full* withdrawal to the border, fulfilling the terms of the Security Council resolution adopted after the 1982 Lebanon War.

Ideally, we would have taken a further few weeks to gradually remove heavy military and logistics equipment ahead of the final troop withdrawal. But when we handed over a pair of military strongholds to the South Lebanon Army, and Hizbollah promptly moved in to take them over, it was clear we needed to speed things up. With the SLA showing signs of collapsing, the head of the northern command supported an immediate withdrawal, and I agreed. Frustratingly, we did have to hold off a further twenty-four hours, in order to ensure that the United Nations staff on the ground could complete their verification process, and UN headquarters in New York could confirm they were satisfied. But on the afternoon of May 23, alongside Mofaz at a command post on the border, I ordered the pullout of all Israeli troops, as well as all remaining vehicles, and other equipment as quickly as possible. I then flew back to Jerusalem for an urgent meeting to secure formal cabinet approval. The field commanders ended up getting it done in *less* than twenty-four hours, mostly overnight, without a single Israeli casualty.

As I should have anticipated, there were accusations from Hizbollah and its allies that our UN-verified withdrawal was incomplete. At issue was a cluster of villages where Lebanon meets Syria, known as the Sheba'a Farms. But as I knew firsthand, they were not part of Lebanon. I'd met their Syrian inhabitants when I helped us take control of the villages at the end of the 1967 war on the Golan. When Syria now publicly supported Hizbollah's efforts to get the UN to say the area was in fact part of *Lebanon*, I decided to call their bluff. Through the Americans, I suggested that Damascus confirm in writing that this part of the Golan was indeed Lebanese. The Syrians never responded.

Equally predictable were the prophets of doom on the Israeli right, who said the Lebanon withdrawal would bury northern Israel in blood. The reality was that in the half dozen years following the pullout, the Israel-Lebanon border was quieter than at any time since the late 1960s. The main personal impact of the withdrawal, however, was to remind me of why I'd run for prime minister in the first place. Despite the challenges, and inevitable setbacks and frustrations, of my first year in office, I was in a position to take action on issues critical for my country's future. On Lebanon, I'd succeeded, mainly because the withdrawal was something we could do unilaterally. With Syria, I'd tried hard to get an agreement, only to find that Assad was unwilling, unable, or perhaps too ill to join in the search for a deal.

I still recognized, however, that no issue was more important to Israel's future than our conflict with the Palestinians. I knew that resolving it would be even tougher than the talks with the Syrians. But the only way to find out whether peace was possible was to try. So on the final day of May 2000, with the Lebanon pullout complete, I flew to Portugal—the site of a US-European summit—to see President Clinton.

# Beyond Oslo

PRESIDENT CLINTON AND I MET FOR A WALK THE NEXT MORNING. My aim was to persuade him that the time had come for a make-or-break summit with Yasir Arafat. I suspected it would not be easy to convince him, and it wasn't.

By the Oslo timetable, we were three years behind in starting work on a permanent-status agreement with the Palestinians, and just six months away from an American election that would choose President Clinton's successor. We could, of course, pursue the Oslo process along its current, meandering path. But even though Bibi had slowed it down, that would mean Israel handing back yet more West Bank land to Arafat—in return for familiar, but still unfulfilled and untested, verbal assurances that he wanted peace. Each successive Israeli withdrawal reduced his incentive to engage on the difficult issues like final borders, refugees, or Jerusalem. I couldn't justify that, either to myself or my country. The second option was the summit. While there was no guarantee it would succeed, it *would* force Arafat to negotiate on the core issues before the departure of an American president who had a grasp of the issues and characters involved, and a personal commitment to converting the promise of Oslo into a genuine peace.

The obvious risk, for both Clinton and me, was that we'd greatly heighten expectations yet fail to get an agreement. But I argued there were risks in *not* holding a summit, and not just the danger of missing the opportunity to secure a breakthrough toward a final peace. Even if our effort failed, at least we would know that an agreement with Arafat was impossible. In fact, amid the diplomatic drift since Oslo, it was clear there was no other way that we *could* know.

Strolling with the president in Lisbon's spring sunshine, I tried to summon up an image that would bring both of us back to the starkly different reality of our conflict with the Palestinians. Only two weeks earlier, Arafat's own police force, with weapons *we* had agreed to under Oslo, had opened fire on Israeli security forces as I was trying to get Knesset approval for returning three villages that *he* wanted. And that wasn't even the worst of it. After I took office, I'd ordered a full-scale intelligence review of the security situation with the Palestinians. The conclusion had been delivered to me six months earlier: plans were well under way by cells in the West Bank and Gaza for armed attacks against Israeli soldiers and terror strikes inside Israel. "It's like two families living in the same house, and it's on fire," I said. "All of us are rushing to put it out. But there's this fireman, from the other family in the house, who rushes onto the scene—*a firefighter with a Nobel Peace Prize*—and we have no way of knowing whether he's got matches and gasoline in his pocket." We had to find that out, I said. We had to establish whether we were *all* firefighters and could put out the flames.

Clinton and I had gotten to know each other well. In one-on-one conversations like this, we called each other by our first names, though I was careful to address him as "Mr. President" when others were there. I had no doubt that he wanted to put out the fire every bit as much as I did. But I also realized he had emerged frustrated, and bruised, from our last joint effort at peacemaking with Hafez al-Assad. I'd pushed him hard to meet Assad in Geneva, over the objections of some of his closest aides that it was likely to go wrong. The aides were vindicated. Assad ended up delivering an extraordinary personal rebuff to the president. Now, I was again asking him for a summit, and I knew that Madeleine Albright, Dennis Ross, and others would be highly skeptical of risking a repeat of the experience with Syria. "I understand they'll have doubts. I understand their reading of the risks," I told President Clinton. "But I'm convinced crucial issues are at stake, which justify the risks. Let's move forward."

Clinton was also skeptical. With Arafat due to visit him in Washington in a couple of weeks, he said that I first had to give the Palestinian leader *something*: the three villages, a prisoner release, or perhaps unfreeze tax revenues that we'd been holding back as leverage. Otherwise, he was certain Arafat would refuse to attend a summit. Even if Arafat said yes, Clinton felt we would need a draft document with broad areas of agreement before a diplomatic "endgame" could begin. I disagreed on that point. If we tried to produce such a document, there would never be a summit. In fact, we'd never get a draft document worth anything. "Neither side is going to commit itself on issues like borders, refugees, or Jerusalem," I said, pointing out that even in our back-channel talks, the only forum in which there had been a hint of progress, those issues had barely been touched.

He conceded that "pre-negotiation" would never crack the main issues. But he still said that before he could contemplate a summit, he would need Madeleine Albright and Dennis Ross to talk in detail with us and the Palestinians. "There has to be a firm basis to work on," he said. Even then, he was almost certain Arafat would resist the idea of a summit. And on that last point, he proved right. I spoke to the president by phone after Arafat's trip to Washington. "He thinks you're trying to trap him into a summit, and that when it fails, I'll blame *him*," he told me.

The next day, the stakes increased dramatically. For months, military intelligence had been warning of the potential for Palestinian violence. But the report that landed on my desk was more specific. It said Arafat and his security people were preparing for a violent confrontation. A few days later, we got an even more worrying report. It not only contained further details about their preparations, but said Arafat was telling those around him that Israel's prime minister had long opposed Oslo and wasn't interested in peace. I summoned my security team: Mofaz as chief of staff and the heads of military intelligence, Mossad, and the Shin Bet. I began by reiterating the directive I'd given them several months after becoming prime minister: to put in place everything required to ensure we were ready to deal with a major explosion of violence, even a campaign of "full-blown terror," if necessary. But I also told them Arafat was wrong to say I did not want peace—a suggestion that, if he truly believed it, I found particularly frustrating. In almost every one of our face-to-face meetings since I became prime minister, I'd emphasized to him that both of us faced a historic opportunity to bring an end to the conflict, and we needed to be ready to take the difficult decisions to make that happen. I told my security chiefs that my one, inalterable "red line" in negotiations would always be Israel's national and security interests. But as long as those were protected, I wasn't just interested in reaching an agreement. I was determined to do everything possible to try to get one.

+ + +

A few days later, a final round of American diplomacy around the idea of a summit got under way. Not in Washington or Jerusalem or Ramallah or Gaza, but in Kochav Yair. Nava and I still spent almost all our weekends there. We valued the quiet, or at least the slightly quieter, time away from Jerusalem or Tel Aviv. Some of my oldest army friends lived there as well: Danny Yatom, as well as Shaul Mofaz and Uzi Dayan, who was now deputy chief of staff. Newer colleagues, too, like Yossi Ginossar, a Shin Bet veteran who spoke fluent Arabic and, after working in the West Bank and Gaza in the late 1960s, became one of the first Israelis to hold secret talks with Arafat, building up a personal relationship with him. Under both Rabin and Peres, Yossi had been a valuable liaison with the Palestinian leader—and now, under my premiership as well.

The summit seemed to me more important than ever. I knew Arafat was never going to be enthusiastic. But if President Clinton was persuaded that at least a framework agreement for peace was within reach, I had confidence he would make the effort. I had allowed Gili Sher and Shlomo Ben-Ami to go to Washington the week before for exploratory talks with Dennis Ross. Now Clinton had sent Dennis to Israel, with Madeleine Albright to follow at the end of the month, and their impressions would be critical to his decision on whether to bring me and Arafat to Camp David.

We agreed to meet Dennis and his team at Danny's house in Kochav Yair. By the time I'd made the pleasant Shabbat-afternoon stroll from our house, a few streets away, they were in the back garden sipping lemonade and munching on popcorn. I'd met often with Dennis. He'd worked under three US presidents: Carter, Bush Senior, and now Clinton. No American diplomat had been more indefatigably involved in the search for Middle East peace. Whatever his occasional frustrations, I believed that he recognized I was ready to go further than any previous Israeli leader in trying to get that peace, yet knew that he would press me to tell him how far that actually was. Ever the good diplomat, he didn't ask directly. But each ostensibly theoretical question was aimed at establishing whether I could give him enough for a summit to bridge the gaps on key issues. Could I accept a "trade-off between sovereignty and time"? Translation: Could I give the Palestinians sovereignty over a larger part of the West Bank if we signed an agreement that would phase in their control? Could I accept the principle of land swaps? This meant giving Arafat land in areas bordering the West Bank, or in the Negev near Gaza, to compensate, at least partially, for the area we would keep for the major settlement blocs. What about applying my principle of "disengagement" between Israel and the Palestinians to Jerusalem? Meaning Arafat getting control of the predominantly Arab neighborhoods in the east of the city.

Dennis knew my long-standing reluctance to commit to concessions until we got to real, final negotiations with Arafat. "We'll not reveal anything you tell us," he assured me. "We won't turn what you say into opening negotiating positions for Arafat. But if there is going to be a summit, the president wants some answers." To Dennis's frustration, I could give him no specifics, beyond telling him: "You know me. You know I'm serious about this. Of course, we will protect our vital security and national interests. But the problem in making peace won't be us, on the Israeli side, as long as Arafat shows a capacity and a will for decision."

Madeleine Albright visited at the end of June. When she came to see me a day after meeting Arafat, she carried a request from the Palestinian leader: two weeks of "preparatory" talks before a summit. Again, I knew her mission was to bring back enough progress for the president to feel a summit was worth it. But again, I couldn't give her what she wanted. "I know what will happen in preparatory talks," I said. "We'll raise new ideas, which the Palestinians will reject, and ask for more." I don't know what she told Clinton, or Arafat. But Dennis called me the following day. He said that Arafat had agreed to attend a summit, and would leave the date up to the president.

When Clinton phoned me at the beginning of July, however, he still hadn't finally decided to hold the summit. Like Dennis, he probed my position on land swaps and Palestinian sovereignty for at least some Arab neighborhoods in Jerusalem. He asked whether I was ruling out those possibilities if they represented the difference between success or failure. I did not give him a definitive answer. I said we could think through those issues together. But when he phoned again, on July 4 from Camp David, I felt I had to go further. I said that, for his ears only, I was ready to commit to considering limited, symbolic moves on both land swaps and Palestinian sovereignty in part of East Jerusalem, as long as Arafat also proved willing to move forward on addressing the core issues required for a peace agreement.

Clinton's answer was that the summit was on. It would begin at Camp David in one week's time, on July 11.

+ + +

Two days before leaving for the United States, I brought my ministers together. "We can't know what will happen at a summit," I said. "But we have a responsibility to give it a chance, and recognize the situation in which we find ourselves. If we sit idle and don't even try, we'll face an eruption of violence, and never know whether we could have avoided it. If, God forbid, we fail to reach an agreement, there will also be violence. We will face a new reality more difficult than you can imagine. But if we do manage to strike a deal, we are going to change the map and history of the Middle East." I reminded them it would ultimately be up to Israelis, in a referendum, to say yes or no to the terms of any agreement. "If we achieve a breakthrough, I'm confident they will do so, by a landslide."

I said I would hold fast to a number of principles. There would be "no return to the 1967 lines," meaning that we would draw a new border with the West Bank to accommodate the largest settlement blocs. They were mostly around Jerusalem, or just beyond the 1967 border, and over the years had in practical terms become part of Israel. Tens of thousands of people lived there. As the Americans and even the Palestinian negotiators recognized, no Israeli government, Labor or Likud, could or would agree to make them part of a Palestinian state. The second principle was that "Jerusalem will remain united." It would not be cut into Jewish and Arab halves as had happened between 1948 and 1967. That, I knew, might prove tougher to carry through. But even if I had to concede a degree of

Palestinian control in parts of east Jerusalem, I expected to be able to retain Israeli sovereignty over the city. The third principle was that there would be "no foreign army west of the Jordan River." In other words, if we did hand back at least the major part of the West Bank, it would be demilitarized, and we would retain security control over the Jordan Valley. Finally, we would not "accept responsibility for the birth of the refugee problem and its solution." Though there could be a "right of return" into a new Palestinian state, we would not agree to rewrite the history of the 1948 war by sanctioning the resettlement of hundreds of thousands of Palestinians inside the State of Israel.

I think it was the very fact we were talking about a comprehensive peace agreement that made it so hard for my Orthodox and right-of-center coalition partners. They didn't see the attraction of coming to final terms of peace. They knew that under any final deal, there *would* be a Palestinian state. We *would* give up the great majority of biblical Judaea and Samaria. While most of the settlers would remain, since they lived in the major blocs, those in more isolated settlements around the West Bank would have to be moved. They saw the prospect of a final peace only in terms of what we were giving up. They didn't see what we would *gain*: peace, and international recognition and endorsement for it; and normalcy, the central aim of Zionism. Jews living in a state like any other. Ever since 1967, we had been in control of the daily lives of the Palestinians on the West Bank and in Gaza. That was bad for them. But it had been bad for us too. *Fifty-two years* after the birth of our state, we still didn't have a permanent, internationally recognized border. Rather than dealing with our economic and social issues like other states, we were beset by internal divisions that were in no small part a result of our unresolved conflict with the Palestinians.

Shas, the National Religious Party, and Sharansky's Yisrael Ba'Aliyah were all threatening to pull out of the government because of the summit. Nothing I said could change their minds. Sharansky was the first to declare he was leaving. A few hours later, Shas and the NRP followed suit. If the Likud mustered the required sixty-one votes for the no-confidence motion it was introducing before I got on the plane to the United States, the government would fall. If the parties that had left the coalition, with a total of twenty-eight seats, went along with Arik Sharon, it wouldn't be close. As if that wasn't enough, David Levy, my foreign minister, told me he would not be joining me at Camp David. He wasn't resigning, at least not yet. But he knew that the final decisions at the summit would be mine; he feared it would fail and didn't want to share in the consequences.

None of this meant I wasn't going. Even if the no-confidence vote succeeded, the new Israeli electoral system, with its separate vote for prime minister, meant I would remain in office, at least until the summit was over. But it was important for me to make the case directly to the public. In a nationally televised message, I reminded the country that I'd been elected with nearly 2 million votes. I felt I had a responsibility, and a mandate, that went beyond party politics. "I must rise above the political arguments, and seek out all possibilities on the way to a peace agreement that will end the conflict, and the blood, between us and our neighbors." I made the same points before the Knesset. Of course I wanted parliamentary support, but I was acting on a mandate from the *people* of Israel. When the Knesset votes were counted, thanks to the fact two-dozen MKs abstained, both sides lost. Arik fell seven votes short of a majority. So the government survived. But those opposed to the summit got more votes than we did: 54–52.

There were several consolations as I prepared to fly out from Ben-Gurion Airport. Shas leader Eli Yishai passed me an envelope on the tarmac. Inside was a note from Rabbi Ovadia Yossef, the Shas spiritual leader whom I'd met with privately after the election and a number of times since. He wanted to wish me good luck. Nearly thirty reserve generals also issued a public message of support. And though I made a rule of not paying too much attention to opinion polls, it was undeniably encouraging to see a newspaper survey find that a majority of Israelis—55 percent to 45—believed I was right to go to Camp David and that I had a mandate to make concessions in return for peace.

David Levy came over to talk before I boarded. "I doubt we'll get an agreement," he said. I told him what I was telling other ministers, what I'd told reporters, and in fact what I had told Nava: "The odds are fifty-fifty." The reporters took this as coy, or deliberately deceptive. So I added that it was not because I knew something they didn't. "It's because there are two possible outcomes, and I don't know which one will happen." The gaps of substance were bridgeable. The question was whether both sides were ready for peace, and whether each possessed the political will to make the difficult decisions required to make it possible. I was ready to do so. But I had no way of knowing whether that was true of Yasir Arafat.

But we'd find out at the summit. Camp David was different from Shepherdstown. No reporters would be there. Mobile phones were banned. Each delegation had one landline. We'd also be operating under a time constraint. President Clinton was due to leave for a G8 summit in Japan on July 19. That gave us barely a week. I wondered whether that would be enough, even if both sides were committed to reaching a peace agreement. Yet I hoped it would at least provide the possibility, as it had for Begin and Sadat twenty-two years earlier, to reach a framework agreement.

Numbers were also limited. We and the Palestinians could have only a dozen members in our negotiating teams. Some of my choices were automatic: Danny Yatom; Shlomo Ben-Ami, whom I'd made acting foreign minister in Levy's absence; Amnon Lipkin and Attorney General Elyakim Rubinstein; Gili Sher and his chief negotiating aide, Gidi Grinstein. I also took along a strong security team, including Shlomo Yanai, head of strategic planning at the kirya, and Israel Hason, a former deputy head of Shin Bet. There was another important, if less obvious, inclusion: Dan Meridor. A leading member of the Likud before he'd formed the Center Party at the last election, Dan was more than a friend: he was a man of rock-solid integrity with a strong moral and ethical compass, who put principle over party. He was also a lawyer. Along with Attorney General Rubinstein, I knew I'd have a gifted legal team if we got to the point of considering the specifics of a peace agreement. There was another consideration as well. Both Dan and Elyakim were right-of-center politically. I needed their voices as a kind of litmus for the tough decisions and concessions I might have to consider if an agreement did prove possible.

I was not nervous as we crossed the Atlantic, though even those who knew me best assumed I would be. Nava had sent me off with a list of dietary instructions, almost like a surgeon-general's warning that Camp David might prove hazardous to my health. But I felt ready. I'd gone to every source I could find about the Begin-Sadat summit. I knew there would be periods of crisis and that at certain points I'd have to allow

leeway for my team to explore possible compromises beyond our set negotiating limits. Yet none of this altered my belief that holding the summit was the right thing to do, nor my confidence in being able to play
my part. I did feel a huge responsibility. Decades after our conflict with
the Palestinians had begun, seven years after Oslo, I was attempting, with
the president of the United States, to shape the final terms of peace. I carried the conflicting hopes and fears of Israelis with me.

# Camp David

IF I BELIEVED IN OMENS, I MIGHT HAVE TURNED BACK AS SOON AS WE got to the summit. It was pouring down rain when we reached Camp David a little before ten at night on July 10, after helicoptering from Andrews Air Force Base near Washington. The cabin assignments also came as a surprise. I was given the one that Anwar Sadat had at the first Camp David summit in 1978. Arafat got Menachem Begin's. Still, the cabins themselves, each named for a tree, were large and pleasant. Mine, Dogwood, had a bedroom, two large sitting rooms, and a terrace. I took it as a good sign that it was the same one where Nava and I had stayed during our visit with President Clinton and Hillary right after I'd become prime minister.

With just eight days to address the core issues of decades of conflict, we got down to work the next morning. Clinton began by meeting Arafat, as I went through the Americans' overall strategy for the negotiations with Madeleine Albright, Dennis Ross, and Martin Indyk. I then met the president in his cabin, which was called Aspen. He told me that while Arafat still thought I was trying to "trick him" into an agreement, and didn't think we'd necessarily get a deal, the Palestinian leader did now accept that I was serious about trying. My fear remained that Arafat was not serious. Yet my hope was that the isolated environment of Camp David, and the wide public expectation that we would accomplish what Sadat and Begin had done there before, would help us deliver the breakthrough that I believed ought to be possible. For that to happen, I told the president it was essential that Arafat truly understood the importance of what was at stake. Not just the cost of failure, but what was potentially on offer: the creation of the Palestinian state he sought, with the full acceptance of Israel and the support of the world.

I wish I could say I was optimistic when Clinton led the two of us into Laurel Lodge, the larger cabin a few hundred yards downhill from Aspen, for the summit's opening session. The scene at the front door—with me bustling Arafat ahead, with the intention of allowing him to enter before me—yielded the best-known image from the summit. Captured by the television crews allowed into the compound for the ceremonial opening, it spawned a cottage industry of political speculation and armchair psychoanalysis purporting to decipher what it meant. Some said it was an encouraging sign of "chemistry" between me and Arafat, a not unreasonable guess, since both of us were grinning. Others concluded that because each of us was trying to nudge the other to go in first, it was a sign of underlying conflict: neither of us wanted to allow the other the privilege of appearing to be polite. Still others saw it as an ornate Middle Eastern power play, intended to demonstrate that *I* was ultimately in control of proceedings. In fact, it would turn out to be a singularly apt image of what happened in the days that followed: a reluctant Arafat, an engaged and expectant prime minister of Israel, a smiling and hopeful Clinton.

We actually began on a note of optimism. In my opening statement, I said, "Now is the time for us to make a peace of the brave, to find a way to live together side by side with mutual respect, and to create a better future for our children." Arafat said he hoped that the peace Begin and Sadat had made at Camp David would prove an auspicious example. "With the help of President Clinton, we could reach a deal that is good for both sides."

But it was going to take more than noble words. The details of a peace treaty, or even a framework agreement, would require negotiation. Both Arafat and I arrived fully aware of the shape of the "hard decisions" I'd referred to months earlier when we met in Oslo. On his side, it would come down to whether he was prepared for a comprehensive, final peace. A true "end of conflict," with no get-out clauses, no strings left untied, no further claims on either side. In concrete terms, this would mean abandoning his claim for potentially hundreds of thousands of Palestinian refugees to resettle inside the pre-1967 borders of the State of Israel. And what were Israel's difficult decisions? In return for the end of conflict, I would have to deal away the maximum possible part of the West Bank, certainly well above the 80 percent I'd intimated in my first meeting with President Clinton as prime minister. I would have to accept the idea of land swaps, if necessary, in order to bring the overall percentage as near as possible to the equivalent of the whole of the West Bank. I would have to be flexible on the arrangements to ensure Israeli security oversight over the Jordan Valley. And if a true peace was really on the table, both Arafat and I would have to consider some form of compromise on the most emotionally and symbolically difficult issue of all: the future governance of Jerusalem.

On the first evening, we met as an Israeli delegation to discuss our position for the days ahead. Gili Sher and Danny Yatom helped me keep a clear overall picture of proceedings throughout the summit. Our secure landline was operated by a Shin Bet technician. I assumed the Americans could still listen in, but was fairly confident we were at least beyond the electronic earshot of the Palestinians. I kept myself fully informed of, but at a distance from, the specific work of the five negotiating teams we'd set up to deal with each of the major issues we'd have to resolve if we were going to get an agreement. It would have been impractical for me to have remained fully involved with all of them. Yet I also believed the looser arrangement would allow our negotiators to explore any realistic opportunity for a breakthrough and any sign of flexibility on Arafat's side—without committing me to a formal position until there *was* such flexibility.

For the first couple of days of the summit, there was not only no sign of flexibility, there was little meaningful engagement. Dennis Ross and his team drew up a paper setting out the main issues. For those on which we differed, the Israeli and Palestinian positions were marked with "I" and "P." It wasn't until around midnight on day two that we got a first look at the American draft. The main, unhappy, surprise was Jerusalem. This crucial issue was not marked with "I" or "P." It said outright that there could be two capitals, one Israeli and one Palestinian, within the city of Jerusalem. I was not opposed to the Palestinians calling Jerusalem the capital of their state. But even in follow-up talks after Oslo, when Yossi Beilin and Abu Mazen had explored avenues toward a possible resolution of the Jerusalem question, the maximum understanding was that Israel might expand the existing city limits to accommodate the "two capital" solution. The Palestinian capital would be in Abu Dis, one of the villages Arafat had asked me to hand back in May. The way the American document was worded suggested dividing Jerusalem as it now was: something ruled out repeatedly by all Israeli politicians, of all parties, ever since 1967.

When I phoned President Clinton, he asked me to come talk. We sat on the back terrace of his cabin, looking out incongruously on a beautifully tended golf hole installed by Dwight Eisenhower. I told the president that after all the hours we had spent together, I'd felt blindsided by the inclusion of a proposal on Jerusalem that went beyond anything we'd talked about. "It was my mistake," he replied, obviously already aware through his negotiators of the error. He said that he'd put pressure on them to get the draft finished, and that Dennis hadn't had time to read it through. But it was already being fixed: the word "expanded" would be added to the Jerusalem section. I was grateful for that, but I told Clinton I was concerned that even this "I and P" paper might have the unintended effect of delaying any real progress. Since it was an American document, with the implication that it would be the president's responsibility to frame and forge an eventual agreement, it gave the Palestinians no incentive to engage directly in looking for common ground. I suggested it might be best simply to withdraw the paper. Clinton's answer surprised and encouraged me. "We agree," he said. "The paper no longer exists." It soon turned out the Palestinians were unhappy with it too, but for another reason. On the lookout for validation of Arafat's insistence that Camp David was an Israeli "trap," they were convinced that the paper had Israel's fingerprints all over it. That wasn't true. The one change we'd insisted on was because it misrepresented our position on Jerusalem. Still, since Dennis had added the word "expanded" to the Jerusalem section in longhand, the Palestinians were convinced of Israel's coauthorship.

In fact, three days into the summit, the mood among the Palestinians seemed increasingly aggrieved. As a result, the Americans and even some members of my own team were urging me to show more "personal warmth" toward Arafat. I always exchanged greetings and pleasantries with him at mealtimes in Laurel Lodge, but even there, I admit that I didn't exactly show enthusiasm, much less ebullience. After one dinner, when I'd been placed next to the Palestinian leader, the president's national security adviser, Sandy Berger, asked me why, rather than talking to Arafat, I'd spent almost the entire time chatting with Chelsea Clinton. My response was only half-joking: "Given the choice, who wouldn't?"

It wasn't only that I believed a charm initiative would come over as contrived. I didn't want to risk misleading Arafat, the other Palestinians, and possibly the Americans as well by giving them the impression I was satisfied with the progress of the summit, or felt that we were heading toward any serious engagement and compromise on the core issues. I had met Arafat many times before Camp David. I had made it clear in all of those meetings that I was ready to consider the tough decisions necessary to make peace possible. At Camp David, I was not against meeting Arafat as a matter of principle. I simply felt the time for such a meeting, if it came, would be at the moment that we saw at least *some* signal of a readiness on his part to negotiate seriously.

Still, given the strength of feeling among some of my own negotiators, I felt a responsibility to give it a try. I told Yossi Ginossar, the former Shin Bet officer who was closest to the Palestinian leader among the Israelis, to set up an informal meeting. To Yossi's obvious satisfaction and surprise, I added that I'd be willing to have the meeting in Arafat's cabin if that's what he preferred. The next afternoon, I went there for tea and baklava. Abu Mazen, his top political adviser and the main Palestinian architect of Oslo, was with him, along with a more junior aide who served the tea and sweets. At least this time, Arafat didn't take notes as we spoke. The mood was friendly. We talked in general terms about the importance of peace. But he showed no sign of willingness to engage on the specific question of what was happening, or should happen, in the summit talks. I found the exercise disappointing as a result. But Yossi assured me it would help the atmosphere and would eventually translate into negotiating progress. "I hope so," I said.

It wasn't until day four that real talks began, but still without any indication Yossi's optimism would be borne out. The Americans arranged for negotiating teams from both sides on borders, the refugee issue, and Jerusalem to meet with President Clinton. The Palestinians participated but showed no sign at all of a readiness to compromise. Borders should have been the most straightforward. Assuming we wanted a deal, it was about sitting down with a map and working out how to address both sides' arguments. But Arafat's representative in the meeting—the original Oslo negotiator, Abu Ala'a—said he wouldn't even discuss borders without a prior agreement to land swaps ensuring Palestinian control over an area equivalent to 100 percent of the West Bank. Shlomo Ben-Ami tried to find a way around this. He suggested the Palestinians *assume* that to be the case for the purposes of the meeting, so that at least there could be meaningful discussion of the border, including the provisions Israel wanted in order to retain the major settlement blocs. President Clinton agreed that made sense. He said that without talking about the *substance* of such issues, there wasn't going to *be* a deal. Even Abu Ala'a seemed receptive, according to Shlomo. But he insisted that he would have to ask Arafat first whether it was OK.

On refugees, pretty much the same thing happened. The Americans— and, we assumed at that point, even the Palestinians—knew that a peace deal would be impossible if we agreed to hundreds of thousands of refugees entering Israel, threatening to leave the state we'd created in 1948 with a Jewish minority. But when President Clinton began trying to narrow down details of a compromise resettlement package—how *many* refugees would return, where they would go, and how to arrange international financial support for them—Abu Mazen insisted that nothing could be discussed without a prior Israeli acceptance of the "principle of the right of return." On Jerusalem, according to Gili Sher, the president didn't even try to find common ground on the core issue of sovereignty. Instead he used the formula Shlomo Ben-Ami had suggested for borders, telling each side to proceed on the assumption sovereignty was decided in its favor, and to concentrate instead on how everyday municipal functions and daily life would be divided between Israel and the Palestinians under a peace agreement.

When I convened our negotiators in my cabin to take stock of the logjam, I was getting more and more skeptical. I told our team that until there was at least *some* movement from Arafat, I didn't want them suggesting any Israeli concessions. We'd obviously get nothing in return. The summit would fail. And despite my repeated insistence both to the Amer-

**Down to work:** REVIEWING PAPERS during my first day in office. WITH HENRY KISSINGER, one of our many meetings both before and since my time as prime minister—a relationship made stronger by a shared understanding that Israel lives in a tough neighborhood, along with a belief in the need to be clear-eyed about one's enemies and unflinching on issues of national security while also ready to explore all realistic opportunities for peace. WITH RABBI OVADIA YOSSEF, the spiritual leader of the Sephardi Orthodox political party Shas, and Eli Yishai, the leading Shas member of the Knesset. Though I was always aware of the limits to Shas support for the difficult decisions we might have to take in order to seek a final peace agreement with the Palestinians, I respected Rabbi Ovadia's immense erudition, his readiness and capacity for open discussion, and the personal support he gave me in my efforts to at least look for the possibility for a peace deal.

**American connections**: REUNITED, during my first visit to see President Clinton as prime minister, with members of my election campaign brain trust, (l-to-r) pollster Stanley Greenberg, James Carville and his wife, Mary Matalin, and Jim Gerstein. WITH PRESIDENT CLINTON and Syrian foreign minister Farouk al-Sharaa for our peace negotiations in Shepherdstown, West Virginia, in January 2000. WITH CLINTON, National Security Adviser Sandy Berger, and Secretary of State Madeleine Albright at the White House.

**Push for peace:** WITH PRESIDENT CLINTON during a key juncture of the Shepherdstown talks, soon overshadowed by media leaks that forced the hiatus in the drive for a breakthrough, which finally ended, a few months later, when a seriously ill Syrian president Hafez al-Assad proved unwilling or unable to contemplate the difficult decisions needed for a peace agreement. THE ICONIC, and serially misrepresented or misunderstood, "shoving match" between me and Palestinian leader Yasir Arafat at the inaugural session of our Camp David summit with President Clinton in July 2000. **Dinnertime diplomacy:** SPEAKING WITH MOHAMMED DAHLAN, Arafat's security chief in Gaza, as President Clinton confers with Arafat, aided by the American delegation's translator, Gamal Hillal. WITH PRESIDENT CLINTON in the early stages of the summit.

Rescue mission: WITH ARAFAT and Palestinian negotiator Saeb Erekat, our acting foreign minister Shlomo Ben-Ami, and Danny Yatom before a dinner at our home in Kochav Yair a few weeks after the collapse of our efforts at Camp David. BEING VISITED by Jordan's King Abdullah, and briefing him on Arafat's unreadiness to engage meaningfully at the summit and my concerns that he was about to turn back to violence. WITH POPE JOHN PAUL II as he kindles a torch of remembrance at the Yad Vashem Holocaust memorial in Jerusalem.

**Diplomatic bonds**: (from top left) Nelson Mandela on a visit to Jerusalem a few months after I became prime minister, during which he stressed the need, in the Middle East just as in South Africa, to ensure that the *hope* for a political resolution and for peace was not snuffed out—a view I said I shared but also emphasized would depend not just on what I, or Israel, did, but on Arafat and the Palestinians. Toasting Hillary Clinton in the prime minister's residence in Jerusalem during a visit in late 1999, a relationship that would deepen in later years when I was Israel's defense minister and Hillary was Secretary of State. With Vladimir Putin, shortly before I became prime minister—a leader I found then and in a number of meetings since to be a strong, laser-focused defender of what he sees as Russia's strategic interests, though not, as I've sometimes told American friends, one I'd like to run my country or that they should want to run theirs. With Britain's prime minister Tony Blair in the first months of my premiership, renewing a relationship that began a few years before as I tried to make our Labor Party, like his, more electable. With George W. Bush's Secretary of State, Condoleezza Rice, during a visit to Jerusalem when I was defense minister. With my longtime friend Secretary of State Leon Panetta during a joint visit in 2012 to one of the launch sites of our Iron Dome anti-missile defense system.

**Personal time:** JOINED BY MY FATHER at a celebration in Jerusalem honoring outstanding soldiers on the fifty-third anniversary of Israeli independence in 2001. PLAYING ONE of my favorite Beethoven pieces in the prime minister's residence. WITH NAVA on our way to our first visit to the Clinton White House shortly after I took office.

**Duty of defense**: WITH (L-TO-R) GABY ASHKENAZI, head of the northern command; chief of staff Shaul Mofaz; and field officers and troops ahead of our withdrawal of all Israeli forces from Lebanon in May 2000. VISITING YOSSI AVSHALOM, a man wounded in a terrorist attack near Nablus on the West Bank in October 2000 in the explosion of violence that became known as the second intifada. **At the door**: USHERING IN ARIK SHARON to the prime minister's office after he won the election in February 2001 and succeeded me as head of Israel's government.

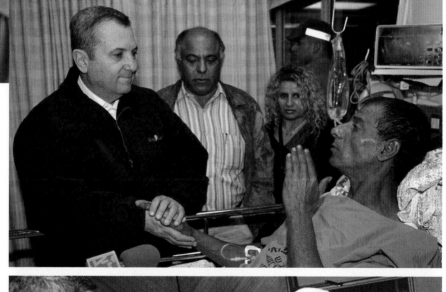

**Allies and Iran**: As DEFENSE MINISTER with then-Senator Barack Obama on a visit to Israel during the 2008 US presidential campaign, during which we spoke at length about the challenge posed by Iran's efforts to develop a nuclear weapon. WITH PRESIDENT GEORGE W. BUSH and Laura Bush and my wife, Nili, during their May 2008 visit to mark Israel's sixtieth anniversary—during which Iran also came up, and President Bush, with customary directness and colorful language, let Prime Minister Ehud Olmert and me know of his unequivocal opposition to any Israeli military action against the Iranian nuclear facilities. WITH MY ULTIMATE ALLY—Nili—in Tel Aviv during the final stages of writing this book.

icans and Palestinians that without an agreement any Israeli suggestions would be null and void, that didn't mean they would simply be forgotten. The result is we'd actually be in a worse situation than before Camp David. Politically, I'd find myself in much the same position as President Assad after the leak of the American draft from Shepherdstown: apparently ready to consider giving Arafat the great majority of the West Bank, without the slightest sign he was ready for a full and final peace. In addition, anything that we put on the table here would handcuff future Israeli governments if and when an "end of conflict" agreement became possible.

Still, when Dennis Ross learned from my negotiators what I'd decided, he was frustrated and upset. He came to see me on Saturday morning—day five of what was looking increasingly like a stillborn summit. "This summit was *your* idea," he said, reminding me that the president had agreed to it over the reservations of many of his own aides. He told me that at a minimum, I had to give it a chance by giving *him* my true negotiating "red lines." Either that, or give my negotiators more leeway to explore compromises. I did not want to make Dennis's job any more difficult than it already was. I assured him I remained ready to engage fully if we ever got to the real substance of a possible deal. "But I can't do what you've asked me," I said. "Not when Arafat is simply holding firm and not showing a willingness even to *look* for compromises."

Fortunately for my relationship with the president—though not for the prospects of an agreement—Clinton had considerably more sympathy with my position after his next meeting with both sets of negotiators that afternoon. It was a return encounter with Abu Ala'a on territory and borders. Shlomo Ben-Ami now produced a map of the West Bank with our proposed breakdown into the areas that would be controlled by a Palestinian state, the part Israel would retain to accommodate the major settlements, and territory that we suggested would go to the Palestinians after a transitional period. The part we had earmarked for Palestinian control was now a bit over 85 percent of the West Bank. But while Abu Ala'a had told Clinton he would ask for Arafat's permission at least to negotiate, he clearly hadn't received it. He refused to talk about the map, or even respond to Clinton's suggestion that the Palestinians present a map of their own, until we did two things: accept the principle of land swaps and reduce the size of the territory we were suggesting for the settlement blocs. To Shlomo's, and I'm sure even more so to Abu Ala'a's, astonishment, the president exploded. He told Abu Ala'a that to refuse to provide any input or ideas was the very opposite of negotiation. It was an "outrageous" approach. He stormed out.

It was late that evening when the first move toward the "make-or-break" situation I had hoped for seemed to occur, though still with much more likelihood of break than make. The president decided the only way to make progress was to sequester a pair of negotiators from each side overnight. Their task would be to search in good faith for the outlines of a possible peace agreement. They were to update Arafat and myself and then report to Clinton the next day. Then, we'd see where we were. I agreed to send Shlomo and Gili Sher, my former back-channel negotiators. I knew that whatever guidelines I gave them, they would probe beyond them, just as they'd done in the back-channel talks. They were negotiators. They were also smart, creative, badly wanted an agreement, and like me believed it ought to be possible. Though I would retain the final word to approve or reject what they suggested, I knew that only in a legal sense could it be null and void. I also recognized, however, that we had to be willing to push further, both to find out for certain where the Palestinians stood and to convince the Americans we genuinely wanted an agreement.

Shlomo and Gili left a little after midnight for Laurel Lodge. Marine guards were posted at the doors, with orders that neither negotiating team was to leave until morning without notifying the president's staff. Mother Nature provided a further incentive to stay inside, since it was again raining buckets. The negotiators talked through the night and the next morning as well. It wasn't until early afternoon that Shlomo and Gili came to my cabin to report on how they'd done. As I'd anticipated, both of them had ventured beyond concessions that I was ready to consider, at least at a time when we weren't even near to a final peace deal. Taking the president's instructions to heart, they'd said they were willing to consider full Palestinian sovereignty over two Arab neighborhoods in East Jerusalem, and even some form of Palestinian authority and control in the Christian and Muslim quarters inside the walls of the Old City. They had dropped our insistence on Israeli control over the Jordan Valley, suggesting that we hold on to only a small segment of the border with Jordan. They had gone beyond the share of the West Bank allocated to a Palestinian state on the map that Abu Ala'a wouldn't even look at. Now, they suggested around 90 percent. But when I asked what the Palestinian negotiators, Saeb Erekat and Mohammed Dahlan, had proposed in return, the answer was almost nothing. They had taken notes. They had asked questions. The one Palestinian proposal, from Saeb Erekat, was on Jerusalem: Palestinian sovereignty over *all* the city's predominantly Arab areas, and Israeli sovereignty over Jewish neighborhoods. In other words, a division of the city.

Even though I was concerned that Gili and Shlomo had gone so far, especially on Jerusalem, I'd reached the point where I doubted that even that would matter. We were now in day six of the summit, barely forty-eight hours from President Clinton's departure for the G8 summit, and we were negotiating only with ourselves. Knowing that the president planned to go see Arafat, I sat down and wrote him a note—emotional not just because I did it quickly, but because of how deeply let down I felt by the Palestinians' deliberate avoidance of a peace deal, which, with genuine reciprocity, should have been within reach. "I took the report of Shlomo Ben-Ami and Gilead Sher of last night's discussion very badly," it began. "This is not a negotiation. This is a manipulative attempt to pull us to a position we will never be able to accept, without the Palestinians moving one inch." I reminded President Clinton that just as he was taking political risks, I was too. "Even the positions presented by our people last night, though they are not my positions, represent an additional risk," I said.

I said I doubted there would be another Israeli leader willing to engage in serious efforts for a final peace agreement with the Palestinians after what had happened here. Unless things changed dramatically, I was not prepared for us to throw out further suggestions, or consider painful concessions. "I do not intend to allow the Israeli state to fall apart, physically or morally. The State of Israel is the implementation of the dream of the Jewish people, for generation upon generation. We achieved it after enormous effort, and at the expenditure of a great deal of blood and sweat. There is no way I will preside at Camp David over the closing of this saga." I told the president that I still believed that we faced a "moment of truth."

But only if he could "shake" Arafat, and get him to sense the enormity of the stakes—an independent Palestinian state, versus more, and undoubtedly deadlier, violence.

And if it did come to armed conflict? "When the people of Israel will understand how far we were ready to go, we will have the power to stand together, unified, in such a struggle, however tough it will become, even if we will be forced to confront the entire world. There is no power in the world that can force on us collective national suicide. Peace will be achieved only if there is a willingness to negotiate on both sides. I am sure the people of Israel, and the American people, will understand it when the details will be revealed."

Clinton had already left for Arafat's cabin by the time Danny Yatom went to deliver the letter. But the president, too, was in a more sober and downbeat mood by the time that meeting was over. Late that night, having read my note, he joined me on the balcony of Dogwood. He looked exhausted. "It was the toughest meeting I've ever had with Arafat," he said. Clinton said he had told the Palestinian leader that only one side, the Israelis, had so far been negotiating in good faith. If Arafat was not prepared to make a genuine effort to reach an agreement, then there was no choice but for all of us to go home. Now, both the president and I were left to wait and see what, if anything, Arafat came up with in reply.

"I've been through battles, and danger, in my life," I said. "But in terms of my responsibility, today, for me as well, was probably the toughest. Shlomo and Gili went beyond what I could live with. If this offer can't move him, then I believe we are left to prepare for war." I told the president he didn't even need to phone me after hearing from Arafat if all he offered was some clever half-reply. Only if it was serious and substantive. I also reminded him that while he'd promised Arafat that he would not "blame" the Palestinians if the summit failed, that had been on the basis of both sides negotiating in good faith. That wasn't happening.

Finally, I touched on an immediate concern if the summit broke up. For months, the Palestinians had been talking about simply "declaring" a Palestinian state. The Americans had insisted neither side should resort to unilateral action in a conflict whose resolution depended on mutual agreement. The Europeans had been less explicit. I told President Clinton I could speak only for how I would respond if a state was indeed declared without a peace deal. "We will extend Israeli sovereignty over the major settlement blocs. We will establish a security zone in the Jordan Valley, and let them know that there will be a heavy price should they attack any of the outlying settlements." In other words, Palestinian unilateral action would prompt unilateral Israeli action. "And the confrontation will begin."

+ + +

Clinton seemed, if not completely revived, considerably more upbeat when he came back to see me an hour later. He told me that he had received the Palestinians' answer. The way he described it to me, Arafat had agreed to leave President Clinton to decide the amount of West Bank land that would go to a Palestinian state, a figure he now told me that he was assuming would end up at around 90 to 92 percent. The trade-off, he said, would be a limited, "symbolic" land swap. Arafat also wanted control of the Jordan Valley, but had agreed to begin negotiating on Israeli security needs there as soon as possible. Then came Arafat's counterconditions, which appeared to bother the president much less than they did me. Everything would be contingent on an unspecified "acceptable outcome on Jerusalem." And despite Clinton's emphasis that any meaningful agreement had to include a formal declaration that the Israeli-Palestinian conflict was "over," Arafat insisted that could come only after the terms of whatever we agreed were fully implemented. I remained skeptical, but Clinton seemed genuinely encouraged, and I didn't want to risk closing off this first hint of progress. I suggested that we could address Arafat's reluctance about an "end of conflict" statement by providing an American guarantee that the terms of the deal would be implemented.

Still, it was clear that any hope of real progress rested on by far the most difficult issue: Jerusalem. Across party boundaries, even across divisions between religious and secular, nearly all Israelis viewed the city as not just our capital, but the centerpiece of the state. It had been divided after 1948. The Old City and the site of the ancient Jewish temple had been under Jordanian rule for nineteen years when our forces recaptured it in the Six-Day War. It was under a Labor government that the area around the temple's surviving Western Wall, left uncared for under the Jordanians, was cleared and a stone plaza put in place for worshipers—at the expense of parts of the old Moroccan Quarter. It was under Labor, too, that Israel unilaterally expanded Jerusalem's city limits to take in more than two-dozen adjacent Arab towns and villages on the West Bank. No Israeli government since then, Labor or Likud, had deviated from a shared pledge that Jerusalem would remain Israel's undivided, sovereign capital under any eventual peace agreement.

Yet when I met Clinton the next morning in Laurel Lodge, he insisted we had to find some room for flexibility. He said that, of course, Israel would retain sovereignty over the Temple Mount: the site of the Western Wall and, above it, the Al-Aqsa Mosque complex. "But without damaging your sovereignty," he argued, "we have to find a way to *draw a picture* for Arafat that includes some measure of Palestinian control in part of the city."

"Could you agree to Arafat having an office, maybe, inside the walls of the Old City?" he asked me. What about a form of administrative control in some of the outlying Arab neighborhoods in East Jerusalem? I replied that I couldn't possibly answer any of his questions until and unless it was clear that Arafat accepted our sovereignty over—and our national and religious connection with—the Temple Mount. Yet I said I understood that we would have to reach some compromise agreement on the city if we were ever going to have a chance of a peace agreement. "But it's an issue that is difficult for every Israeli," I told him. Before I could even begin to see whether there was a way forward, I would have to talk it through with my entire negotiating team. Then, we could discuss it.

For the next five or six hours, we had the most open, serious, searching discussion I've experienced in my public life. It began on the terrace of my cabin at two in the afternoon and went on until well after sundown. I opened by saying what each of us already knew: Jerusalem was the most emotionally charged and politically complex issue of all. Our maximum position coming into the summit had been that we would again expand the municipal boundaries of the city, as we'd done after the 1967 war, in order to accommodate two separate "city councils." One would be in Abu Dis, just to the southeast of the Old City, almost literally in the shadow of the Temple Mount. The understanding was the Palestinians would be free to rename the village, referring to it by the Arabic name for Jerusalem: Al Quds. I said that we should use that position as a starting point and discuss how, or whether, we might go further. All I added was the need to be aware of what was at stake. I didn't know whether peace was within reach. I was still deeply skeptical. But if it was, we had to accept that Jerusalem would be key. And if the summit failed, for whatever reason, what inevitably awaited us was confrontation.

Israel Hasson, the Shin Bet veteran, spoke first. He saw two choices. Either we could retain Israeli sovereignty over a "united Jerusalem" with functional, day-to-day autonomy for the Palestinians in their neighborhoods, or we could in effect divide the city: "divide sovereignty." He didn't say which he favored, only that it was essential that we make the decision now if we could, however difficult or reluctant Arafat was as a negotiating partner. Otherwise, we'd never be able to say with certainty whether he was truly equal to the challenge of peacemaking. And if we didn't achieve an agreement with him, the reality was that we'd end up at some stage having to deal instead with the Islamists: Hamas and Islamic Jihad. Oded Eran, the career diplomat whom I'd put in charge of frustrating, formal talks with the Palestinians in the months preceding the summit, said he was convinced that we should give the Palestinians full sovereignty over at least the "outer" Arab neighborhoods in East Jerusalem, which had become part of the city only when we'd expanded the city boundaries after 1967. He said that was in Israel's own interest. We had no historic connection to these Arab villages, and something like 130,000 Palestinians lived there. "Why should we want to annex them?" he asked. It would be like accepting the "right of return" through the back door.

Dan Meridor's voice, for me, was especially important. I knew he was as determined as I was to achieve a negotiating breakthrough. But he was also a former Likudnik and a native Jerusalemite. "I'm against any concessions when it comes to Israeli sovereignty," he said. "Any attempt to divide Jerusalem would be a serious blow, and not just for Jews in Israel." For centuries, Jewish communities all over the world had looked to Jerusalem, prayed for Jerusalem. The yearly Seder meal, on Passover, ends with the Hebrew phrase *Shanah haba b'Yerushalaim*. Next year, in Jerusalem. "What we decide here in Camp David," Dan said, "also affects Jews in New York. In Moscow. In Johannesburg." He urged us to focus instead on offering Arafat as attractive as possible a package of concessions on all the *other* issues. "Then let him decide. But even if sovereignty over Jerusalem means that the deal collapses, I'm not willing to pay that price."

No voices were raised. It was the rarest of political discussions. People offered their views, and listened to others'. Amnon Lipkin pointed out that a large area of what was now inside the boundaries of Jerusalem was not part of the city he'd known before 1967. Echoing Oded Eran, he said, "It's in our interest for as many as possible of the Arab inhabitants to come under the authority of the Palestinians, and as few as possible under our rule." Amnon's bottom line was that we could not give up Israeli sovereignty over the Temple Mount, which, although he was a nonobservant Jew, he called "the cradle of Jewish history." But equally, we couldn't and shouldn't "run the Al-Aqsa Mosque." He was also in favor of agreeing to what Clinton had asked of me: giving Arafat a base in the Muslim Quarter of the Old City. His one caveat was that we should not do any of this unless it was part of a genuine, final peace agreement with the Palestinians.

Danny Yatom urged us to move beyond our emotions and look for a practical solution. "We all know how the boundaries of Jerusalem were drawn," he said, referring to the post-1967 expansion of the city. "They're not holy. It is important to get down to our *real* red lines." Elyakim Rubinstein, the attorney general, was an observant, Orthodox Jew, and more sympathetic politically to Likud than Labor. Israel, in his view, had to retain our hold over the Old City. But in practical terms, he too believed we needed to include "as few Arabs as possible" under Israeli sovereignty. As a result, he was in favor of ceding the outer villages to the Palestinians, adding, "This is a moment of truth."

It was nearly five hours before I brought the discussion to a close. "This is as grave a decision as when Ben-Gurion accepted the partition plan in 1947; the declaration of the state; or the most tense moments of the Yom Kippur War," I said. "Or the decisions which Begin took in this same place." Of course, Begin hadn't even been willing to enter into discussion on Jerusalem. But we were in a different situation. If we were going to get a true end to our conflict, the question of Jerusalem had to be addressed. "We can't delay the decision. We can't avoid it. We will have to decide." My own red line was the same as Amnon Lipkin's: sovereignty over the site of our First and Second Temples. Even shared sovereignty elsewhere within the Old City seemed to me a step too far at this stage, but I didn't rule it out as part of a full peace. "Without disengagement from the Palestinians, without an end of conflict," I reminded our negotiating team, "we're heading toward further tragedy. We can't pretend we don't see the iceberg."

I asked several members of the team, under Shlomo Ben-Ami, to draft a paper based on our discussion. Since I knew that Clinton, and Arafat too, could do nothing of substance until I'd resolved how far to go on Jerusalem, I went to see the president. I told him about our session. I said that we were now crystallizing what had been said into a formal position, and I hoped to be able to return in a few hours with "the furthest point we can go." Clinton said that would be a critical moment in the summit. If we *could* find common ground, he said, Israel would have achieved what had eluded it under Rabin, and even Ben-Gurion: "end of conflict, and Jerusalem recognized internationally as your capital." I told him that the discussion with my negotiators had been moving and illuminating. "I could see how much it weighed on everyone." But I added that I still did not feel anything of a similar nature, or remotely as serious, was happening on the Palestinian side. I also said that in deciding how to proceed, I couldn't ignore political realities back home. I would have to get any major change in our position concerning Jerusalem through the Knesset, even before putting a peace agreement to a referendum.

"When will you get back to me with your paper?" he asked. I said I'd try by midnight. I also asked him whether he could delay going to the G8 summit in Japan, for which he was due to leave Camp David on the morning of the nineteenth. That meant we had just one full day left. I said even if the plan was to resume our talks afterward, I couldn't move on Jerusalem right before we recessed. It would mean "putting my last and best offer on the table" and running the risk of leaks in Israel while Clinton was gone. He said that he had to go to the G8, but would try to put off leaving for a further day. Then, he asked me to draw up a list of questions for him to present to Arafat so that we could solidify our understanding of how far *he* was ready to go for peace.

I had Shlomo get busy on the list of questions, but it took time. We reconvened around eleven at night to discuss both the questions and the Jerusalem package. Though it retained Israeli sovereignty over the entirety of the Old City, it did give the Palestinians a greater measure of control over other areas of East Jerusalem than any Israeli government had been willing to consider in the past. Still, almost everyone in the negotiating team could live with it, assuming it became the critical element in a final peace. Dan Meridor alone remained firmly opposed, though Elyakim Rubinstein also had some reservations. Even Dan said he understood the importance of getting a peace agreement, if indeed it was possible, and our readiness to discuss new proposals on Jerusalem.

When I left for Clinton's cabin at about 1:00 a.m. on Wednesday, I had no idea I was about to enter the most difficult meeting—and the only real fight—I had with him during our long effort to achieve a Middle East peace. I brought Shlomo and Danny with me, which meant that Madeleine Albright, Dennis Ross, and Sandy Berger stayed as well. I sensed tension in all of them, in large part, I soon discovered, because they took exception to the more than twelve hours we had spent discussing and refining our position on Jerusalem. I think Clinton expected a formal offer from us. Since I'd been guided by his request for a list of questions for Arafat, however, that is what we came to him with. As we'd discussed, I wanted finally to elicit some sign of whether Arafat, too, was ready to make difficult decisions.

The questions were specific. "Will you accept an agreement that stipulates the following," it began, and proceeded to outline the kind of peace we could accept. The points included not just Jerusalem, but areas I knew would also be sensitive for Arafat, such as the right of return and formal agreement to an end of conflict. We went further than before in some areas. One of the outer East Jerusalem neighborhoods would be under Palestinian sovereignty. The rest of the city would remain under Israeli sovereignty, but most of the other Arab villages would be subject to a system of Palestinian administration. The Haram al-Sharif, the mosque complex above the wall of the Jewish temple, would be under Palestinian "administrative and religious management." We also suggested "special arrangements" implying a Palestinian presence in the Old City, but again under Israeli sovereignty. The questions envisaged eventual Palestinian control in the Jordan Valley, with an Israeli security zone for twelve years, rather than our proposal in pre-summit talks for thirty years. Then, explicitly, we proposed a question to Arafat to confirm my understanding with Clinton that the "right of return" would apply not to Israel proper, but to a Palestinian state on the West Bank and Gaza. Finally, the document said, "I understand that such an agreement constitutes an end of conflict, and a finality of all mutual claims."

After he read it, the president blew up. Far from the "bottom lines" he'd apparently hoped for, but which I'd never thought were expected at this stage, I seemed to be retreating from ideas Shlomo and Gili had presented in their all-night session with the Palestinians. Given the ground rules of that exercise, they'd felt able to go beyond anything we'd actually agreed, and in some areas beyond what they knew I could support. As a result, the list of questions assumed Israel would keep a little more than 11 percent of the West Bank, nearly 1 percent more than Shlomo had mentioned. Shlomo and Gili had also raised the possibility of up to three of the outer Jerusalem villages coming under full Palestinian sovereignty. "You keep us, and Arafat, waiting for thirteen hours," Clinton fumed, his face nearly scarlet. "And you want me to present something *less* than you've already offered." He said he wouldn't do it. "This is not real. It's not serious." He said that he'd gone to Shepherdstown in search of what was supposed to be an endgame with the Syrians. Then to Geneva to see Assad, "where I felt like a wooden Indian, doing your bidding. I will *not* let it happen here. I will simply not do it."

I tried to keep my voice steady when I replied. I explained that the issues we were addressing went to the heart of Israel's interests, its future security, its identity and definition as a nation. I had a responsibility to tread carefully. Then, my voice rising too, I came back to what I felt was the real problem. Arafat and his negotiators had been sitting and waiting for me and my team, and probably Clinton as well, to deliver more and more concessions with no sign that they were willing to move on anything. "I find that outrageous," I said. I did not expect Arafat to respond with equal concessions. After all, Israel had most of the tangible assets. "But I did expect him at least to take a small step once we had taken ten. We have not seen even this. This is the kind of behavior parents would not tolerate in their own children! We don't expect Arafat to accept this, but I *do* expect him to present a counterposition."

Clinton remained adamant he couldn't go to Arafat with a retreat from our earlier ideas. "My negotiating team moved beyond my red lines," I told him. The overnight talks were supposed to be nonbinding and assumed that *both* sides would make a genuine attempt to get an agreement. "I can't see any change in Arafat's pattern. We take all the risks." I said I doubted that Arafat expected to hear that we had decided to "give him Jerusalem." In any case, the Israeli public hadn't given me a mandate to do that. But I would still move in Arafat's direction, *if and when* I got any sign he was willing to do the same.

The president's anger eased. He suggested he caucus with his negotiators and figure out what to do next. I felt bad about what had happened: not about the list of questions, or my insistence that we could not offer major concessions with no sign of reciprocity. But I did regret that it had left the Americans so frustrated, and Clinton so angry. He had invested huge amounts of time and brainpower, and political capital, in the search for peace.

He phoned me at about three thirty in the morning and asked me to come back. This time, I went alone. We sat on the terrace of Aspen. He said again he couldn't go to Arafat with the list we'd drawn up. But having met with his negotiators, he suggested they draft a more forthcoming list of their own—consistent with what Shlomo and Gili had proposed. I agreed, as long as they kept in mind that it had to be something I could ultimately live with, and that it be presented to Arafat as an American proposal. I suggested the president could tell Arafat that he'd try to get me to agree to it, providing Arafat first showed a readiness to move.

The American questions did go further than ours. They asked Arafat whether he would negotiate on the basis of getting Palestinian sovereignty over all the outer Jerusalem neighborhoods, as well as the Muslim Quarter of the Old City and a "custodial role" over the holy sites. But Arafat still said no. He insisted on Palestinian sovereignty over all of East Jerusalem, including the Old City and the holy sites. For a few hours after Clinton's fruitless meeting with Arafat, Dennis and the American team engaged in a rescue effort, adding another carrot. They included the Christian Quarter as well, meaning Palestinian sovereignty over nearly half of the Old City, including the areas where almost all Arab residents lived. Dennis gave the proposal to Shlomo and Amnon Lipkin to bring to me, and asked two of the Palestinian negotiators to take it to Arafat. Even offering sovereignty over the Muslim Quarter went beyond anything I'd proposed. So did a lot of the other American questions. Still, I said that if Arafat ever showed a readiness to move, we'd be willing to consider them in discussions with the US negotiating team—with the exception of the Christian Quarter. But that, too, turned out not to matter. Arafat didn't even respond.

Clinton called me to say we'd reached the end of the road. There were only two options: end the summit and announce we'd tried and failed, or defer Jerusalem and try to get agreement on the rest of the issues. I asked for time to think it over, and he said he'd come see me when I was ready. I was tempted to put off Jerusalem. In the admittedly unlikely event we could get a deal on the other issues, that would undeniably be an achievement. But Arafat's lack of engagement on Jerusalem was yet another sign that he was not ready for the almost equally tough compromises required to resolve the other core issues. And there was no escaping the reality that without a deal on Jerusalem, no agreement we reached would truly represent an end of conflict. Moreover, Jerusalem wasn't just a Palestinian issue. It was of fundamental interest to the whole Muslim world. If we left it unaddressed, we would be putting future Israeli governments in the position of having to negotiate on Jerusalem *after* we'd given back our key negotiating assets and all our leverage.

I accepted now that the search for a full peace treaty, or even a framework agreement, looked all but impossible. Even Shlomo's and Gili's freelancing had produced only a series of no's from Arafat. But I couldn't give up. Much as I'd been resisting it, I needed to give Clinton my *true* bottom lines, even with Arafat still mute and unresponsive. That was the only way we could know with certainty whether peace was possible. If it wasn't, it would also demonstrate powerfully to the Americans that we were not the party that had prevented an agreement.

The president came to see me in Dogwood a little before eleven at night on the eighteenth, less than twelve hours before he was due to take his delayed flight to the G8. I told him I'd decided to do what Rabin had done with Syria. I was going to give him a "deposit" to keep in his pocket, which he would be free to use as the basis for a further, *American* proposal to Arafat, assuming it was part of an agreement with a "satisfactory resolution" of the refugee issue and an explicit end of conflict. He could present it to Arafat as something he was confident of persuading Israel to accept. It went well beyond what I'd offered before, on all the major issues. Under the terms of our "deposit," I was ready to consider Palestinian rule over 91 percent of the West Bank. Our security zone in the Jordan Valley would remain in place for "less than twelve years." And if all went well there, I was prepared for a Palestinian state to have sovereignty over 85 percent of the border area. Seven out of the nine outer Arab neighborhoods of Jerusalem would come under Palestinian sovereignty. The inner neighborhoods would be under Palestinian civil authority, including planning and zoning, and law enforcement. For the mosques on the Temple Mount, I proposed a shared custodianship to include the new state of Palestine, Morocco, and the chair of the Higher Islamic Commission in Jerusalem. I also agreed to consider Palestinian sovereignty over *both* the Muslim and Christian quarters of the Old City.

Clinton, arching his eyebrows and smiling, said what I'd offered was a package of genuine concessions. It was more than he had expected and, he assumed, more than the Palestinians could have hoped for. It had the makings of a potential breakthrough toward a fair and final peace. I told him I hoped so.

Now, it was our turn to wait. The president invited Arafat to Aspen and, from what we heard soon afterward, got no hint of any readiness to reciprocate. He agreed only to talk to his negotiators and get back with an answer. Overnight, the Palestinians sent messages to the Americans asking questions on each of the concessions, though still with no indication from Arafat of a response. Finally, he sent a suggestion that since Clinton was about to fly off to the G8, we take a two-week break to allow Arafat to consult with Arab leaders. To his credit, Clinton knew an escape act when he saw it. He recognized that only by confronting the issues raised by our proposals and showing a willingness to find common ground would we have any hope of success. No recess, Clinton said. He needed a straight answer. Again, not full acceptance necessarily, but agreement to treat the proposals as a basis for negotiating an Israeli-Palestinian peace. Arafat's answer came shortly before dawn. It was "no."

Clinton couldn't quite believe it. He went back to see Arafat, telling him he was making an error on the scale of 1948, when the Palestinians had rejected the partition of Palestine and the creation of an Arab state; or in 1978, when by negotiating on the basis of Sadat's Palestinian-rights framework, they would have ended up with a mere 5,000 Israeli settlers on the West Bank instead of nearly 200,000. What most astonished Clinton was that Arafat was saying no even to using the package as a *basis* for negotiations. Arafat would not budge.

As Palestinian negotiators tried to salvage things by suggesting another trip by Madeleine and Dennis to the Middle East, it was clear that even the Americans were fed up. They knew that one side, at least, had been trying to get an agreement. They couldn't understand why Arafat was unwilling even to accept the proposals as a basis for further talks. When Yossi Ginossar, our most reliable conduit, went to see Arafat, he found him sitting alone and, in Yossi's description, "paralyzed." Clinton finally decided to have one last go. When he did, Arafat not only remained unwilling: to the president's astonishment, he insisted that the ancient Jewish temple hadn't been in Jerusalem at all, but in the West Bank city of Nablus.

I was getting a bite to eat in the dining room in Laurel Lodge when Madeleine showed up. She didn't bother defending Arafat. She was as frustrated as I was. Her message was that after the summit, it was important not to make things worse. A negotiating process had to be kept alive. Then, Clinton sat down with me. He delivered a similar message, but with even greater feeling. "You're smarter than I am," he joked. "You're certainly experienced in war, and I'm not. But I'm more experienced in politics, and there are a few things I've learned along the way. The most important is not to corner your adversaries, and not to corner yourself. Always leave yourself a way out. Don't lock yourself into a losing option." I could see that he was right. I also believed, as strongly now as before the summit, that Israel's *own* interests and its security were not served by an unresolved conflict with the Palestinians. The problem was that, in the absence of an equal commitment on Arafat's side, any continued negotiating process seemed futile.

I packed my bags. I told Danny Yatom to inform the Americans we were leaving and to get our plane ready to take us back to Israel. I let the others in our team know that we were going. A number of them, and several of the Americans as well, urged me to reconsider. But I said I saw no point in staying. What I didn't know, however, was that one of the Palestinians' original Oslo negotiators, Hassan Asfour, had approached Dennis Ross with a new proposal: that we ask Arafat to accept everything except the proposal on the holy sites as a basis for negotiation. Sovereignty over the Temple Mount would be addressed in later, international negotiations. When Dennis brought this to me, my instinct was to say no. Like so much else at the summit, it was an inherently skewed formula: it would involve major Israeli concessions on all the other main issues, *without* securing our absolute minimum need in Jerusalem: sovereignty over the Temple Mount. I didn't say yes. Still, with Clinton's words of advice still on my mind, I said that I'd think it over.

When I met the rest of the Israeli team, almost all of them felt we should stay. The consensus was that especially if violence broke out after the summit's collapse, we didn't want to feel we'd left any stone unturned. At about 11:00 p.m., I phoned the president and told him we would stay until he returned from Okinawa. He was clearly pleased, and asked us to keep working in his absence. When I resisted that, saying that any substantive talks needed his involvement, we finally agreed that talks could continue in search of a formula for the holy sites. On all the other issues, only informal discussions would be held until and unless a way ahead on the Temple Mount was found. If that happened, and *if Arafat* finally accepted the pocket proposals as an agreed starting point, formal negotiations could resume. Clinton accepted this formula. He went to see Arafat and secured—or thought he had secured—his agreement as well.

One of the president's great strengths was his genius for blurring the edges of potential differences in search of common ground. But when edges had to be sharpened, this could lead to confusion. Before leaving for the G8, the president neglected to mention to Arafat our explicit understanding that, with the exception of the talks on the holy sites, nothing would happen until he accepted the concessions that President Clinton and I had delivered as at least a basis for further negotiations. As a result, Arafat's team now set about happily asking questions and probing my negotiators—pushing us to go *further*—but with no more inclination than before to produce any concessions of their own.

When I learned what was happening, I told my negotiators they were not to hold any further formal meetings during the four days Clinton would be away. Dennis's initial response was frustration. Madeleine Albright's was fury. They both made no secret of their view that I was needlessly stonewalling. It wasn't until a few hours later that Madeleine apparently saw the stenographer's record of my conversation with the president before he'd left, confirming the condition that Arafat accept the pocket at least as a basis on which to proceed. That evening, she apologized to me for the misunderstanding, and explained the mix-up to the full Palestinian and Israeli negotiating teams.

I spent most of the remaining three days in my cabin or, when the rain relented, walking through the woods. The Americans appeared to think I was sulking. I wasn't. I was trying to find the least diplomatically damaging way to navigate the period until the president's return. I couldn't see showing up at Laurel at every mealtime, mingling and joking with the Americans and Palestinians, but refusing to enter into any form of negotiations. That would compound the awkwardness, and also be a direct affront to Madeleine. I highly respected her. But I could not in good conscience help her out in her efforts to find at least some, informal, way of moving the summit along in Clinton's absence. If Arafat had failed to show even a scintilla of movement with the president in the room, there was no way he was going to do so with the secretary of state. For the Palestinian negotiators, who were predictably in favor of her efforts, the definition of "new ideas" was whatever further movement they might cajole out of *our* negotiators. On day three of Clinton's absence, I got a note saying that Secretary Albright was on her way to my cabin. I didn't want the needless diplomatic difficulty involved in again telling her I could not sanction freewheeling, and decidedly one-sided, negotiations while Arafat hadn't moved a single inch. So I made myself scarce. Fortunately, I was wearing sneakers. I told Danny to inform the Americans I was out jogging around the perimeter of the large Camp David estate, and went off to do just that.

I told my own delegation I was taking time out to assess where we stood. I did continue meeting with Gili Sher and Danny Yatom. Yet for much of the time, I read. I also did a lot of thinking. I considered the pocket concessions I'd agreed to, the uncertainties and risks I'd been prepared to run, and how to deal with the fact that Arafat, when he had engaged at all, had said no.

Once it was clear to the Americans there would be no talks until the president returned, however, Madeline urged me to go see Arafat, again seemingly of the view that a dash of "personal chemistry" between us might somehow unblock things. The two members of our team who were the least pessimistic about Camp David's outcome, Shlomo Ben-Ami and Yossi Ginossar, also said they thought it was a good idea. It was they who'd pressed me to go see Arafat for tea and sweets earlier in the summit. But that meeting had produced not even a glimmer of negotiating flexibility from the Palestinian leader. Yossi had said at the time that it would help the atmosphere, and pay dividends later on. But that hadn't happened either. "Madam Secretary," I told Madeleine, "eating more baklava with Arafat isn't going to help. The situation is simple: he needs to answer whether he views the president's proposal as a basis for going forward."

When Clinton returned, he promptly got back down to business, attempting one last push to see whether a deal was possible. He phoned me around midnight on July 24, a few hours after he'd arrived. He told me that he had sent an even more far-reaching package to Arafat. Now, he was proposing that all of the outer Arab neighborhoods in East Jerusalem would come under Palestinian sovereignty, in addition to the Muslim and Christian quarters in the Old City. And Arafat would be given "custodial sovereignty" over the Muslim holy sites on the Temple Mount. Though he knew this was further than I could go, it was still broadly within the spirit of the "deposit" ideas I'd agreed he could present. So I didn't object to his offering it under the same ground rules: as American proposals, which the president was telling Arafat he would try to deliver if he accepted them as a basis for serious negotiations. Yet when Clinton phoned me back, around three fifteen in the morning, it was to tell me that Arafat had again said no.

The curtain had finally come down. What remained now was to clear up the set. I did meet Arafat once more, in a joint session with President Clinton, but only for closing statements. The president and I spoke as much in sorrow and frustration as anger. Both of us said we thought a historic agreement had been within our grasp, and that far-reaching proposals had been tabled to make it possible. Arafat responded with words both of us had heard before: effusive toward Clinton, rhapsodic about his "old partner" Rabin, and fulsome in his ostensible commitment to keep trying for peace. But in reality, he'd proved unwilling even to *talk* about the compromises a real, final peace would require.

The president's remarks to the media were, by the standards of post-summit diplomacy, unmistakably clear in making that point. He praised me and the Israeli negotiating team for courage and vision. Essentially, he thanked Arafat for showing up. That was some consolation. But it didn't alter the weight of the message we were carrying home.

There were only two potential deal-breakers on our side, as Arafat had known from the start. The first involved a Palestinian "right of return" to within Israel's pre-1967 borders. This was not just a recipe for the end of Israel as a majority-Jewish state. It would imply a rewriting of the history of how Israel was born: in a *war*, with an almost equal number of refugees fleeing or forced to leave on both sides, after the Arab world took up arms against a UN partition plan that would have created a Palestinian Arab state as well. The second critical issue was Jerusalem. There, I'd stretched our negotiating position almost to breaking point. The "pocket deposit" ideas Arafat ended up rejecting amounted to a breach of an assurance that I and every other Israeli prime minister since 1967 had given: never to redivide Israel's capital. Had we actually got an end-of-conflict deal, I would have had to justify it to Israelis in a referendum. I think I could have done so. But one thing no Israeli leader could give up was sovereignty over the Temple Mount, the centerpiece of our history as a people and Israel's as a state.

Arafat never even engaged in a discussion on the right of return. On the Temple Mount, however, he was explicit. Any peace, any *basis for negotiation* toward peace, had to begin by confirming Palestinian sovereignty. Besides, as he'd told the president of the United States, he'd persuaded himself there never even *was* a Jewish temple in Jerusalem. When I heard about that remark, I was less shocked than Clinton. It struck me as just another way Arafat had of conveying *his* bottom lines. It was a bit like the stories he liked to tell about visiting his aunt in Jerusalem as a young boy and seeing religious Jews praying at the Western Wall. I don't know whether the stories were true. But the point was that while he had no problem with Jews in their long coats and black hats *praying* in the holy city, Jews exercising authority or sovereignty, or a Jewish *state*, was something else entirely. Camp David had made it clear it was something he was not prepared to accept.

The question I now had to confront was what to do next.

# Arafat's Answer

IT DIDN'T FULLY HIT ME HOW DRAINING OUR EFFORTS HAD BEEN UNTIL the morning that the summit collapsed, when President Clinton called me to come talk to him in the living room at Laurel Lodge. When I arrived, Madeleine was already there, sitting on the edge of the sofa. She greeted me with a resigned shrug and a valiant but not altogether successful effort at a smile.

"We *tried*," Clinton said quietly as I took a seat in a wooden chair opposite his. "We gave it everything." The nominal reason for the meeting was to brief me on the communiqué the Americans were going to issue: mostly boilerplate assurances that both sides remained committed to seeking peace, but with an additional "understanding" that neither would take unilateral actions in the meantime. But mostly, Clinton wanted to reinforce his message of a few days earlier: don't "lock yourself into a losing option." Don't close the door. Don't give up. "I won't," I told him, an assurance I echoed in remarks to reporters a few hours later, when I said that while the peace process had "suffered a major blow, we should not lose hope. With goodwill on all sides, we can recuperate."

But I told the president that we couldn't just ignore what had happened at Camp David. Yes, in the event Arafat suddenly had second thoughts about the potentially historic achievement he'd passed up, he would know where to find me. But until and unless that happened, I told Clinton that I assumed my pocket concessions would now be firmly back in his pocket.

And while we couldn't erase them from memory, I said it was important both of us make it clear that, in legal and diplomatic terms, they were null and void. They could not be used to provide Arafat a *new* starting point from which he could make his customary demand for more.

"And I have to tell you that, given what has happened, there's no way I can justify handing him control of more land. I am not going to go ahead with the Wye redeployments in these circumstances."

"You don't have to," Clinton replied. "I'll back you."

Though I never discussed internal Israeli politics with any foreign leader, even the closest of allies, I didn't doubt that the president's support was partly a recognition of what awaited me at home. Even before I'd left for Camp David, the defections from our coalition meant we'd been left with only forty-two seats in the Knesset, nineteen short of a majority. Amid the first, sketchy media reports that we were even *talking* about sharing control of parts of Jerusalem with the Palestinians, there was a chorus of denunciation from right-wing politicians back home. Bibi Netanyahu had largely kept out of the public eye since his resignation after the election. Now, he issued a statement accusing me of having "broken all the red lines held by all Israeli governments." During the president's final push to save the prospects for a summit agreement, Bibi called a news conference. He said he was determined to prevent what he called an impending disintegration of Israeli society. "What we hear from most of the reports out of Camp David does not answer our hopes," he said.

I had no regrets about going as far as I had in trying to reach, at the minimum, a framework agreement. In that sense, it is true the summit had failed. But when I'd urged President Clinton to convene it, I made the argument that if genuine peace was ever going to be possible, we at least had to know whether Arafat was interested in, or capable of, playing his part. That question had, for now, been answered. At least as importantly for Israel, the president of the United States and almost the entire international community recognized we'd done everything realistically possible to reach an accommodation. Diplomatically, the ball was in the Palestinians' court.

There was a final achievement as well—little noticed or remarked upon in the days immediately after Camp David, but hugely significant. A taboo had been broken. For the first time, all Israelis recognized what their political leaders, both Labor and Likud, had long known, if not publicly acknowledged: a formal, final peace with the Palestinians would require us not just to withdraw from the great majority of the West Bank, but to find a formula for sharing power in Jerusalem. Many Israelis still believed that was a price too high, and not just Likudniks. A couple of weeks after the summit, Leah Rabin told an Israeli newspaper that her late husband would be "turning in his grave" if he'd known the concessions I'd been ready to consider on Jerusalem. I found the remarks hurtful, but I understood them. In a way, they drove home the point I'd made to Clinton during the summit: *all* Israelis had a deep, emotional attachment to our historic capital. "Yitzhak would never have agreed to compromise on the Old City and the Temple Mount," Leah said. There is no way of knowing for sure, of course, what Rabin would have done had he been in my place at Camp David. Yet the major change from what had happened at the summit was that even those Israelis who found a compromise on Jerusalem unacceptable now recognized that, if they *did* want to negotiate a definitive end to our conflict with the Palestinians, talking about it was unavoidable.

As our El Al 707 descended over the Mediterranean for our approach back to Ben-Gurion Airport, I faced the more immediate issue of ensuring my government's survival. This was partly in case, against all odds, Arafat showed a readiness to revive the search for peace—but also because of the far more likely prospect that he would choose violence.

+ + +

Since the Knesset was about to go into recess until late October, I would have a three-month window to reshape and stabilize my coalition—but only if we could survive a no-confidence motion introduced by Arik Sharon after Camp David. We did weather it, barely. Arik needed a majority of the Knesset's 120 seats to bring down the government. The vote ended in a 50–50 tie; the other twenty MKs abstained or didn't show up. This was not because of any enthusiasm for my efforts to get an agreement at Camp David, but because of a *lack* of enthusiasm for an early election in which they feared losing seats.

Yet at least I could now focus on the challenge of the inevitably altered situation with Arafat after the summit's collapse. My main concern was the possibility of violence. Even before returning home, I'd phoned Shaul

Mofaz and Avi Dichter, a former Sayeret Matkal soldier who was now head of the Shin Bet. "Let's hope the violence doesn't come," I told them. "But if it does, make sure we are ready." Though there was no sign of violence in the weeks immediately after the summit, there was equally little sign of diplomatic engagement by Arafat. Obviously relieved at the way Camp David had ended, he returned to Gaza to a hero's welcome, proudly proclaiming that he had refused to "give up" Jerusalem. It was vintage Arafat: the "general" in his starched uniform and keffiyeh, fresh from the diplomatic equivalent of the battlefield, triumphant against the odds. It was the role he liked and played best. His next move was to take the show on the road: to Arab, European, and world capitals, pleading that he had been the "victim" of summit chicanery in which President Clinton and I had presented him with a deal no self-respecting Palestinian could accept. He was also campaigning for international support for a move, in contravention of the final Camp David communiqué, to "declare" a Palestinian state unilaterally in mid-September.

I spoke personally to Tony Blair and French president Jacques Chirac, as well as to King Abdullah of Jordan and Egypt's Hosni Mubarak. I also dispatched Shlomo Ben-Ami, Amnon Lipkin, Yossi Beilin, and Shimon Peres, who was minister of regional cooperation in the coalition, on a series of diplomatic visits to make sure the true story of what had happened at the summit was understood. As a result, the globetrotting Arafat received an almost unanimous rebuff for the idea of a unilateral declaration of statehood. He was told that if he really wanted a state, he should return to the negotiating table with Israel.

By the time I went to New York in early September—joining the largest collection of world leaders ever assembled, for the UN's Millennium Summit—there seemed little chance of that happening. I met privately with a number of world leaders before delivering a brief address to the more than 150 presidents and prime ministers. I was at pains to take the high road. Looking straight at Arafat from the UN podium, I said, "We are at the Rubicon, and neither of us can cross it alone." Jerusalem, "the eternal capital of Israel," was calling out for a "peace of honor, of courage, and of brotherhood"—a peace recognizing that the city was also sacred to Muslims and Christians the world over. When Arafat spoke, it was almost as if the summit had never happened. "We remain committed to our national rights over East Jerusalem, capital of our state and shelter of our sacred sites, as well as our rights on the Christian and Islamic holy sites," he declared. He didn't mention Jews, beyond a bizarre reference to the two-thousandth anniversary of the birth of Christ "in Bethlehem, Palestine." I couldn't resist remarking to one of the American negotiators that I'd always thought Jesus grew up as a Jewish boy, making thrice-yearly visits at festival time to the temple in Jerusalem, at a time when there was not a church, much less a mosque, in sight.

I assured President Clinton I was not giving up altogether on the prospects for reviving peace negotiations, in part because I believed it was critical for Israel to retain the diplomatic, political, and moral high ground we had earned in the eyes of the international community from the concessions we had been willing to consider. When the president suggested drafting a final American paper, based on Camp David though presumably with an even more generous proposal for the Palestinians, I did not object. Still, I told him I doubted that a new American proposal would make any difference to the Palestinian leader. If it didn't, I believed at some point all our talk about an end of conflict would give way to conflict. The only question was when.

Tragically, I got the answer only weeks after my return from the UN.

+ + +

At the urging of the Americans, I invited Arafat and his negotiating team to a private dinner in Kochav Yair on September 25. The atmosphere was surprisingly warm, for which a lot of the credit, as well as culinary praise, has to go to Nava. "Very cordial, even congenial," Nabil Shaath told reporters after the dinner, nearly forty-five minutes of which I spent talking alone with Arafat on the terrace out back. Each of us spoke to Clinton by phone for about ten minutes near the end, and the president was obviously pleased to hear us sounding upbeat about seeking to avoid a return to violence and narrow any differences on the forthcoming American negotiating paper. On the *substance* of our differences, by mutual agreement, Arafat and I didn't say much to each other. Yet I did try to impress on him that time for a negotiating breakthrough was getting short. His monosyllabic reply—yes—was at least better than the alternative. Clearly, the Americans hoped it might still leave the door open for progress.

The request that had come across my desk a few days earlier need not have changed that. Even though Sharon had failed, for now, to bring down the government, he was keen to make political capital from the collapse of Camp David. He now declared his intention to pay a visit to the Temple Mount. The Mount—or as it was called in Arabic, Haram al-Sharif—was part of Israel. The unsubtle point of Arik's visit was to dramatize his determination to keep it that way. The target of this political theater was not Arafat or the Palestinians. It was the Israeli public, me, and my government. In a perfect world, I would have liked to find a way to block the visit. In a democracy, it wasn't that easy. The only way I could do so was on the grounds it was a threat to public order or security, a judgment in the hands of our police and security services. I duly asked for the views of Avi Dichter of the Shin Bet and Shlomo Ben-Ami, who in addition to being interim foreign minister was minister of internal security, in charge of the police. Both came back with the same answer: although we'd all be happier if Arik stayed down on his farm in the Negev, there was no basis, from our available intelligence, to argue that his visit would pose a major public-order issue. When Shlomo contacted Jibril Rajoub, Arafat's West Bank security commander, Rajoub had only two requests, and Shlomo agreed. The first was that the visit not occur on a Friday, when the mosques would be full of worshippers; the second, that Sharon and his entourage not enter either of the mosques on the Haram. Our chief of police informed Sharon of the conditions, and he agreed. When he went, for about half an hour under police escort on Thursday morning the twenty-eighth, he complied.

At first, we thought it would prove a one-off media stunt. But that evening, Danny Yatom brought me an intelligence report with evidence that Arafat's Palestinian Authority was planning for wide-scale violence after Friday prayers, in protest over Sharon's visit. Danny called Dennis Ross. Madeleine Albright called Arafat, to urge him to ensure this didn't happen. But as Dennis would remark later, "Arafat didn't lift a finger to stop it."

The trouble began the next day, shortly after Friday prayers. It was also the eve of the Jewish New Year, and the Western Wall area was crowded. As people poured out of the mosques, a number began hurling stones, some of them the size of small boulders, onto the Jewish worshippers and police below. One knocked out the highly experienced, steady-handed commander of the Jerusalem police, which I'm sure contributed to making the confrontation that followed even worse. By the end of the day, dozens of Israelis and Palestinians were injured. Five Palestinians lay dead. Though the media almost instantly labeled it a new "intifada," this one was very different. It was not a burst of anger, however misdirected, by stone-throwing youths convinced that a road accident in Gaza had been something more sinister. There had been no serious unrest on the day of Arik's visit. We would later learn this was a deliberate campaign, waged with guns and grenades, by Hamas and Islamic Jihad, the Fatah offshoot Tanzim, and Arafat's own police force.

The media had changed, too, in the thirteen years since the first intifada, with the rise of 24/7 news broadcasters, including the Arabic-language Al Jazeera. Images of pain and suffering and fear stoked anger on both sides. None, in the first days of the violence, was more powerful, or heartrending, than the picture of a terrified twelve-year-old Palestinian boy named Mohammed al-Durrah, sheltered by his father as they took cover from the cross fire in Gaza. The facts of the incident, as best we could establish immediately afterward, were that the Palestinian security forces had opened fire on Israeli troops near the settlement of Netzarim. Ten Palestinians, including the little boy, lost their lives when the soldiers returned fire. We later established with near certainty that the boy had in fact been killed by *Palestinian* gunfire. But even if we'd been able to prove that at the time, I'm sure that in the increasingly poisonous atmosphere, it would have made little difference.

Nor would it have changed the next, deeply disturbing escalation: the spread of the violence into Israel itself, with unprecedentedly serious clashes between our own Arab citizens and the police in the Galilee, in Wadi Ara, in the main mixed Arab-Jewish cities, and in the Negev. Beyond the political implications, the demonstrations of solidarity with the Palestinian violence presented a security challenge of a different order: to the ability of the Israeli police, and by extension the government, to ensure basic law and order inside our borders. The worst of the clashes lasted barely a week. But they left thirteen Arab Israeli protesters dead, sparking demonstrations as far afield as Jaffa as well as ugly incidents of mob violence by Israeli Jews against Arabs in some areas.

President Clinton tried his best to help us halt the violence on the West Bank and in Gaza. I doubted the Americans would succeed, but I was fully ready to join in their efforts. About ten days into the new intifada, I attended a crisis meeting with Arafat, mediated by Madeleine Albright and Dennis Ross, at the US ambassador's residence in Paris. It was nominally under the aegis of French president Jacques Chirac, but the understanding was that Madeleine would be in charge. Far from showing any willingness to end the violence, Arafat at first simply lied. He said the Palestinian violence was in response to an unprovoked assault by Israeli troops and demanded an international "protection" force. There was a particularly bizarre moment when I read out the names of individual Tanzim leaders whom we had intercepted organizing the attacks. Arafat pretended he'd never heard of any of them, almost as if I was reading from a zoology textbook about species of polar bears. This was a man who had been awarded the Nobel Peace Prize. What he really deserved was an Oscar.

Terror had to be confronted. I ordered Mofaz to make sure we took all necessary steps to respond, and we did so. But people were *dying*. Needlessly. We ended up agreeing to a US-led fact-finding commission, as well as a number of steps to separate the Palestinian attackers and Israeli units. I reaffirmed our policy of insisting that Israeli soldiers use live fire only if they felt their lives were under threat. Arafat undertook to order his security forces and Tanzim not to participate in the violence. He even phoned Gaza with what we were given to understand were explicit orders. But it was all for show, as we discovered when we were invited to the Elysée Palace to meet Chirac. The French president had clearly received advance word from Arafat about his demand for an international "protection" force, presumably with a role for the French. To my surprise and frustration, and Secretary Albright's as well, Chirac insisted that no agreement was acceptable without that happening. Then he turned to me, demanding to know why the violence had left nearly 400 Palestinians dead, but barely two-dozen Israelis, if the Palestinians were the aggressors. "Mr. President," I said, "just several weeks ago we were prepared to go very far in order to put this entire conflict behind us. It is Mr. Arafat who rejected the proposal, even as a basis for negotiations. Just a *basis* to seek peace. He then deliberately turned to terror. We are protecting ourselves, and our soldiers. Are you really saying that you'll be happy for us to agree to end it only when another three hundred and fifty Israelis are killed? I'm not playing that game. Arafat started this. He has to stop it. We know he can, and we hold him responsible if that does not happen."

It did not happen, and on the evening of October 7, I delivered an ultimatum: "If we don't see a change in the patterns of violence in the next two days, we will regard this as a cessation by Arafat of the peace process." That did, briefly, have an effect. When Clinton reinforced my message later in the day, Dennis told me that for the first time, he sensed that Arafat realized he had to act. But if so, it didn't translate to any major change on the ground. And with an appalling act of murder three days later, it was too late.

That outrage came in Ramallah. Two Israeli reservists took a wrong turn and ended up driving into the town. They were taken to the Palestinian police station. Hundreds of people broke in and stabbed them, gouged out their eyes, and disemboweled them. In a chilling image broadcast around the world, one of the murderers brandished the blood-stained palms of his hands in a gesture of triumph. Since I was defense minister as well, I spent the hours that followed in the kirya. I was furious. Though it was clear the murderers had by now fled, I issued an order for all of them to be pursued and, no matter how long it took us, brought to justice. Or, if that wasn't possible, killed. I also ordered attack helicopters into action for the first time, though with advance warning to local Palestinians in the areas we targeted. We destroyed the Ramallah police station, as well as a militia base near Arafat's headquarters in Gaza.

As Israelis took in what had happened in Ramallah, it is hard to say which emotion was more powerful: disgust or fury. There were growing calls for us to hit back with the full force of the Israeli army—though no suggestion from politicians, the media, or even our military and security professionals of any specific steps, beyond what we were already doing, that were likely to prove more effective in bringing the violence to an end. When Clinton asked me to join him, Arafat, King Abdullah of Jordan, and UN secretary-general Kofi Annan for a summit in Sharm el-Sheikh, I of course agreed. But I doubted it would produce any practical results, and sadly, it didn't: just boilerplate promises from Arafat that, within only days, turned out to be hollow. The Palestinian attacks intensified, and we responded. The only, brief, lull came when Arafat feared the Americans would cancel his scheduled visit to Washington to see Clinton on November 9. I was due to follow him three days later.

I met Clinton and Dennis Ross over dinner in a little kitchen area attached to the Oval Office, and both seemed surprisingly upbeat. The president said he'd told Arafat the broad points that would be in the new American negotiating paper. It was Camp David–plus. Assuming all issues in a final peace were agreed, the Palestinians would now end up, after a land swap near Gaza, with a "mid-90-percent" share of the West Bank. On Jerusalem, the guiding principle would be "what is Arab will be Palestinian, and what is Jewish, Israeli." On the Temple Mount, the Haram al-Sharif, each side would have control of its own holy sites. Finally, though Palestinian refugees would be free to return in unlimited numbers to a new Palestinian state, there would be no right of return to pre-1967 Israel. The president told me that after he'd run all this by Arafat, he and Dennis had asked whether "in principle" these were parameters he could accept. Arafat had said yes.

I assume they expected a response from me as well. But I told them I couldn't give them one. What concerned me now was the violence. Until it was reined in, I would not be party to rewarding Arafat diplomatically. I urged the Americans to make ending the violence their focus as well, because if they didn't get tougher on Arafat's noncompliance with anything resembling a de-escalation, Israel would do so.

+ + +

Since the Knesset had returned before my trip to Washington, I'd needed first to make sure my government would survive. The obvious, or at least the most mathematically secure, choice would have been a deal with Sharon. Especially since the lynching in Ramallah, there were calls from politicians on all sides for a unity coalition between Labor and Likud. Arik definitely wanted in. The main issue remained the peace process. I didn't find Arik's specific objections to Camp David hard to deal with. As I'd said from the start, the failure to reach an agreement at the summit meant that any concessions I'd considered were null and void. The package Arafat had ultimately rejected had not even been presented by

me. It was an American proposal. Besides, it was obvious no serious negotiations were going to happen anyway for the foreseeable future. Arik,
however, said he wanted not just a "full divorce" from Camp David. He
insisted we formally declare an end to the entire Oslo process.

I told him that was a price I was not prepared to pay for his support.
Despite the failure of the summit—and the terrible human cost on both
sides from Arafat's choice of violence over diplomacy—there was a wide
international recognition that it was the Palestinians, not Israel, who were
responsible. For us to end the Oslo process meant inviting accusations
we'd never intended to reach a peace agreement in the first place, and that
it was *Israel* that was closing the door. We would also risk forfeiting
the American support we'd secured by our efforts to reach a peace deal,
an asset all Israeli governments would benefit from in other circumstances
and contexts in the future.

More than a few people around me urged me to bring Arik into the
coalition anyway. None was more insistent than my old friend Yasha
Kedmi, the burly and ebullient Russian immigrant I'd had under my
company command in the War of Attrition and with me on my tank at
the Chinese Farm in the 1973 war. He had got to know Arik shortly after
arriving from the Soviet Union and had become both an adviser on all
things Russian, and a friend of his, over the years. With me as well. In
fact, he'd been a great help to me during my election campaign. He was
convinced that, especially given the remote prospects for a renewal of the
peace process and the security challenge the country faced, Arik would
prove a reliable partner, as well as strengthening the position of my government. To this day, Yasha, and a number of other friends, believe that
saying no to Sharon at the time was a major political miscue. In retrospect, they were probably right, but I thought differently at the time.

Still, I had an alternative, however potentially fragile, to a coalition
with the Likud. Alarmed at the prospect of having Sharon in the government, the Oslo-era doves in Labor, led by Yossi Beilin, worked out a
new deal with Shas. The Sephardi Orthodox party was still not prepared
to rejoin the cabinet, but it did promise a "safety net" in the Knesset to
ensure we would not have to worry about no-confidence votes while confronting the Palestinian violence. I knew Shas's support might waver. Yet
as Clinton continued to insist we make one final attempt to get a peace

deal, skeptical though I remained about the prospects, I wasn't prepared to put Israel in the position of appearing to stonewall his efforts. Though the Palestinian campaign of violence was getting worse, I authorized Shlomo Ben-Ami, Gili Sher, Amnon Lipkin, and Yossi Ginossar to stay in contact with the Palestinian negotiators.

By late November, I believed that the chances of a peace agreement with Arafat were so microscopic as to border on nonexistent; my own prospects for retaining sufficient support to be an effective prime minister much beyond Clinton's departure were not much better. It was not just Arik and the Likud, but other parties on the right that were actively attempting to bring down the government. I was being squeezed politically: by opposition to the concessions, especially on Jerusalem, I'd been willing to consider in pursuit of a peace agreement, and by the ever-worsening Palestinian violence. Shlomo Ben-Ami put it best, saying that in the view of most Israelis, "Arafat's response to Camp David was not peace, it was an intifada."

The irony was that the military and security response that we put in place was proving effective, if not in ending the campaign of Palestinian violence, then at least in limiting the number of Israeli casualties. By the time I left office, a total of thirty-nine Israeli lives would be lost. Every one of them was a painful tragedy. Every one of them was one too many. In the year that followed, however, five hundred would be killed. Still, I recognized that this was scant consolation amid the prevailing national mood of anger and frustration.

There were five separate motions of no-confidence working their way through the Knesset. I could have quashed them all at a single stroke, since Arik, both publicly and privately, was conveying to me his continuing interest in joining a unity coalition. But I again decided against it. Nor was I ultimately prepared to take another obvious way out, by insisting that any early election be not just for a new prime minister but for a new Knesset, something very few sitting Knesset members wanted to see happen. I recognized that to bring down the Knesset along with me would be unfair to the country, not to mention my own Labor Party, which still had the largest number of parliamentary seats. In pursuing my peace efforts with Hafez al-Assad, and at Camp David, I'd insisted I was acting on the mandate I'd received in the prime ministerial election. If the peace efforts had failed, or if a significant part of the country felt I was wrong to have tried in the way I did, surely the responsibility for that, too, should fall on me.

I remained confident I had been right to make the efforts with Arafat, with Assad, and, of course, to have followed through on my pledge to withdraw our troops from Lebanon. But believing that you are right, even if later events might bear you out, was not all that mattered in politics. You had to be able to bring the public with you. It was clear my support was ebbing away, most frustratingly for me from my former campaign allies on the left. Looking ahead to the challenges Israel would face during Clinton's final period in office and afterward, I knew I could not go further without seeking a fresh mandate from the country, however unlikely the prospects now seemed.

Deciding to do so was a decision that was probably easier for me than for other politicians. Privileged though I felt as prime minister to be able to pursue what I felt deeply were Israel's national interests, the trappings of office were not that important to me. I'd gone into politics to *do* things, not for the photo opportunities. I still believed it was important to see the final diplomatic push by Clinton through to its end. But I knew an early election for prime minister wouldn't happen overnight. It would involve a couple of months' preparation.

+ + +

When I called a news conference on December 9, the media, and the country, assumed that it was about the Palestinian violence and the ups and downs of the Clinton initiative, and I did talk about both. But at the end, I said, "There are those who doubt the mandate I received from the citizens of Israel. I have decided to seek a new mandate—to lead the State of Israel on the road to security, peace, and a proper civic and social agenda." I said I would go see the Israeli president the following morning. "I will formally resign, and run for a special election, at the head of the Labor Party, for the prime ministership of Israel."

The election was set for February 2001. The last act in President Clinton's attempt at a breakthrough actually came after the American election, and just a month before George W. Bush would succeed him. In practical terms, any final agreement would now almost certainly be impossible before inauguration day, so Clinton's final negotiating paper was framed as a set of parameters that, if agreed to by both sides, were intended to set the stage for a final deal. On December 23, Clinton presented the draft to both sides' representatives at the White House.

The president emphasized that this was no longer the starting point for further argument on the basic shape of a peace deal. This was his considered judgment of what would constitute a fair agreement. He was presenting it on a take-it-or-leave-it basis. If either side said no, he would withdraw it, and it would not be binding on President George W. Bush.

He proceeded to lay out his proposal. It now envisaged the Palestinians ending up with between 95 and 97 percent of the West Bank. Israel's military presence in the Jordan Valley would be for a maximum of six years, after which our soldiers would be replaced by an international force. On refugees, the solution Clinton proposed would "make it clear there is no specific right of return to Israel itself" but recognize "the aspiration of the Palestinian people to return to the area." He proposed a joint endorsement by Israel and the Palestinians of the right of refugees to return to a new Palestinian state. In Jerusalem, Arafat would have sovereignty over the entirety of the Old City except for the Jewish Quarter and, of course, the Western Wall and the "holy space of which it is a part." Finally, the president said, this would be a *final* peace: an end of conflict and, once implemented, an end to any further claims. He wanted replies from Israel and the Palestinians within five days. Dennis Ross added that, while both sides could come back with reservations, if any of these fell outside the substantive limits of President Clinton's parameters, the response would be interpreted as a "no" and our search for an agreement would be over.

Clinton's latest proposals went beyond even what I was willing to have him keep in his pocket at Camp David. Opposition politicians in Israel, and even a few of our cabinet ministers, promptly objected to the formula for Jerusalem. I told the critics that I too would have preferred to say no to Clinton's ideas on Jerusalem. Or to say "yes, but" and proceed to insist on fundamental changes. Yet, as Dennis had made clear to both sides, that would have placed Israel in the position of rejecting the entire Clinton paper, something I was not prepared to do.

I sent word to the president that we accepted his ideas. We did raise reservations—nearly thirty in all. But none fell outside his parameters for a peace agreement. At first Arafat asked the Americans for more time. Then he went to Washington to see Clinton. There, he presented his "reservations." They were not just outside the Clinton parameters: they rejected outright two key elements. Arafat said there could be no Israeli sovereignty over the Western Wall of the ancient temple. Nor would he agree to any compromise on the right of return.

So that was his final answer. As one Palestinian leader remarked to me amid the still-escalating terror attacks a couple of years later, the Palestinians had "needed a Ben-Gurion, but we got an Arafat." He didn't mean Ben-Gurion the Zionist, but the statesman who at crucial moments like the partition vote in 1947 could give up his maximalist hopes and dreams in order to secure a better future for his people. Arafat felt much more comfortable, more secure, when the suicide bombers were calling the tune. Then he could whip up the crowds with promises of "marching on Jerusalem" or jet around the world telling everyone that Israel was denying his right to a state.

+ + +

We now knew an agreement was impossible. For many on the Israeli left, my ostensible allies in the forthcoming election campaign against Arik, that was hard to accept. Particularly for Yossi Sarid of Meretz, and to a certain extent Yossi Beilin too, as a key figure in the original Oslo process, the only explanation for our failure to get a deal had to be that we hadn't negotiated well enough. The idea that Arafat didn't want a two-state peace was anathema to them. So was the political platform I said that I hoped to implement if I was reelected as prime minister. Maybe, at some point in the future, a negotiated peace would be possible. But for now, I believed we had to move on, both in order to keep the situation on the ground from getting worse and to act in Israel's own long-term political and security interests. I said we should unilaterally disengage from most of the West Bank and Gaza.

The idea was straightforward. The Palestinians' unwillingness to accept even the final Clinton parameters, driven home with murderous ferocity by the explosion of violence, should not be allowed to paralyze Israel politically. While reserving the right of our army to continue to operate anyplace, anywhere, in order to forestall or confront terror attacks,

I proposed that we delineate a disengagement line that would meet our fundamental security needs as well as ensure a solid and stable overall Jewish majority within the territory we retained. We would keep our area around the major settlement blocs, as well as the outer East Jerusalem suburbs; a further security strip along the Jordan River; and several other strategically important points. In all, that would mean retaining control of around 20 percent of the West Bank, yet without any of the major Arab towns or cities. Though deliberately stopping well short of the share of the West Bank Arafat could have secured through a negotiated peace, it would remove Israeli troops and settlers from most of the territory. It would give the Palestinians ample room to set up a state if they so chose, and conceivably to expand its area if some future Palestinian leader had more of the "Ben-Gurion" in him. Until then, it would allow both of our peoples to get on with their lives and focus on their own political, social, and economic challenges.

There was a second, critically important part to what I proposed: the construction of a physical security fence along the new "disengagement line" with the West Bank. It was the suggestion rejected under Rabin, accepted under Peres amid the Hamas bombings in the 1996 election campaign, but never followed through on. Even under the new arrangement I envisaged, Israeli troops would retain the freedom of action to respond to, or preempt, terror attacks with targeted operations inside the West Bank. But the physical barrier would hugely increase our ability to halt the attackers before they could strike.

Even if I'd been able to bring those on the political left behind the plan, this election campaign would be a lot tougher than in 1999. Since Knesset members weren't running for their seats, the Labor machine lacked its usual incentive to put up posters, knock on doors, or get out the vote. Arik, however, benefited from the enthusiasm of Likudniks and other right-wing activists who saw an opportunity to retake control of Israel's political agenda.

Long before election day, I knew my time as prime minister was up. Before the campaign, an old friend of mine, a leading Israeli journalist, had even tried to talk me into withdrawing. "You're going to lose, Ehud," he said. "Why, after making all this effort for peace, after doing your best, do you want the last act to be losing to Arik?" I'd never seen the objective as just staying in office. If that had been the case, I wouldn't have put the chances of a peace deal with Syria to their final test. I wouldn't have gone to Camp David. I also would have accepted Arik's serial offers to join a unity coalition. But never in my life had I walked away from a challenge. I certainly wasn't going to retreat in the midst of Palestinian violence, and when Israel still faced key decisions on how to move on from Arafat's unreadiness to negotiate an end to our decades-old conflict.

I did regret being unable to rely on the support of two key constituencies that had helped deliver my landslide victory barely eighteen months earlier: my own Labor Party and the Arab citizens of Israel. I had no trouble understanding one major reason that many Israeli Arabs were abandoning me. The clashes in the Galilee at the start of the new intifada had left more than a dozen of their community dead. As an official inquiry would later conclude, there was blame on all sides. A number of Arab members of the Knesset had played a part in inciting the violence. Yet the police had been unprepared, and they had used excessive force. As I said publicly before the election, I, as prime minister, was ultimately responsible, and I formally expressed my sorrow for what had happened. Yet the roots went deeper, to the economic and social disadvantages still faced by many Arab citizens, and the difficulty in resolving those problems calmly and collectively as long as Israel remained in a state of war with its Arab neighbors.

For many in Labor and others on the political left, it was as if, despite Arafat's repeated rejections of ever more forthcoming terms of peace, they couldn't bring themselves to believe he really meant it. So by default, I was to blame for not delivering peace. I was accused of relying too much on a close circle of aides and negotiators I'd known from my time in the army, of not giving a negotiating role to Labor veterans of the Oslo negotiations like Yossi Beilin, and of being insufficiently sensitive to Arafat's needs in the negotiating process. Typical of the argument was a broadside by the journalist and historian Tom Segev, in *Haaretz*, which accused me of an "incredible arrogance" that had "led to an historic mistake. Rather than continue on the Oslo road, Barak put it into his head that he could reach a final settlement and try and impose it on the Palestinian Authority President." The truth was that I did not try to "impose" anything on Arafat. I was indeed openly critical of some aspects of the "Oslo road" because it was inexorably leading to a situation where, after the final Wye redeployments, Arafat would have control over the great majority of the West Bank *without* having to commit to any of the assurances that even most on the Israeli left would define as the minimum required for peace. Now, of course, we knew that was something the Palestinian leader was not prepared to do.

When election day came, not that many on the left actually voted against me. Nor did the Israeli Arabs. Rather, in large numbers, they simply didn't vote. In percentage terms, Arik's victory was even more decisive than mine over Bibi. He got more than 62 percent of the vote, while I received barely 37 percent. But the turnout was the lowest in Israeli history. Arik received *fewer* votes than I had in 1999. Around half of the 1.8 million people who had supported me stayed at home.

I conceded defeat after the first exit polls and announced that I would be stepping down as head of the Labor Party. Still, since the election had been only for prime minister, Labor remained the largest party in the Knesset. Mathematically, Arik might be able to cobble together the required sixty-one-seat majority with an assortment of smaller parties. But without Labor as ballast, his government would be even more precarious than mine. When I triggered the election, he'd let it be known that if he won, he hoped to include Labor in his government, with me as his defense minister. Even though I'd announced I was stepping aside, he phoned me the morning after the election to make that argument again. He said Israel needed a strong government, especially to confront the escalating violence. Having a person with my background, whom he knew well and trusted, in the defense portfolio was important. I didn't say yes. Unfortunately, I failed to do what I should have done: I didn't immediately say no.

When the public learned about Sharon's interest in a unity government, Labor descended into bickering. Some of my former ministers were against the idea of joining any Likud-led government. Most of Labor's central committee did seem in favor of joining. But given the scale of my election defeat, many wanted to do so without me. The bottom line was that I soon realized the idea of joining the new government was unworkable, and I publicly confirmed that I would indeed resign.

Several weeks after Arik formed his government—including Labor, with Shimon Peres as one of four deputy prime ministers—he invited me to his office. He wanted to ask my views on a sensitive security question. That took barely fifteen minutes. But I raised another issue that I argued would have more far-reaching implications. It was the idea of building the security fence around the major portion of the West Bank. I'd tried to make the case for doing so during the election campaign, and I'd lost the election. "Now I'm turning to you. When I left office, thirty-nine Israelis had been killed in this new intifada. Now, there are *seventy*. When the number reaches seven hundred, there's no doubt you'll decide to build this fence. But to your dying day, you won't be able to look yourself in the mirror and explain why you waited for another six hundred and thirty Israelis to die first."

He did eventually start building it, but by then more than five hundred further lives had been lost, and Israel had been hit by an act of terror that, even by the standards of this still-escalating intifada, was truly obscene. In March 2002, suicide bombers murdered thirty people, mostly elderly, as they were celebrating the annual Passover Seder in a hotel dining room in Netanya. Arik hit back two days later with Israel's largest military operation on the West Bank since 1967. Israeli forces retook major Palestinian towns, placed Arafat under de facto siege in his headquarters in Ramallah, and imposed curfews and closures. In June, the government formally approved the security fence. Another year would pass, and a further five hundred Israelis would be killed, before the major part of the barrier was in place. Only then did the number of casualties begin to fall.

I tried to steer clear of public criticism of Arik's government. One of the lessons I'd learned as prime minister was how easy it was to second-guess from the outside. No prime minister can act exactly as he might plan or want to. The most you can do is make sure you understand and analyze the issues and follow your instincts, experience, and conscience to come as near as possible to doing what you believe is right. You will inevitably make mistakes and misjudgments. I certainly did. At least some of the criticism I received was deserved. I was at times too inflexible. I was less good at schmoozing with—or, perhaps more importantly, delegating to—others in the government or the party. I suspect it's no coincidence that the man who brought me into government in the first place was often criticized for the same things. By character, instinct, and experience, Rabin too remained less a politician than a military man. Yet toward the end of his second period as prime minister, he did get better at delegating to people around him and creating an atmosphere that encouraged teamwork, even when he knew he could not accept or act on everything they might suggest. During my term as prime minister, I was much less good at that.

But another thing Yitzhak and I shared was a determination to set specific goals and do everything possible to achieve them. I promised to get the army out of Lebanon. With the Palestinians, I arrived in office convinced that the process begun in Oslo was both a huge opportunity and a potential dead end. I was determined to focus on the end goal: initially, at least, a framework agreement, and over time a final resolution of our conflict. Ever since the outbreak of the Palestinians' first intifada, I believed this was as much in Israel's own interest as theirs. Yet when I entered office, we also had clear intelligence that a new and more violent intifada might not be far off. And we still had no way of knowing whether *Arafat* was ready for an agreement under which two states would live side by side in peace. I felt it was my duty to find out, and, if the answer was yes, to put an agreement in place that delivered real peace and also safeguarded Israel's core national and security interests. I felt the same way about Syria and Hafez al-Assad.

When I left office, I believed I had achieved the most important goals of my premiership. We were out of Lebanon. Though we couldn't achieve the peace agreements I had hoped for, it was not for lack of trying. Nor had I neglected the parallel imperative: to make sure our army and security services were prepared for a new campaign of Palestinian violence. Along the way, Israel had succeeded in demonstrating to the world that it was able and willing to consider painful compromises, and that it was the Arab leaders who, at least for now, were unequal to the challenge of making peace. If I'd been able to retain the backing of the voters who made me prime minister in 1999, we might even have moved ahead on unilateral disengagement from the Palestinians, dramatically altering the trajectory of our relationship. Yet even without that, Camp David did delineate the terms of any future peace arrangement. When and if conditions allowed a resumption of serious negotiating efforts, the shape, and indeed most of the details, of a final peace between our peoples were now clear.

I was on holiday in the summer of 2001 when Bill Clinton phoned me. The *New York Times* had run a piece on how and why the summit, and the subsequent negotiations through the end of the year, ended in failure. When I later read the article, by Pulitzer Prize–winning reporter Deborah Sontag, I found it a meandering mix of opinions garnered from an assortment of Americans, Europeans, Israelis, and Palestinians, including Arafat himself, with the overall conclusion that Clinton and I had not offered as generous a deal as was assumed and that it was somehow unfair to suggest the Palestinians deserved blame for rejecting it. There had been several other articles in various publications along the same lines. I didn't see much point at this stage in setting the record straight. To the extent the content of the *Times* piece bothered me, it was a simple, but important, error of fact. Quoting Arafat himself, Sontag wrote that during the back-patio discussion I had with him at the dinner in Kochav Yair shortly before the new intifada, he'd "implored me to block Mr. Sharon's plans" to go to the Temple Mount. In fact, Arafat hadn't raised the issue at all, and he presumably knew that we had liaised with his own West Bank security chief in an effort to prevent the visit from becoming a catalyst, or in this case a pretext, for violence.

Yet the revisionist history about our peace efforts left Clinton not just frustrated, but genuinely puzzled. What the hell were these people talking about? he asked me. Why were they missing the forest for the trees? "The true story of Camp David," he said, "was that for the first time in the history of the conflict, you and I, the prime minister of Israel and the president of the United States, placed on the table a proposal, based on Resolutions 242 and 338, very close to the Palestinian demands. And Arafat refused to accept it as a basis of negotiations, walked out of the room, and even turned to terrorism." All the rest, President Clinton said, was gossip.

All of it was now irrelevant, too. His parameters were off the table. Palestinian violence against Israelis was getting ever deadlier. And I was out of politics. When I delivered my final remarks to a Labor Party meeting, I was asked whether I was leaving politics for good. I replied that I would always remain a member of Labor. But I saw my role as a bit like when I'd left the army. "I'm a reserve officer," I said, adding that I hoped I would not be called back to duty anytime soon.

# Voice for the Defense

I HAD ONLY A GENERAL IDEA OF WHAT I WOULD DO NEXT. "SOME-thing in business" describes it best. But I sought the advice of a friend who, rather than leaving politics, had just entered it. Colin Powell was now the second President Bush's secretary of state. "Why don't you go on the lecture circuit?" he said. The short answer was that it hadn't oc-curred to me that I'd be any good at it. But it turned out to be energizing and interesting both for me and, it seemed, the audiences I spoke to. It was also lucrative. I'd deliver four lectures in a week and end up making two times what, until that point in my life, I had earned during a full year. I was also invited onto a number of company boards. I turned down those that even appeared to present a conflict of interest. But I did get involved in an area where I believed my range of experiences, along with my firsthand grasp of geopolitics, might be relevant: high-level in-vestment decisions and venture capital.

The result of this activity was a dramatic change in lifestyle. Nava and I got to spend more time with our daughters. We vacationed overseas for the first time. We also decided to build a new home, and the place that we chose gave me my first experience of how far I was from being a "pri-vate citizen" in the eyes of the Israeli public. When it became known we were planning to move to Kfar Shmaryahu near Tel Aviv, one of the wealthiest places in Israel, all hell broke loose. How *could* you? I was asked. I couldn't resist joking that I just wanted to be close to my voters.

Likud supporters were about as rare in Kfar Shmaryahu as panhandlers. Along with Mishmar Hasharon, it was the only place where I'd polled around 80 percent even in my election loss to Sharon.

Israel had changed dramatically from the kibbutz-centered pioneer society of my youth. Greater Tel Aviv, in particular, was thriving economically, and the rising crop of millionaires, whether from traditional business or in the burgeoning technology sector, included its fair share of former kibbutzniks. Still, socially and culturally, a puritanical streak remained, a sense that there was something not quite right about people raised on a socialist ideal becoming personally well-off. Not to mention that I had been head of the Labor Party. And prime minister. While I understood why people felt this way, I found much of the personal criticism unfair. I had devoted more than four decades of my life to serving my country. I'd behaved with scrupulous honesty while in office, and was avoiding any business involvement that could present a conflict now that I'd left. I saw nothing wrong with earning money through honest endeavor, and using the proceeds to provide economic security for myself and my family, and to give our grandchildren a better start in life than Nava's or my own parents had been able to do.

In the end, we didn't move to Kfar Shmaryahu because of an even more profound change in my life: I separated from Nava, after more than thirty years together. When we had begun plans to move, I laughed off a warning from a psychologist friend that decisions like building a new house could lead to a deeper reassessment of your life. But that is at least in part what happened. There were also other changes that caused me to stop and take stock. My father had passed away soon after I left office. Professionally, I was exploring new areas and developing new interests. Nava and I had been happily married since our twenties. We had three wonderful daughters, and a first grandchild. Yet the more I thought about where we were in our lives, the more I felt our future paths were pulling us in different directions. The separation was difficult, though at least Nava knew that it had nothing to do with another woman, or another relationship. I did imagine that I might one day meet someone else, but was equally prepared for that not happening. I certainly didn't expect it anytime soon.

A few weeks after our separation, I was visiting the Knesset for a discussion about fixing Israel's broken electoral system. In the audience was a member of one of the civic associations pressing for reform: Nili Priell, who, as a young Nili Sonkin, had been my first, and only, serious girlfriend before I met Nava. We spoke for a few minutes afterward. We agreed to meet again, and catch up with each other's lives, a week or so later. Both of us now had grown children. Since she was divorced, we were both on our own. There is, I assume for everyone, something impossible to replicate about a first love. Nili and I were given an unlikely second chance. That seemed to me an extraordinary gift. It still does.

Yet if my personal life seemed full of new promise, the same could not be said of the country I'd served for my whole adult life, or of the political party I'd led into government. The continuing construction of the security fence along the West Bank did slightly reduce the *number* of Palestinian attacks: from nearly fifty in 2002 to about half that in 2003. But not the human toll they claimed. The suicide bombers who did get through—from Hamas, Islamic Jihad, and Fatah's Al-Aqsa Martyrs' Brigade—struck wherever they could inflict the most terror and death: at bus stations, on buses, in shopping centers, restaurants, and cafés. Over a twelve-month period, beginning with a bombing of Tel Aviv's main bus station at the beginning of January 2003, they murdered 145 men, women, and children. It would not be until two years later, when the West Bank fence was nearing completion, that the attacks, and the deaths, were finally brought down dramatically.

The Labor Party had finally left Arik Sharon's coalition in late 2002. But in Israel's 2003 election—reverting to the old rules again, with a single vote for party and prime minister—Arik and the Likud won resoundingly. They doubled their Knesset seats, to thirty-eight. Labor, now with only nineteen seats, again turned to Shimon Peres as interim party leader.

I didn't miss the political limelight. But by mid-2004, with the first sign of a major change in policy toward the Palestinians, I felt I had a contribution to make. What first prompted me to dip my toes back into politics were the ever more obvious signs throughout 2004 that Arik Sharon's coalition, and his hold on the Likud, were unraveling. Part of his problem was a steady drumbeat of corruption allegations around Arik and his two sons, Omri and Gilad. But he also seemed to be undergoing a welcome political conversion, to the need for a more profound political "disengagement" from the Palestinians, something I'd long advocated. He had endorsed President George W. Bush's "road map" for resuming the peace process. Yet with Yasir Arafat aging, ailing, and even less inclined to consider the difficult decisions he had shirked at Camp David, Arik went one, dramatic step further. He raised the idea of unilaterally withdrawing Israeli forces and settlements from Gaza—ensuring a showdown with the rank and file of the Likud and other parties on the right. His main Likud rival, very much back in frontline Israeli politics, was his finance minister: Bibi Netanyahu. Though Bibi remained on board until the last moment, and actually voted in favor of the pullout, he dramatically resigned from the cabinet in August 2005, a week before it happened, declaring: "I am not prepared to be a partner to a move which ignores reality, and proceeds blindly toward turning the Gaza Strip into a base for Islamic terrorism which will threaten the state."

To this day, Bibi, along with many Israelis across the political spectrum, draws a direct line between our pullout from Gaza, Hamas's takeover and its violent purging of Fatah's old guard, and the periodic wars we've had to fight since then in response to Hamas rocket fire into Israel. The moral: Arik was wrong to withdraw. But the Islamists' ascendancy was happening anyway. It was Hamas attacks that had provided the spearhead in the campaign of violence following Camp David. Arafat's own influence was also inexorably on the wane by the time he passed away, in Paris, at the end of 2004, to be succeeded by Abu Mazen.

I do not know of a single senior figure in Israel with any military experience who believes that we would be more secure today if we still had thousands of soldiers and settlers inside Gaza. Arik's security judgment was the right one. I was also encouraged by his parallel announcement of a small, token withdrawal from a few small settlements in the northern part of the West Bank. My regret was that he did not go further toward the kind of major West Bank disengagement I'd been arguing for, and that the Gaza pullout was insufficiently thought out. On a political and diplomatic level, I believed we should have followed the model of our troop withdrawal from Lebanon—involving detailed prior consultation with, and political support from, the UN and key international allies. I also felt it was important to ensure that, while we would obviously need offshore patrols to prevent arms and munitions from getting in, we allowed and encouraged an environment in which the Gazan economy could function and grow after we left. Though we left Gaza, we effectively sealed off and blockaded one of the most densely populated, economically strapped, and politically febrile strips of land on the face of the earth.

Still, it was an important first step toward the kind of wider disengagement that would prioritize Israel's own security interests, and political and social cohesiveness, until and unless conditions allowed for a serious new effort for a final peace deal. I was heartened when Shimon led Labor back into Arik's coalition at the start of 2005 to ensure he'd have the support necessary to go through with the Gaza withdrawal. And while I did make a brief attempt to return as party leader later in the year, when it was clear I wasn't going to win, I threw my support behind Shimon and against longtime labor union leader Amir Peretz, who was running on a platform to take Labor out of Sharon's government.

But Peretz won the leadership election and followed through on his pledge to leave the cabinet, forcing Arik to call an early election for March 2006. That, and the most ambitious and ill-fated Israeli war in Lebanon since 1982, was the reason I ultimately found myself back in the Israeli government.

+ + +

On July 12, 2006, Hizbollah fired rockets from southern Lebanon as cover for an ambush of two Israeli Humvees on our side of the border. Two soldiers were killed, and two others abducted. A few hours later, when an Israeli armored unit crossed to look for the kidnapped soldiers, an explosive charge blew up one of our tanks, killing four of its crew members.

Arik Sharon was no longer prime minister by then. With Bibi marshaling opposition inside the Likud to the Gaza disengagement, he had formed a new centrist party called Kadima, along with prominent Likud moderates and buttressed by a Labor heavyweight: Shimon Peres. But before the election, Arik suffered a pair of strokes and lapsed into a coma from which he would never emerge. His notional deputy, the veteran Likud politician and former Jerusalem mayor Ehud Olmert, suddenly found himself prime minister. Kadima won the May election comfortably, ending up with twenty-nine seats, followed by Labor with nineteen and leaving the Netanyahu-led Likud with only twelve. Olmert formed a coalition, including Labor, which had undeniable political ballast: Shimon was one of his deputy prime ministers, along with Haim Ramon. A gifted lawyer, longtime Likudnik, and strong backer of the Gaza plan, Tzipi Livni, was foreign minister. Amir Peretz, as head of Labor, was given the Defense Ministry. But without Sharon himself at the helm, the government was about to face a military crisis with virtually no military experience around the cabinet table.

Olmert called an emergency cabinet meeting on the evening of the Hizbollah attack, and just before it was due to convene, my phone rang. It was Shimon, with whom I'd become closer of late, especially after I'd supported him in his last Labor leadership contest. "Shalom, Ehud," he said when I answered the phone and, without small talk or preliminaries, asked me, "What do you think we should do?"

I said I couldn't offer specific suggestions without knowing the full details, but I could advise him on the right *process* to follow when the chief of staff, the former air force chief Dan Halutz, briefed the cabinet. "*Push* him," I said. "When he presents his recommended action, ask him for his assessment of what Hizbollah will do in response. When he, or the head of military intelligence, has given you the range of possibilities and told you which is the most likely, say, OK, let's assume that happens. What's our *next* step? How is that going to lead us to our main objectives? And what *are* the objectives?" Newspaper reports the next morning said that Shimon pressed the chief of staff about each further stage of the operation and about the aims that we wanted to accomplish. The reply, the reports suggested, was that once the military operation *got* to the later phases, they could discuss it.

From the first reports I received through my army contacts, I feared the operation would go badly. There was no doubt we could inflict damage on Hizbollah. But there were no clear answers to the questions Shimon had raised. The initial Israeli air force response had been put in place several years earlier, when I was prime minister. Codenamed Operation Cinnamon Sticks, it was designed to take out the fixed Hizbollah missile sites we had been able to identify. We knew its limitations. As in the case of Saddam Hussein's Scud missiles during the Iraq war, a lot of the rockets were fired from mobile launchers. But in one exercise we'd conducted, the known "Hizbollah" sites were replicated in the Galilee. They were destroyed in forty-three minutes. I had no doubt this part of the plan would succeed, and it did. In the early hours of July 13, it took only thirty-four minutes to destroy the nearly sixty launchers whose location our military had pinpointed.

But Operation Cinnamon Sticks was designed as a first step in a far wider assault on Hizbollah and other targets, including major infrastructure installations, deeper inside Lebanon. It was part of a plan for a full-scale war, if the government decided that was necessary. As the early public statements by Olmert and other ministers made clear, they did not intend to start a war—and weren't even aware they were in one, at least at the outset. They didn't mobilize reserves. They didn't formally declare an emergency, much less a war—the two options under Israeli law to facilitate a reserve call-up and other measures during a conflict.

They certainly didn't have a coherent plan. When Hizbollah fired hundreds of missiles at Israeli towns and cities, our operation intensified not by plan or military logic, but improvisation, and the government would soon find itself in Israel's longest single armed conflict since 1948.

I felt it was not appropriate for a former prime minister to criticize Olmert publicly while Israeli troops were in action. Two days in, I told a television interviewer that the government had every right to respond and was doing so effectively. Olmert phoned to thank me. When he, like Shimon, asked what I thought the government should do next, I was straightforward: "Do your best to bring things to an end as soon as you can." I said that Halutz and the other generals would be caught up in the operational details, which made his role and that of the cabinet even more critical. "In any operation, you'll have an idea about what represents a satisfactory exit point. But there will be a temptation, when you get close to that point, to take just one more step, to keep going until you're absolutely sure you've reached it." Resist that temptation, I told him.

In pure military terms, there was a choice that had to be made in responding to the Hizbollah attack: a deliberately limited and fairly brief operation, or a full-scale war with the aim, from the start, of inflicting major, lasting damage on the Shi'ite militia force and the Lebanese state from whose territory it operated. We ended up doing neither. The result was an operation that lasted thirty-four days, nearly twice the length of the Yom Kippur War. Our air force flew 12,000 missions, more than in

1973 and nearly twice as many as in the 1982 Lebanon War. Hizbollah fired about 4,000 rockets into Israel—from a stockpile we estimated to number nearly 14,000—and not just at the border settlements but as far south as Hadera and Haifa, keeping hundreds of thousands of Israelis under effective siege. More than 120 Israeli soldiers and 44 civilians were killed. So were hundreds of Hizbollah fighters and, inevitably, many Lebanese civilians as well, with a predictable surge of criticism from much of the outside world. Only President Bush and Britain's Tony Blair steadfastly reminded the critics of how the war had actually begun.

The one putative victory for Israel was the UN cease-fire resolution that Tzipi Livni helped to negotiate in August. At least on paper, it contained a commitment to a "long-term solution" including the disarmament of Hizbollah and the "unconditional release of the abducted Israeli soldiers, which has given rise to the current crisis." But as Israeli newspapers began speaking to the returning soldiers and officers, a picture emerged not just of a long and difficult war, but a lack of clearly communicated military objectives and an often chaotic chain of command, which ended up costing Israeli lives. Our final advance alone, shortly before the cease-fire, claimed the lives of some thirty soldiers. And for *what*? many Israelis soon asked themselves. One of the newspapers most supportive of the operation at the beginning summed up the feeling of most of the country at the end: "If you don't win, you lose. Hizbollah survived. It won the war."

Without the botched handling of the war, I might well have remained a private citizen. But when the commission of inquiry released its report in April 2007, three people were singled out: Olmert, Amir Peretz, and Halutz. Olmert was portrayed as a military novice who'd gone into battle without understanding the wartime role and responsibilities of a prime minister. Halutz's "excess of charisma" was held responsible for keeping ministers, and military officers as well, from questioning his judgment or pressing him for alternatives. Amir Peretz was found to be the wrong man in the wrong cabinet post at the wrong time. Of the three, only Halutz seemed ready to take personal responsibility. Even before the report came out, he resigned. Olmert and Peretz were determined to stay put, despite calls to quit not just from the opposition but from Tzipi Livni. Inside Labor as well, the war produced a clamor for change. When a vote for party chairman was held in June 2007, I was chosen to return in Peretz's place.

Within days, I replaced him as defense minister as well. The main item in my in-box would not be Lebanon, however. The Mossad had uncovered a threat hundreds of miles farther away: a construction site in northeast Syria along the Euphrates River, where the Syrians, with technical help from North Korea and funding from Iran, were building a nuclear reactor.

+ + +

I had gotten to know Olmert fairly well over the years, initially when I was in the kirya and both he and Dan Meridor, then another rising Likud politician, were members of the Knesset's defense committee. But from the day I returned to the Israeli government in June 2007, tension grew between us over how and when to deal with the Syrian nuclear site. It was not about *whether* we should take military action to destroy the reactor. An immutable, core assumption in Israel's security strategy was the need to retain our ability to deter, and if necessary defeat, our enemies. A nuclear Syria—or Iraq, or Iran—would dramatically alter the balance of power in the region, at obvious risk to Israel. Syria posed a particular threat, as part of an increasingly close alliance with Iran and with Hizbollah in Lebanon.

The question was how and when to strike. Olmert wanted to attack within a few weeks at most. I understood the reasons for his sense of urgency. We obviously had to act before the reactor became operational. In addition, there was always the risk the Syrians would find out that we were aware of their nuclear facility and put their forces on higher alert. But I argued that we needed to think through the plan carefully. The operational challenge was complex. We needed a fail-safe way to destroy the reactor, and we had to do it in such a way as to avoid a full-scale military confrontation with Syria, and probably Hizbollah too, if we could. Neither of those prerequisites was yet in place.

A bit as had happened with the recent Lebanon war, we were facing a choice between two off-the-shelf plans from the kirya. One involved using a large military force and was likely to draw us into a major conflict with Syria. The other was a smaller, targeted operation, but it remained untested and there was no certainty it would destroy the reactor. I knew, from our intelligence people, that we still had time to seek other options. They said that we'd know if the reactor was getting nearer to becoming operational, in which case we would obviously have to choose between the two existing attack plans. But, meanwhile, I ordered intensive work to develop alternative approaches aimed both at ensuring the destruction of the reactor and minimizing the chance of a clash with the Syrians or Hizbollah.

Over the next two months, Olmert got more and more frustrated that we hadn't yet attacked. We held dozens of meetings, sometimes two or three a day, usually chaired by the prime minister, sometimes by me as defense minister. I always began by saying that there was no doubt we had to destroy the reactor—something I felt was particularly important to emphasize because Olmert had begun implying to the few ministers and senior officers involved in our planning that I was actually against an attack. I wasn't. I just wanted to make sure we had the right options in place when the time came to strike.

Finally, in early September 2007, that moment arrived, amid signs from our intelligence reports that the window for an attack was closing. Fortunately, we had two new, much more robust, operational alternatives to choose from when Olmert called the cabinet together to approve the attack. The ministers voted in favor. They left the precise timing to the prime minister, foreign minister, and defense minister: Olmert, Tzipi Livni, and me. The three of us met immediately after the cabinet discussion. Olmert and I both felt that the risk of possible leaks justified attacking that night. Tzipi had certain reservations regarding the attack plan we'd chosen, but I turned to her and said: "We all agree it has to be destroyed. Are you sure you're comfortable with an attack being ordered by Olmert and me, while you chose to abstain?" She thought it over, and added her approval.

We struck just after midnight, in an intricately coordinated air raid that evaded not only a Syrian response, but Syrian notice. The reactor was destroyed. Although even today some details remain subject to Israel's military secrecy regulations, accounts published abroad in the weeks and months that followed painted an accurate picture. In the aftermath of the strike, Israel deliberately made no public comment. We refused to say whether we'd had anything to do with an attack. As we'd hoped, this gave Syrian president Bashar al-Assad both the space and good reason to deny it had happened—in fact, to deny he'd been trying to make a nuclear weapon—and removed any compelling reason for him to retaliate.

+ + +

In the spring of 2008, domestic political issues again took center stage. It became known that the Israeli police were investigating Olmert's relationship with an American businessman named Moshe Talansky. The suggestion, initially in a New York paper and then the Israeli press, was that Olmert had taken bribes. In his first public response, he didn't deny receiving money from Talansky. But he insisted it was all a part of election campaign contributions.

Publicly, I reserved judgment. Privately, I urged him to take a leave of absence and clear his name. Yet with other ministers convinced that would make things worse, I held off doing anything else until there seemed to me no choice, after Talansky gave evidence, as a witness, in Jerusalem's District Court. Though he genuinely seemed not to have expected anything specific in return, he did say that he had given Olmert something like $150,000 in cash. I called a news conference the next day. I didn't say whether I thought Olmert was guilty. I did say that I believed he couldn't continue leading the country while resolving his "personal matters." Things finally came to a head in September 2008. When Kadima held fresh leadership elections, Tzipi Livni won. Olmert confirmed he would step aside for his successor, but under Israeli law, he would remain prime minister until she either succeeded in forming a new government or called early elections. She did try, valiantly, to assemble a new coalition. But Bibi Netanyahu was holding parallel talks with the Orthodox parties that were critical to her assembling a parliamentary majority, in effect telling them that if they held out and he won the next election, they'd be much better off. He was ready to match and raise every assurance of a ministerial seat or budgetary concession Tzipi was prepared to offer. In the end, she threw up her hands, saying she refused to draw out a process that was not so much a negotiation as organized extortion. I am sure she won the respect of many Israelis for taking an all-too-rare stand on principle. She certainly won mine. But I was not alone in wondering whether it was worth the price if Bibi did prevail in an early election and return as prime minister in a Likud-led coalition.

The election was set for February 2009; Olmert would remain in charge until then. We'd long been discussing the increasingly worrying situation in Gaza. After Arik pulled out, an election had placed Hamas in power, after which the Islamists embarked on a violent purge of Fatah loyalists. Arms smuggling through tunnels from the Sinai had become rife. Rockets from Gaza were now landing on southern Israel. Hundreds of thousands of Israelis were living with the reality of a warning siren and a rapid dash into their shelters. For a while, amid negotiations through Egypt to end the rocket fire, we limited ourselves to sending small ground units into Gaza to target the source of specific rocket attacks. But that was always going to have only a limited effect. It also ran the risk of our soldiers being abducted or killed.

Pressure was building for a major military operation. With the election drawing nearer, Bibi reminded voters regularly that he'd been against the pullout from Gaza, and insisted we should now hit Hamas hard. Olmert and Tzipi, and most of the cabinet, were also in favor of military action. I was too. But I held to my view that we first needed a defined mission and a clear plan. Operationally, I told the cabinet, we were perfectly capable of taking over Gaza. But what *then*? Unless we were prepared to resume open-ended Israeli control, we'd be left with no one to run Gaza afterward. The obvious candidate, Egypt, was even less interested than we were in assuming responsibility for the more than 1.5 million Palestinians who lived there. I doubted that even Arafat would have been ready to do so. But relations had only worsened, since his death in 2004, between the Fatah old guard in the Palestinian Authority on the West Bank and the Hamas overlords in Gaza. I doubted very much that Abu Mazen would want to get involved. I did send an aide to see him and ask whether, in principle, he was open to reassuming control of Gaza following an Israeli takeover. His answer was unsurprising and unequivocal: no.

I secured cabinet support for the more limited aim of restoring a period of calm for Israeli citizens in the south. I said the military operation had to be as sharp and short as possible, and end with some kind of political understanding that the rockets would stop for a significant period of time. The final plan was presented to ministers a few days before the operation. It would begin with surprise air strikes and a naval bombardment, followed by a limited ground incursion to hit remaining Hamas targets outside the major refugee camps. The whole operation was intended to last, at the very most, two weeks, with diplomatic efforts through Egypt to secure a lasting cease-fire and, ideally, prevent Hamas from resupplying its rocket stockpiles through its smuggling tunnels from the Sinai.

When we launched Operation Cast Lead on the morning of December 27, nearly all the Hamas forces were where we'd expected them to be. Two waves of air strikes, with over a hundred jets and attack helicopters, killed 350 Hamas fighters and members of its police force. We destroyed Hamas's headquarters and dozens of its government and police installations. The attacks continued in the days that followed. We took a range of actions designed to minimize civilian casualties. We dropped leaflets before bombing sorties and phoned residents to warn people to clear out. We fired light missiles before heavier ordnance was used. Still, I realized that civilian casualties were unavoidable—if only because Hamas, like Hizbollah in Lebanon, deliberately fired its rockets from civilian areas, sometimes even near schools or hospitals. Civilian casualties were obviously tragic in themselves. They also made it inevitable that the longer the operation went on, the more likely we were to face international criticism and diplomatic pressure to bring it to an end. That was an additional reason I had insisted that the operation be well defined and time-limited.

Olmert and Tzipi soon fell prey to the same self-defeating temptation that had worried me during the meandering war against Hizbollah. Our ground incursion began a few days into the operation. The intention was to stay for a few more days and then, responding to inevitable international appeals, call a halt to a campaign that had already achieved nearly all of its targets. Perhaps wanting to balance the failures in Lebanon with "success" in Gaza, Olmert wanted us to continue and expand our attacks deeper into Gaza. I reminded him that we'd *agreed to* the aims beforehand. All of us recognized we were not going to retake and retain control of Gaza. And the longer we stayed, the less clear any gains of the operation would be. Yes, our ground forces had so far faced virtually no resistance or casualties. "But that's *because* we're outside the main populated areas," I said. "The deeper we get in, the better it will be for Hamas. They gain simply by surviving, just like Hizbollah." Yet Olmert kept insisting that we'd succeeded so far, so let's not stop.

It wasn't until January 17, three weeks after the operation began, that we announced a cease-fire. Militarily, the operation was a success. While Hamas launched nearly 3,000 rockets into Israel in the twelve months before our attack, there were only 300 in the year that followed. But politically and diplomatically, the extra week reduced, rather than helped, the chances of reaching an understanding for a longer-term reduction of the attacks. To the extent there was any political gain, it was to burnish Tzipi Livni's credentials as a tough potential prime minister ahead of the election. I am certain that was not her intent. Of all the politicians I've known, she is among the least interested in such games, especially with lives at stake. But it was one of the effects.

She did win the election, in a photo finish, with opinion polls suggesting she'd been effective in shaping the campaign as a choice "between Tzipi and Bibi." Kadima got twenty-eight Knesset seats to twenty-seven for Bibi and the Likud. But not only had the Likud gained an extra fifteen seats; the far-right, stridently anti-Arab party Yisrael Beiteinu, led by a former Likudnik named Avigdor Lieberman, now held fifteen seats. Our Labor Party result was an undeniably disappointing thirteen, a loss of six seats. Overall, the coalition math clearly favored Bibi. So he was given the first crack at forming a government, which he did.

Though I was not surprised when he asked me to remain as defense minister, and to keep Labor inside the coalition, that was not an easy argument to make to my reduced Knesset contingent. They saw joining Bibi, especially in a government with the right-wing Lieberman as foreign minister, as a betrayal of all the efforts that they and I had made to achieve peace with the Palestinians. Still, the decision on whether to join the coalition ultimately rested with the party's central committee, almost every one of whose members was on a local government council or a member of another publicly funded body. For them, the choice was between a share of power, however limited, and the wilderness of opposition. We joined Bibi's government.

I was in favor of our doing so, but for more complicated reasons. I recognized that Bibi was often more interested in politics than policy, and perhaps above both of those, in the tactical maneuvering required to consolidate his own political position. But I knew he wasn't intellectually shallow, as many of his critics suggested. I believed he was capable of doing what he felt best for Israel and had a basic pragmatism to guide how he got there. I hoped that, as part of his government, I could help us address two key policy priorities. The first was to ensure at least *some* peace process with the Palestinians. That, in turn, would win us the diplomatic support, especially from the Americans, we would need to tackle an even more pressing challenge.

We'd been aware of Iranian efforts to get nuclear weapons for a number of years. Certain steps were taken to delay them from doing so, but they were now getting steadily closer. In fact, as defense minister under Olmert, I'd directed the new chief of staff, Gaby Ashkenazi, to develop a plan for a surgical strike to destroy the most important facilities in the Iranians' nuclear network. But it became clear we didn't have the operational capability, in part because we lacked the necessary bunker-busting bombs and the midair refueling capacity to get us to Iran and back. I'd sought help from the Americans, in meetings with defense secretary Bob Gates, CIA director Mike Hayden, national security adviser Steve Hadley, and President Bush himself. While not explicitly mentioning that we were planning military action against Iran, I sounded them out on the prospects of getting more heavy munitions, and possibly leasing US tanker aircraft.

In our final meeting with President Bush, during a visit to Israel in June 2008, he made it clear to Olmert and me that he knew what we were up to. Olmert hosted a private dinner for the president. Afterward, Bush asked to talk privately. Olmert poured us each a glass of whiskey and lit a cigar, and we sank into brown leather armchairs. Smiling, the president looked straight at me, and said to Olmert, "This guy scares the living shit out of me when he tells me what you want."

He told Olmert how I'd asked for heavy munitions, tankers, and a variety of other military equipment. "Remember. I'm a former F-16 pilot," he said. "I know how to connect the dots." Then, turning more serious, he added, "I want to tell both of you now, as president, the formal position of the US government. We are totally against any action by you to mount an attack on the nuclear plants." The effect was all the more dramatic because of his administration's support for our attack on the reactor in Syria the year before. "I repeat," Bush said, "in order to avoid any misunderstanding. We expect you not to do it. And we're not going to do it, either, as long as I am president. I wanted it to be clear."

Olmert said nothing, so I replied. "Mr. President, we're in no position to tell you what the position of the United States should be. But I can tell you what I believe history will have to say. I'm reminded by what we call, in field artillery, 'bracketing and halving.'" I said that in the wake of the al-Qaeda attack on the Twin Towers, he had fired one shell long, in Afghanistan, and another one short, in Iraq. "But when the time came to hit the real target—Iran—it ended up you'd already spent two terms, and all your political capital." He seemed neither insulted nor unsettled by my remark. He simply nodded. Perhaps, in part, because he was pretty sure that we lacked the ability to attack the Iranian facilities anyway.

We had now been working intensively for more than eighteen months to acquire that capacity. Yet we *still* hadn't succeeded when I became defense minister in Bibi's government in May 2009. From the day his government took office, I was determined to do all I could to change that.

# Final Act

THERE WERE ONLY TWO WAYS WE COULD STOP THE IRANIANS FROM getting a nuclear weapon: for the Americans to act, or for them not to hinder Israel from doing so. Either was going to be a lot harder if there was tension with the new American president, Barack Obama, who hoped to revive the peace process. So I hoped that political pragmatism, if nothing else, would nudge Bibi toward a reengagement with the Palestinians.

Within weeks of our taking office, Obama launched an effort to restart negotiations, declaring it "intolerable" that the Palestinians still didn't have a state. He was explicit about what he expected of us, calling for a halt to all settlement construction on the West Bank. The main issue wasn't new settlements; there had been almost none in recent years. It was the expansion of existing ones. The Jewish population on the West Bank had been about 190,000 when I became prime minister. In the decade since, the number had grown to 315,000—more than half a million if you counted the Jewish neighborhoods inside the expanded, post-1967 boundaries of Jerusalem. The expansion of the settlements—"natural growth" as we euphemistically called it—was what President Obama now wanted Bibi to end.

With each passing year since Camp David, the pro-settlement right wing in Israel had become more confident and influential. The rise of Avigdor Lieberman's Yisrael Beiteinu party was the latest sign, but there had also been a move rightward in the Likud itself. For Bibi to say yes to a settlement freeze would mean putting aside his short-term political interests in recognition of the importance of our alliance with the Americans. He'd actually done this twice during his first term as prime minister: agreeing to give the Palestinians control of most of Hebron, and accepting further withdrawals under the Wye River agreement. But amid predictable protests from the right, he'd retreated from his Wye commitments. I knew that his default response to Obama's call for a settlement freeze would be "no." And it was, delivered first to the cabinet and then in public.

In repeated meetings with Bibi in the weeks that followed—both one-on-one and within the informal group of ministers and aides known as the Group of Eight—I tried to persuade him that we needed to show *some* sign of engagement with Obama's efforts, if only because of America's key role on Iran. I wasn't entirely alone in this. One ally was Dan Meridor, who had rejoined the Likud before the election. Another was more unexpected: Lieberman. He was never going to accept a settlement freeze. Not only did his heart and political interests lie on the West Bank: he lived there. But as foreign minister, he was worried about creating the impression of blanket Israeli intransigence toward a popular new American president, and isolating ourselves internationally, if we didn't go some way to help restart talks with the Palestinians.

Though Bibi showed no signs of retreat on the settlement freeze, he did accept that broader point. Ten days after Obama's Cairo speech, Bibi delivered an address of his own, at Bar-Ilan University, in which he publicly accepted the idea of a Palestinian state for the first time. He'd ruled it out as recently as the month before in White House talks with the president. The shift was dismissed as trivial by the Palestinians. I disagreed, believing it was significant. But I had another serious concern about the "peace plan" Bibi announced: a precondition that the Palestinians "clearly and unambiguously recognize Israel as the state of the Jewish people." That made no sense to me. We hadn't asked Egypt or Jordan to grant us explicit recognition as a Jewish state when making peace with them. Even when Bibi had briefly tried to open negotiations with Damascus in his first period as prime minister, he'd never felt the need to ask it of Syria either. To the extent there was any logic in demanding it from the Palestinians, Bibi's reasoning seemed to be that this would neutralize recidivist claims to all of Palestine, especially since we had around 1.5 million Arab citizens living inside our pre-1967 borders. But as I told Bibi, that was a red herring. There was a far more straightforward, legally binding answer to that concern: a peace treaty, like the ones with Egypt and Jordan, that declared an end to our conflict and to further claims on either side.

My main concern about the precondition was its implications for Israel. Bibi's new approach contradicted the central thrust of Zionism: that after centuries of powerlessness and persecution, Jews would finally take control of their own destiny. We now had our state. It was more than six decades old. "Why do we need the Palestinians, or *anyone*, to validate us as a Jewish state?" I asked Bibi. "Why propose something that implies the Palestinians somehow have a say in what kind of state we choose to be?" Yet the more I pressed him, the clearer it became that the substance didn't much matter. His move was political and tactical, aimed at staking out a position of power in the diplomatic process. Besides, he didn't expect any new negotiations to make real progress anyway.

As defense minister, I did have scope for taking some steps with the Palestinians on my own. With Bibi's knowledge and tacit acceptance, I established a particularly strong relationship with Abu Mazen's prime minister, Salaam Fayyad. A respected economist, he operated on the assumption that neither violence nor negotiations seemed likely to lead the Palestinians to statehood as things now stood. He saw his role as putting in place the institutions, infrastructure, economy, internal security, and stability needed for an eventual state to succeed. He was trying to do for the Palestinians what Ben-Gurion had done before 1948. He and I met and talked often but discreetly—sometimes in Jerusalem, sometimes in my office in the kirya, sometimes over dinner in my thirty-first-floor flat in central Tel Aviv. I remember one dinner in particular. I led him toward the window after we'd eaten. Since the West Bank was barely a dozen miles away, we could see the twinkling lights of Ramallah. Smiling, he said, "Ehud, why do you need Ramallah when you've got Tel Aviv?" I smiled back. He knew my views: Israel *didn't* need Ramallah. I was more convinced than ever that it was in our *own* interest, by treaty if possible and unilateral disengagement if not, to remove Israel from all of the major towns and cities of the West Bank.

I issued a standing directive in the kirya that we should agree to anything Fayyad asked for, as long as there was no security reason to say no. We ended up arranging a direct source of fuel supply to Jenin, on the northern edge of the West Bank, and built new terminals to handle it. We facilitated construction permits for a new industrial zone. For a conference of international economists and businesspeople, we set up VIP treatment at Ben-Gurion Airport and limousine transport to the conference venue. I believed that if Fayyad succeeded in what he was trying to accomplish, it would benefit not just the Palestinians, but Israel too. Bibi was agnostic on Fayyad's efforts. Yet he recognized they did no harm. In a way, my support for them was politically convenient. To the extent the international community, especially the Americans, appreciated our efforts to help the Palestinians, Bibi and others in the government could, and did, claim credit. When there were complaints from the right, Bibi could, and did, say, "It was Barak."

My part in our relations with the Americans was more politically delicate. As I continued to prod Bibi toward accepting a settlement freeze during the summer and autumn of 2009, my de facto role became to help smooth over the increasingly rough edges in our ties with the Obama administration. I knew some of its key figures from earlier incarnations in their public lives and mine, including Secretary of Defense Bob Gates, who had been President George H. W. Bush's deputy national security adviser in the first Iraq war and head of the CIA; and Hillary Clinton, who was now secretary of state. During a series of early trips to the United States as defense minister, I met Gates, Hillary, and other senior administration figures. In part because they were aware that I favored agreeing to a settlement freeze, they clearly found it easier to talk to me than to Bibi. On one visit, to my regret and Bibi's evident frustration when I'd come home, the press highlighted this dramatic difference in mood. Emerging from talks with me at the State Department, Hillary Clinton told reporters our talks had gone "wonderfully." She added: "As longtime friends do, much was said. And much didn't need to be said." Still, the Americans understood that it was Bibi's actions that ultimately mattered. He, not I, was prime minister.

I was as heartened as they were when he finally announced a settlement freeze in November 2009. It was hedged with several conditions.

Rather than be open-ended, it would last for ten months as a way to boost efforts to restart negotiations. It would apply to new construction, not work already under way. And it would exclude the post-1967 neighborhoods inside the expanded city limits of Jerusalem. Like his other moves, it was dismissed as insignificant by the Palestinians. Though there was a formal restart of the talks, they went almost nowhere during the period of the freeze, which Bibi cited as a reason for not extending it further. From then on, the negotiations produced even less. This was not entirely Bibi's fault. Abu Mazen remained steadfastly, deliberately passive. Obviously not inclined to take the risk of further widening his rift with Hamas in Gaza, at the beginning of the Obama administration he was content to echo Washington's argument that nothing could happen until there was a settlement freeze. Once the freeze was announced, he went through the motions, avoiding all the difficult issues, in the expectation the Americans would ensure the freeze was renewed. President Obama's initial Mideast moves had made it easier for Abu Mazen to avoid serious engagement: in contrast to past US presidents, he'd placed almost all of the onus for progress on Israel. But the effective stalemate also suited Bibi. It became more evident as the months went on that his aim was simply to keep things chugging along and to avoid any major diplomatic crisis.

He appointed an old personal friend, a lawyer named Yitzhak Molcho, as our negotiator. I finally realized how pointless the exercise was when, during a visit to the United States, I found myself in New York at the same time as Molcho. We met at the Israeli consulate and he briefed me about the state of the negotiations. With Molcho still in the room, I phoned Bibi in Jerusalem on the secure line. I said I'd just been updated on the talks, and it seemed clear there were a number of suggestions that Israel could make, with no domestic political risk but with every prospect of improving the atmosphere and accelerating progress. "Yitzhak is one of Israel's top lawyers," I said. "He's struck dozens of deals in his life. But he strikes a deal when that's what his client wants. *You* are the client. If you tell him: bring me back the best deal you can—not a peace treaty, just a deal on a specific issue—he'll do it. But if his brief is simply to negotiate, he can go on negotiating forever. And it's pretty clear to me that's his brief." Bibi insisted I was wrong. He said that what I saw as wasting time was actually prudence, to make sure the negotiations bore fruit. But his approach never changed. Whenever it came up in our Group of Eight discussions, I could usually count only on Dan Meridor, and occasionally a handful of others, to argue in favor of any form of initiative on our part. In private meetings, Bibi did sometimes engage in discussion about what Israel might do. But he then invariably steered the conversation elsewhere, insisting the *real* issue was the Palestinians' lack of interest in making peace.

For the immediate future, I too saw little chance of an agreement. But the longer the vacuum lasted, the harder it would become to revive a serious effort to reach a two-state compromise. The dithering, delay, and deadlock suited Bibi politically since it meant he didn't have to consider concessions that were sure to anger his coalition partners on the right. But much of the Israeli public seemed equally untroubled by the lack of serious talks. Ironically, this was in part due to the security framework I oversaw as defense minister. Intermittent outbreaks of violence always remained a threat. Yet the West Bank fence, along with our military, police, and intelligence measures, meant it was highly unlikely we'd see a return to full-blown terror. I was now also working to obtain US support for Israel's development of new anti-missile weapons to greatly reduce the threat from Hamas in Gaza. The overall result was that the conflict with the Palestinians no longer affected the day-to-day lives of most Israelis.

Still, the effect of the negotiating stalemate on our relations with Washington did matter, both for our security cooperation on things like the antimissile weapons and, crucially, the challenge that had led me into Bibi's government in the first place: keeping Iran from getting a nuclear weapon.

+ + +

The Iranians were producing more and more yellowcake, building more advanced centrifuges, accumulating more low-enriched uranium. They were getting better at hiding and protecting the network of facilities being used to try to produce a nuclear weapon. But in the early months of Bibi's prime ministership, the question wasn't *whether* to take military action against Iran—something I knew, from Bob Gates and others, that the Obama administration viewed no more favorably than George W. Bush. It was to ensure that we actually had the military capacity to strike before the Iranians entered their "zone of immunity"—the point at which the amount of damage we could do, and the delay we could cause, to their nuclear program would be too negligible to be worth the operational, political, and diplomatic risks from such an attack.

I began working, both with the kirya and the engineers and technological experts in our military industries, to ensure we had a military option: the required means and munitions, and a workable plan for an attack if we decided to launch one. It wasn't until mid-2010, a year into Bibi's government, that I was confident we'd reached that point. Our experts estimated that if we struck now, we could set back the Iranian nuclear efforts by several years. Given the Iranians' knowledge that we could always attack again, that meant we might very well succeed in ending their nuclear program altogether.

It was then that the question became whether we *should* launch a strike. Answering it was like a contest of three-dimensional chess, involving both an internal debate among Israel's political and military leadership and discussions with the Obama administration, whose priority was to negotiate a halt to Iran's nuclear program. On all major security decisions in Israel, two ministers always mattered most: the prime minister and defense minister. Neither Bibi nor I doubted we had to be ready to strike if that proved necessary. Nor did Foreign Minister Lieberman. Even for us, it was an option to be considered only when all other ways to rein in the Iranians had failed. We agreed on two other preconditions as well. First, we would need to secure international legitimacy, most of all from the Americans, for a clear act of self-defense. Second, we'd have to demonstrate a compelling urgency to act when we did, with the approach of an Iranian "zone of immunity" against Israeli military action.

Ideally, we hoped the US-led campaign of economic and diplomatic pressure would get Iran to abandon its nuclear ambitions, as had happened with Libya. Or, as in South Africa, that a change in nuclear policy might come from a change in regime. Yet we couldn't count on either. And there was no doubt in our minds that a nuclear Iran represented a hugely serious threat. If the Shi'ite Muslim regime in Iran did get a nuclear weapon, Sunni Arab states like Egypt and Saudi Arabia, and Turkey as well, would inevitably try to go nuclear, dramatically unsettling the regional security picture. Neither these other states nor Israel could assume that Iran was developing a bomb as a mere act of deterrence.

Especially in a crisis threatening the survival of the ayatollahs' rule, Iran might use the weapons it was developing or even send a nuclear device in a container smuggled on board a commercial vessel docking in one of Israel's ports.

While few in Israel disputed the seriousness of the threat, a number of top political and military figures had deep misgivings about military action. Given the need for secrecy, most of our discussions took place within the Group of Eight, often also including the chief of staff and other generals from the kirya. Dan Meridor and Benny Begin, a minister without portfolio, were opposed to an Israeli attack from the start. They feared it could have unpredictable and possibly dire implications for the region, as well as for our relations with the wider world. Dan raised a further concern: that an Israeli attack might intensify Iran's effort to get a nuclear bomb, only now with political cover, because it would argue it was acting in self-defense. In fact, regularly updated reports we were receiving from our intelligence experts suggested that if we did attack, some Iranian retaliation was inevitable. But the options would be limited. They would probably involve, at worst, a period of escalated use of two familiar weapons: terror operations abroad and missile attacks by its Lebanese proxy, Hizbollah, in southern Lebanon.

Those ministers who opposed a strike argued that we should rely on American economic and political pressure to deal with the threat. And if that failed, on *American* military action.

In November 2010, the internal debate came to a head at a meeting involving the Group of Eight as well as the chief of staff, the head of military intelligence, and the commander of the air force. We convened in a Mossad facility near Tel Aviv. The meeting began with a presentation by the generals of our attack plan. There was still a core of ministers opposed, led by Dan Meridor and Benny Begin. But the confidence and detail with which the plan was laid out, and the fact that Bibi, Lieberman, and I were in favor of being prepared to act, gave me the sense that a majority would back military action if it were deemed necessary. The proviso would be the need for the chief of staff, and ideally the heads of military intelligence and Mossad, to sign off on the operational viability of the plan.

That proviso soon ended any prospect of an Israeli attack, at least for now. Bibi, Lieberman, and I withdrew into a side room to talk with the chief of staff, Gaby Ashkenazi, as well as the heads of military intelligence, the Mossad, and Shin Bet. We emphasized that no final decision on whether to attack had been taken. That would require a further meeting with the Group of Eight, and then the full cabinet. But we asked each of them for their views on the operation. We knew they had political reservations along the lines of those voiced by Dan Meridor. On an issue of this magnitude, it was accepted practice that military and intelligence commanders could weigh in on the political implications. But their formal role was operational and professional. Ashkenazi and the other generals conceded that in every area—planning, materiel, training, and intelligence—our attack plan was far ahead of where it had been a year earlier. Yet Ashkenazi, in particular, concluded that the preparations had not yet "crossed the threshold of operational capability."

This left me fuming inside. I respected the considered opposition of ministers like Dan or Benny Begin, and had no problem with the chief of staff or other generals expressing concerns about the political or geo-strategic implications of an Israeli attack, even though our intelligence assessments suggested these were almost certainly unfounded. What I found astonishing was Ashkenazi's suggestion that the "operational threshold" had not been crossed. Yes, this would be a demanding mission. It was not without risks—no operation was. But having followed every stage and detail of the preparations—and as a former chief of staff and intelligence chief myself—I believed it was simply wrong on a *professional* level to say that we lacked the capacity, and a workable plan, for a military strike if the order was given.

Our discussions continued in the months ahead alongside a further refinement and strengthening of the attack plan. So did Iran's progress toward its "zone of immunity," which we now believed would begin late in 2012, a couple of years away. As that point drew ever closer, we faced the need to decide finally whether military action was possible and necessary.

The delay in reaching that point, however, had serious implications for my role as Labor leader. Since the negotiations with the Palestinians were stuck in neutral, I was under pressure from many within Labor to pull out of Bibi's government. What on earth was the point of staying? they asked. All I was doing, from their perspective, was giving Bibi political cover for abandoning any serious effort to get a peace agreement. That argument was entirely reasonable. My frustration was that, due to the need for military secrecy, I could not explain my real reason for believing we needed to stay in the government: the fact that we were at a critical juncture in deciding whether to take military action against Iran's nuclear program. To a mix of consternation and anger among many Labor colleagues, I ended up taking what seemed to me the only realistic option. In January 2011, I left the Labor Party. With three other of our ministers in the government—who were, of course, aware of the ongoing Iran discussions—I set up a new "centrist, Zionist" party called Ha'Atzmaut, or Independence. We remained in Bibi's government.

+ + +

For the "international legitimacy" an Israeli attack required, we had to secure from the Americans at least their *understanding* that we might feel it necessary to act, a goal not helped by steadily rising tensions between the Obama administration and Bibi. Ever since the initial pressure for a settlement freeze, right-wing politicians and commentators, and Bibi himself, had taken to portraying President Obama as fundamentally unsympathetic to Israel. Then, after the Republicans' victory in the midterm congressional elections in November 2010, Bibi went a step further, deepening his already-close ties with Republican congressmen and senators and with their major financial patrons. This overt meddling in the internal politics of our closest ally was not just a breach of long-standing tradition, but of common sense. Members of the administration began privately calling Bibi "the Republican senator from Rechavia"—a reference to the Jerusalem neighborhood where the prime minister's official residence was located.

Yet in spite of this, my main contacts in the administration—first Bob Gates and then his successor as secretary of defense, Leon Panetta—never wavered from their commitment to the principle that Israel needed to retain our "qualitative military edge" over any combination of threats we might face, nor to the $3 billion package of annual US aid that underpinned it. We were even able to agree on additional US backing for our increasingly effective range of anti-missile systems: the Arrow, against long-range ballistic missiles, developed in coordination with the US defense contractor Raytheon; "David's Sling," to target enemy forces' mid-range missiles, cruise missiles, and aircraft; and our new Iron Dome system, integrating sophisticated Israeli radar and guidance technology and designed to deal with the missile threat from Hizbollah on our northern border and Hamas in Gaza. It had not yet been used in battle, but from test firings, we were confident it could destroy incoming rockets with nearly 90 percent success.

By late 2011, the issue of Iran had taken on much greater urgency. There was still no sign the American-led diplomatic efforts were succeeding in removing the nuclear threat. As for an American military strike, though the president intermittently declared that "all options" remained on the table, I knew from senior administration members that it was extremely unlikely to happen. Iran, meanwhile, had been producing thousands more centrifuges, more uranium, and building heavier protection around its key sites. The "zone of immunity" was now closer than in 2010.

By now, most of the key players in Israel agreed we had to be prepared to take military action if there was no alternative way to rein in the Iranians. Along with Bibi, Lieberman, and me, Benny Gantz, Ashkenazi's successor as chief of staff, had signed off on the attack plan. The strike force we were assembling was also better equipped, trained, and prepared to mount a complex—and, very likely, successful—military operation. The damage to Iran's nuclear ambitions would be considerably less than if we had acted earlier. But our intelligence analysts still estimated we could deal a meaningful setback to the Iranians' program.

Yet there were still voices of opposition within the inner group of eight: not just Dan Meridor and Benny Begin but the minister for strategic affairs, Boogie Ya'alon, and Finance Minister Yuval Steinitz. That meant we could not yet count on passing a resolution to go ahead with the operation. There was also a further, more immediate problem as we approached the turn of the year. A major joint military exercise with the Americans, agreed on two years earlier, was due to take place in Israel in April 2012. It would include Patriot missile batteries, naval vessels, and thousands of uniformed US personnel. The focus, of all things, was on defense against a missile attack from Iran. In late 2011, I'd contacted Leon Panetta to see whether we could delay it. Though I didn't say why, I assumed he understood that we were at least considering military action. He also realized that if we did launch an attack, it was in the Americans' own interest for their troops to be as far away from Israel as possible. We agreed to reschedule the exercise for October 2012. That meant that if we decided to attack, we'd have until well into September, when significant numbers of US troops would begin to arrive.

As we weighed our final decision, I held a series of high-level meetings in Washington: with Panetta, national security adviser Tom Donilon, Hillary Clinton, and President Obama himself. Though not explicitly saying we were contemplating an attack, I explained the reasons we believed Israel's fundamental security interests might make it necessary. The message from all of the Americans I met was that the administration shared our basic goal: to prevent, or at least seriously impair, Iran's drive to get a nuclear bomb. But they continued to believe that nonmilitary pressure was the best way to achieve that.

The Americans knew we were skeptical that the nonmilitary route would work, and that we were deeply worried about the implications of failing to stop Iran's nuclear efforts. I discussed our thinking—and, in general terms, our plans—with Panetta. I assumed that he probably had a pretty good idea of the broad contours of what we were contemplating, since US radar systems and electronic intercepts had the capacity to record the volume and nature of air force exercises we'd been conducting over recent months. Leon and I knew each other well, having first met when he was President Clinton's White House chief of staff and then when he was made head of the CIA at the start of the Obama administration. In one of our early meetings at CIA headquarters in Langley, there had been a small bunch of grapes on his desk, and I plucked a few and popped them into my mouth with obvious enjoyment. Now, at the Pentagon, he had a big bowlful ready whenever we met. The fact that he opposed an Israeli military operation made him no less of a pleasure to deal with. He was calm and even-tempered. He had an encyclopedic grasp of issues of defense, intelligence, budgets, and policy. He was a proud, patriotic American. He was also always rock-solid on America's commitment to Israel's security. It's worth remembering that, in spite of our insistence from 1948 onward that we would never ask others to do our fighting for us, even as Leon and I were meeting, US radar operators were working around the clock to provide us with early warning against any incoming Iranian missiles. Patriot batteries were routinely ready to deploy in Israel on short notice in case of an attack. AEGIS naval vessels were also usually in the Mediterranean and were able to reinforce Israel's Arrow missile defense system with sea-launched weapons.

Panetta made no secret of the fact he didn't want us to launch a military strike, which would undo the many months of intensive work the Americans had devoted to building international political and economic pressure on the Iranians. He urged me to "think twice, three times," before going down that road. But he recognized that Israel would be affected far more dramatically by a nuclear Iran. "It's your conflict. It's your neighborhood," he said. At one point, he asked me outright: "If you do decide to attack the Iranian facilities, when will we know?"

I told him that, realistically, we couldn't give him more than a few hours' notice. But I did recognize our responsibility not to leave the Americans in the dark. They were a key ally, and their personnel might be at risk from any Iranian retaliation. "We know your command-post deployment and the communications protocols with your forces," I told him. "We'll make sure you have enough time to tell your people. We won't endanger a single American life, any of your personnel."

My most important meeting was with the president. Though I knew him less well than I did Panetta, we had met on a number of occasions. The first time was when he was still Senator Obama, on a visit to Israel during the 2008 presidential campaign. As defense minister, I escorted him to Sderot, the town in southern Israel bearing the brunt of Hamas rocket attacks from Gaza. Back in Jerusalem, we spent a half hour talking at a corner table in the lobby of the King David Hotel—about Iran. I argued that a nuclear Iran was a challenge not only for Israel and the Middle East, but America, too. I urged him, if elected, to convene an early meeting including operational specialists and security experts on what the Iranians were seeking to do and what could be done to stop them— by diplomatic means or, if necessary, by force. Also, what the Iranians could, or more relevantly could *not*, do in response to an American or an Israeli attack, since our intelligence assessments suggested their options for retaliation would be fairly limited. Obama struck me from that first meeting as coolheaded, independent-minded, highly intelligent, and intensely cerebral. Though we didn't go into the details of the Iranian nuclear threat, he talked at length about the implications for the region, and about broader Middle Eastern security challenges. He displayed a grasp of the cultural and political nuances of an increasingly diverse and complex world that was more impressive than many of the other American political or military leaders I'd met.

When he and I now returned to the issue of Iran, in the White House, he had an undeniable command of the details of Iran's nuclear program, and of the American military options, should he choose to use them. He opened by summarizing the US position. He emphasized that he, too, was determined to keep Iran from developing a nuclear weapon. The difference, he said, was that we seemed to feel an urgent need to reach a decision on military action. In Obama's view, such a move would be both premature and potentially harmful to the coalition he'd helped to assemble to exert diplomatic and economic pressure on Iran.

Maybe you had to be an Israeli to truly understand our urgency. In the early years of the state, the explanation we gave for our preoccupation with security—our near obsession, as some non-Israelis saw it—was that we were surrounded by Arab countries pledged not just to defeat us, but eliminate us from the map. While Egypt or Syria, Jordan or Iraq could afford to lose an Arab-Israeli war, Israel's first defeat would be its last. That picture had changed dramatically over the decades. We no longer had to worry about the prospect of losing a war. The "qualitative military edge" we possessed over all enemy armies in the region ensured that. As Israel's chief of staff, prime minister, and now defense minister, I had made it a major priority to safeguard that advantage, not just through our alliance with the United States but with the remarkable domestic resources we possessed in advanced technology, manufacturing, design, and invention. But the new-order challenge represented by Iran was not just theoretical or academic: a nuclear Iran would almost certainly lead to a nuclear Saudi Arabia, Egypt, and Turkey, introducing a whole new order of instability and danger to the region. Beyond that, only the most naïve observer would exclude the possibility that if the Iranians did get a nuclear weapon, circumstances might arise, however remote they now might seem, in which they might use it.

I was not about to lecture President Obama on this. While Bibi liked to portray him variously as weak, naïve, or tone-deaf to the interests and security of Israel, I knew he was none of these things. Yet I did, in a deliberately nondidactic way, raise the issue of our different perspectives on the Iranians' getting nuclear arms. "You see it in the context of the whole world," I told the president. "If Iran, in spite of all our efforts, gets a nuclear weapon, yes, it will be bad. But for you, it's just one more nuclear state. It won't dramatically change the situation for America. For us, it can evolve over time into a real, existential threat."

He agreed that we inevitably looked at the situation differently. But after pausing a few seconds, he said, "Ehud, think of it this way. You get to school in the morning and there's this big, nasty bully. You can take him on, maybe give him a black eye. But you have this bigger, stronger friend, who can knock him out cold. The only problem is that your friend won't be there until the afternoon."

I would have liked nothing more than to wait for our "bigger, stronger" friend, especially since I knew through my contacts in the American military and intelligence establishment how much more effective an American attack would be. During the first couple of years that Israel worked on acquiring the capability for a military strike against Iran, the Americans had been no more ready than we were. They had the tanker aircraft and the heavy bombs, but their *plan* was so obviously prone to lead to a wider conflict that it would never have received the go-ahead from President Obama, or probably any president. I used to joke with colleagues in the Pentagon that while Israel's idea of a "surgical operation" was the equivalent of a scalpel, they seemed to favor a chisel and a ten-pound hammer. By the time I met the president in 2012, that had changed. Under Gates and Panetta, an intensive research-and-development effort and enormously improved planning and testing had yielded results. The Americans now had high-precision heavy munitions we couldn't dream of, and stealth air-attack capabilities we also lacked. Our assessment was that they had the operational capability to launch an attack that, within a period of hours, could push the Iranian nuclear program back by years, and that, even if the Iranians knew the strike was coming, they'd be powerless to stop.

"Our problem, Mr. President," I said, "is that we can't be sure our friend will show up in the schoolyard. Since Iran is already very nearly in a zone of immunity against an Israeli attack, we can't afford to wait until the afternoon. By then, with *our* capabilities, we won't even be able to give the bully a black eye." I said I trusted what he'd just told me. "I'm sure it genuinely reflects your intentions now. But there are no futures contracts in statesmanship. There's no way that you, or any leader, can commit yourself to what will happen in a year or two. When the moment of decision arrives, nothing will be able to free you from the responsibility to look at the situation as it is *then*, with *American* interests in mind."

He accepted the point but reiterated his view that "kinetic action"—US security-speak for a military strike—would not only remove his ability to exhaust the nonmilitary alternatives. He said it wouldn't be in Israel's interests, either. "We hear that even people high up in your military, in military intelligence and the Mossad, are against it."

I couldn't deny that. "We highly respect our top people in the military, and in intelligence. We make a point of listening to them before taking action," I said. "But here's the difference. When they look up, they see Netanyahu, or me. When Bibi and I look up, we see heaven. Whoever is up there, we clearly can't go to Him for advice. *We* are responsible for Israel's security."

The president smiled, but brought the discussion back down to earth. When he again urged us to consider the American position in any decision, I replied, "Mr. President, I feel compelled to tell you frankly how I see the situation. We highly appreciate, and are grateful, that America supports Israel in so many ways. I believe we're doing our best to support American interests in the Middle East as well. But when it comes to issues critical for the security and future of Israel, and in a way for the future of the Jewish people, we can't afford to delegate responsibility even to our best friend and ally. When we face such situations, we have to decide on the basis of our own sovereign responsibility, and act on our decisions. I would expect the United States, and you as its president, to respect that position." He did not seem especially happy with what I'd said. But he showed no anger. Though we differed, it was clear he understood and respected our position. In any case, I believed it was important to convey to him honestly, face-to-face, where Israel stood on Iran. Or at least where I stood.

+ + +

With our joint exercises pushed back until the fall, the logical time for us to consider an attack was the summer of 2012, when the conditions were optimal. Operationally, we were ready. Politically, Dan Meridor and Benny Begin, who were against military action, had not changed their minds. If anything, they seemed more strongly opposed. Ironically, they now argued that because we'd *waited* so long, the Iranians were too close to their zone of immunity. Several senior members of the military and security establishment, though in agreement over the technical aspects of the attack plan, also retained political reservations. But the decision in effect rested with Bibi and me, as long as we could secure the support a majority in the Group of Eight and the wider cabinet. The fact that we were contemplating going ahead in those circumstances, even with some key voices still opposed, was not unprecedented in Israel. When Menachem Begin ordered the bombing of Saddam Hussein's nuclear reactor in 1981, he'd acted against the advice of the heads of both the Mossad and military intelligence, the chairman of our nuclear energy commission, and of Shimon Peres, who was head of the Labor opposition.

As we neared our final, formal decision, however, we were forced into another delay, by a series of unrelated tensions in the region during the summer of 2012, with ripples that were still being felt when small American advance teams began arriving for the joint exercises. As more American soldiers and sailors arrived, I finally realized that an Israeli strike would not be possible. This wasn't because I doubted the damage it could still do to Iran's nuclear efforts, but because of the damage it would do to our ties with the United States. No matter how we might explain our attack, with the joint exercises about to begin, it would come across as a deliberate attempt to implicate our most important ally in a potential conflict with Iran, against the explicit wishes and policy of President Obama and the US government.

I felt this even more strongly when, a few weeks later, I was approached by one of Bibi's close allies. He sounded me out on the possibility of launching our strike against Iran *after* the joint exercise was over: barely two weeks before the 2012 US election. Politically, he implied, Obama would feel *compelled* to support Israel's action, or at the very least to refrain from criticizing it. In other words, we would be setting a political trap for the president of the United States. My reply to this last-gasp suggestion of a way for us to attack the Iranian sites required no hesitation, and just two words: "No way."

With Israeli military action now in effect off the agenda, Bibi's approach to other diplomatic and domestic issues seemed guided by a mix of anxiety, pessimism, and passivity. Almost everything he did seemed increasingly designed to create a kind of grand narrative to reinforce his support on the right and solidify a base that he figured would sustain him in office. At its core, the narrative presented a picture of vulnerability and victimhood: a "fortress Israel" threatened by terror, missiles on its northern and southern borders, and now potential nuclear annihilation from Iran, while our main ally, the United States, was under the sway of a president who neither understood nor fundamentally supported us. In day-to-day policy terms, this allowed Bibi to insist we couldn't *risk* serious engagement with the Palestinians. On domestic issues as well, like the widening gap between those at the top of our high-tech economy and a painfully squeezed middle class, the sense of crisis he encouraged gave him license to hunker down, warn of impending doom, and do virtually nothing.

Effective though the narrative was politically, it bore no resemblance to reality. Yes, President Obama disagreed with us on issues of policy—both the peace process and how to deal with Iran. But he was unquestionably committed to America's alliance with Israel. I had dealt face-to-face with four US presidents: both of the Bushes, Bill Clinton, and now Obama. In terms of Israeli security and intelligence concerns, none of them, except for President Clinton, had proved as consistently supportive as Obama. Israel faced an array of security challenges, and a nuclear-armed Iran would make things harder. But we were a regional superpower with a military as effective as any in the world and a high-tech economic sector justifiably compared to Silicon Valley.

Every few weeks, Bibi, Lieberman, and I would meet for a wide-ranging discussion on the patio of the prime minister's residence. On several occasions, I raised my objections to the skewed image Bibi was promoting of our country. It wasn't just inaccurate, I told him. It struck me as a betrayal of the core tenet of Zionism: the importance of Jews controlling their own destiny. "We *are* in that position now," I said. It was nonsensical to argue we were so threatened by everything around us that we couldn't "risk" taking the initiative required to disentangle ourselves from the Palestinians on the West Bank. "I don't get you," I said, turning to Lieberman as well. "Your *rhetoric* suggests you have spines of steel. But your behavior is living proof of the old saying that it's easier to take Jews out of the *galut*, than take the *galut* out of the Jews." *Galut* is Hebrew for the diaspora. "The whole Zionist project was based on the idea of taking our fate into *our own hands*, and actively trying to change the reality around us. But you behave as if we never left the *galut*. You're mired in a mind-set of pessimism, passivity, and anxiety, which, in terms of policy or action, leads to paralysis. Of course, there are risks in any action, any policy initiative. But in the situation where Israel finds itself, the biggest risk of all is being unable or unwilling to take risks, as if we are somehow on the brink of destruction."

I was especially upset by Bibi's increasing use of Holocaust imagery in describing the threat from Iran. "Just think of what you're saying," I told him. "You're prime minister of the State of Israel, not a rabbi in a *shtetl*, or a speaker trying to raise funds for Israel abroad. Think of the implications. We're not in Europe in 1937. Or 1947. If it is a 'Holocaust,' what's our response: to fold up and go back to the diaspora? If Iran gets a bomb, it'll be bad. Very bad. But we'll still be here. And we will find a way of dealing with the new reality."

Though Bibi and I had known each other for more than half a century, I had to accept that nothing I could do or say would change his approach. With the next Israeli election months away, in January 2013, I confided to Nili, and then my closest aides, that I was not going to run for a seat in the Knesset. Israeli military action against Iran was off the agenda, at least for the foreseeable future. The diplomatic process with the Palestinians was stalemated. I could see no point in remaining in the government.

Like my last period in Olmert's government, my final few months were dominated by finding a way to end Hamas attacks from Gaza. During one twenty-four-hour period in November 2012, Hamas launched more than one hundred rockets at towns in the south. Especially since our military response would be the last during my time as defense minister,

I was determined that, this time, it would have a strictly defined objective and a finite time frame. The overall objective hadn't changed since Olmert's premiership: to hit Hamas hard; bring down the number of rocket attacks to as near zero as possible; and reach an understanding, through the Egyptians, that established a period of calm on our border for as long as we could. Bibi's "victimhood" narrative notwithstanding, one aspect of the military balance in the south was now dramatically different. We had Iron Dome, which I was confident would help deal with the inevitable shower of Hamas rockets that would follow our initial attack. Again, it was essential to start with a quick, unexpected, damaging first strike. Then, through sustained air bombardment, to keep up enough pressure to secure the political arrangement we wanted. And, unlike under Olmert, to end the operation as soon as we'd achieved its aim.

On the afternoon of November 14, we launched a targeted air strike on Hamas's de facto chief of staff, Ahmed Jabari. We'd gone after Jabari in the past but for one reason or another had failed. We also hit nearly two-dozen other Hamas targets, including all of the missile sites we had identified. The whole operation lasted a week. Hamas fired nearly 1,500 rockets into Israel, not just locally manufactured Qassems but longer-range Iranian Fajr-5s and Russian Grads. For the first time since the 1991 Gulf War, several were targeted at Tel Aviv and Jerusalem. Fortunately, they were not significantly more accurate than in the past. More than half landed in fields or orchards. And with Iron Dome deployed around our major towns and cities, more than 85 percent were intercepted.

We hit nearly 1,500 targets over the seven-day period, mostly launchpads, Hamas government installations, and weapons stores, but also a number of apartment complexes being used by Hamas as bases or firing points. Bibi rightly pointed out that we were forced to fight a fundamentally asymmetric battle. While Israel began with the principle of directing our fire *away* from civilian areas, Hamas based its launchers in precisely those places. So it was not easy. At one point, we announced a call-up of reserves. We hinted at a possible ground incursion. But both Bibi and I had agreed on the need to avoid that if at all possible, and we did so. Though there were inevitable civilian casualties, most of the Palestinians killed were Hamas fighters and leaders, including not just Jabari but the head of Hamas's rocket program. By limiting ourselves to air strikes and naval fire, the Palestinian death toll was around 150, about one-tenth of what it had been in 2008. Six Israelis, including four civilians, lost their lives. On November 21, a cease-fire was announced.

With the election approaching, and my time in public life drawing to a close, I had no illusion that this latest military operation, or future ones, would bring us closer to the negotiated peace with the Palestinians that had eluded us since Oslo. Nor was I confident that, having been unable to mount a military strike of our own on Iran, Obama's "bigger, stronger kid" in the schoolyard would take military action. I trusted him to do all he could to use diplomacy to constrain Iran's efforts to get a bomb; I also feared he might fail. Even if he succeeded, I figured the best case would be an agreement that delayed the Iranians' development of a weapon—at least on paper. My hope remained that Israel's relationship with the Americans would be sufficiently strong for us to reach a formal understanding of what form of surgical military strike each of our countries might take if Iran didn't honor the terms of a negotiated deal.

When I first left political life after my election defeat in 2001, I'd described my status as the equivalent of a reserve officer. I said—and believed—it was unlikely I'd return for the foreseeable future. But I knew then that it wasn't impossible. This time was different. When I announced I was leaving politics, five days after the Gaza cease-fire, I pointed out that I had spent the greater part of my life as a soldier and had never had a burning desire to be a politician. I believed that what I'd attempted, and achieved, in government would prove to have safeguarded and strengthened Israel, but I also recognized that important challenges and decisions still lay ahead. So did our unfulfilled dream of being a country not just strong, secure, and prosperous, but socially just and at peace. Yet I believed it was right to draw a line under my time on the political front line. Though my dedication to a democratic and ultimately peaceful Israel would never waver, I expected that whatever contribution I might make would no longer be on the battlefield, in the kirya, or around the cabinet table.

# Epilogue

## Crossroads

IT IS NOW NEARLY FIVE YEARS SINCE I LEFT GOVERNMENT, AND ISRAEL is facing the deepest crisis of my lifetime, and its own. The issue is not about an individual prime minister. It's not about left or right, Ashkenazi or Sephardi, secular or religious, rich or poor. It is—to borrow a word often used, and abused, in Israel over the past few years—*existential*. It is about whether the country whose birth I witnessed, for which I fought for thirty-five years, and in whose government I served for nearly a decade can survive as a democracy under the rule of law, true not only to Jewish history and traditions but to the moral code at its core. Whether we can still aspire to be a "light unto the nations," or even a light unto ourselves.

The cause to which I've devoted my life—redeeming the dream of Zionism in a strong, free, self-confident, democratic Jewish state—is under threat. This is not mainly because of Hizbollah or Hamas, ISIS, or even Iran, all of which I feel confident in saying, as a former head of military intelligence, chief of staff, and defense minister, are real yet surmountable challenges. The main threat comes from inside: from the most right-wing, deliberately divisive, narrow-minded, and messianic government we have seen in our seven-decade history. It has sought to redefine Zionism as being about one thing only: ensuring eternal control over the whole of biblical Judaea and Samaria, or as the outside world knows it, the West Bank, even if doing so leaves us significantly less secure. In the past few years, it has also proven ready to erode, vilify, demonize, or delegitimize any check or criticism that might impede that goal: a free press, open debate, universities, the rule of law, even the ethical code of the Israeli military.

The ideological engine of the government has been driven by far-right politicians like Avigdor Lieberman and, above all, Naftali Bennett, the leader of a religious-nationalist party called Jewish Home. A former aide to Bibi Netanyahu, Bennett embodies the "Greater Israel" agenda, the idea that there is a divine imperative for Jews to settle and permanently control the entirety of Judaea and Samaria. During my final period as Bibi's defense minister, he was head of the joint settlement council on the West Bank, and led the drive against our agreeing to President Obama's call for a settlement freeze.

The *political tone* of the government has been set by Bibi. Well before the emergence of Donald Trump or Steve Bannon in the United States, he pioneered the tactic of denouncing the media for purveying "fake news" and fomenting some grand, left-wing conspiracy to unseat him. He has gone after academics in Israeli universities, the judiciary, human-rights organizations and other NGOs, as well as a number of our top generals, in a similar vein. Other ministers have threatened the independence of the Supreme Court. They've backed a statute to retroactively "legalize" 4,000 settlers' homes built on privately owned Palestinian land on the West Bank. They have brought pressure on university faculties through a "code of ethics" that has nothing to do with ethics and everything to do with combating Bibi's phantom "conspiracy." And they have demonized people from the left and "the Arabs"—including the Arab citizens inside Israel's pre-1967 borders.

Why do I see all of this as part of an *existential* threat to the founding purpose of Israel? Bibi himself should know at least part of the answer. He and Yoni were raised by a devoted follower of Ze'ev Jabotinsky, one of the towering figures of pre-state Zionism. Jabotinsky envisioned an Israel stretching from the Mediterranean across the Jordan River, encompassing all of Judaea and Samaria, as well as present-day Jordan. But his position was rooted in a belief that the Arabs of Palestine would never accept, or willingly coexist with, a Jewish state. Jabotinsky was also a classic nineteenth-century liberal intellectual. No less than David Ben-Gurion, he saw a future state of Israel as a democracy, culturally vibrant and pluralistic, governed by the rule of law. The prospect of an Israeli government eroding all of that, and taking aim at any individual or institution standing in its way, would have appalled him.

Even more fundamental to the threat is the central policy aim that has been driving the government that was formed after the election in 2015: to kill off any remaining possibility of a Palestinian state and ensure that only *one state*—Israel—will exist on the biblical land of Palestine. Even just a few years ago, when I ended my time as defense minister, there was a fairly broad, if tacit, political consensus among Israelis, from center left to center right, about the main element of any eventual political resolution of our conflict with the Palestinians. There would be two states. Israel would, for national security reasons, retain the Jewish neighborhoods in Jerusalem and the large "settlement blocs"—almost all of them around Jerusalem or fairly close to our 1967 border, and within the security fence that was finally completed under Arik Sharon's prime ministership. But consensus had never been achieved on the nearly one hundred smaller settlements in more isolated areas of Judaea and Samaria. While the largest of these contains a few thousand residents, some have only a couple of dozen families. In all, they account for barely one-fifth of all West Bank settlers. Their aim was always political. It was to surround the main Arab towns and cities and to prevent the establishment of a geographically viable Palestinian state. Far from being an asset to Israel's security, they are a burden. They are, as intended, a political roadblock: not just to a negotiated peace with the Palestinians, but to the kind of unilateral Israeli disengagement on the West Bank that I, and increasingly others, have advocated as a fallback as long as such an agreement proves impossible.

Beyond the damage to our security, the "one state" that the pro-settlement ideologues envision would be a Jewish state, or so they would have us believe. Yet beyond the fact that it would still have the Star of David on its flag, that's a delusion. The combined Arab population of the West Bank, Gaza, and pre-1967 Israel is already nearing—or by some estimates, has surpassed—the number of Israeli Jews. The demographic trends point toward a "Jewish" state in which Jews will inexorably become a minority. I suppose it's theoretically possible the one-state advocates would safeguard the democratic norms and institutions that the early Zionists, whether pro-Ben-Gurion or pro-Jabotinsky, took as a

given. But that, too, requires believing in a fantasy: that they would extend the right to vote to an additional 3 million or more Palestinians on
the West Bank.

During all my years in public life, I reacted with a mix of horror
and anger to the blinkered, or sometimes simply anti-Semitic, ideologues abroad who accused Israel of engaging in "apartheid." But many
in Israel and abroad point to the fact that Palestinians, unlike Arabs
within our pre-1967 frontiers, are subject to a structurally different legal
and political system than Jewish settlers who may live just a few hundred yards away from them on the West Bank. The settlers are Israeli
citizens. They are governed by, and enjoy full rights under, Israeli law.
The West Bank Arabs are subject to the civil regulations of the Palestinian Authority, overlaid by Israeli occupation. As long as this was an interim arrangement, with the understanding that our ultimate goal was a
political resolution of our conflict with the Palestinians, that was defensible. But under a *one-state* vision, it will become harder and harder to
rebut comparisons made with the old South Africa. A Jewish minority
ruling over an ever-increasing, largely voteless, Arab majority will also
be a recipe for deep division among Israelis and violence with the Palestinians. Even, possibly, a kind of permanent civil war: a Middle Eastern
Belfast or Bosnia. It will pose a new political challenge for Israel as well.
The demand from Palestinians and their supporters will no longer be for
a state of their own. It will be for a simpler, more straightforward principle,
one carrying much greater resonance in America, Europe, and democratic countries around the world: one person, one vote. Majority rule.

+ + +

The fork in the road for Zionism came in 1967. Like most Israelis, I was
far too caught up in the aftermath of our victory in the Six-Day War to
take much notice. Israel's sense of vulnerability, the feeling that our existence always hung in the balance, seemed gone for good. Within the space
of a week, we had defeated the combined armies of Egypt and Syria and
Jordan. The territory under our control had more than tripled. We felt
secure and, yes, proud to have turned the tables on enemy states that had
vowed to erase our country from the map since 1948. Even the many
Israelis who, like me, were not religiously observant felt an emotional

tremor, and a deep sense of connection, on visiting the Western Wall of the ancient temple in the Old City of Jerusalem, or the places in Judaea and Samaria where the story of the Jewish people began.

When the first West Bank settlements were established in the decade following the Six-Day War, I don't recall feeling there was anything wrong. The decision was taken under Labor prime ministers: Levi Eshkol, Golda Meir, and then Yitzhak Rabin. The two initial sites—Gush Etzion in the Bethlehem hills south of Jerusalem, and Kiryat Arba on the outskirts of Hebron—seemed, in a way, the closing of a circle, the righting of past wrongs. Gush Etzion was where "The 35" were killed in January 1948, shortly before I turned six years old, and where the remaining defenders were murdered and mutilated a few months later. Hebron was one of the oldest areas of continuous Jewish settlement in Palestine, until dozens of Jews were killed there in 1929. Soon afterward, the British authorities evacuated the surviving members of the community.

I don't even recall worrying that Kiryat Arba was promoted, organized, and set up by a group of Orthodox rabbis whose settlement agenda was not rooted in security, like Labor's, but in Jews' *religious* right to all of biblical Israel. I still thought of religious Zionism in terms of its early guide and leader, Avraham Yitzhak Kook. The first chief rabbi of Mandatory Palestine until his death in 1935, Rav Kook was not just a towering Torah scholar, but a subtle and probing intellect. For him, the prospect of a Jewish state on our ancient land was an almost miraculous gift from God. But faced with the reality that most of the Jews at the forefront of making it happen were *non*religious, he chose to embrace rather than denounce, denigrate, or try to delegitimize them. He did not condone their failure to keep the laws of Judaism. But he concluded that if God had chosen nonobservant Jews as part of our return to our land, a mere human being, even a chief rabbi, was hardly in a position to second-guess Him. In terms of the two major themes of Jewish and Zionist thought—the importance of the unity of the Jewish people, *Am Yisrael*, and of *Eretz Yisrael*, the Land of Israel—Rav came down on the side of the people over the land. In fact, I, as many other nonreligious Israelis, always insisted that we have a natural, historic right to have a Jewish state in the biblical land. The debate was always about to what extent that "right" should be exercised given the realities of security, international legitimacy, and other considerations.

In the years after the 1967 war, that changed. Kiryat Arba, the other religious settlements that followed, and the nationalist-religious movement organizing them, known as Gush Emunim, took their inspiration from the late Rav Kook's son, Rabbi Zvi Yehudah Kook. For the younger Rabbi Kook, it was the *Land* of Israel that held primacy. By the mid-1970s, Gush Emunim had begun to dominate the settlement enterprise. Even then, since Rabin was prime minister, that set off no real alarm bells for me. Rabin was guided by Labor's "Alon Plan," under which virtually all settlement activity would be limited to three security bands: along the 1967 border with the West Bank; on the ridge of hills running down its midsection; and in the Jordan River valley. The assumption was that when we finally managed to make peace with Jordan, the rest of the West Bank, including all the main Arab towns and cities, would revert to King Hussein's rule.

When Menachem Begin and the Likud supplanted three decades of Labor-led government in 1977, the Alon Plan was shelved. Begin believed that Judaea and Samaria were, and must remain, part of Israel. He imagined a limited form of self-government for the Palestinians, but was inalterably opposed to the establishment of a Palestinian state. Crucially, he also included a former army general in his cabinet who proved eager to foreclose any such possibility on the ground. Arik Sharon had made little secret of wanting to become defense minister. When Begin instead made him agriculture minister, he brought a military single-mindedness to his role as settlement czar. Arik was no more religiously observant than I. When he argued in favor of the settlement program, it was still primarily on the grounds of security. But he knowingly co-opted Gush Emunim's enthusiasm, determination, and religious sense of purpose. It was Arik who backed and helped implement the plan to establish dozens of new settlements explicitly intended to encircle the major Palestinian population centers of the West Bank, and to foreclose the possibility of a geographically coherent Palestinian state.

Nearly forty years on, Arik is no longer with us. It is worth remembering that his last major policy initiative was a unilateral pullout of all

Israeli troops and settlers from Gaza. He also ordered the evacuation of four isolated settlements in the northern part of the West Bank, in a preliminary signal he might apply the Gaza model to a broader Israeli disengagement from Judaea and Samaria as well. Though I knew Arik well, I can't say whether he would have followed through on that. But I do know that both prime ministers who followed him—Ehud Olmert, and Bibi as well, at least pro forma, came to recognize the difficulty of reconciling permanent Israeli control over the West Bank with a political resolution of the Arab-Israeli conflict. They also understood the corrosive effect of that unresolved conflict on Israel: the widening chasm between the pro-settlement right, especially those for whom ensuring our hold over the Land of Israel was an unarguable divine mission; and those who would choose the unity of the *people* of Israel over the drive to settle every inch of the land. Why did I believe that Bibi might have understood this? I've heard him say so, in so many words, in our conversations over the years. Yet maybe he didn't mean it. Certainly, his words have not been borne out by action. On the policy litmus that divides those Israelis who aspire to some form of political resolution with the Palestinians from those who don't—the hundred-or-so isolated settlements in Judaea and Samaria intended to prevent any realistic prospect of a Palestinian state and ensure open-ended Israeli control of the entirety of the territory— Netanyahu has sided with the pro-settlement religious nationalists.

I'm not sure how much of this has to do with ideology. I suspect it's primarily a political judgment, motivated by an overarching determination simply to hold on to office. What began as a "Fortress Israel" approach during the years I spent in his government became, in the years after 2015, more like Fortress Bibi. In his mind, he was not just prime minister. He was the embodiment and existential defender of the state, standing alone and defiant against an array of purported "enemies" near and far. At home, the favored targets were rival politicians, "leftists," the media, academia, the courts, human-rights groups—and, of course, the Arabs. Abroad, the ire and invective were often aimed at genuine adversaries, like Hamas and Hizbollah, Syria and Iran. But also, until the day Barack Obama left the Oval Office, at the president of Israel's most important foreign ally.

With the accession of Donald Trump, the official line was that all would now be well with the Americans, because they had a president with whom Israel's prime minister was on good terms, both personally and politically. Yet the fabric of our decades-old alliance has rested not just on a single president. It has relied on deeper bonds: with both major political parties, the American public, and institutions like the US military and the national security community. Bibi's willingness to trample on long-accepted norms of engagement with the United States during the Obama administration could not help but have longer-term ramifications.

The effect became clear in his handling of the nuclear deal with Iran. To my dismay, no less than Bibi's, President Obama ultimately decided against the use of America's own military option to prevent the Iranians from going nuclear. The Americans and their international partners secured a negotiated agreement to limit key aspects of the nuclear program for between ten and twelve years. I felt it was a bad deal at the time, and still do. It conferred international recognition on Iran as a major regional power, without constraining its development of missiles, or its support of terror. It also left open the possibility, indeed the likelihood, that Iran will resume its move to become a nuclear weapons state when the deal runs out, or even before. Still, as the details of the agreement began to become clear in 2015, its provisions to curb Iran's nuclear program did appear, at least on paper, more comprehensive and effectively policed than I had expected.

When it was announced, Israel faced the question of how to respond. Even had Labor been in power—even if I'd been prime minister—there would have been an obvious need to register our concern about a deal that relied on the compliance of an Iranian regime openly hostile to Israel and actively supporting Hizbollah and Hamas. But since the US administration already knew of these reservations, the real imperative was to use the political leverage this gave us to reach new understandings on how we could safeguard ourselves against the possibility of a nuclear Iran. We needed to reach agreement with the Americans about what kind of military strike we, or they, might have to take if the Iranians again moved to get nuclear weapons. With the approaching renewal of the ten-year agreement on American military and security aid to Israel, it was also essential to ensure that the continuing possibility of an Iranian nuclear threat was fully taken into account.

What Bibi did instead was astonishing. There was obviously no possibility that the US administration, having finally hammered out the terms of the Iran deal, was going to abandon it. Yet he chose to place himself in unprecedented, open, public opposition to President Obama. With the support of his Republican Party friends—and *without* the prior knowledge of the administration—he was invited to address a joint session of Congress. He used his speech to attack the Iran agreement as posing the risk of Armageddon for Israel, the Middle East, and America itself. Obama and those around him were predictably furious at this act of political grandstanding by the leader of their closest ally in the region. Nor did it escape their notice that the address to Congress came only weeks before Israel's March 2015 election.

The stunt carried a real price for our security. A few months later, the renewal of the military aid package was announced: a total of some $38 billion over ten years. That sounded like an enormous sum, and it was. But in real terms, it wasn't any more than the amount we were already receiving, taking into account the additional help that Congress, at the urging of the Obama administration, had provided for Israel's missile defense programs. From my continuing contacts with high-level Americans, it was clear that without the deep tension in the administration's relationship with the "Republican senator from Rechavia," the package could have been worth up to an additional seven billion dollars.

Still, it played brilliantly with the constituency Bibi clearly valued most: his religious-nationalist, pro-settlement allies at home. So did another example, not long afterward, of what I suppose can be called his "Alt Zionism." He backed out of a meticulously negotiated arrangement to set aside a small area at the Western Wall in Jerusalem where men and women could pray together, something that is anathema to the strictly Orthodox but of importance to millions of Conservative, Reform, and Progressive Jews in the United States. That decision, like Bibi's embrace of the one-state "solution" for the West Bank, spoke volumes about his elevation of short-term politics above serious policy considerations. We have always held up Israel as a state not just for those who live there, but for those in the diaspora for whom it is a powerful symbol, and those who might one day become Israelis themselves. Now, we were in effect telling the non-Orthodox majority of American Jews, the largest and most important diaspora community, that they could not pray according to their own traditions at the holiest site in Judaism.

+ + +

Still, to paraphrase the words of Israel's national anthem, *Hatikvah*, I remain firmly convinced that there are reasons not to lose hope.

One of the unexpected pleasures of having spent the last few years working on this book is that I've found myself retracing not just my own life but Israel's, step by step, since our shared infancy. I realize that a cemetery will seem an odd place to find reason for confidence in Israel's future. But a few months ago, on one of my visits to Mishmar Hasharon, I took a walk through the little graveyard at the edge of the kibbutz where I was born and lived until I left for the army as a teenager. Stopping in front of the rows of gravestones, I was reminded of the extraordinary assortment of young men and women drawn together in the early years of the kibbutz by the shared purpose of Zionism. By a shared dream, really, since none of them could be sure it would happen. I thought of how they persevered, and of the immense sacrifices many of them made. The tombstones told the story: of my own mother and father; the parents of my kibbutz schoolmates; Bina, the metapelet, or kibbutz caregiver, who looked after us in our early years; my schoolteachers. And a reminder of the ultimate sacrifice: a dozen childhood friends and neighbors who lost their own lives, or their children's, in defense of Israel on the battlefield.

My mind went back to two memories of my father. The first was from a few weeks after my fourth birthday, in the spring of 1946, when the state was yet to be born and Holocaust survivors were being smuggled past the British authorities into Palestine. Many came in through a cove a few miles from Mishmar Hasharon. Though almost all of them were moved on to other towns or settlements further inland, a few stayed on in our kibbutz. One was a woman named Anka. To my eyes, she looked gaunt and frail and quite old, although she was barely thirty at the time. For the first couple of weeks she was with us, I took little notice of her. Without being told what she or the others had endured, even the youngest of us somehow knew it would be wrong to stare. But gradually, I became aware of something odd. After each evening meal, she would take an entire loaf of bread, tuck it into the folds of her ill-fitting kibbutz cloth-ing, and hurry back to her room. I couldn't understand it. There were shortages of many things on the kibbutz. But at its center, near the com-munal dining hall, was our bakery, which served not just us but the whole area for miles around. We *always* had bread. Finally, I asked my father why she was doing it. He turned very serious when he answered. He didn't want to lie to me, but he could find no words to describe the Nazis' slaughter of millions of Jewish men, women, and children to a son so young. Crouching down to my level, he said quietly, "Ehud, with what this young woman has gone through in her life before she came here, she can never be sure there will be bread tomorrow."

The other memory was from nearly a decade later. The occasion was my bar mitzvah, the Jewish rite of passage for boys when they reach the age of thirteen. Mishmar Hasharon, like other kibbutzim, was not only nonobservant. We were ideologically nonreligious. Yet our whole school class, boys and girls, gathered in front of the children's home for a group ceremony, as our parents and the other grown-ups looked on with pride. Given the age range among us, I was one of the nearest to my actual bar mitzvah date. The traditional entry into adulthood for girls in Judaism comes a year earlier than for boys, at age twelve, and several of the girls were not far short of turning fourteen. The girls wore blue skirts. We wore white dress shirts and dark blue trousers. One of the girls gave a short speech on behalf of us all, saying how we hoped to put what we had expe-rienced and been taught as children to the service of the kibbutz, and of Israel.

Then came, for me, the most memorable part. My father, usually so reticent in public, had been chosen to deliver a few words on behalf of all of the parents.

"Dearest children," he said, "our hearts are too narrow to contain all the feelings of mothers and fathers on this celebration of reaching the age of *mitzvot*"—the Hebrew word for the 613 obligations in the life of a reli-gious Jew. "Only yesterday we stood by your cots, gazing in wonder at the renewal of creation, and looking, dumbfounded, upon beaming babies' faces, gripped by tingling anticipation and nervous joy . . . And suddenly you have sprouted and become grown people!"

The world, he said, had not welcomed our arrival "with cries of joy, or shouts of 'hooray!' You were brought into the world under leaden skies, in the shadow of the horrors of the Holocaust. Our brothers in European lands were subjected to desolation and destruction, and the threat of devastation also loomed over those of our nation dwelling in Zion. In those dark days, we saw in the light of your eyes a ray of hope that the sun would shine again." He went on to talk about the 1948 war, when "a mighty wave burst our borders" and threatened to "wipe away the hope" of a Jewish future in Israel. And how it was only the steadfastness and courage of mere children, not that much older than us, who had kept that from happening: "a generation with the morning dew still in their eyelashes, and childhood laughter still in their mouths, who carried the nation's fate on their backs."

That, he said, was the soil into which we had been planted. And yet, somehow, it had brought forth fruit. "The morning of your lives did not cloud over. Nor was the sunshine dimmed. You have grown older, taller, like new saplings before the arrival of summer." Now, he said, it would fall upon us to write the next chapter in our country's story. The Jewish *people's* story as well, as he made clear by how he ended his speech. He did not quote from Theodor Herzl, the founding inspiration for the Zionist movement, or Ben-Gurion. Instead he ended with a prayer, albeit with touches of the kibbutz sprinkled in as well. "Please, God," he said, "prepare their steps as they walk forward so that they do not stumble or fall. For they are still soft and delicate. Give their hands strength to carry the burden of generations on these promised shores. And give understanding in their hearts, so that they gain knowledge and wisdom, handicraft and practical skills, to complete the work we have started, and to achieve what we have not managed to do." Finally, he said, "awaken in them, from above, the spirit of yearning for the glory of mankind, just as rain drips from heaven into the furrows of the thirsty fields."

Recording his words now in writing, six decades later, I know I have every one of them right. That's because I still have the copy, in his own neat Hebrew script, which he gave me as a gift that evening. At the top, he wrote: "Welcome speech from the parents, at the bar mitzvah for Ehud's class." Then, above the words of the speech itself: "For you, my son. With lots of love."

+ + +

It is not just nostalgia that brings me back to these memories. It is because they so powerfully capture what motivated early Zionism and the early Zionists—and how far our government's Alt Zionism has moved away from what they stood for and sacrificed for. In the Palestinians' eyes, Mishmar Hasharon was probably a Jewish settlement not that different from those Arik began planting throughout the West Bank in the late 1970s. But for the settlers of my parents' generation, the ultimate aim was not to secure every inch of the Land of Israel: it was to redeem, reinvigorate, and rededicate themselves to the *People* of Israel. Today's settlement ideologues would argue that they, too, are pioneers, seeking to establish and defend what they view as the basic *security* of the state. Yet that's not true, certainly of the dozens of fairly isolated settlements they've established deep in Judaea and Samaria.

The real drive for these settlers is a sense of divine mission. Nor are they shy in contrasting themselves with the early Zionists, so many of whom were not religiously observant. In fact, some of them insinuate that the early settlers were not really, fully, truly Jews. Yet my father's bar mitzvah speech encapsulated the sense in which he and almost every other adult I grew up with remained in touch with their Jewishness, their history, their traditions. When we entered high school, we also studied a range of Jewish texts, especially the supreme source of Torah commentary and religious legal tradition, the Talmud. I can still remember one of our teachers quoting a phrase used over the centuries by some of our greatest sages: that there are "seventy faces" to the Torah. In other words, our scripture invites multiple interpretations, often contradictory, yet all valuable—a precept central to the vitality, and the argumentativeness "for the sake of God," that have always underpinned Judaism. It also reflects the inherent modesty, the openness to other views and insights that the elder Rav Kook brought to early religious Zionism. It is that, above all, that our unprecedentedly right-wing government appears to have lost.

What I firmly believe has *not* been lost is the power of Zionism itself: the unlikely story of how Israel was born, how we survived, and, even against the toughest of challenges, emerged not just stronger in military terms, but more resilient, vibrant, and renewed. For me, never has the arc of our history been so vivid, or felt so personal, than at an event I attended in the spring of 2001. It was only a few days before I left office as prime minister. It was a graduation ceremony, to honor the air force's latest group of fighter pilots. As it got under way, I watched the cadets who would soon get their wings march in and take their places. Including, I noticed, a young woman with a ponytail. We had no female fighter pilots at the time, so I asked one of the air force commanders who she was. "Her name is Roni Zuckerman," he said. "She's an ace. One of the top five in the entire class. She'll be commissioned as an F-16 pilot in another three months." And he added: "She's from *Lohamei HaGetaot.*" In English, the phrase means "ghetto fighters." It's the name of a kibbutz in northern Israel, founded a year after the state by Holocaust survivors, including some of the few young resistance fighters who lived to fight on after the Nazi SS moved in on the eve of Passover 1943 and began killing the remaining Jews of the Warsaw Ghetto and burning it down, block by block. I knew, without having to ask, who young Roni's grandparents must be: Antek Zuckerman and Tzivia Lubetkin. All Israelis knew of them. They were commanders of one of the main Jewish resistance groups. Tzivia was one of the leaders of the ghetto uprising, while Antek was leading the effort to smuggle in weapons before the Nazis' final assault. A year later, they led some 300 survivors from the ghetto in a further Warsaw uprising against the Germans.

As I watched Roni take her place with the other cadets, I felt tears well up in my eyes. My own grandparents had perished inside the Warsaw Ghetto. Now, I was prime minister and defense minister of a strong, sovereign Israel of which they could not even have dreamed. And I had the privilege of seeing the granddaughter of two of the leaders of the Warsaw uprising against the Nazis take her place as a fighter pilot among the elite defenders of our state.

Seventeen years have passed since that moment when tears welled up in my eyes on the air force dais. In those years, the State of Israel has continued to grow stronger economically and militarily. During this period, I served as defense minister in two governments. We overcame the second intifada, brought quiet to our northern border, and triumphed over most of the threats that had menaced us in the past. Many of our enemies have become weaker; others have become covert allies. At the same time, Israel has grown prosperous, world-renowned for its leading-edge technologies. And yet during those years, the one-state process has also advanced, almost unimpeded, and is now nearing the point of no return.

Today, we must return to the dream that allowed Antek Zuckerman and Tzivia Lubetkin to survive the inferno of the Warsaw Ghetto and build a Jewish democratic state in the land of our forefathers. Today, my generation must say to our children and grandchildren the very same words that my father said to me on my bar mitzvah. And we must work together with Roni Zuckerman and her generation, so that Israel can continue to enjoy not only air supremacy, but also a deep sense of moral clarity, Jewish purpose, and universal mission. The threats we face may have changed enormously over the last seventy years, but the challenge has remained the same: to defend our lives, preserve our heritage, and uphold Israel as a model nation.

There is a quote, from Herzl, that has been repeated by so many Israeli and Jewish leaders over the past seven decades that I fear it has become a cliché. That doesn't make it any less true, however, nor less relevant to the critically important fight now under way to ensure that Israel has a strong, secure, democratic, and prosperous future.

"If you will it," Herzl said, "it is not a dream."

# Acknowledgments

When I embarked on this project more than three years ago, I had read many a political memoir. But I'd never written one, and could not have done so without the unstinting support, insight, skill, and dedication of others around me.

Any acknowledgments must begin with Ned Temko, whom I first met through a publishing titan and friend of Israel, the late George Weidenfeld, in London. Ned has made it nothing less than his mission to help me tell my story. Over many months, three continents, and more cigars than I thought possible for one man to consume, he has listened to me, captured my voice, challenged my arguments and assumptions, and helped me bring back to life ideas, people, and events spanning three-quarters of a century with remarkable clarity. That he knew Israel's history, and had covered or written about many of the events in the latter part of this book, certainly helped. But what was even more important to me was his dogged insistence on getting the story right. I cannot thank him enough.

Ned also introduced me to Israel's premier literary agent, Deborah Harris, and her indefatigable New York–based partner, Flip Brophy. Any author would be fortunate to have just one terrific agent, let alone two of them. Together, they organized meetings with the best, brightest, and most accomplished of New York editors and publishers, and helped find the ideal home for the book: St. Martin's Press.

From the outset, Tim Bartlett, executive editor at St. Martin's, was absolutely central to making the book happen and, at every single stage along the way, making it better. He was not just a meticulous, knowing, and thoughtful editor. He became a friend. Alongside him, Laura Clark, George Witte, and Sally Richardson championed the project from the start. Alice Pfeifer, Tim's assistant, was always there to answer questions both large and small with professional aplomb. The publicity team of Dori Weintraub and Leah Johnson took an early interest in the book, and impressed me with their energy and creativity. Donna Cherry, as production editor, kept the book on schedule while ensuring the necessary attention to every last detail, while Meryl Levavi brought care and creativity to the design and the photo sections of the book. Gene Thorp, the cartographer, did a wonderful job producing three beautiful maps. Finally, copyeditor Bill Warhop deserves enormous thanks for the meticulousness, precision, and care with which he approached every paragraph, indeed every word, of the manuscript.

The choice and quality of the photo layouts must be credited to Ricki Rosen. Drawing on her decades of experience as a top photojournalist, her editorial eye, and her dedication to getting every detail right, she helped narrow down the choice of photographs from an initial mountain of hundreds, from dozens of different sources, stretching back to my childhood years in Mishmar HaSharon.

Especially during the home stretch of the project, a special, warm note of thanks is due to my friends Heather Reisman and Gerry Schwartz. In Israel, I relied on the invaluable help of a number of wonderfully supportive family members, friends, and old comrades. Professor Danny Michaelson and Rafi Friedman—Sayeret Matkal colleagues who were with me as we drove ever deeper into the Sinai at the start of the Six-Day War—helped, along with my younger brother and fellow sayeret veteran Avinoam, to find half-century-old pictures from that period in our lives. Reserve Major-Gen Moshe Ivry and Dr. Nahum Gat, officers in my battalion at the Chinese Farm, generously helped to locate photographs from the 1973 war. Dana Mizrahi Braude helped bring together other photos from the archives of the Ministry of Defense, while Pinchas Leviathan offered a trove of valuable pictures and historical information from the kibbutz museum in Mishmar Hasharon.

Two other Sayeret Matkal veterans—Aviram Halevy, field commander, fighter, senior intelligence officer, and unofficial historian for the unit; and Mookie Betzer, my comrade-in-arms on countless missions—helped to correct any inadvertent errors of detail and generally to make sure I got the story of the sayeret's formative years right.

Four other friends kindly read the manuscript and helped make it better in many places and many ways: Professor Itamar Rabinovich, the distinguished historian and diplomat who was centrally involved in Israel's Middle East diplomacy and, above all, our efforts to reach an agreement with the Syrians; Ari Shavit, one of Israel's leading writers and journalists, who contributed valuable insights on both the content and the style; Dan Margalit, one of our country's preeminent television anchors and commentators, who provided enlightening suggestions and, in some places, trenchant yet always useful criticism; and Danny Yatom, a former head of Mossad, who was my deputy when I commanded Sayeret Matkal as well as one of my top advisers during my time as prime minister. Over many decades, Danny has provided cogent, honest, and unfailingly helpful insights and suggestions. Throughout the writing of this book, he did so again.

I'd also like to thank Norman Menachem Feder and Navot tel Zur of the Israeli law firm Caspi, and its senior partner, Rami Caspi, who handled the legal side of the project with their customary attention to detail, which would otherwise have escaped nonlawyers like me.

Yoni Koren was alongside me as my senior aide during most of my time as a senior general in the military, including my period as chief of staff, and also after I entered the political arena. His contribution to the book came not only from his razor-sharp memory for detail, but an understanding of the human side of the story and an unwavering dedication to help see the project through. And, in so many ways, that would have been impossible without the help of Moran, my tireless, always cheerful secretary, always able to find a solution to almost any problem, and always ready to take on yet another challenge.

Finally, and by far most importantly, my gratitude goes to my wife, Nili. She was involved in the project from the very start, utterly convinced it was important, and resolved to do whatever was necessary to help make it happen. My own natural tendency, as she can confirm, is never to do today what can be left until tomorrow. Or the next year, or the next decade. For a project of this scale, without Nili, that might easily have stretched to infinity. Yet with her firm, calm, decisive voice in my ear at every key moment, procrastination was not an option. Still less was the prospect of giving up. The completion of the book was as much down to her as to me. Along the way, I learned to respect her good judgment on every aspect of the project, including the style, structure, flow, and content of the book itself. I know now, even more, why I love her so much.

# Photo Credits

Frontispiece: author's private collection

1.1 Top: author's private collection; middle: Government Press Office (no photographer listed); bottom: Kibbutz Mishmar Hasharon Museum

1.2 Top: Government Press Office (no photographer listed); bottom left: Government Press Office (no photographer listed); bottom right: author's private collection

1.3 Top: Government Press Office (no photographer listed); middle: Avinoam Brog; bottom: Rafi Friedman

1.4 Danny Michaelson

1.5 Top: author's private collection; bottom: author's private collection

1.6 Top: Ilan Ron/Government Press Office; bottom: Israel Navy

1.7 Top: author's private collection; middle: author's private collection; bottom: IDF & Defense Establishment Archives

1.8 Top: author's private collection; bottom: author's private collection

2.1 Top: author's private collection; middle: author's private collection; bottom: IDF & Defense Establishment Archives

2.2 Top: Government Press Office (no photographer listed); middle: Nathan Alpert/Government Press Office; bottom: Ofer Lefler/ IDF & Defense Establishment Archives

2.3 Top: author's private collection; middle: Roi Bushi/ IDF & Defense Establishment Archives; bottom: author's private collection

2.4 Top: Tzvika Israeli/Government Press Office; bottom left: Paul Richards/Getty; bottom right: author's private collection

2.5 Avi Ohayon/Government Press Office

2.6 Top left: Menahem Kahana/AFP/Getty; top right: author's private collection; middle: UK Defense Ministry; bottom: Ricki Rosen

2.7 Top: Avi Ohayon/Government Press Office; bottom: Avi Ohayon/Government Press Office

2.8 author's private collection

3.1 Top: Yakov Saar/Government Press Office; middle: David Karp; bottom: author's private collection

3.2 Top: author's private collection; middle: Avi Ohayon/Government Press Office; bottom: author's private collection

3.3 Top: White House photographer; middle left: Avi Ohayon/Government Press Office; middle right: White House photographer; bottom: White House photographer

3.4 Top: Amos Ben Gershom/Government Press Office; middle: Avi Ohayon/Government Press Office; bottom: Avi Ohayon/Government Press Office

3.5 Top left: Avi Ohayon/Government Press Office; top right: Amos Ben Gershom/Government Press Office; middle left: Yakov Saar/Government Press Office; middle right: Moshe Milner/Government Press Office; bottom left: Yakov Saar/Government Press Office; bottom right: US Department of Defense Archives

3.6 Top: Yakov Saar/Government Press Office; middle: Yakov Saar/Government Press Office; bottom: Yakov Saar/Government Press Office

3.7 Top: Avi Ohayon/Government Press Office; middle: Moshe Milner/Government Press Office; bottom: Avi Ohayon/Government Press Office

3.8 Top: Moshe Milner/Government Press Office; middle: White House photographer; bottom: author's private collection

End photo: Moshe Milner/Government Press Office

# Index